THE HORRORS OF ADANA

THE HORRORS OF ADANA

Revolution and Violence

in the Early Twentieth Century

—————

BEDROSS DER MATOSSIAN

Stanford University Press

Stanford, California

STANFORD UNIVERSITY PRESS
Stanford, California

©2022 by the Board of Trustees of the Leland Stanford Junior University.
All rights reserved.

Printed in the United States of America on acid-free, archival-quality paper

Library of Congress Cataloging-in-Publication Data

Names: Der Matossian, Bedross, 1978- author.
Title: The horrors of Adana : revolution and violence in the early
    twentieth century / Bedross Der Matossian.
Description: Stanford, California : Stanford University Press, [2022] |
    Includes bibliographical references and index.
Identifiers: LCCN 2021033159 (print) | LCCN 2021033160 (ebook) |
    ISBN 9781503608177 (cloth) | ISBN 9781503631021 (paperback) |
    ISBN 9781503631038 (epub)
Subjects: LCSH: Armenian massacres, 1909—Turkey—Adana İli. | Ethnic
    conflict—Turkey—Adana İli—History—20th century. | Political
    violence—Turkey—Adana İli—History—20th century. | Public
    sphere—Turkey—Adana İli—History—20th century. | Courts-martial
    and courts of inquiry—Turkey—History—20th century. | Turkey—
    History—1878-1909. | Turkey—History—Mehmed V, 1909-1918.
Classification: LCC DS51.A2 D47 2022 (print) | LCC DS51.A2 (ebook) |
    DDC 956.6/20154—dc23
LC record available at https://lccn.loc.gov/2021033159
LC ebook record available at https://lccn.loc.gov/2021033160

Cover photo: Figures among destroyed buildings in the city of Adana, 1909.
Ernst Jackh Papers, Rare Book & Manuscript Library, Columbia University.
Cover design: Rob Ehle
Typeset by Newgen in 10.25/15 Adobe Caslon Pro

To my young daughters,
KNAR *and* YERAZ
May they grow up in a peaceful world free
of violence, hate, and bigotry

CONTENTS

ACKNOWLEDGMENTS

This book would have been impossible to write without the help of family, friends, colleagues, librarians, archivists, and various organizations. I am indebted to all of them. First of all, I would like to thank the Department of History at the University of Nebraska–Lincoln (UNL) and its chair, James Le Sueur, for their support. My colleagues in the department have been a source of inspiration in the completion of this project. I specifically want to thank Tim Borstelmann, Barb Bullington, David Cahan, Deirdre Cooper Owens, Breana Garretson, James Garza, Jennifer Garza, Vanessa Gorman, Margaret Jacobs, Jeannette Jones, Tim Mahoney, Gerald Steinacher, William G. Thomas III, and Alexander Vazansky.

Marc David Baer, Ronald Grigor Suny, Mehmet Polatel, Michelle Tusan, and Christine Philliou read drafts of this book. Their comments and constructive criticisms were very helpful in shaping the final version–I am indebted to them all. I would also like to thank the two anonymous reviewers for their outstanding feedback on earlier versions of the manuscript; their thoughtful comments brought the book into fruition. Tom Aldrich read and commented very closely on multiple drafts. His suggestion and comments were extremely useful in shaping this book.

This project would not have been possible without the support of Kate Wahl, Stanford University Press (SUP) editor in chief. Caroline McKusick, the assistant editor at SUP, played an important role in submitting this project to SUP. I would also like to thank Jessica Ling and Charlie Clark, production editors. Special thanks to Adriana Smith for copyediting.

In the course of researching and writing this book, I was the recipient of multiple grants that enabled me to complete this endeavor. I would like to thank the College of Arts and Sciences at UNL for the ENHANCE grant; the Calouste Gulbenkian Foundation-Armenian Communities Department and its director Razmik Panossian; and the Harris Center for Judaic Studies at UNL for supporting this project through travel grants that enabled me to conduct research in multiple archives. The assistance given by the staff of archives, libraries, and research institutions was extremely valuable for the completion of this book. I would like to thank the directors and staff of the Presidency's Ottoman Archives in Istanbul, Turkey; the Ministère de l'Europe et des Affaires étrangères, Centre des Archives diplomatiques in La Courneuve and Nantes, France; Archives jésuites (AJV), Vanves, Paris; The National Archives, UK; the Armenian National Archives and its director, Amadouni Virabyan; the archives at the Madenataran Library; the Armenian Genocide Museum-Institute Archives and its former director Hayk Demoyan in Yerevan, Armenia; the Armenian Revolutionary Federation Archives in Watertown, MA, and its director, George Aghjayan; the United States National Archives in College Park, MD; the Minnesota Historical Society Archives (United States); the Rare Book & Manuscript Library at Columbia University in the City of New York; the American Board of Commissioners for Foreign Missions (ABCFM) Archives, Cambridge, MA; the Gulbenkian Library in Jerusalem; the National Association for Armenian Studies and Research (NAASR) in Belmont, MA; the Archives of the Armenian Patriarchate of Jerusalem (AAPJ); the Armenian Research Center at the University of Michigan–Dearborn and its director, Ara Sanjian; and the AGBU Nubar Library in Paris and its director, Boris Adjemian, for their indispensable help and assistance in providing me with most of the primary sources that I needed for this research. I would like to thank Graham S. Haber, senior photographer at The Morgan Library & Museum, for producing the copy of the photograph of Hagop Babigian. Special thanks to Sylvie Merian for providing me with a copy of the interview with her grandmother Alice (Babikian) Maremetdjian, the daughter of Hagop Babigian, the deputy of the Ottoman Parliament (1908–9).

On a personal level I would like to thank Sebouh Aslanian and Jean Cahan, who have been longtime friends and a source of unconditional support and encouragement. I would also like to give special thanks to Barlow Der Mugrdechian, Richard Hovannisian, Marc Mamigonian, Seda Ohanian, and Uğur Ümit Üngör for providing unconditional support in the course of writing this book. The following individuals have been particularly helpful: Sossie Andezian, Christos Argyropoulos, Ari Ariel, Stephan Astourian, Karen Barkey, Michael Bobelian, Tamar Boyadjian, Serhat Bozkurt, Talar Chahinian, Yaşar Tolga Cora, Asya Darbinyan, Lerna Ekmekcioglu, Rachel Goshgarian, Edita Gzoyan, George Hintlian, Mary Hoogasian, Elizabeth Johnston, Hilmar Kaiser, Haig Kazazian, Raymond Kévorkian, Shushan Khachatryan, Rashid Khalidi, Sergio La Porta, Suren Manukyan, Harutyun Marutyan, Vartan Matiossian, Mihran Minassian, Sato Moughalian, Claire Mouradian, Devin Naar, Tsolin Nalbantian, Katia Peltekian, Greg Sarkissian, Linda Sayed, Vahram Shemmassian, Ari Şekeryan, Nader Sohrabi, Victoria Stamadianou, Vahé Tachjian, Nader Uthman, Ani Voskanyan, Keith Watenpaugh, Heghnar Zeitlian Watenpaugh, İpek Yosmaoğlu, and Malina Zakian. I would like to thank Andreas Batalas and Alexandra Stamadianou for translating the relevant Greek newspaper articles. Special thanks to Patrick Hoehne for meticulously preparing the maps.

　　None of this would have been possible without the support of my family. First of all, I am indebted to my family in Jerusalem: my mother, Haiganush; my aunts Osanna and Salwa; my sister Victoria; my brother Mihran; my sister-in-law Naira; my nieces Talar and Kohar; and my nephew Vartan, who have been a source of encouragement and support. My father, Vartan, passed away few years ago without being able to witness the completion of this book. I am sure he would have been elated to see the book in its final form. Similarly, my family in the US has been a source of constant support. I would like to thank my father and mother in-law, Jerair and Shakeh Siyahian, and my sisters-in-law Ani and Aida Siyahian for genuinely supporting me in my academic career.

　　This book would not have been written without the affection, care, and unconditional support of my inimitable wife, Arpi Siyahian. Working on the theme of massacre and genocide is never an easy task. She made the writing process much easier by providing doses of love and encouragement on a daily basis. Our young daughters, Knar and Yeraz, have been the source of constant joy and inspiration, and it is to them that I dedicate this book.

NOTE ON TRANSLITERATION
AND TRANSLATION

Titles of books, periodicals, and concepts in Armenian, Arabic, Hebrew, Greek, Ladino, Ottoman Turkish, Russian, and Turkish are transliterated according to the Library of Congress Transliteration System. Except for the translations from Greek, done by Andreas Batalas and Alexandra Stamadianou, all translations are mine.

THE HORRORS OF ADANA

INTRODUCTION

ON THE NIGHT OF THURSDAY, SEPTEMBER 19, 2019, TURKISH
locals in the Seyhan District of Adana Province attacked and looted shops
belonging to Syrian refugees in response to rumors that a Syrian man had
tried to rape a Turkish boy. The rumor had spread very quickly on social
media. The mob yelled, "Down with Syria, damn Syria!"[1] The police later
caught the suspect, who according to the Adana governor's office, was a
fifteen-year-old Turkish citizen with thirty-seven past criminal offences. The
police detained 138 subjects for causing extensive damage to Syrian businesses, or instigating such acts on social media, and contained the situation.
This was not the first time that Syrian businesses were targeted in Turkey; for
example, in July of the same year, dozens of Syrian shops were looted by an
angry mob over rumors that a Syrian boy had verbally abused a Turkish girl.[2]
With the arrival of 3.5 million refugees since the beginning of the Syrian civil
war, intercommunal tensions in Turkey have been high.

Such violent outbursts are not solely the result of rumors; they represent underlying political and socioeconomic anxieties. Furthermore, they
are endemic in more than just one society, religion, culture, or geographical
region. In the course of history, similar acts of violence have taken place—
in the form of blood libels, riots, pogroms, massacres, or, in extreme cases,
genocides—in different parts of the globe. From the St. Bartholomew's Day

massacre (1572) to the pogroms of Odessa (1905) and from the Sabra and Shatila massacre (1982) to the Gujarat massacres (2002), history is rife with such violent episodes. These acts of violence share similar societal stressors that become heightened due to major political or economic crises or upheavals. The outcome of these stressors is conditioned by local exigencies. The factors leading to the escalation of these tensions include, but are not limited to, competition over resources, xenophobia, wars, nationalism, influxes of refugees, land disputes, economic envy, and the proliferation of rumors. Specific events—minor or major, fabricated or true—can then become catalysts that mobilize dominant groups against vulnerable minorities.

More than one hundred years ago, the province of Adana, in the southern section of the Ottoman Empire and of present-day Turkey, witnessed a major wave of violence that took the lives of thousands of people. More than twenty thousand Christians (predominantly Armenian, as well as some Greek, Syriacs, and Chaldeans) were massacred by Muslims, and around two thousand Muslims were killed by Christians. Starting from the premise that no such horrendous act happens in a vacuum, the aim of this book is to understand the full complexity of these massacres. However, I would like to stress at the outset that this is not a definitive history of the massacres. The enormity and the complexity of crimes such as massacres and genocides make it impossible to write a definitive history; any scholar who claims to do so would do no justice to history. Each village, town, and district that was struck by the massacres could itself be the topic of a monograph. Hence, this book attempts instead to interpret these events through a thorough analysis of the primary sources pertaining to the local, central, and international actors who were involved in the massacres as perpetrators, victims, or bystanders. Unlike other works on the topic, this book analyzes the event through the lenses of both Ottoman and Armenian history and with an interdisciplinary approach. As Jacques Sémelin argues in his seminal work *Purify and Destroy*, "'massacre' as a phenomenon in itself is so complex that it requires a multidisciplinary examination: from the standpoint of not only the historian but also the psychologist, the anthropologist and so on."[3]

Adana, located on the Mediterranean coast in southern Anatolia, was one of the most significant economic centers in the Ottoman Empire at the beginning of the twentieth century. With a diverse population of Muslims

(Turks, Kurds, Circassians, and Arabs) and Christians (Armenians, Greeks, Syriacs, Chaldians, and Arabs) and a large population of seasonal migrant workers, it was the hub of cotton production in the Ottoman Empire. At the end of April 1909, in a period of two weeks, brutal massacres shook the province of Adana and its capital, the city of Adana.[4] Images of Adana after the massacres show unprecedented physical destruction of a once prosperous city. Local Armenian businesses, churches, residences, and living quarters were totally destroyed. The violence that began in the city of Adana soon spread across the province and poured beyond its borders eastward into the province of Aleppo. In terms of the number of victims, this was the third-largest act of violence perpetrated at the beginning of the twentieth century, following only the Boxer Rebellion (1899–1901) and the genocide of the Herero and Nama between 1904 and 1907 in the German colony of Southwest Africa. The central Ottoman government immediately sent investigation commissions and established courts-martial to try the perpetrators of the massacres. However, these courts failed to prosecute the main culprits of the massacres—a miscarriage of justice that would have repercussions in the years to come.

Despite the massive bloodshed of the Adana massacres, most of the major books on late Ottoman and modern Middle Eastern history fail even to mention these events.[5] Where the massacres are considered in the historiography, the contested nature of the events has led to competing narratives. While the Armenian historiography broadly argues that these massacres resulted from a deliberate policy orchestrated by the Committee of Union and Progress (CUP), the leading Young Turk party, Turkish historiography generally claims that these events were the result of a well-planned Armenian uprising intended to reestablish the Kingdom of Cilicia.[6] Many Armenian and European historians have agreed that the Adana massacres represent a "dress rehearsal" for the Armenian Genocide (1915–23).[7] The prominent historian Raymond H. Kévorkian, in his monumental volume on the Armenian Genocide, discusses the background of the Adana massacres and, based on circumstantial evidence, incriminates the CUP. He concludes by saying:

Who gave the order? Who told high-ranking civilian and military officials, as well as the local notables, to organize these "spontaneous riots"? Was it

the authorities, the state, the government, the CUP? Everything suggests
that it was only the sole institution that controlled the army, the government,
and the main state organs—namely, the Ittihadist Central Committee—that
could have issued these orders and made sure that they were respected. In
view of the usual practices of this party, the orders must have been communicated, in the first instance, by means of the famous itinerant delegates sent
out by Salonika, whom no vali would have dared contradict.[8]

Kévorkian's assessment of the massacres takes into consideration the view-
point of the Armenian intelligentsia at the time. Many Armenian scholars
adhere to his approach. This consensus notwithstanding, it is important to
keep in mind that Armenians were not passive objects who lacked agency; on
the contrary, they were active subjects in their own history, a perspective that
is usually sidelined in the Armenian Genocide historiography.

With this book, I offer a necessary corrective to these narratives. Through
a consideration of the Adana massacres in micro-historical detail, I also offer
a macrocosmic understanding of ethnic violence in the Middle East and beyond. Outbreaks like the Adana massacres do not occur sui generis; they are
caused by a range of complex, intersecting factors that are deeply rooted in
the shifting local and national ground of political and socioeconomic life. In
addition, I do not intend to privilege one factor over another in explaining
these massacres. The most important factors leading to the Adana massacres
were the Young Turk Revolution of 1908, which shook the foundations of the
"fragile equilibrium" that had existed in the empire for decades; the emergence of resilient public spheres after three decades of despotic rule in which
the public sphere was largely repressed; and the counterrevolution of April
13, 1909. The contestation of the legitimacy of the state's power during the
counterrevolution resulted in intense social violence that fed directly into the
massacres.[9] A major question that this book strives to answer is how and why
public spheres in postrevolutionary periods become spaces in which underlying tensions surface dramatically, creating fear and anxiety about the future
that manifests in violence.

Official narratives often attempt to explain such events as manifestations
of "ancient hatreds." They argue that these "ancient hatreds" manifest themselves in times of crisis when political or socioeconomic tensions ignite. In

the case of the Middle East, rudimentary explanations of conflicts hinge on tropes such as sectarianism, Muslim-Christian conflict, or the clash of nationalisms. Such dull "explanations" only serve to perpetuate what authorities would like to hear. A question that every historian of this region should ask is, if "ancient hatreds" were the reasons behind conflicts and massacres, why did these episodes of violence begin in the nineteenth century? It is only in the second half of the nineteenth century, in the wake of internal and external transformations, that we see ethno-religious or "sectarian" violence manifest itself in the Ottoman territories. Hence, the "ancient hatreds" approach—as in the case of Yugoslavia—does not hold water in the case of the Ottoman Empire or the modern Middle East.

Furthermore, this book refutes the claim that certain cultures and religions are predisposed to violence—an idea that was and remains prevalent in the way some Western scholars and Orientalists view Islam. Even a prominent scholar of the Armenian Genocide did not shy away from certain Orientalist tropes in explaining the Armenian Genocide.[10] The literature on genocide and massacres in recent decades has demonstrated that, in particular circumstances, ordinary men and women from many different religious and cultural backgrounds are capable of barbaric crimes.[11] Instead of perpetuating the idea that certain human beings have a biological predisposition to commit crimes, I suggest that scholars should examine how and why a rationalized society suddenly erupts at a particular juncture in history to produce massacres. Having said that, it is important to highlight that scholars should be cautious about normalizing violence as an inevitable process in such cases.

Massacres, Riots, and Pogroms

In historical cases where violence has been used disproportionately against vulnerable groups, there is always a conceptual contention between the "perpetrators" and the "victims" in terms of labeling the event. Both the Ottoman state and Turkish revisionist historiography have employed what Edip Gölbaşı has called "Ottoman linguistic camouflage," or the practice of referring to these massacres as "riots," "events," "revolts," or "uprisings" in order to exclude them from the category of massacres.[12] This "Ottoman linguistic camouflage" blankets the large number of Ottoman documents from the period that were consulted in writing this book. The effect of this rhetoric is to shift the blame for the violence onto the victims. Both the Ottoman and Turkish states have used what has been called "the provocation thesis" in an attempt to justify the violence of the Ottoman state. In short, they argue that the decision to attack the Armenians was a result of Armenian provocation.[13] According to Paul Brass, the winning side in periods of mass violence is not only the one which "inflicts the most damage and suffers the least from crowd violence, but the one which succeeds in labeling it a riot."[14] Furthermore, as empirical surveys have shown, riots, pogroms, and lynchings are themselves not spontaneous forms of violence by a group; rather, they are planned by their leaders. According to Sémelin, the idea of spontaneous outbreaks of mass violence "is more often than not mere propaganda, wielded by the powers-that-be in seeking to mask their primary responsibility in the outbreak of violence."[15]

In this light, I deem it necessary to clarify my choice of the word *massacres* over *riots* or *pogroms* in referring to the two waves of violence that took place in April of 1909 in the province of Adana. *Riot* is defined by the Oxford English dictionary as "violence, strife, disorder, tumult, *esp.* on the part of the populace," and "a violent disturbance of the peace by an assembly or body of persons: an outbreak of active lawlessness or disorder among the populace." Riots are triggered by grievances of certain sectors of society, ranging from poor working conditions to racial conflicts or injustice. As we will see in this book, due to the number of victims and the involvement of local government officials, *riot* is not a suitable term to describe the mass violence in Adana, although it was adopted by the local and central authorities in order to deny the events the status of massacres. *Pogrom* is a Russian word deriving from the word *pogromit*, meaning "to break or smash," and "conquer."[16] Historically, the term is linked specifically to antisemitic violence that erupted against the Jews of the Russian Empire in 1881–82, 1903–6, and 1919–21 (although it was eventually used in describing all anti-Jewish waves of rioting in Eastern Europe).[17]

The term *massacre* was used in the nineteenth century by European governments and elites to indicate "the loss of innocent human lives on a vast scale caused by a deliberate act."[18] Its historical usage in the context of the Ottoman Empire has been discussed in depth elsewhere.[19] What interests us here is its social-scientific definition. Philip G. Dwyer and Lyndall Ryan define a massacre as follows:

> The killing [of] one group of people by another group of people, regardless of whether the victims are armed or not, regardless of age or sex, race, religion and language, and regardless of political, cultural, racial, religious or economic motives for the killing. The killing can be either driven by official state policy or can occur as a result of the state's lack of control over those groups or collectives on the ground. Massacres, in other words, can occur with or without official state sanctions although the state, especially in the colonial context, often turns a blind eye to the killing of indigenous peoples by groups of settler-colonizers that are geographically removed from the center of power and over which it has little or no control.[20]

Dwyer and Ryan argue that massacres usually take place in a short period of time and tend to be confined in geographical space.[21] They are not necessarily directed by the state; different cases of massacres show that the violent episode can be initiated from above and/or from below, attesting to the fact that it is "a dynamic process which can easily get out of hand."[22]

Following Jacques Sémelin, I would like to emphasize that a massacre is not an aberration beyond rational discourse, as is accepted in some circles; rather, it is a rational act with its own internal logic and should be studied as such.[23] It is important here also to distinguish between massacres and genocide. While the latter aims at eliminating a communal group from a social structure, the former seeks to change the behavior of the targeted group through intimidation.[24] Although genocides may include one or several massacres, massacres are not synonymous with genocide.[25]

The violence examined in this book clearly falls into the category of political massacres. However, political bodies are not only confined to a state and its agencies but may also include non-state actors such as mobs, gangs, factions, parties, paramilitary groups, and communal groups. According to Robert Melson there are four types of political massacres: "massacres perpetrated by the state against domestic communal groups; massacres perpetrated by the state against foreign communal groups; massacres perpetrated by non-state actors against domestic communal groups; and massacres perpetrated by non-state actors against foreign communal groups."[26] What interests us here are the first and the third categories. As we will see, in both phases of the anti-Armenian violence, massacres were perpetrated by some local government as well as non-state actors against an indigenous communal group. It is important to reiterate that the aim of a massacre is not the extermination of a communal group but the reinstatement of the status quo, to which the victimized group represents a challenge. It is also worthwhile to note that the act of massacre is not a manifestation of power by the perpetrator group; on the contrary, it is an expression of weakness, in which the perpetrator feels obliged to resort to mass violence.

Reforms and Violence

During the nineteenth century, the Ottoman Empire initiated a series of reforms to increase its political power and preserve its territorial integrity. This defensive developmentalism was intended to strengthen the state through centralization, radical military reform, and new legal norms rationalized along Western lines. These reforms extended rights to all Ottoman subjects, regardless of creed or religious affiliation, and had a profound impact on Christians and Jews by pledging equality among the empire's subjects, Muslims and non-Muslims alike.[27] But through these reforms, religious identity also became increasingly politicized. The economic, political, and social gains made by Christians challenged the traditionally dominant position of Muslims in Ottoman society. As a result, political and socioeconomic conditions on the ground changed dramatically, leading to the emergence of intercommunal tensions and culminating in violence, massacres, and civil wars in the region of the Fertile Crescent, Anatolia, and the Balkans.

In some regions, the violence became sectarian. Historian Ussama Makdisi has suggested that sectarianism in Lebanon was a by-product of "modernity." The Lebanese attempted to work out their place in a rapidly transforming world order by adopting categories of identity that had been privileged and sometimes imposed by Western diplomats and missionaries.[28] Makdisi's work challenges the views that sectarian violence was simply an Islamic response to Westernization or an outcome of the social and economic inequalities among the different religious groups in Lebanon. In her study of the Ottoman Balkans, İpek Yosmaoğlu explains the shift from sporadic to systematic and pervasive violence in Ottoman Macedonia in the nineteenth century through a social history of the "Macedonian Question."[29] In her work, Yosmaoğlu demonstrates how national identities replaced the polyglot associations that had formerly defined people's sense of collective belonging, although she argues that national differentiation was a by-product, and not the cause, of violent conflict in Ottoman Macedonia.

Economic changes in the nineteenth century also contributed to the escalation of interethnic tensions. Leila Fawaz has discussed the civil war that began in Mount Lebanon in 1860 and spread to Damascus. She argues that uneven economic growth affected not only inter-sectarian but also intra-sectarian relations. She contends that the upsetting of the continuously renegotiated, finely tuned balance between the region's central state power and the forces of regional autonomy resulted in the civil war.[30] Fawaz argues that conflict in the region cannot be explained without analyzing the regional and international currents, and specifically their impact on local autonomy. Furthermore, she demonstrates the important role of the communal balance between social and political institutions in the region and the way it was disrupted by the intervention of Europeans.

A lack of in-depth academic analysis, beyond essentialist and rudimentary explanations, is especially evident in the limited scholarship of the Adana massacre at its centenary. This book follows in the footsteps of the fine works mentioned above by demonstrating that the violence in Adana was much more complex than dualistic and superficial analyses would have it. The dichotomy of Muslims versus Armenians encourages vast essentializations of the parties involved in the conflict and obfuscates a sound analysis of the socioeconomic and political factors that led to the massacres. By analyzing the changes in the sociopolitical, religious, and economic structures in the region, this book provides multicausal and multifaceted explanations of the events that unfolded in Adana. The book examines the violence and struggles for power in terms of failures and successes in the public sphere and more generally in relation to the 1908 revolution, using primary sources in a dozen languages. The Adana massacres are considered not as part of a continuum of Armenian massacres leading to the Armenian Genocide but as an outgrowth

of the ethno-religious violence that was inflicted on the region in the nineteenth and early twentieth centuries. While much work has been done on
understanding ethnic violence in the Ottoman Balkans and the Arab Middle
East prior to World War I, there is a lacuna in such studies in the region of
Anatolia.[31] This project aims to fill this gap. This book analyzes the history
of the massacres through four interrelated themes: dominant and subaltern
public spheres, rumors, emotions, and humanitarianism and humanitarian
intervention.

Dominant and Subaltern Public Spheres

The concept of the public sphere, which is very much associated with the experience of Europe and North America, was introduced by Jürgen Habermas
in *The Structural Transformation of the Public Sphere*. Habermas's study of the
public sphere (*Öffentlichkeit*) focused on what he calls its modern "bourgeois"
form, or the "liberal model of the bourgeois public sphere," which emerged
and flourished in eighteenth- and early nineteenth-century Europe before
going into decline during the remainder of the nineteenth and the twentieth
centuries.[32]

Since its translation into English in 1989, which coincided with the collapse of the Soviet Union, *The Structural Transformation of the Public Sphere*
has drawn the attention of many scholars from a variety of fields who have
criticized and modified the theory in different ways. Habermas himself has
revisited his approach and admitted that his theory of the bourgeois public sphere is a "Eurocentrically limited view."[33] Some scholars have argued
that the public sphere came into play well before the late eighteenth century,
while others have pointed out that Habermas failed to examine other, non-
liberal, non-bourgeois, competing public spheres.[34]

Geoff Eley and Mary Ryan have provided historians with crucial and
influential formulations by rejecting Habermas's idea of the public sphere as
being confined to the bourgeoisie and by analyzing the political and public
activities of other social groups in nineteenth-century Europe and America.[35]
For Eley, the public arena was a place in which different and opposing publics maneuvered for space and from which certain publics (including women,
subordinate nationalities, the urban poor, the working class, and the peasantry) may have been excluded altogether. In the case of Adana prior to the

Revolution of 1908, the most significant of such marginalized publics was the Armenians.

Eley has also demonstrated that the participation of these counter-publics in the public sphere was fragmented, contested, and competitive: "this element of contest was not just a matter of coexistence, in which such alternative publics participated in a tolerant pluralism of tendencies and groupings. Such competition also occurred in class-divided societies structured by inequality."[36] Nancy Fraser has elaborated on this issue of subordinate groups in stratified societies, which she terms "subaltern counter-publics," in order to indicate "parallel discursive arenas where members of subordinated social groups . . . formulate oppositional interpretations of their identities, interests and needs."[37] This definition aptly describes the counter-publics of the post-revolutionary period in the Ottoman Empire.

Furthermore, whereas Habermas presumed that identities would be formed in private before their entry into the political public sphere, scholars have subsequently argued that this is not the case. In particular, Craig Calhoun has criticized Habermas's treatment of public activity as rational-critical discourse posterior to identity formation or expression.[38] He argues that the identities of groups are in part formed and revised through their participation, rather than settled in advance.[39] Hence, public spheres provide an important medium for the enactment of social identities and, for the purposes of this discussion, can be seen as a medium that precipitates ethno-religious tensions between dominant and nondominant groups—tensions that may manifest as violence, including massacres.

Thus, the critique of Habermas's theory has elicited new dimensions of understanding the public sphere. First, it revealed the exclusionary nature of the Habermasian public sphere in its classical liberal form and argued for the existence of multiple public spheres or publics as opposed to one dominant public sphere. It further pointed out that, because of historiographic biases, historians had considered only the politics and history of the dominant public sphere. Second, these new approaches argued that counter-publics or subaltern counter-publics exist in competition, both against and within the dominant public sphere. Third, this modified theory indicated that the public sphere is an arena not only for rational-critical discourse, but also for the formation and enactment of social identities. These approaches will help us to better understand the formation of dominant public spheres as well as subaltern public spheres in the postrevolutionary period.

The Public Sphere and the Ottoman Empire

The discussion of how the public sphere operated in the Ottoman Empire and continues to operate in the Middle East remains in its infancy, and this study will not attempt a comprehensive history.[40] Both the premodern and the modern forms of the public sphere existed in the Ottoman Empire, but they appeared against a different background and were affected by different factors from those in the European milieu. In particular, autonomous institutions that did not exist in the European milieu functioned as the ultimate mediums for the creation of the Ottoman premodern public sphere. For example, in the seventeenth and eighteenth centuries, *waqf*s (religious endowments) constituted important elements of the public sphere and of the social organization that gave substance to civil society in the Ottoman Empire. Haim Gerber argues that the *waqf* was so pervasive in Ottoman society "that one is almost tempted to view it as a key institution in the way the cockfights were seen by Geertz to be a key institution in Balinese society."[41] Another example would be the coffeehouses of the early modern period, which played a significant role in forming "the cultural public sphere."[42] According to Selma Akyazıcı Özkoçak, in addition to providing the only public space for poorer inhabitants of the cities, the coffeehouses "served as a principal location for the social, political, and cultural discourses of the Ottoman elite."[43]

The Ottoman public sphere entered its modern form during the nineteenth century with the development of peripheral capitalism and the construction of urban spaces, which was accompanied by the proliferation of scientific and literary societies. As a result, literary public spheres emerged, including the press, in general, and newspapers, in particular. These outlets dominated the expansion of Ottoman public sphere(s).[44] In tandem with the development of an official Ottoman press in the nineteenth century, the private press flourished, helping to create subaltern public spheres and counter-publics. Through these private, ethno-religious publications, non-dominant groups began to discuss issues pertaining both to their communities and to Ottoman politics.[45] This transformation of literary public spheres into political public spheres in the modern sense among both dominant and

nondominant groups reached its peak with the promulgation of the Ottoman Constitution in 1876.[46]

In 1878, Sultan Abdülhamid II dissolved the Ottoman Parliament, de-
railed the constitution, and established one of the most sophisticated espio-
nage systems in the history of the empire in an attempt to put an end to the
political public sphere. Despite his efforts, weak forms of both dominant and
marginal public spheres nonetheless continued to exist, the latter strengthened by political activists in exile and their clandestine cells in the empire. By
the beginning of the 1880s, journalistic activities had shifted from the Levant
and Anatolia to Paris, Geneva, London, Tbilisi, and Cairo. In those cities,
an exilic Ottoman public sphere formed, in which exiles of different ethnic
backgrounds debated the future of the empire, using means of expression
ranging from print media to public gatherings.[47] Influenced by the European
intellectual and political currents of the nineteenth century, they strove to
reform the empire's political system by adopting the tool that had transformed the West into a successful political entity: namely, constitutionalism
and parliamentary rule.

After the Young Turk Revolution of 1908, this exilic public sphere tran-
sitioned into a homeland public sphere as political exiles returned home. The
revolution allowed for an immediate boom in serial publications among the
empire's many ethnic groups.[48] The press played the most important role in
this new public sphere, with more than two hundred periodicals published in
İstanbul alone during the first year after the revolution.[49]

Rumors

One of the most important factors that precipitated the violence in Adana
was the spread of rumors—both before and after the revolution—regarding
the so-called Armenian uprising for the reestablishment of an Armenian
kingdom. With the development of public spheres in the post-revolutionary
period, and the consequent escalation of intra- and interethnic relations,
these rumors attained new heights. Agents provocateurs used the limitless
liberty that came with the public sphere to disseminate these rumors to all
classes of society.

A rumor can be defined as an "unverified account or explanation of
events, circulating from person to person and pertaining to an object, event,

or issue of public concern."[50] In their study "Rumor Dynamics in Ethnic Violence," Ravi Bhavnani, Michael G. Findley, and James H. Kuklinski argue that rumors possess two features that make them especially suited to the promotion of violent action. First, they argue that rumors often lack verifiability when verification is most needed. Second, rumors can invoke emotions by giving form to existing intergroup animosity. Thus, rumors solidify the boundaries of the crowd, giving them a sense of bonding and affirming their "authenticity" while preparing them for an imminent violent onslaught on the other group. In this situation, conformity serves as an especially critical mechanism; members of the crowd often follow the majority belief without questioning the veracity of the rumor. Consequently, the "path from heightened emotions to impulsive, violent behavior is short."[51] In the case of interethnic violence, rumors come in an extreme form that creates panic, elevates already existing negative emotions, intensifies distrust, and justifies physical brutality toward the other ethnic group.[52] This situation becomes more volatile in settings—such as Adana—where ethnic groups live in close proximity to one another and interact frequently. This theory is borne out by the way in which the massacres of Adana began in an urban setting where false rumors then enabled the violence to spread to the periphery. In addition, it was due to these rumors that the emotions among the Muslim population were heightened, leading to the assault on the Armenian population. Rumors provide a "fertile medium in which propaganda can put down the roots of 'shock arguments' and appear 'credible' to a disoriented and traumatised population."[53]

Emotions

Until recently, emotion-based approaches have been marginalized in historical and social-scientific studies of ethnic violence. The main purpose of an emotion-based approach is to compare and assess the different motivations within the perpetrator group. According to Thomas Brudholm and Johannes Lang, emotions are "powerful social and political forces that can be harnessed and shaped in the service of collective action."[54] In the contexts of political upheavals, emotions often motivate people toward violent action by creating an "us versus them" mentality. Thus, it is difficult to thoroughly understand historical change during turbulent periods without considering the role of emotions. In his study of ethnic violence in Eastern Europe in the twentieth century, Roger D. Petersen identified four emotions that motivate individuals to commit violent actions against another ethnic group: fear, hatred, resentment, and rage. Despite the fact that many of these motives overlap in the case of Eastern Europe, Petersen argues that the resentment motive, which is "centered on a belief and sense of unjust group status, provides the best predictive and descriptive fit toward a variety of cases of ethnic conflict in Eastern Europe."[55] In the case of the Ottoman Empire, Petersen's models could be beneficial to an understanding of the different phases of the ethno-religious violence that began in the second half of the nineteenth century. However, the emotion-based approach to assessing and analyzing ethnic violence has been marginal thus far in the historiography of the Ottoman Empire.

Ronald Suny is one of the first historians to take an emotion-based approach, in his excellent analysis of the Armenian Genocide.[56] Suny refers to the emotional world of the Turks vis-à-vis the Armenians, in which sentiments of fear, anger, resentment, and hatred were part of the mental universe, as an "affective disposition." According to him, this affective disposition is what enables a perpetrator group to commit crimes against another ethnic group. In the case of Adana as well, affective disposition played an important role in the enactment of violence. In the emotion of fear—or as Séme-lin calls it, "imagined fear"[57]—anger, resentment, and rage were combined and directed against the Armenians, who were believed to be "preparing an uprising" to erect an Armenian kingdom by massacring the entire Muslim population of Adana. Thus, the Muslim population of Adana constructed the Armenians as seditious, disloyal, treacherous, subversive, deceptive, and sinister. The present book demonstrates the extent to which such an affective disposition was characteristic of the reaction of the Muslim population toward the Armenians in the pre- and postrevolutionary periods that culminated in the twin massacres. However, while the majority of the Muslim population genuinely feared Armenians through an affective disposition, even to the point of considering them an existential threat, agents provocateurs manipulated this for their ultimate objective of scapegoating Armenians in order to discredit the new constitutional regime. In this context, the propaganda machine played an important role in manufacturing emotions. According to

Sémelin, propaganda can be used to arouse "fear, mistrust, and resentment and then provoke a reaction of vigilance, pride, and revenge." For him, the propaganda machine "is first and foremost a device for fabricating public emotion as dictated by political leaders whose words it relays and amplifies."[58]

Humanitarianism and Humanitarian Intervention

The Adana massacres also demonstrate the limitations of humanitarianism and humanitarian intervention on behalf of the Armenians of the empire in the late Ottoman period. Historians Michelle Tusan, Davide Rodogno, and Keith Watenpaugh have elucidated our understanding of humanitarianism and humanitarian intervention, or the lack thereof, in the nineteenth- and early twentieth-century Ottoman Empire.[59] Rodogno defines humanitarian intervention as

> a coercive diplomatic and/or armed (re)action against massacre undertaken by a state or a group of states inside the territory of a target state. Its main motivation is to end massacre, atrocity, and extermination or to prevent the repetition of such events. It is an ex post facto event whose objective is to protect civilian populations mistreated and unprotected by the target-state government, agents, or authorities.[60]

Rodogno argues that the idea of intervention to end massacre emerged "as a way to protect the right to life of a restricted group of people in the early nineteenth century, prior to the creation of a proper legal definition of the intervention."[61] However, the intervention on the part of Europeans to save the lives of their "Christian brothers" in the Ottoman Empire was selective. While in some cases in Greece, Lebanon, and Crete, European humanitarian intervention did take place, in other cases it failed despite strong evidence of horrendous massacres. The Armenian case represents the most important example of the latter. The answer as to why humanitarian intervention did not take place in some cases is complex. Rodogno argues that if intervention "threatened to destabilize the international system . . . the European powers would not intervene to end massacre." In the nineteenth century, this international system required that "before undertaking an intervention, European powers had to reach a collective agreement guaranteeing that none of them would unilaterally benefit from the intervention."[62]

In addition, the humanitarian interventions that did occur aimed only at saving selective Christian communities and did not deal at all with the suffering of the Muslim populations of the Balkans or the Caucasus. In the European view, it was always the Muslim who killed the Christian. Watenpaugh argues that the "evident lack of response to Muslim suffering by Western humanitarians, or even the acknowledgment of Muslim suffering, colored the way modern humanitarianism was encountered in the late Ottoman period and into the interwar era in Muslim majority states."[63] Most of the European consular records consulted for this research do not mention the conditions of the families of the Muslim refugees in the post-massacre periods. The global press covered in this book was also silent on this topic; their coverage mostly dealt with the plight of the Christians of the empire by providing detailed graphic descriptions of the massacres. According to Watenpaugh, this modern humanitarianism was based on a "sentimental missionary narrative," which "adopted religious vernacular to describe the suffering of non-Muslim minorities."[64]

The European humanitarian effort to alleviate the suffering of the Armenians of the empire goes back to the second half of the nineteenth century. The British, followed by the French, played the most important role in this process. The Armenian Question in the second half of the nineteenth century became one of the most important humanitarian causes in the Victorian period (1837–1901).[65] The European media played a key role in shaping public opinion about the Armenian Question. In Britain, it became part of the everyday public discourse.[66] With the signing of the Paris Peace Treaty following the Crimean War (1853–56), humanitarian intervention became an official part of British imperial diplomacy.[67] With the internationalization of the Armenian Question following the Berlin Peace Treaty of 1878, sentiments in favor of humanitarian intervention in the Ottoman Empire were heightened. Tusan argues that "Humanitarianism, as articulated in this period, was not a neutral or benign ideology of universalist altruism. Along with the impulse to defend the rights of others came the moralizing liberalism of the Victorian period that was influenced both by strident evangelicalism and orientalism."[68]

The Hamidian massacres put the British principle of humanitarian intervention as "comprising a necessary part of foreign policy to its most difficult test to date."[69] The British government, through publishing government reports in the form of Blue Books based on records of its consulates in the region, disseminated knowledge about the horrors of these massacres.[70] The British press covered these civilian massacres extensively and "represented humanitarian intervention as a duty of the British Empire, a guidepost of the pax Britannica."[71] As Tusan and Rodogno have demonstrated, the British response to the Hamidian massacres also catered to domestic political debates about the empire's status in the world.[72] However, in this case, no humanitarian intervention by any European power took place. What did occur were diplomatic maneuvers to force the sultan to agree on a reform package.

Despite the lack of humanitarian intervention in the Adana massacres, we see an extensive network of local, regional, and international humanitarian efforts to alleviate the suffering of the Armenians of Adana. The public sphere created after the revolution played a crucial role in spreading the news about the massacres both nationally and internationally and in communicating the need to aid the victims. The Armenian Patriarchate and Armenian organizations along with the Ottoman state, different ethno-religious groups, and international organizations from different countries sent financial and material aid to help the thousands of refugees in Adana.[73] British vice-consul major Charles Doughty-Wylie and his wife Lilian played a dominant role in this effort. In the midst of the catastrophe, Armenians, in Watenpaugh's words, felt a "sense of communal humiliation" and resisted the "culturally effacing effects of international humanitarianism."[74]

Why did the British fail to act? Tusan aptly argues, "The failure of the British Empire to live up to its self-imposed responsibility resulted from the tension between pragmatism and idealism which gradually weakened the moral imperative and humanitarian impetus that sustained the commitment to protect minority rights over the course of the late nineteenth and early twentieth centuries."[75]

The Young Turk Revolution of 1908

Nineteenth-century reforms led to the growth of a constitutional movement in the Ottoman Empire between 1865 and 1878, primarily represented by a group of intellectuals calling themselves the Young Ottomans.[76] They were central to the short-lived first Constitutional period (1876–78), which was disrupted when Sultan Abdülhamid II (1876–1909) prorogued the parliament, suspended the constitution, and established a despotic rule.[77]

Armenian hopes rose during this period as a result of the Treaty of San Stefano, signed on March 3, 1878, which ended the Russo-Turkish War (1877–78). Article 16 of the treaty stipulated that the Russian forces occupying the Armenian-populated provinces in the Eastern Ottoman Empire would withdraw only with full implementation of reforms. Article 16 reads:

> As the evacuation of the Russian troops of the territory they occupy in Armenia, and which is to be restored to Turkey, might give rise to conflicts and complications detrimental to the maintenance of good relations between the two countries, the Sublime Porte engages to carry into effect, without further delay, the improvements and reforms demanded by local requirements in the provinces inhabited by the Armenians and to guarantee their security from Kurds and Circassians.[78]

However, as a result of Great Britain's objections to the terms of this treaty, the Russians were forced to sign a new treaty, the Treaty of Berlin, on July 13, 1878. Article 16 was altered to become Article 61, which also stipulated the removal of all Russian forces from the region but did not include an effective enforcement mechanism for the reforms. To the above text, Article 61 appends: "[The Sublime Porte] will periodically make known the steps taken to this effect to the powers, who will superintend their application."[79] Efforts by the Armenian leadership to amend the article proved futile. After the Treaty of Berlin, the Armenian Question became internationalized. However, the condition of the Armenians did not improve, even with the stipulations of Article 61 of the Treaty of Berlin. On the contrary, frequent attacks by the Kurdish tribes on the Armenians, heavy taxation, friction with newly immigrated Muslims from the Caucasus and the Balkans, corruption in the administration, and the failure of Armenian efforts to solve these problems diplomatically led to the emergence of Armenian revolutionary groups.

In 1885, the Armenakan Party was founded in Van, becoming the first party to engage openly in revolutionary activities.[80] It was followed by the Social Democrat Hunchakian Party (Sōts'ialistakan Dēmokratakan Hnch'akean Kusakts'ut'iwn, or Hnchak), founded in Geneva, Switzerland, in August 1887, and named after its journal, *Hnch'ak* (Bell). The party's platform

focused on counteracting the depredations taking place against the Armenians in the eastern provinces of the empire. They used the means of agitation, terror, and propaganda to achieve their objectives.[81] Due to internal
crisis and ideological differences, a group from the party detached itself from
the main organization to form a new party. In 1898, this faction named itself
the Reformed Hnchakian Party (Verakazmyal Hnch'akean Kusakts'ut'iwn).

The most prominent of the Armenian revolutionary organizations
was the Armenian Revolutionary Federation (Hay Heghap'okhakan
Dashnakts'ut'iwn) or ARF, founded in Tbilisi in 1890. Also known as Dashnak, or Dashnakts'ut'iwn, its official organ was called *Droshak* (Flag). In its
first congress, the party put forth a vision of political and economic freedom
in Turkish Armenia (*T'rk'ahayastan*).[82] This would be accomplished through
propaganda, the arming of the population, and violent acts against corrupt
government officers. All of these revolutionary parties had clandestine cells
in the eastern provinces of the empire. While the Dashnaks had a very strong
presence in provinces such as Van, the Hnchaks were predominant in the
region of Cilicia. These groups used various tactics to achieve their goals,
ranging from assassination of Ottoman officials to major demonstrations
aimed at bringing the attention of European governments to the plight of
the Armenians.

The Hamidian regime responded to the revolutionary activities of the
Armenians in the eastern provinces with brutal collective punishment, resulting in well-orchestrated massacres of more than two hundred thousand
Armenians from 1895–96 at the hands of the Hamidiye Regiments and
Kurdish brigands, as well as local actors. The Hamidiye Regiments were
created by Sultan Abdülhamid II as an irregular militia composed of select Kurdish tribes ordered to protect the empire's eastern border from Russian incursions, to suppress Armenian activities, and to bring the region into
the Ottoman fold.[83] Through these massive waves of massacres, the sultan
aimed to preserve the status quo in the eastern provinces and to abort any
attempts by the European powers to alter the situation. The Kurdish beys
and the Hamidiye chieftains looted hundreds of town quarters and villages
and seized thousands of acres of Armenian land. Although Adana was not
targeted during those years, the collective memories of these massacres were
deeply entrenched in the psyche of Armenians in Adana.[84]

Meanwhile, the Young Ottomans' legacy was carried on by another influential group that played a dominant role at beginning of the twentieth century. Called the Young Turk movement, it emerged in the Ottoman Empire and in its expatriate communities. Its main political party, the Committee of Union and Progress (CUP), became a powerful political force. With the aid of the Ottoman Third Army, located in Macedonia, the Young Turks staged the Young Turk Revolution of 1908. They reinstated the Ottoman Constitution of 1876 and opened the parliament, launching the Second Constitutional Period (1908–18). With its slogans of freedom, brotherhood, equality, and justice, the 1908 Revolution ushered in a new dawn for all the ethnic groups that had "suffered under the yoke" of the ancien régime.[85] When news of the revolution reached the city of Adana, a euphoric atmosphere erupted. Muslims and Christians began decorating the streets and houses and visiting each other. The masses shouted, "Long live the sultan! Long live freedom!" Prayers were held in honor of the sultan and the Ottoman nation across the city.[86] But when these festivities subsided and the postrevolutionary political process got underway, the real test of the new era began.

After the revolution, the growth of Adana's public sphere not only enabled political activism within formerly outlawed groups but also contributed to an escalation of ethnic tensions. The new physical and verbal manifestations of Armenians in the public sphere—in the forms of cultural and political processions, the bearing and selling of arms in public, theatrical presentations, and publication of print media—alarmed the dissatisfied elements of the population, who began to use the same media to air their anxieties about, and discontent with, the newly created order. This book, by giving voices to all the parties involved in the event, demonstrates how the reinstatement of public spheres in postrevolutionary periods can become a double-edged sword. While adherents of the new regime would use the medium of the public sphere to pursue conventional politics, the elements opposing the new regime would use it for the incitement and mobilization of malcontents, with the aim of destabilizing the existing order.

The Young Turk Revolution of 1908 led to drastic changes in the dynamics of power among the different regions of the empire, disrupting the power balance that had existed for decades. It led to the creation of a large, dissatisfied class that had benefited from the ancien régime and had now lost power. This disruption in power dynamics and the tensions among political forces within the empire led to a violent backlash by reactionary forces in a counterrevolution on April 13, 1909.[87] The trigger for the counterrevolution was the assassination of Hasan Fehmi, the editor of one of the dominant opposition papers, *Serbesti* (Freedom), which was extremely critical of the CUP. I have argued elsewhere that the counterrevolution led to the demise of the Ottoman dream that the revolution had striven to achieve.[88] Furthermore, it became an excuse for the CUP to take drastic measures in strengthening its grip on power in the name of preserving the empire. The counterrevolution represented variegated groups formed by liberals and religious elements as well as low-ranking military officers. Despite their different objectives, they had one goal in common: to oust the CUP leadership from the capital. Thus, as opposed to its presentation in the historiography, the counterrevolution was not a manifestation of religious fanaticism but a "multi-actor, multi-vocal event that brought together groups with a variety of interests who finally articulated their demands in the same voice, but this time in the language of religion."[89]

The counterrevolution was quickly subdued in the capital by the Action Army, and other pockets of uprising in the provinces were quelled within a few days due to the strong presence of the CUP. In contrast to its failure in prosecuting the real culprits of the massacres in Adana, the state was successful in trying those responsible for the counterrevolution.[90] In the province of Adana, however, the effects of the counterrevolution spun violently out of control, leading to the Adana massacres. Public space in Adana became a vehicle through which political, social, and economic anxieties were manifested or transformed in conjunction with the counterrevolution. As this book will demonstrate, emotions played a significant role in transforming the triggering incidents into a series of full-scale massacres.

The reaction of the central government and the CUP toward the real perpetrators of the Adana massacres was lenient, as was demonstrated by the decisions of the courts-martial. Justice was achieved nominally, as most of the key architects of the massacres received light sentences, while about fifty Muslims (some of them innocent) and six Armenians were sentenced to death, and many more were sentenced to imprisonment with hard labor. It seems that the CUP, having just recovered from the counterrevolution, chose not to take drastic action against the primary perpetrators of the massacres for fear of the wider effects in the region of such a course, which could have endangered its political existence.

———

This book is divided into eight chapters. In the first chapter, I discuss the historical background of Adana Province, concentrating mainly on the nineteenth century. In order to understand the roots of the violence, this chapter examines the sociopolitical and economic changes that took place in this period. In addition, the chapter explains the centrality of Cilicia to the Armenian national past, which became yet another factor in escalating the tensions. For more than six centuries prior to World War I, the city of Sis (modern-day Kozan, Adana) was the center of the Catholicosate of the Great House of Cilicia. Cilicia was also the location of the last Armenian kingdom (1198–1375). Taken together, these centuries-long associations with the Armenian people meant that the area was of particular cultural significance to them.

The second chapter discusses interethnic relations in Adana during the Hamidian despotic period (1878–1908). Despite the fact that the public sphere in Adana—as in the other provinces of the empire—was restrained due to extreme censorship by the Hamidian regime, a weak form did exist. In this period, Muslim notables in Adana began to play an important role in disseminating (mis)information about the grandiose plans of the Armenians to reestablish the Kingdom of Cilicia. Although Adana was spared during the Hamidian massacres due to good relationships between some of the local Muslim notables and the Armenians, there were, nonetheless, serious tensions in the province.

The third chapter discusses the impact of the 1908 Young Turk Revolution on intra- and interethnic politics in Adana and the ways in which the revolution changed the political and societal structures across the region. It begins with a brief overview of the impact of the revolution on the different provinces of the empire before focusing on its impact in Adana and exploring the reactions of different sectors of the local society, ranging from the ecclesiastic leadership to the class of notables and from Armenian political parties to CUP members. Understanding postrevolutionary changes in power dynamics and the growth of subaltern public spheres is crucial for understanding the escalating ethnic tensions and violence that followed. Hence, this chapter concentrates on the development of the public sphere in Adana and the ways in which rumors played a substantial role in the buildup of tensions.

Chapter 4 discusses the first wave of the massacres in depth, detailing how they began as sporadic incidents but developed into widespread violence. The keg of violence exploded in an urban setting and then spread to different parts of the periphery. Armenians in a few places resorted to self-defense, but with limited success. Rumors allowed the idea of an Armenian uprising to quickly take root; thus, it could be said that the massacres in the periphery were a reaction to the "Armenian rebellion" in Adana. By situating the massacres in the context of the counterrevolution, this chapter scrutinizes the starting point—a brawl that took place between an Armenian and a Turk in the neighborhood of Şabaniye—and reconstructs the successive phases of the massacres while analyzing their progression. This chapter also examines another salient feature of the Adana massacres—the role of emotions—and provides an analysis of the disparate motivations of the participants in the massacres, which included soldiers, reservists, Circassians, Avşars, Afghans, Cretan refugees, and *fellahin* (Muslim agricultural workers). It also discusses the spread of the violence to various districts of the Adana and Aleppo provinces, showing how provincial officials in these districts incited the Muslim population to violence by alleging that an Armenian rebellion was imminent.[91]

Chapter 5 examines the second wave of massacres in the city of Adana. The public sphere in the inter-massacre period became an instrument for the opponents of Armenians to further incite the masses in Adana by explaining to them what had clearly happened in the failed "revolt." Despite the declaration of martial law by the vali (governor) of Adana, the public sphere was not restrained. On the contrary, the public discourse—mostly propagated by the *İtidal* (Moderation) newspaper—fomented more anger and hostility toward the Armenians, who were portrayed as undesirable elements and as an "existential threat" to the Muslim population. In massacres, the tool of propaganda is used to disqualify the victim; in the words of Sémelin, it is "advance killing with words."[92] In critical periods, emotions can easily be manipulated by agents provocateurs with the aim of mobilizing the masses toward attacking targeted groups. In the case of Adana, the revolutionary activities of a handful of Armenian *fedayees* (freedom fighters) were presented by agents provocateurs through a magnifying glass. As a result, the majority of the Muslim population sincerely came to believe in an Armenian uprising, whereby European military intervention (British and French) would lead to the reestablishment of the Kingdom of Cilicia.

Chapter 6 considers the local and international humanitarian aid efforts that were rendered to the victims of Adana, as well as the local, regional, and international reactions to the massacres. It discusses the reasons why humanitarian intervention did not take place on behalf of the Armenians. As more than twenty thousand remained homeless after the massacres, the task of feeding and taking care of the survivors was a daunting one. Some European consuls and missionaries as well as Armenian organizations worked relentlessly to alleviate the misery of the Armenians. Appeals for aid were heard from Athens to Jerusalem, from Manchester to Berlin, and from New York to Lausanne. International, national, and local organizations engaged in intensive fundraising efforts for the Armenians. Despite its relatively slow action, the Ottoman government, too, participated in aiding the victims of massacres. This chapter also demonstrates how, although these massacres have since fallen into obscurity, the international press covered them extensively at the time.

Chapter 7 analyzes the abortive steps taken by the imperial authorities to bring the perpetrators of the Adana massacres to justice. The CUP, which had just returned to power after the counterrevolution, sent investigation commissions to the region and ordered the establishment of courts-martial. This chapter discusses the work of those investigation commissions, the mechanisms through which the courts-martial functioned, and the reasons for their failure to institute justice. It also discusses the dramatic and instructive story of Hagop Babigian,[93] an Armenian member of both the CUP and the parliament who served on one of these investigation commissions. The disappearance of Babigian's report on the investigations, and his death three days before he was scheduled to testify in the parliament about the massacres, occurred under mysterious circumstances. Babigian's fate raised major questions during the period about the real culprits behind the massacres.

Chapter 8 examines the workings of the courts-martial. It analyzes the
legal system and the types of crimes that were committed. Furthermore,
it discusses the sentencing of the primary culprits complicit in the Adana
massacres and demonstrates the various reactions of the Armenians and
the Muslims to the verdicts of the courts-martial. With the appointment
of Ahmet Cemal Paşa, a member of the CUP Central Committee and kaymakam (district governor) of Üsküdar, as the governor of Adana, a new phase
began. Public order was restored, and an attempt was made to reconcile the
parties. Through his strong persona, Cemal Paşa improved the situation in
Adana by effectively implementing the humanitarian work and constructing
houses for the Armenian refugees.

The concluding chapter situates the Adana massacres in the larger context of ethno-religious violence in the region and beyond. Although each
case of ethno-religious violence is unique, understanding the commonalities
between them will give scholars better tools for examining such phases of
violence. For this reason, I arbitrarily compare the Adana massacres to two
other phases of violence inflicted on minority groups: the pogroms of Odessa
of 1905 and the massacre of the Sikhs of 1984. This provides a more global
perspective on massacres in terms of underlying causes, perpetrators, and
abortive justice. Finally, I briefly address the question of how better to understand the Adana massacres in relation to the Armenian Genocide, while
bearing in mind their individual trajectories rather than simply viewing the
first event as foreshadowing the second.

CHAPTER 1

A FRAYED TAPESTRY

The Transformation of Adana in the Nineteenth Century

The Ottoman province of Adana constitutes a large section of the historical territory of Cilicia, which lies along the northeastern shore of the Mediterranean Sea.[1] To the south, it is bounded by the Mediterranean; to the west, by the provinces of Konya and Ankara; to the north, by the provinces of Konya, Ankara, and Sivas; and to the east, by the province of Aleppo.[2] One of the most important features of its geography is the Cilician plain, considered to be the most fertile plain in the region. It extends from the Gulf of İskenderun (Alexandretta) in the east to the Lamas Su (Lamas River) in the west.[3] The fertile soil of the Cilician plain enables a high level of cereal and cotton production.[4] The territory is surrounded by three mountain chains—the Taurus to the northwest, the Anti-Taurus to the northeast, and the Amanus to the east—and its plain is crossed by three rivers: the Tarsus, Seyhan, and Ceyhan.[5]

Historically speaking, it has not been a particularly habitable area. The majority of the region's marshes were once a breeding ground for dangerous, fever-bearing insects.[6] The plain's climate was exceedingly hot and humid during the summers, which led the local population to move to the orchards in search of better air quality.[7] Travelers of the nineteenth century reported that public life in Adana and Tarsus practically came to a halt during the summer, when much of the population abandoned the cities for the cooler mountain pastures (*yayla*).[8]

This chapter provides a historical background of the region of Cilicia and its significance to the Armenians. It will demonstrate how the various political, socioeconomic, and demographic changes that took place in Adana in the nineteenth century created a contentious environment in the region. Competition over resources, agrarian conflict, economic envy, ethno-religious tensions, power struggles, and modernization, among other factors described in this chapter, led to an atmosphere of distrust, anxiety, fear, and hatred. Unlike in other provinces, these feelings were suppressed in Adana during the Hamidian period. However, the 1908 Revolution opened a Pandora's box that led to the public manifestation of these anxieties. Hence, in order to understand the contentious postrevolutionary situation, it is important to examine in detail the ways in which regional, as well as global, economic and sociopolitical transformations shaped the region of Cilicia in general and that of Adana in particular.

The History of Armenians in Adana

Armenian presence in Adana goes back to the period of Tigran the Great (r. 95–55 BC). As a result of reforms implemented by Emperor Justinian, the Byzantine emperor in Armenia during the 530s AD, a significant wave of Armenians joined their cousins who were already in the region.[9] Later, in the middle of the seventh century, Adana was occupied by the Arabs. Thereafter, it frequently shifted between Arab and Byzantine rule. The emergence of Armenian communities at this time was augmented by waves of voluntary and involuntary migrations under the Byzantine Empire as a result of the Seljuk invasion of the region. The defeat of the Byzantine Empire at the hands of the Seljuks in the Battle of Manzikert in 1071 was a turning point in the region's history.[10] The outcome of that battle led to the migration of Armenian dynastic families such as the Artsrunis, the Rupenians, and the Hetumians from Armenia proper to Cilicia, culminating in the establishment of an Armenian principality (1080–1198) and the Armenian Kingdom of Cilicia (1198–1375), which had its capital in Sis (Kozan).[11] The Battle of Manzikert also paved the way for a massive flow of Turkic tribes from the east to Anatolia. Hence, the strong presence of Armenians in Cilicia under Ottoman rule goes back to the period of the Armenian Kingdom of Cilicia.

The Armenian Kingdom of Cilicia, which lasted until 1375, represented an important chapter in Armenian history and is known as the Armenian Silver Age.[12] This kingdom was the first independent Armenian state with direct access to the Mediterranean Sea to exist outside the borders of historic Armenia. Cilicia was characterized by extensive commerce (especially with Genoa and Venice), cultural rejuvenation, and diplomatic relations between the Crusaders representing the West and the Mongols representing the East.[13] It would take more than half a millennium after the fall of the Armenian Kingdom for an independent Armenian government to be established (1918–20).

Cilicia also had significant religious meaning for the Armenians, since it housed the Holy See of the Catholicosate in Sis, its capital.[14] As a result of the Seljuk invasion of Armenia, the Holy See moved in 1292 from Echmiadzin to Sis under the patronage of the Armenian Kingdom of Cilicia.[15] When the kingdom collapsed in 1375, the Church Assembly decided to transfer the Holy See back to Echmiadzin, its traditional location.[16] However, the Catholicos of Cilicia in Sis continued to function until World War I, when it was transferred to Lebanon.[17] During the Ottoman period, the Catholicos had jurisdiction over his own diocese and several others, including the archbishop of Adana, who presided over the bishops of Payas, Haçin, Zeitun, and Aintab.

In addition to the Armenian Apostolic community, Adana had an Armenian Catholic community dating to the seventeenth century, resulting from Italian and French missionary activities. Even though the primate of the Armenian Catholic Church resided in Bzomar, Lebanon, from 1742 to 1867, he bore the title of the Patriarch of Cilicia. In 1849, the number of Armenian Catholics in Adana reached two thousand. The first Armenian Catholic church in Adana, Anarat Heghut'iwn (Immaculate Conception), was built in 1851. A few years later, the church bought agricultural land and a farm in the village of Şeyhmurat to generate revenue for the church and its community.[18] Adana also had a small Armenian Protestant mission, which was established in the mid-nineteenth century.[19] In 1866, the first Protestant church was built in Adana, followed by the establishment of the Protestant American Girls College.[20]

After the collapse of the Armenian Kingdom, Cilicia was incorporated into the Mamluk Empire and became the core territory of the Ramadanids.[21] During his Egyptian expedition in 1516, the Ottoman sultan Selim I incorporated the *beylik* (principality) of Adana into the Ottoman Empire, although the Ramadanids were not removed from power but remained in control of the region as vassals of the Ottomans. They maintained the administration of the Ottoman *sancak* (district) of Adana in a hereditary manner until 1608.[22] From that time onward, Adana constituted a regular province (*eyalet*) under a tax collector (*mütesellim*) appointed by the sultan. Despite this change, however, the power of the Ottoman government in the region remained very weak.[23]

During the eighteenth century, Adana was inflicted with several rivalries among the local *derebey*s (feudal lords),[24] who controlled Cilicia autonomously, levying taxes, raising troops, and acting as kaymakams of the Ottoman government. An important power among the *derebey*s were the Kozanoğulları, a Turkmen tribe,[25] whose position was strengthened by an informal alliance with the Armenian Catholicos of Sis.[26] Such alliances were cemented by the common interest of the Kozanoğulları and the Armenian notables in defending their traditional autonomy against the encroachment of İstanbul, although the Armenians paid a high price for maintaining relations with the Kozan beys.[27] In addition to paying a hefty annual tribute, the Armenian Catholicosate of Sis also suffered as a result of conflicts among the *derebey*s. For example, Catholicos Kapriel Achabahian was killed on September 10, 1770, as a result of the inter-tribal rivalry between the Kozanoğulları and the Divanoğulları.[28]

In addition to the *derebey*s, there were approximately twenty-six pastoral, nomadic tribes in Cilicia.[29] These tribes moved seasonally with their herds. In the summers, they moved to the plateaus surrounding Cilicia; in the winters, they moved to their winter quarters inside Cilicia.[30] These tribes had rather disruptive relationships with the sedentary population—particularly with the Armenians. When they wintered on the foothills of the Taurus and the Çukurova, they came into contact with Armenians engaged in crafts, agriculture, viticulture, horse-breeding, and mining.[31] As a result of the liberty enjoyed by these tribes, the security and economic development of the local

population suffered immensely.[32] Several attempts by the Ottoman government to settle the tribes failed, until the forced settlement of 1865.[33]

Adana under the Egyptian Occupation

In 1831, in line with his expansionist policies, the Egyptian ruler Muhammad
Ali sent his son, İbrahim Paşa (1789–1848), to Syria, which was "historically
seen as an extension of Egypt."[34] Shortly afterward, İbrahim established his
headquarters in Adana. In 1833, as a result of the Treaty of Kütahya, both the
Syrian provinces and the district of Adana were ceded to him, and he became governor of the two provinces. In less than a decade, however, thanks in
part to the intervention of the European powers, the Egyptians were forced
to evacuate Syria. Through the Convention of London in 1840, Europeans
forced Muhammad Ali to return both Syria and Adana to the Ottomans. As
a result, Adana became part of the province of Aleppo.

Some of the most significant outcomes of İbrahim Paşa's time in Syria
and Adana were the social and governmental innovations he introduced
there and the effects of those innovations on the socioeconomic and demographic statuses of the region. Under his rule, more freedom was granted to
the non-Muslim population of the region, government monopolies were established, and direct taxation and military conscription were introduced. The
Muslim population resented these reforms and revolted beginning in 1834,
with rebellions breaking out against the Egyptians in northern Syria, Lebanon, and Palestine—particularly in Jerusalem. In Syria, the repercussions of
İbrahim's policies, coupled with the Tanzimat Reforms, led to both civil war
in Mount Lebanon and the Damascus Massacres of 1860.[35]

İbrahim's forces in Cilicia numbered around twenty thousand men, allowing him to introduce major economic changes in the region through mining as well as agriculture. He requested mining engineers from the Austro-
Hungarian government in order to find ore in Lebanon and Mount Tarsus
and invited the Austrian mining engineer Joseph Russegger to the region.[36]
İbrahim also reopened the mines in Tarsus and Amanus and built new roads;
developed the port of Mersin; exported a massive amount of timber from the
mountains of Rhosus, Amanus, and Tarsus to Egypt; and introduced sugar-
cane while investing heavily in agriculture.[37] İbrahim ordered the draining of

the swamps to advance Cilicia's agricultural system and developed its cotton culture at a time when Egypt was dominating regional cotton production. Thus, the commercialization of cotton in the second half of the nineteenth century and the transformation of Cilicia into a major cotton-producing region alongside Egypt can be traced back to İbrahim's agricultural policies.[38]

The demographic changes that took place under İbrahim's rule were no less significant. He began a serious tribal sedentarization process by implementing the policies that his father had successfully carried out in Egypt.[39] In addition to these reforms, Muslim and Christian Arabs were settled in the region both as expert laborers and as workers in the fields.[40] The expert laborers consisted of Christian Arabs, who became commercial and industrial merchants. The field workers consisted of fellahin.[41] Thus, Arabs and even North Africans began to settle in the area, upsetting a finely tuned demographic balance, which included Armenians and both nomadic and sedentary tribes.[42]

İbrahim Paşa also developed the city of Adana during this period, turning it into the urban center of Cilicia and building a city infrastructure that would continue to develop into the second half of the nineteenth century. Historian Stephan Astourian argues that Egyptian rule during this period "revealed that the economic potential of Cilicia was great and that its exploitation depended on competent administration."[43] Indeed, after the retreat of İbrahim Paşa, the region deteriorated, as the Ottomans were unable to maintain the Egyptian reforms, leading to anarchy.[44] From 1840 until 1867, Adana was ruled by fifteen different *mutasarrıf*s (governors of sancaks) and was part of a *paşalık* (a territory governed by a *paşa*) connected to Aleppo.[45] In 1867, it became an independent province.

After the Egyptian occupation ended, the Ottoman Empire witnessed major transformations that shaped the political as well as the socioeconomic dynamics of the region. These transformations included administrative reforms, economic development, sedentarization and pacification, population growth resulting from the influx of refugees, and changes in the land codes.

Administrative Reforms

As part of the Tanzimat Reforms, the Vilayet Law of 1864 (*Teşkil-i Vilâyet Nizamnâmesi*) was introduced, replacing the *eyalet* system. This represented a fundamental change in Ottoman administrative structure in the provinces:

MAP. 1. The vilayets of Adana and Aleppo in the nineteenth century. This map shows the borders and subdivisions of the Adana and Aleppo vilayets, as well as important settlements. Map by Patrick T. Hoehne.

the empire was now divided into *vilayet*s (provinces), each of which was divided into *sancak*s (districts), *kaza*s (subdistricts), and *nahiye*s (subdivisions of a kaza). Under this new system, the vali, who was appointed by İstanbul, became both the governor and the general commander of the province. In each province, new departments were established, including bureaus of economic services; postal services; foreign affairs; public works; service, trade, and agriculture; and public education, among others.[46] Each province had three advisory bodies, which included Muslims, Christians, and Jews. In 1865, Adana and the districts of Payas and Kozan were attached to the province of Aleppo.[47] In 1867, however, Adana was detached from the province of Aleppo and became part of a separate province that also contained Payas and Kozan.[48] In that year, the province of Adana consisted of the districts of Adana, Mersin, İçil, Kozan, and Cebel-i Bereket.[49]

In the second half of the nineteenth century, Armenians were very active in Cilicia's provincial administration, working primarily in the central

districts.[50] There were two to three Armenians on the province's Administrative Council representing the Apostolic, Catholic, and Protestant communities. In addition, three to six Armenians were elected to administrative
roles in the municipality of Adana. After the provincial reforms, two Armenians served as mayors of Adana: Krikor Bzdigian (1877–79) and Sinyor
Artin (1879–81).[51] Armenians in Adana were also employed in the control of
revenue and expenditure, in the taxation department, in the Ottoman Bank,
in the local branch of the Agricultural Bank (Zirâat Bankası), in public debt
administration, in the court of appeal, in commerce, as chief engineers of the
province, in the post office, as operators of telegraphic services, and as railway
station masters in Adana, Mersin, and Tarsus.[52] In regions such as Haçin,
where Armenians constituted the majority, they entirely controlled the municipality.[53] Armenians also were active in the police force and in the fields of
agriculture, public health, and education.[54]

Economic Development

The economic transformation of Cilicia was part and parcel of the wider,
major economic changes of the nineteenth century. As the Ottoman Empire emerged as a semi-peripheral region in the global economic system, certain regions and groups benefited more than others. With the signing of the
Anglo-Ottoman Convention of 1838, the Ottoman state abolished monopolies in foreign trade and prohibited exports of any commodity. In addition,
the treaty removed internal tariffs previously imposed on British merchants
and allowed them to settle in any region of the empire.[55] While Christians
and Jews benefited from this agreement by gaining protection from European powers, Muslim merchants found themselves at a disadvantage, since
they were required to pay taxes from which non-Muslims were exempt.[56]

This free-trade treaty played an enormous role in increasing agricultural
production for export, aiding in the development of Cilicia as a cotton-
producing region.[57] It is impossible to discuss the economic transformation
of Cilicia without considering the role of cotton. Cotton, which came to be
known as "white gold" (ak altın), became the area's most important commodity, radically reshaping both regional and international trade. Cotton production was not a novelty in Adana; its roots went back to the fourteenth
century. Until the second half of the nineteenth century, however, it was

produced only for domestic use. Cotton production in the region was crucial to the emergence of Mersin,[58] located in the southern part of the province of Adana, as a major regional port city.[59] As a result of Cilicia's massive production of cotton, the port replaced that of İzmir as the main port for cotton exports of the Ottoman Empire.

Agricultural production in the region generally followed a predictable rhythm. Fields usually were plowed in October for the main winter crops, barley and wheat; while barley was harvested at the end of April, wheat was reaped in June or July. In summer, the main crops were cotton and sesame, which usually were sown in the spring.[60] The plowing of cotton began in April, and the picking began in the fall, around October. These agricultural operations on the plain of Cilicia were the major source of income for the region's poor people. Normally, somewhere between 60,000 and 120,000 migrant workers came to Adana from across the eastern provinces to work the land each spring.[61] Most of the migrant workers were Muslim (Kurds, Turks, Arabs) and Armenian peasants from Diyarbekir, Urfa, Harput, Bitlis, and as far away as Mosul.[62] These workers returned home after a few months of work: the income generated during that period was sufficient to sustain them for the rest of the year.[63] Seasonal labor also fitted the semi-nomadic tribes' lifestyle, allowing them to resume their traditional migrations during the majority of the year.[64] Historian Hilmar Kaiser argues that the concentration of such a large number of seasonal workers from different backgrounds led to major problems. Fights took place between different work gangs, usually with blunt instruments.[65]

The American Civil War of 1861–65 had a huge impact on Adana. When cotton production was disrupted in the American South, Great Britain's main cotton supplier,[66] the Ottoman government took steps to capitalize on the situation. For example, in 1863, the Ottoman government of Sultan Abdülaziz (1861–76) allowed the import of agricultural machinery without taxes, and the Ottoman Trade Office published fourteen thousand copies of a pamphlet on how to improve the production of cotton. Knowing the important role Armenians played in cotton production, the Armenian newspaper *Kilikia* (Cilicia) translated these orders into Armenian.[67] In 1866, with the aim of encouraging cotton production, the government distributed free American cottonseed to the peasants.[68]

The commercialization of Cilicia's agriculture during the second half of the nineteenth century necessitated the use of many types of modern machinery. In particular, demand for agricultural machines for cotton factories and mills increased considerably.[69] The first factory equipped with cotton gins in Adana was founded in 1864 by the French engineer Justin Daudet.[70] By the end of the nineteenth century the Greek Trypani family followed suit by entering the cotton business. Thereafter, they became owners of the most important factories and machines in Adana. Trypani and his sons also established a steam-powered spinning mill that competed with the Greek Mavromatis family's workshop in Tarsus.[71]

By the end of the nineteenth century, 19 hydraulic presses, 45 oil presses, and 33 tanneries—all of which included modern machinery—served the needs of the area.[72] In 1909, the British traveler David Fraser noted that the province of Adana contained approximately 450 cotton-ginning machines, 18,000 spindles, 200 looms, 10 flour mills, 60 threshing machines, 4 steam plows, and 1,000 reaping machines.[73] Most of this machinery was British and imported by the Trypani firm. Fraser noted, "[Although] there is not a born Briton at Adana or Tarsus, our reputation for the manufacture of machinery seems to have remained undiminished."[74]

Toward the beginning of the twentieth century, Germany also played an important role in supplying machinery to the region. By 1909, nearly thirty German companies served Cilicia's needs for modern machinery. Fraser wrote that the annual migration of laborers decreased in 1909 because "the resident population, aided by steam-plows, steam-threshers, and reaping machines, were able to undertake the labor themselves." According to him, this was "a magnificent object-lesson in the utility of agricultural machinery, by which it would be well if other provinces could profit. One reaping-machine, which can be purchased for £15, is said to do the work of forty men."[75] Fraser's commentary focuses entirely on the efficiency of these operations, failing to note the negative impact this modernization process had on the poor migrant workers being replaced by those machines. Some of those migrants would find an outlet for their anger and frustration in the massacres that took place in April of that year.

Although European and American concerns were heavily involved in this mechanization process, we should not underplay the role of local actors in Cilicia.[76] For example, most of the machinery imported from the larger English and German firms was operated by indigenous people.[77] Additionally, Adana's local merchants greatly facilitated agricultural mechanization.[78] These included Abdülkadir Bağdadizade, one of the major landowners in Adana, who worked with foreign companies such as the German Levantine Cotton Company (Deutsche-Levantine Baumwolle-Gesellschaft) of Dresden.[79] Adana's bankers, both native and foreign, also contributed significantly to the commercialization of agriculture. A branch of the Ottoman Bank had opened at the end of the 1880s.[80] In 1888, an imperial decree established the Agricultural Bank in Adana with the aim of lending money to cultivators. Foreign banks followed suit.

The province of Adana not only supplied cotton to the rest of the Ottoman Empire but increasingly produced a substantial amount for the global market. This upward trend in exports continued in the early years of the twentieth century. From 1904 to 1906, Fraser estimated that the total annual export and import trade of Mersin averaged £1.5 million (equivalent to around £180 million in 2021).[81] According to the data reported in an Armenian newspaper in 1907, between thirty-five thousand and fifty thousand bales of cotton were exported from Adana that year.[82] In exchange, in addition to financial payment, imported goods came through the port of Mersin from the United Kingdom, Egypt, Cyprus, America, Austria-Hungary, Belgium, France, Germany, Greece, Italy, Russia, Spain, the rest of Turkey, and other countries.[83] The largest portion of these imports were machines, specifically machines used in cotton production and manufacturing. The United Kingdom's imports were valued at £670,830, followed by Turkey's at £124,590, and then Egypt's at £60,690.[84]

The figures above demonstrate the massive increase in cotton production and exports during the second half of the nineteenth century, locally, regionally, and globally. They also demonstrate the extent to which the local population—ranging from migrant workers to the agents of international companies—were involved in the production, intensifying the level of internal competition for the benefits of these developments. Christians (Armenians and Greeks) were the chief beneficiaries. This fact, coupled with the introduction of modern means of production, led to uneven distribution of profits, causing much anxiety among the Muslim communities represented by local notables, refugees, tribes, and migrant workers. Thus, with the advancement of cotton production and exports, economic envy toward non-Muslims in the region—especially toward Armenians—also increased.

Development of Transportation and Communication

The development of transportation and communication in the second half of the nineteenth century and at the beginning of the twentieth century also contributed immensely to the province's economic advancement. The railway system led to rapid acceleration in the import of goods and the export of agricultural material, chiefly through the port of Mersin. In addition, steamer lines incorporated the province into regional and global economic systems.

Railways developed rapidly during this period. In the 1880s, the Mersin–Adana line (which passed through Tarsus) was established to develop trade and commerce.[85] By the beginning of the twentieth century, there were three railways in Adana. The first was the Mersin–Adana line, the second was the Baghdad Railway, and the third was the İskenderun–Toprakkale (a town in the district of Osmaniye) line.[86] The most important of these was the Mersin–Adana line, which was directly connected to cotton exports from Mersin. The railway was constructed in 1886, for the most part with British capital, and for some years was worked by a British company in which French interests were subsequently represented. In 1905, however, virtual control of the Mersin–Adana line was obtained by a German group, although the railway retained an Anglo-French directorate.[87]

The port of Mersin also was well connected with other parts of the empire through steamer lines. In the beginning of the twentieth century, various steamer lines operated by foreign powers ran between Mersin and several other ports. These were the British Khedivial, Prince, Asia Minor, Ellerman, Egypt, and Levant lines; the French Messageries Maritimes line; the Russian Navigation et Commerce line; the Italian Florio Rubattino line; the German Deutsche Levant and Atlas lines; the Dutch Royal Nederlandais line; the Belgian Adolf Deb line; the Austrian Lloyd line; and the Greek Pantaleon and Cozzika lines.[88]

Communication also developed quickly and expansively during this period. Telegraph offices could be found in Adana, Mersin, Tarsus, İskenderun, Karataş, Misis, Ayas, Sis, Yarsuat, Erzin, Dörtyol, and Payas. The first four of these cities had international service. Adana was a directing station for local lines through communication with Konya, İstanbul, and İskenderun.[89] The development of communication and transportation played an important role in advancing Armenian economic superiority in the region of Cilicia while enabling the transfer of information in a striking speed. These developments would play a significant role in the dissemination of rumors leading to fear and anxiety in the different districts and subdistricts of the province that culminated in massacres against the Armenians.

Armenians in the Economy

Armenians played an important role in Adana's economy in the second half of the nineteenth century and the beginning of the twentieth century. For example, the most important cotton exporters in Adana were the Ashikian-Bakalian, Pambukchian-Donikian, Shadrigian, Sofolikidis (Greek), and Gulbenkian families.[90] The cotton factory of Calouste and Badrig Gulbenkian in the city of Adana played an important role in the city's economy. An enormous sock factory was owned by the Babigian-Chakmakchian and Parigian families.[91] Of the four wheat factories in Adana, the Ashikian-Bakalian factory was equipped with the most modern technology.[92] Two of the four ice factories belonged to the Ashikian-Bakalian and the Pambukchian-Donikian manufacturing businesses.[93] In the sesame business, Maghserchi Hagop was prominent. Construction equipment was imported by Avedis Avedisian and Mihran Keshishian, among others.[94]

Armenians were also active in the economy of the other districts of the province. A branch of the Gulbenkian company was located in Mersin, along with the commercial houses of N. Ghazanchian and the Frengian brothers.[95] The cotton factory in Mersin belonged to the Zelveyans.[96] Bedros S. Urfalian was in the business of importing construction materials. Many Armenian families and businesses were involved in textile imports.[97] In Tarsus, the Shalvarjians owned modern machinery for cotton processing and manufacturing; the largest wheat factory, which produced sixty-thousand kilograms of wheat a day, also belonged to them.[98] In Dörtyol, which was famous for its oranges, Armenians played an important role in the business of picking, processing, packaging, and transporting oranges. Among such businesses was the Armenian-owned Yepremian factory, which had about one thousand employees.[99] The oranges were exported to İzmir, İstanbul, and Odessa, among other cities.[100] In addition to these Armenian industrialists, there were many Armenian traders and artisans concentrated in Cilicia's major cities. Outside the district of Adana, they had an influential presence in Tarsus, as well as in the subdistricts of Haçin, Sis, İçil, and Payas. Most of these important businesses were destroyed and looted during the massacres.

The economic development of Cilicia in the second half of the nineteenth century made it one of the world's most attractive regions for European powers interested in investments overseas. In their global economic rivalry, Great Britain, France, and Germany all competed over the region. This competition, and the abundance of cotton in the area, elevated the importance of the province of Adana in particular, making it one of the most strategically economically desirable areas within the Ottoman Empire.

Sedentarization and Pacification

The settlement and pacification of the nomadic tribes and the dismantling of the *derebeys*' power in the Adana region took place in the context of the Tanzimat Reforms and the Crimean War (1853–56).[101] A recent study on the settlement and pacification of the tribes argues that the real catalyst for the settlement campaign was the murder of American missionary Jackson Coffing in 1862 near the region of Payas. The murder led to a diplomatic crisis, causing the Ottoman government to take measures designed to bring law and order to the region.[102] One of the aims of the Tanzimat Reforms was the centralization of the administration, bringing all the regions of the empire under İstanbul's control. The region of Cilicia, which had been under the control of the *derebeys* for centuries, was initially outside this centralized control.[103] For example, during the Crimean War, İstanbul needed to recruit forces from the region, but because the local tribes were not under the government's control, this aim was not realized.[104]

In 1863, the Reform Division (Fırka-i Islâhiye) under the command of Derviş Paşa—who also was the commander of the Ottoman Fourth Army—was established to address this situation.[105] According to contemporaneous historian Ahmed Cevdet, who was appointed director of the division's civil issues (*umûr-ı mülkiyye*), its aim was to bring the region into the "circle of submission."[106] More specifically, the goal was to pacify the region from

İskenderun to Maraş to Elbistan; from Kilis to Niğde to Kayseri; and from the *eyalet* of Adana to the borders of the *eyalet* of Sivas. Both Derviş Paşa and Cevdet were able to gain the trust of some of the tribes, which facilitated their work.[107] According to Christopher Gratien, the more ambitious aim behind the process of restoring order and pacification was to spread "civilization" (*medeniyet*) in the countryside.[108]

Initiated in early 1865, the Reform Division's expedition to the area consisted of about 9,000 infantry, 2,000 cavalry, and six pieces of artillery. It was, in fact, bigger than İbrahim Paşa's army.[109] According to Cevdet, this force included Kurdish, Circassian, and Cretan Muslim battalions, which came from Aleppo, Crete, Maraş, and Adana, raising the number of battalions to eleven.[110] On May 27, 1865, the Reform Division arrived on the coast of Adana, and the next day it docked at the port of İskenderun. Between 1865 and 1866, the Reform Division succeeded in bringing Çukurova, Gavur Dağı (Cebel-i Bereket), and Kozan Dağı under the control of the state. It also successfully settled the nomadic tribes in the newly established towns and villages, such as Osmaniye, İslahiye, İziye, Dervişiye, and Cevdetiye.[111] Its strategy was one of reconciliation rather than punishment: a declaration was sent to all the region's leaders, asking for submission in exchange for being pardoned.[112] A general amnesty was granted to all who had failed to pay taxes, evaded military service, or been disloyal to the sultan.[113] In November 1866, the division's commanders returned to İstanbul for the winter, leaving their troops posted in garrisons throughout Cilicia. There was very little resistance from the tribes, and most of the *derebey*s had given up without a fight.

Six years after the beginning of the campaign, Archbishop Bedros Der Melkonian published a book titled *Patmut'iwn Azatut'eann Hachēnoy i Dserats' K'ōzaneants'* (The history of the salvation of Haçin from the hands of Kozanoğulları), in which he described the complicated situation of the Armenians during the campaign.[114] According to that book, a certain Mkrtich Bayramian Ağa from Haçin played an important role in providing directions to Derviş Paşa. Der Melkonian relates that Archbishop Bedros, prelate of Haçin, initially made the other leaders take an oath of loyalty to the Kozanoğulları.[115] However, when the Armenian notables returned to Haçin, they decided to contact [Kurt] İsmail Paşa, one of the commanders of the Reform Division, and escaped from Haçin to surrender to him. İsmail Paşa demanded that Archbishop Bedros attend an audience with him. At first, the prelate of Haçin refused to comply. As a result, two Ottoman battalions besieged Haçin and denied its population, as well as the surrounding villages, access to salt and wheat, leading to a famine. On July 10, 1865, the *mufti* (a Muslim legal expert who is in charge of Islamic affairs for a province or district) and Turkish and Armenian notables went to see İsmail Paşa. He received them and told them: "From now on you are our subject, if the Kozanoğulları harm you, or bring financial damage, and if we cannot help you at that time, it is our duty to pay you ten times more from the state treasury."[116]

When law and order had prevailed in Haçin, Derviş Paşa began the task of dispersing the Kozanoğulları. At the same time, a cholera outbreak hit the army.[117] Once Derviş Paşa became aware of the outbreak, he handed the important task of dispersion over to İsmail Paşa and returned to Sis, traveling from there to İstanbul. By the time Derviş Paşa arrived in İstanbul, the Reform Division had achieved its main objective: pacifying the region of Kozan. This accomplishment led to the division of the region of Kozan into four subdistricts: Sis, Belenköy, Haçin (Saimbeyli), and Kadirli. Although the major tribe of Çukurova, the Avşars, requested settlement in the town of Aziziye, near the border of Sivas, they ended up near the Uzunyayla, where refugees from the Caucasus were also settled.[118] Meanwhile, Tatar refugees were settled in the town of Kadirli. As a result of these measures, some unsettled tribes moved to Aleppo. Gradually, the tribes became accustomed to sedentary life and centralized Ottoman rule. Thus, by settling the nomads of Çukurova, Kozan, Gavur Dağı, and Kurtdağı, the division brought all these areas under state control.

As a result of the Reform Division's initiatives, the region was pacified and attracted a sizable number of new immigrants, such as Turkmens and Circassians, who sought refuge from other parts of Anatolia and the Caucasus.[119] Vital Cuinet estimated the number of Circassian immigrants during this period to be between twelve thousand and thirteen thousand.[120] These newcomers were broken up into small groups and dispersed among the Armenian, Kurdish, and Alevi concentrations in the southeast, disrupting the shaky demographic balance that had existed in the region. The towns of Hassa, İslahiye, Osmaniye, Reyhanlı, Kadirli, and Kozan all emerged as a result of the policies of settlement enforced by the division.[121]

An Influx of Refugees

Sedentarization programs in the second half of the nineteenth century co-incided with a massive influx of refugees from Crimea and the Caucasus.[122] This combination radically reshaped rural life.[123] The arrival of hundreds of thousands of Muslim refugees from these regions and—later, during the Balkan Wars—from the Balkans, fleeing war and persecution, dramatically changed Anatolia's demographic structure.[124] The first period of migration from Crimea and the Caucasus took place between 1858 and 1863.[125] Later, between 1877 and 1891, 28,730 refugees were sent from İstanbul to Adana.[126] In the case of Adana, the arrival of refugees led not only to demographic changes but also to land shortages, competition over resources, and the rise of ethno-religious tensions.

In response to the arrival of the first of these groups, the Nogay refugees,[127] the Refugee Commission (Muhacirin Komisyonu) was established.[128] Cevdet Paşa reported that, in 1866, the commission ordered that the Nogay refugees be settled in the region between Mersin and Adana.[129] By settling them in Adana, the government aimed to increase agricultural production in the region. This initiative was facilitated by the ease of transport between Mersin and Adana; Adana was located on the Mediterranean and the existing Mersin–Adana line made it a relatively straightforward operation.[130]

One of the premises for the commission's decision was that there was a surplus of uncultivated, vacant land in the Adana area.[131] While seeking a location to settle the refugees, the government had sent letters to local administrations asking for information about available land and had received answers from various regions, including Adana.[132] In fact, some of the supposedly vacant lands near Adana actually belonged to Armenians. For example, in 1906, the Telan property, which belonged to the Armenian Catholicosate of Cilicia, was allocated for the refugees.[133] This decision became a major source of conflict between the government and the Catholicosate, leading to the resignation of Cilician catholicos Sahag II Khabayan at the beginning of 1909 in protest against the government's measure.[134]

There were two waves of Crimean-Caucasian migrations to Adana.[135] As mentioned above, the first refugee group, which arrived in Adana between 1859 and 1861, were Nogays, approximately 20,000 of whom were settled in Adana.[136] In 1869, about 1,500 Karaçays (a Turkic ethnic group) and Circassians joined that first wave after leaving their homes in the North Caucasus and arriving in Adana as refugees.[137] The second wave of migration began as a result of the Russo-Turkish War of 1877–78 (93 Harbi). Kemal H. Karpat, who typically overestimates such figures, argues that half a million refugees arrived in the empire from the Caucasus between 1881 and 1914.[138] Some of those who arrived in Trabzon were sent to Adana in 1877.[139] According to Talat Paşa's notes, during the Russo-Turkish War, 29,785 Muslim refugees (5,922 households) arrived in Adana.[140] After the war, an additional 6,381 arrived in the province.[141] In 1891, approximately 5,000 Circassian refugees were also sent to Adana.[142] They were followed in 1902 by refugees from Crimea and Karabağ.[143] Some 400 of the refugees from Karabağ were settled in the Çiftlik-i Hümâyun villages in Çukurova.[144] In 1904, about 900 Crimean Muslim (Tatar) refugee households were settled in Adana.[145]

This influx of refugees had extensive effects on the area's communities. Some of the arriving refugees were settled in existing villages, while new villages were established for others. For example, in 1894, with the settling of the Circassian refugees, the village of Burhaniye was established.[146] As a result of the population increase, some villages became towns and some towns became boroughs.

In order to support them, the Refugee Commission distributed fifty dunams of land between Mersin and Payas or Kozan and Feke to each refugee family.[147] These families also received deeds to their new land, wheat and barley, an ox, and money to buy agricultural equipment.[148] In the process of their arrival and settlement, these refugees faced many hardships: transportation issues, climate problems (especially humidity and heat in the summer), epidemics such as malaria and especially the cholera outbreaks of 1890 and 1894, and sociopolitical friction with the local tribes.[149] As a result of the weather, in particular, some refuges left the Adana region for other provinces.

Thus, between 1867 and 1907, approximately twenty thousand Tatar, Kazak, Karaçay, Azeri, Kabartay, Circassian, Chechnian, Abhazian, Dağıstani, Karabağı, Tbilisi, Baku, Izabetol, and Dostof refugees were settled in Adana.[150] Interestingly, there is no mention in Turkish historiography of how the arrival of these refugees affected local Armenians—particularly of the extent to which these refugees were settled on land previously belonging to Armenian peasants. Astourian argues that the goal of Ottoman refugee-settlement policies during this period was clear: to settle Muslim immigrants from the Balkans and the Caucasus in the six eastern provinces (Erzurum, Harput, Sivas, Diyarbekir, Van, and Bitlis), which were inhabited by a dense Armenian population.[151] The aim was to change the population balance in favor of the Muslims.

The Population of Adana

The region of Cilicia encompassing Adana had an extremely diverse ethno-religious population, including Circassians, Kurds, Turkmens, Yuruks (of Oğuz Turkic descent), Romani (Roma) fellahin,[152] Ansariyeh,[153] Afghans, Armenians (Gregorians, Catholics, and Protestants), Orthodox Greeks, Orthodox Arabs, Arab Muslims, Latin Catholics, Europeans, Maronites, Chaldeans, Syriacs, and Jews.[154] Each of these groups did, however, have a tendency to congeal in larger concentrations in certain areas. In 1882, for example, the Armenian population in the province of Adana totaled about 280,000, concentrated mostly in the districts of Adana, Kozan, and Cebel-i Bereket.[155] Christian and Muslim Arabs from Syria, meanwhile, had settled in Mersin, where they formed the bulk of the population.[156]

Due to a lack of reliable sources and discrepancies among existing sources, it is difficult to provide a precise figure for the Armenian population of Adana in the nineteenth and early twentieth centuries; the figures provided by Armenian, European, and Ottoman sources do not match.[157] Most historians have relied on the Ottoman censuses for their accuracy, but these censuses represent Muslims as a monolithic group and break Christian populations down into different denominations. Astourian suggests that the censuses after the Treaty of Berlin were compiled with political consider-ations in mind.[158] Indeed, an examination of the total number of Armenians in the census of 1881–82 reveals a dramatic decrease.[159] The Ottoman census of 1914 places the number of Armenians living in Cilicia at 124,513 out of a total population of 936,087; of those Armenians, 58,027 were reported as residing in the province of Adana and the district of İçil.[160] According to the Armenian Patriarchate's census of 1914, however, there were 249,971 Armenians in Cilicia, with 119,414 of them living in Adana and İçil.[161] The difference between these figures demonstrates why census information became a contentious issue. Regardless of these discrepancies, it is clear that Armenians did not comprise a demographic majority in the province prior to the Adana massacres; in the postrevolutionary period, they probably comprised about 40 percent of the population.

It is, however, important to mention that, as a result of the economic boom in Adana and the demand for migrant workers, Armenians did migrate in large numbers to Adana, creating a strong Armenian settlement there. While most of these immigrations occurred for economic reasons, the Muslim leadership of Adana's postrevolutionary anti-Armenian discourse portrayed this process as part of a grandiose political plan engineered by Armenian religious and political leaders to populate Adana with Armenians in order to establish an independent Armenian entity that would have the support of the European powers.

Agrarian Reforms and the Land Question

The sedentarization process, along with the arrival and settlement of refugees in the region of Adana and other regions of the eastern provinces, led to a dramatic rise in competition over resources. Land was the most important source of conflict between the area's different ethno-religious groups. In the final two decades of the nineteenth century, this conflict led to the mass transfer of Armenian properties and their dispossession under the rule of Sultan Abdülhamid II. Thus, the land shortage constituted the most important aspect of the Armenian Question that arose in the second half of the nineteenth century.

According to historian Mehmet Polatel, land disputes accelerated after the 1890s. The Ottoman government initiated a systematic policy of settling immigrants on lands previously belonging to Armenians, most of whom had been scattered after the Hamidian massacres of 1894–97.[162] Polatel argues that, while conflict over land had generally been local in origin prior to the Hamidian period, it was orchestrated by the Ottoman government during the Hamidian period. Specifically, land conflicts in the pre-Hamidian period were characterized by conflicts between local elites (ağas and beys) and peasants. Whereas the Armenian peasants claimed customary and prospective rights to the lands, the power holders claimed that they had historical right to the disputed lands.[163]

The agrarian reforms in the second half of the nineteenth century, which were part of the Tanzimat Reforms, also had a huge impact on conflicts in the region. The most important of these reforms was the Land Code of 1858, which aimed at extracting taxes from the peasants and curbing the power of intermediaries such as notables, tribal leaders, and prominent landowners. The land code required the registration of land and the granting of title deeds (*tapu*), and in general, it led to the commodification of land.[164] As a result, by the 1870s, Christians and Jews could buy properties in Cilicia, and Armenians began buying large tracts of land.[165] This changed agrarian relations in the region, leading to niche overlap and the polarization of interethnic relations.[166] At the same time, the resettlement of Muslim refugees from Crimea and the Caucasus intensified interethnic polarization and competition over scarce resources. These conflicts took place between armed Muslims and an unarmed Christian population that the Muslims "associated with the Christian enemies who had expelled them from their previous homelands."[167]

Astourian disagrees with the idea that Cilician Muslims resented Cilician Armenians because Armenians had benefitted from the Ottoman Empire's semi-peripheralization in the global economic system. Rather, based on two reports of the oppression suffered by the Armenians in the eastern provinces sent to the Sublime Porte, he contends that the majority of the "oppressive acts" toward Armenians involved land usurpation by ağas, beys, ulemâ (Muslim scholars), and sheikhs.[168] These acts took place in the villages, which were detached from the global economic system, rather than in the towns.[169] Astourian presents the sequence of events as follows: In the region of Adana, Armenians began buying large landholdings in the 1870s. Within a few years, they—along with Greek residents—became major landowners in the province. Armenian economic success in the region led to resentment from a variety of actors, including Muslim refugees, Turkish beys, and Kurdish ağas, leading to acts of violence targeting Armenians.

Reports sent to the government by the Armenian Patriarchate demonstrate that many of the groups involved in oppressing the Armenian peasantry were composed of Muslim refugees settled in areas populated by

Armenians, Kurdish beys, and Avşar tribes, among others.[170] During the Hamidian period, the state took two dubiously legal measures to confiscate property: the authorities confiscated land belonging to Armenian peasants whose taxes were overdue, and the Agricultural Bank seized the land of those who could not repay their loans.[171] Polatel's research demonstrates that these confiscated properties were allocated to Muslim refugees from Crimea, the Caucasus, and the Balkans. The sedentarization of Kurdish tribes and their subsequent need for land was another reason for the expropriation of Armenian-owned land. In general, after the 1878 Treaty of Berlin, altering the demographic character of the eastern provinces by dispossessing Armenians became an important aspect of the Hamidians' centralization and homogenization policy.[172]

After the Young Turk Revolution of 1908, Armenian leaders lobbied extensively for the return of the lands confiscated during the Hamidian period. In 1909, the Armenian deputies of the Ottoman Parliament established the Commission of Usurped Lands to analyze 134 reports presented to the Ottoman government between the years 1890–1910.[173] The commission suggested that the expropriation, abuse, and violence inflicted on Armenians were part of a systematic policy initiated by the state, with the ultimate aim of impoverishing the Armenian peasantry and forcing them to emigrate. These policies did, in fact, lead to a massive emigration of Armenians from their ancestral homeland. According to the commission, 741,000 hectares of Armenian land had been usurped or confiscated during the previous decades.[174] However, the Young Turk regime failed to provide a remedy to the land question, and none of these lands were returned to their original Armenian owners.

The Armenians of Adana experienced their share of land confiscation. For example, in Payas, lemon fields belonging to the Armenian Catholicosate were confiscated by the government.[175] In Kars Pazarı, Sarkis and Panos Karamanoğlu's private 945 dunams, including one farm and a vineyard, were forcefully confiscated by Haji Rejib İsmailoğlu.[176] In Hamidiye, the land and farm of the Karasarkissians were forcefully confiscated by local Turks in 1895.[177] In Kars Pazar, fifty-seven parcels of land belonging to about fifty Armenians, including four walled properties (*arsan*), nine shops, and four homes were confiscated by force.[178] In addition, one of the two mills belonging to the Armenians in Enderun, Adana, was confiscated by force by Yaycıoğlu

Hacı Davud.[179] In 1901 in Dörtyol, lands belonging to the Armenian peasants of Nacarlı were forcefully confiscated by Rumelian refugees who had been settled in Hamidiye. These refugees built seventy wooden houses on the lands, and in the following years, the land confiscation expanded.[180]

Conclusion

This chapter has demonstrated the major transformations that took place in the province of Adana as the result of global economic changes, centralization reforms, the sedentarization of nomadic tribes, migrations, and immigration. Adana's complex population composition, geographical positioning, developing economy, and administrative reforms turned the province into a major hub for refugees and migrant workers. In the second half of the nineteenth century, Armenians arrived in Adana in large numbers, seeking better opportunities. These changes resulted directly from the region's modernization, especially the acceleration of cotton production. While modernization introduced machinery that greatly accelerated the pace of production and helped Adana become one of the most important economic centers in the region, it also led to decreased demand for migrant workers, causing anxiety and anger among the people who had relied on itinerant labor in the fields for a living. The region's migrant workers had benefited immensely from the premodern agricultural system. Thus, mechanization devalued labor in favor of capital.

As this chapter has also explained, the dramatically increased competition for resources in the region became the source of ethno-religious conflict. The Ottoman government's policy of settling Muslim refugees from Crimea and the Caucasus in Armenian-populated regions created major tensions. Meanwhile, the sedentarization of nomadic tribes such as the Avşars increased contention and friction among their members, Armenians, and immigrants. Armenian economic success in the region also increased the resentment of the Muslim lower-middle classes. Thus, Adana's participation in the global economic system seems to have brought it more harm than benefit.

These tensions appear to have been contained during the Hamidian period. Despite minor incidents, Adana did not suffer the fate of the other provinces inhabited by Armenians during the Hamidian massacres of 1894–96, during which approximately two hundred thousand Armenians were killed.[181] Nevertheless, the impact of these massacres on Armenian migrant workers was evident.[182] In 1896, no Armenian migrant workers arrived in Adana from the regions that suffered the massacres, leading to a heavy decline in grain and cotton production.[183]

In the next chapter I discuss in detail interethnic relations in Adana during the Hamidian period until the Young Turk Revolution of 1908. The chapter analyzes the phenomenon of the "weak public sphere" and its counterpublics and demonstrates that, despite the existence of a weak public sphere, tensions between the different ethno-religious groups were restrained.

CHAPTER 2

AGITATION AND PARANOIA

Adana during the Hamidian Period

IN 1878, SULTAN ABDÜLHAMID II (1876–1909) PROROGUED THE parliament, suspended the constitution, and established a despotic regime that lasted for thirty years. Through a sophisticated surveillance system and strict censorship, he attempted to suppress dissident movements and stifle their voices in the empire. However, despite the fact that the public sphere was restrained, a "weak public sphere" existed. This weak public sphere was semilegal and limited. It was confined to the educated elite and political activists, who shared their ideas in gatherings. It resembled the public spheres that existed in other autocratic monarchies of the time, such as in the Austro-Hungarian Empire.

The aim of this chapter is to investigate the limits of the weak public sphere and to analyze interethnic relations in Adana in this period by highlighting the political and socioeconomic anxieties that existed. The chapter demonstrates how the weak public sphere in Adana became the arena of intra- and inter-religious contentions. These tensions in Adana were not simply based along Christian versus Muslim lines—tensions and alliances transcended ethno-religious boundaries and classes. Through this weak public sphere, notables and their acolytes in Adana played an important role in disseminating rumors about the purported Armenian uprising. In addition, the chapter highlights the personal animosities of the key stakeholders in Adana during the Hamidian period and the role that they played in fomenting anxieties and escalating interethnic relations. Thus, the tensions that would resurface during the postrevolutionary period had their origins in the Hamidian period, but due to the tight control of the weak public sphere by the regime, and the governor's pro-Armenian inclinations, these tensions did not burst into a vortex of violence.

In the prerevolutionary weak public sphere, exiled activists from different backgrounds sought to counter the dominant element's discourse through pamphlets and newspapers that were smuggled to their respective suppressed ethno-religious communities in the empire. Within the region of eastern Anatolia, Armenian revolutionaries were the most active in distributing these materials in the six provinces as well as in the region of Cilicia. The empire declared these publications illegal and seditious, taking all necessary measures to both confiscate them and apprehend those responsible for their distribution. The state also considered the ecclesiastic orders to be complicit in these seditious activities, viewing churches as hiding places for political activists and weapons. Under such circumstances, the activities of Armenian political activists, especially those of the Hnchaks in the province of Adana, did not go unnoticed.

Geostrategically, Adana is both located on the coast of the Mediterranean, through which prohibited materials were disseminated to central Anatolia, and proximate to Cyprus (controlled by Britain after 1878), which was one of the hubs of Armenian revolutionary activity from which agents were sent to the southern section of the empire. Correspondence among the grand vizier, the Ministries of Police and the Interior, and officials from the province of Adana during the Hamidian period speak to the Ottoman state's anxiety regarding even the minutest incidents taking place in Cilicia.[1] For example, on November 29, 1891, the grand vizier Ahmed Cevad Paşa wrote to the Ministry of Police regarding seditious activities by Armenians in Adana. In that telegram, he ordered the ministry to investigate Armenians who were planning a large-scale uprising in the city.[2] Thus, the rumor that Armenians would stage a revolt, which would play an important role in justifying the massacres of 1909, was enshrined in the imaginations and collective memories of the state, the provincial administration, the Muslim notables, and the Muslim population of Adana well before the postrevolutionary period. The fear was that Armenians would revolt to reestablish the Kingdom of Cilicia.

Supposedly, this would take place with the aid of the European powers in general, and that of the British in particular.

Other correspondence confirms that this was a recurring source of concern. On May 31, 1892, the Ministry of the Interior sent a telegram to the grand vizier reporting that an Armenian by the name of Artin Mazmanoğlu from Adana, having been questioned by the police, had stated that the Armenians were planning a revolt that would last until Easter and that the British fleet would come to their aid. Mazmanoğlu claimed that the patriarch of the Armenian Church, who was also at the time the Catholicos, had written to the British and spent time in Adana with the aim of establishing a seditious organization headed by Garabed Gökderelian, a Hnchak activist and an influential Armenian notable in Adana. Consequently, Gökderelian was exiled to Acre by the order of the authorities.[3] While most of these allegations seem unfounded, they nevertheless played an important role in fomenting paranoia about the Armenians.

In another example, in August of 1896, the minister of the interior wrote to the grand vizier, reporting that a reliable Armenian source had notified him that leaders of the Armenian revolutionary committees of Zeitun and Suwaydiya had convened a meeting in which they planned to arrive from both land and sea to initiate an uprising in Kozan and Haçin, and then move on to attack Adana. The plan, supposedly, was to carry out the attack when the tribes of Kozan and the surrounding areas retreated to their summer camps (*yayla*). The revolutionaries of Zeitun and Haçin would move on Cilicia from the north, and those of Suwaydiya would move in from the south on either August 8 or 15. The minister suggested that notice should immediately be sent to the provinces of Adana and Aleppo, allowing them to take necessary defensive measures.[4]

From the perspective of the Ottoman authorities, British Cyprus was the center of revolutionary activities, from which Hnchak revolutionaries would infiltrate the province of Adana. The minister of the interior reported to the grand vizier that Armenian committees both in British Cyprus and in other countries were planning a huge uprising. Hence, he argued, the coasts of Adana and Beirut needed to be restricted.[5] As a result, the Sublime Porte sent a telegram to the province of Adana ordering that impactful measures be taken on the coasts and, most importantly, that one or two

ships permanently roam the coast from Mersin to Aley (Lebanon) and from
İskenderun to Mersin.[6] The Ottoman government was particularly attentive
to Armenians arriving from the harbor of Mağusa in British Cyprus.[7] These
Armenians apparently were smuggled to Adana in rowboats (*kayak*). On
April 16, 1908, Bahri Paşa, governor of Adana, sent a telegram to the Sublime
Porte in which he reported that a Cypriot ferryman named Mehmed Suri
asserted that many Armenians were being brought to the coast of Karataş
in this manner. Bahri Paşa asked that a gunboat or ship be sent immediately
to monitor the sea nearby.[8] Since Mersin was the main port of Adana, the
activities of Armenians also were carefully monitored there.[9]

The rumors of an Armenian uprising in Adana were connected to Ottoman anxieties about the rising number of Armenians in the province. As
mentioned in the previous chapter, by the end of the nineteenth and the
beginning of the twentieth centuries, Armenians began to migrate to Adana
from surrounding provinces. This was primarily due to Adana's economic
boom after it became a center for cotton production. Many others fled the
Hamidian massacres to find a safe haven in Adana. Letters published in the
Armenian press by influential community members were instrumental to
this influx of Armenian migrants. For example, after the revolution, Avedis
Gulbenkian, one of the wealthiest Armenians of Adana, published a letter
in İstanbul's Armenian daily newspaper, *Biwzandion*, urging wealthy Armenians who were Ottoman citizens to buy properties and build factories in
Adana. He wanted Armenians "to benefit from the current circumstances;
they would do a great favor to our suffering nation and I will be happy to
provide more details about the condition of the province and its status."[10]
However, the arrival of Armenian families in Adana raised serious alarm in
Ottoman government circles and among local Muslim elites, who thought
they perceived more sinister motives behind this influx of Armenians. Indeed, this suspicion would be reported as a justifying fact on numerous occasions after the first wave of the Adana massacres, particularly in the influential local CUP newspaper, *İtidal*, which argued that the settlement of
Armenians in Adana was part of a larger project to create an independent
Armenian state there.[11]

The Ottoman government's policy of settling Muslim refugees in
Armenian-populated areas, beginning before the revolution, was a solution

to this perceived demographic threat. For example, on September 27, 1892, a telegram from the Ministry of the Interior to the province of Adana and the Refugee Commission addressed the increasing Armenian population in the province, asserting that this increase was occurring with the aim of "carrying out seditious activities" and suggesting that Muslim refugees from Rumeli and elsewhere be settled gradually (*peyderpey*) in the empty and *mîrî* (state-owned) lands of the districts—including Sis, Payas, Çöl, Merziçun, Yumurtalık, Zeitun, Çayla, Ocaklı, and Maraş—where there were a large number of Armenians.[12] The government's concerns over this issue did not fade after the revolution, and the strategy of diluting Armenian influence through Muslim resettlement continued. A communiqué from the grand vizier to the vali of Adana on March 25, 1909, encouraged countering Armenian settlement in the empty lands near Sis and Kozan with the settlement of Muslim tribes in that region.[13]

Despite the central government's concerns, interethnic relations in Adana prior to the revolution seem to have been better than in other regions of the empire.[14] One of the factors contributing to this dynamic was the cordial relationship between Armenian leadership and the vali of Adana, Bahri Paşa.[15] Ali Münif Bey, the CUP member and the Adana deputy in the Ottoman Parliament in 1908, argued in his memoir that the good relationship between the vali and the Armenians of Adana emboldened the Armenian revolutionary activities in the region. He accused Bishop Moushegh Seropian, the prelate of Adana, of benefiting from this friendship to organize the Armenian revolutionary activities in Cilicia.[16] Armenian sources from the period indicate that political imprisonment was rare in Adana during Bahri Paşa's twelve-year tenure and that he was a fine politician.[17] Indeed, he was able to effectively administer Adana and its surrounding areas while gaining the confidence of the Yıldız Palace, but he was not always able to avoid discord with the local notables and the ulemâ.[18] In 1900 and 1901, he was forced to contend with a series of inspections and investigations stemming from their complaints to the Ottoman government. For example, on December 4, 1900, the local ulemâ and the notables of Adana sent a telegram to the central government accusing Bahri Paşa of illegal activities.[19] In response, the government ordered that an inspection commission be sent to Adana.[20] In another instance, on January 14, 1901, a telegram signed by many people from the center of Adana and sent to the Ministry of Justice also complained that Bahri Paşa was behaving illegally. In response, the grand vizier ordered the commander in chief of Adana to initiate necessary investigations into the matter.[21] In addition, the Ministry of the Interior sent an investigation commission to Adana to examine complaints against the vali.[22]

Although relationships between the Armenians and Turks of Adana were enacted in important, quotidian ways by the province's citizens, no discussion of Armenian-Turkish relations in the province of Adana just before and after the revolution would be complete without a survey of the most influential individuals involved. To that end, we begin with a discussion of arguably the foremost Armenian in Adana during that period: Bishop Moushegh Seropian.

Bishop Moushegh Seropian

Bishop Moushegh Seropian was born in İzmit in 1869, graduated from Armash Seminary (Armash is a town near the Sea of Marmara), and became a priest in 1895, joining the Cilician congregation. He was ordained as a bishop on October 28, 1906, without the knowledge of the patriarchate, leading to a series of disputes between the Armenian Patriarchate and the Cilician Catholicosate.[23] Seropian, who was a Hnchak revolutionary leader before assuming the position of the prelate of Adana, was a dominant stakeholder in both the prerevolutionary and postrevolutionary periods in Adana. He was also a major source of concern for the government and Muslim notables, particularly after the revolution. The rumor was that, in the Armenian conspiracy to reestablish the Armenian Kingdom of Cilicia, Seropian planned to "appoint himself as the king of Cilicia."[24] It is unclear whether there is any truth to these allegations, but it is certain that the state had already made up its mind about Seropian's character by the time he was appointed prelate; prior to his tenure in Adana, he had been an active member of the Hnchak party, before leaving the party as a result of a falling out with the other members.[25]

As prelate of Adana, Seropian developed good relations with the vali, Bahri Paşa.[26] Nonetheless, various elements of the Ottoman state had serious reservations about him, arguing that Seropian had been involved in seditious activities and was the object of several complaints when he had

served as prelate of Arapgir (Malatya) prior to his appointment as the prelate of Adana. The minister of the interior recommended that the grand vizier not appoint him to Adana and send him to another place instead.[27] On
December 23, 1905, the Ministry of the Police wrote to the Ministry of the
Interior asking that Seropian be removed from his position in Adana because he was engaging in harmful activities, including contacting Armenian
revolutionaries, and requested that he be put under constant surveillance. The
telegram argued that, when Seropian was in İstanbul, he was constantly in
touch with the Armenian revolutionaries Levon Kirishdjian and Dr. Naza-
reth Daghavarian.[28] It also asserted that, when he was the prelate of Arapgir,
Seropian had tried to convert a Muslim boy to Christianity. Seropian had
been removed from his position and replaced as a result of these allegations.
Since then, his movements had been followed very closely.[29] On December 8, 1906, the extraordinary commandership of Adana and Aleppo sent a
telegram to the commander in chief opposing the elevation of both Seropian
and a certain Garabed from Aleppo to the bishopric, declaring them both
seditious people (*erbâb-ı fesâddan olub*).[30]

Despite the central government's reservations about Seropian, his friendship with Bahri Paşa was so strong that even Turks asked Seropian to advocate before Bahri on their behalf.[31] Because of this friendly relationship,
Seropian was able to ensure that an Armenian market, several Armenian
schools, and a couple of important Armenian churches were built during his
tenure. In an extraordinary session that took place on November 29, 1905,
the political, economic, and religious assemblies of the Armenian Diocese of
Adana decided to name the Armenian market the Bahri Paşa Market (Bahri
Paşa Çarşısı).[32] Bahri Paşa, in an interview after the Adana massacres, said:

> Our friendship [with Bishop Seropian] had begun for simple reasons; the
> similarities of ideas and character were the pivot of our friendship. I have
> found in the character of Bishop Seropian the smart, working, sincere, and
> vehement clergyman with whom I had sympathized so much. I used to look
> with satisfaction at the wearying labor that he was giving to his flock. Un-
> der my personal responsibility and in the most difficult conditions, I imple-
> mented the Mousheghian School and the building of a market of 46 depart-
> ment stores, a church in Hamidiye, a church in Osmaniye, a school in Bahçe,

FIGURE 1. Bishop Moushegh Seropian, 1911. Source: Moushegh Seropian, *Manch'ēsdri Hay Gaghut'ē* (Poston: Tpagrut'iwn Azgi, 1911).

FIGURE 2. The Bahri Paşa Market (Bahri Paşa Çarşısı), 1906.
Source: BOA, Y.A.HUS 505/22.

and a school in Chorkmarzban [Dörtyol], as well as a church in Mara; all
of these were built by the individual efforts of Bishop Seropian and with
my support. My thoughts about his intellectual and administrative abilities
are so high that I would have wished for him to become the patriarch, as I
expressed to Bishop Tourian, who came to visit me.[33]

This cordial relationship between the Armenians and the vali, which contributed to Armenian progress, was viewed with animosity by some Turkish
notables. Seropian elaborated on this situation in his memoirs, which were
written less than a month after the Adana massacres. Seropian said that,
during the prerevolutionary period, journals were sent to the Yıldız Palace
by spies in Adana claiming that he was working to transfer Armenians from
around the world to Adana.[34] Seropian believed that the hostility of Adana's
Muslim ağas toward their Armenian neighbors was motivated by Armenian economic success and that this attitude led Abdülkadir Bağdadizade,
one of the most influential Turks in Adana, to form a group to counteract

Armenian influence in Adana.[35] The main aim of the group was to bring the vali and the officers under its influence in order to hinder Armenian economic development.

Abdülkadir Bağdadizade

Abdülkadir Bağdadizade was a member of the province's Administrative Council and a prominent businessman who owned large tracts of lands in Adana, Mersin, and Tarsus.[36] His conflicts with the Armenians were a matter of extensive public record. In one particularly dramatic incident, Bağdadizade had a major property dispute with the influential Armenian Garabed Gökderelian, who was a member of the court of appeals (istinaf mahkemesi). In late December of 1891, this dispute took a violent turn when weapons were used by the adherents of both sides.[37] Many complaints about Bağdadizade—not only by Armenians—were sent to the central government. Most of these complaints dealt with his alleged illegal activities, corruption, and meddling in judicial affairs.[38]

Bağdadizade denied these accusations by asserting that the Armenians were complaining about him because he was cracking down on their seditious activities. In an inflammatory petition sent to the grand vizier in March 1894, Bağdadizade repeated the rumor that the Armenians intended to recreate the Kingdom of Cilicia. He claimed that revolutionary groups in Europe had sent Andon Rshduni, a Hnchak activist, from Cyprus to Mersin for the sake of fomenting an Armenian uprising and that subsequent investigations had revealed that Adana's previous prelate, Fr. Mgrdich, was the head of an Armenian revolutionary committee. He noted that Mgrdich had been exiled to Ankara and that his second-in-command—who happened to be Garabed Gökderelian—had been exiled to Acre. Bağdadizade argued that Armenians were preparing to revolt by gaining influential political positions in the province and becoming prominent in business.[39]

In line with his friendship with Seropian and interest in advancing Armenian welfare, Vali Bahri Paşa was especially opposed to Bağdadizade and his clique, which included Ali Gergerlizade and Hafız Hüseyin Efendi. Bağdadizade and Gergerlizade in particular seem to have caused a great deal of trouble for the vali. When he had both men removed from the province for a time, the Ministry of the Interior decided to send them back to Adana.

On April 1, 1902, Bahri Paşa sent a telegram to the ministry arguing that Bağdadizade and Gergerlizade were members of a seditious party and that their presence in Adana would cause disturbances. He asked the ministry to reexamine its decision and to send them to a different province.[40] However, his efforts did not yield any results.

Garabed Gökderelian

Bağdadizade's archrival was Garabed Gökderelian, whose own problems with the local government stretched back to the previous vali, Faik Bey. According to Ottoman documents, Gökderelian was arrested on charges of murdering the second-in-chief of police, Hacı Resul, together with his accomplice, Stepan Arzuyan, who went by the nickname "Haygoni" and who was an officer of the revolutionary Hnchak party in Adana and the surrounding area. Both men received the death sentence, but the sentence was commuted for good behavior.[41] On July 14, 1898, Haygoni was released for self-reform (*ıslâh-ı nefs*), while Gökderelian remained in prison.[42]

Imprisoned for more than a decade in Adana, Gökderelian relentlessly petitioned the government for his release. On January 20, 1896, he sent a telegram to the grand vizier complaining about his arrest and asserting his innocence.[43] In response, the government contacted the sitting vali of Adana for clarification.[44] Faik Bey replied that Gökderelian was not innocent.[45] On March 26, 1902, Gökderelian sent another letter to the grand vizier in which he denied the allegation of murder, lamented the amount of time he had spent in prison, and denied belonging to a revolutionary committee.[46] In yet another letter, he claimed that he was arrested and sentenced to death because he was a target of his political enemies, who intended to keep him in prison until the election of the Sis Catholicos had taken place.[47]

On August 21, 1902, an ex-informer from Adana named Faik Bey sent a letter to the grand vizier reporting that the new vali of Adana, Bahri Paşa, accompanied by Colonel Hüseyin and Superintendent Kazim Beys, was facilitating Gökderelian's escape by removing him from the prison and keeping him in a room in the Agricultural Bank. In addition, Faik Bey claimed that Gökderelian, with the aim of "confusing public opinion," had been distributing harmful papers that had been smuggled into the country by a seditious Armenian committee.[48] A couple of weeks later, the minister of the interior

FIGURE 3. Garabed Gökderelian, 1910.
Source: *Zhamanak* (February 14, 1910, no. 397, 1).

wrote to Bahri Paşa asking him about the veracity of this news. Bahri Paşa
replied that Gökderelian had been moved to receive medical treatment after
two men had attacked and injured him in prison at the incitement of Abdülkadir Bağdadizade and his son Abdurrahman Efendi. Bahri Paşa explained
that Gökderelian's cell was in the police station rather than the Agricultural
Bank, and that he was under full supervision.[49]

A few years later, in April of 1905, Gökderelian again petitioned the sultan, arguing that he was being mistreated because his position as a member

of the appeals court did not sit well with his adversaries. He again refuted the allegations against him and noted that his numerous petitions remained unanswered. He argued, "[I have] been imprisoned for the past ten years for a crime for which I should not have been imprisoned for even ten minutes and, according to fate, I was convicted as a criminal, rather than being rewarded." Gökderelian asked for imperial compassion and his release.[50] When he was ordered to appear in İstanbul on October 27, 1906, Gökderelian was arrested in Beşiktaş and returned to Adana.[51] However, Bahri Paşa, the former vali of Adana, interceded on Gökderelian's behalf, and he was finally released, although he was kept under surveillance. Later, he fled to Cyprus to escape this scrutiny.

After the revolution, when political activists were allowed to return from exile, Gökderelian returned and became one of twelve founders of the Young Turk party, the CUP, in Adana. He also became an important component in the continued rumors of an impending Armenian uprising in Adana. Certain sectors of the local population considered him an "omnipotent figure" who was planning to attack Adana with the aid of "thousands of Armenian fighters" and to reestablish an Armenian kingdom there. The prelate of Adana, Moushegh Seropian, despised Gökderelian and criticized his activities.[52]

The Telan Farm Conflict

In addition to these interpersonal conflicts among major Armenian and Muslim political figures, the other major source of tension between Armenians and both local and central elements of the Ottoman government in the province of Adana concerned Telan Farm, which was owned by the Armenian Catholicosate of Sis and located in the district of Kozan, northeast of the city of Adana.[53] The farm had belonged to the previous Catholicos, Mgrdich Kefsizian, and was passed on to the Catholicosate after his death.[54] The farm consisted of ten thousand dunams, of which five thousand dunams were used for agricultural purposes to sustain the priests of the Noravank (New Monastery) near Sis and of which five thousand dunams were swampland. The local authorities had considered it empty land to be used to settle refugees. It seems that the Ottoman government was concerned about Armenians using the lands to settle Armenians from other provinces, and in order to prevent this, the Refugee Commission of Adana wanted to

settle Muslim refugees on the land. The Ottoman government intervened in
the growing conflict concerning Telan Farm in a ciphered telegram sent to
the province of Adana on June 22, 1906. In that telegram, the grand vizier
declared that none of Telan Farm's ten thousand dunams should be allocated
for settlement by either Armenian or Muslim refugees.[55]

The farm was, however, of utmost importance to a monastery that was
struggling to support itself. In a letter written on May 31, 1903, to the Catholicos of Echmiadzin, the Catholicos of Sis, Sahag II, described in detail
the monastery's dire financial situation.[56] The Catholicos contended that the
monastery had not yet benefited from the farm property in Telan being be-
queathed to it.[57] He argued that, unless the sultan were to step in and declare
Telan Farm the monastery's property, the monastery would be unsustainable.
He also suggested that an Armenian benefactor or another rich person could
allocate a large sum of money to the monastery, not as a contribution, but
rather as an investment, cultivate the land for a long period of time, establish a cotton factory, convert the wetlands to croplands, and gain more than
double their capital while still creating income for the monastery.[58]

On June 2, 1906, the grand vizier informed the Ministry of the Interior
that Telan Farm should be used solely for agricultural purposes to help the
priests of the monastery and that by no means should Armenians be settled
there (*kat'iyyen Ermeni iskân edilmeyup*).[59] Finally, the sultan fulfilled Catholicos Sahag II's wishes, allocating Telan Farm to the monastery by official
order on June 22, 1906. Despite this, the local government refused to accept
the order.

Letters from Adana's Armenian officials testify to the difficulties created
by this stalemate. After visiting the monastery, Bishop Seropian wrote to
Maghakia Ormanian, the Armenian patriarch of İstanbul, describing the
monastery's desperate situation and suggesting that an agricultural school
be established on Telan Farm.[60] He also described the unsettled nature of
the conflict over the farm, noting that, so long as the imperial edict (*irâde*)
had not been handed to the local authorities, nothing could be built on the
land, despite the property's ownership and cultivation by the monastery.[61] On
October 25, 1905, Catholicos Sahag II also sent a letter to Patriarch Maghakia Ormanian, in which he described the Noravank Monastery's dilapidated
condition and noted that the vali's letter to the Ministry of Justice regarding

the Telan Farm conflict remained unanswered. His level of frustration is notable in this letter: he declared his intention to resign in protest if the farm
was allocated for some other purpose.[62]

While the Armenian leadership was fighting for the future of Telan
Farm, the Refugee Commission in Adana decided to allocate the farm to
Muslim refugees (*muhâcir*). In the aftermath of this decision, the province's
Armenian officials repeatedly appealed to the central government for assistance. On April 26, 1906, Ormanian explained that the property had been allocated to Muslim refugees and that, unless this action was reversed, Sahag II
would follow through on his intention to resign. Ormanian argued that, since
the imperial edict had declared that the farm belonged to the monastery, the
government was obligated to intervene.[63] As a result, an imperial edict was
sent to Adana confirming that the property belonged to the monastery.[64]
On July 5, 1906, Sahag II sent a telegram to the Ministry of Justice thanking
it for the edict.[65] On August 25, 1906, Ormanian sent another letter to the
Ministry of Justice and Confessions (Adliye ve Mezâhib Nezâreti), informing officials there that the imperial edict sent to the province of Adana had
confirmed that Telan Farm belonged to the Noravank Monastery.[66] Nonetheless, the local government remained reluctant to implement the order.[67]
On the contrary, they decided to allocate the farm to settle Muslim refugees.
On February 5, 1907, Ormanian sent a letter to the grand vizier protesting
this move, despite the imperial decision to allocate it to the monastery.[68] The
Telan Farm conflict would continue to become a source of contention in the
postrevolutionary period.

Conclusion

Despite the restraint of Adana's public sphere by extreme censorship on the
part of the Hamidian regime, a weak form of the public sphere persevered.
The weak public sphere in Adana was frequently the site of intra-religious
and inter-religious contentions. Notables in Adana engaged in disseminating
(mis)information about the grandiose plans of the Armenians. On the part
of Armenians, revolutionary activists who were smuggling contraband articles in the form of pamphlets, newspapers, books, and even weapons played
an important role in countering the state's discourse by providing Armenians
with an alternative vision that totally contradicted the status quo.

Although conditions for the Armenians of Adana during the Hamidian period seem to have been better than those of Armenians in other provinces, serious tensions existed in the province.[69] The conflict between the faction of Bahri Paşa and Seropian and that of Bağdadizade and the personal antagonism between Bağdadizade and Gökderelian were important factors in the rise of tensions. Competition over land and the Refugee Commission's decision to settle Muslim refugees on Armenian land at Telan Farm also raised the province's political temperature.

The situation in the province would continue to intensify as a result of the Young Turk Revolution of 1908, which led to a sudden rupture of the prerevolutionary restraints that had dictated the limits of the public sphere. In the strong public sphere that emerged, the subaltern publics took on a new attire. The next chapter deals with the impact of the revolution on the province of Adana and demonstrates the ways in which the new public sphere served as a medium not only for the enactment of social identities but also for the drastic escalation of interethnic tensions. While far-reaching economic modifications took place in Adana over a period of half a century, political change took place more rapidly as a result of the revolution, causing serious and abrupt shifts in power structures. In short, the revolution opened a Pandora's box of economic and political anxieties that had been swelling for decades.

CHAPTER 3

BAD BLOOD, THWARTED HOPES

Contesting the Public Sphere in Postrevolutionary Adana

IN ORDER TO UNDERSTAND THE DEVELOPMENT OF ADANA'S public sphere after the Young Turk Revolution, it is necessary to consider the revolution's impact on the dynamics of power within the Anatolian provinces. The revolution caused major changes in Adana's already tenuous power equilibrium, leading to an erosion of social and political stability and producing much dissatisfaction within some segments of the population. The sudden mushrooming of CUP cells and clubs in the provinces caused extreme anxiety among the notables and the ulemâ who identified and collaborated with the ancien régime. Some members of the ancien régime joined the CUP bandwagon in order to preserve their interests and positions—however, despite having branches in most of the Anatolian and Arab provinces, the CUP was not in full control of the political situation in these regions. Thus, within the provincial CUP branches there were individuals connected with the ancien régime who sought to preserve the status quo while pretending to represent the new order.

A major factor in the deterioration of intra-ethnic relationships among Muslims in Anatolia was the dismissal of local officials belonging to the ancien régime and their replacement with CUP members or officials who were loyal to the CUP. In the new public sphere, this contributed greatly to the rising tension between the CUP and the figures of the ancien régime, as a whole stratum of notables who had benefited from the previous order lost power. Hence, one cannot understand the changes in Adana after the 1908 Revolution without considering these regional waves of discontent, especially in the Anatolian and the Arab provinces. What distinguished Adana from other provinces was its geographical position, its historical and religious importance to the Armenians, its economic and agricultural centrality to Anatolia—which attracted thousands of migrant workers arriving from Haçin, Erzurum, Bayburt, and Bitlis—and its complex ethnic composition, all of which contributed to the deterioration of interethnic relationships.

This chapter addresses the impact of the revolution in Adana and discusses the ways in which it led to drastic changes in the power equilibrium that had previously existed in the province. These changes in the dynamics of power, the active participation of Armenians in the public sphere through political and cultural activism, the deterioration of the political situation, and the spread of rumors all exacerbated interethnic tensions. The formation of the new public sphere was enabled by institutions and mediums that had not existed in the prerevolutionary period; these included political clubs, literary and educational societies, auditoriums, the press, public processions, lectures, and theaters. Through these institutions and mediums, Armenians expressed their ideologies, ideas, and feelings in an unrestrained manner. The freedom of expression enjoyed by such nondominant groups did not sit well with the dominant group, which clung to its prerevolutionary status. Thus, the new public sphere affected momentous changes to the status quo, heightening fear, anger, and distrust among the Muslim population of Adana. The revolution also created a social-emotional conundrum by sparking a clash between euphoric sentiments of both freedom and camaraderie and dark feelings of anger and resentment. This emotional conflict played an important role in the escalation of ethno-religious relations, electrifying the atmosphere in Adana.

"Long Live the Sultan! Long Live Freedom!": Celebrating the Revolution

One of the first introductions of the Armenians—as well as other nondominant groups—into the public sphere was through revolutionary festivities. As in other provinces, in Adana the proclamation of the constitution was received by a certain sector of society with great jubilation. On Sunday, July 26, a procession of locals paraded around, celebrating the constitution. A few days prior to this, a special train decorated with Ottoman flags and flowers and resounding with cries of "Long live the Sultan!" had set forth from Adana to Tarsus, where speeches were given by Turks and Armenians hailing the constitution amid cries of "Long live the constitution!" The next day, people carrying flags and banners in Armenian and Turkish walked to the governor's mansion in Adana, where the vali and İhsan Fikri, the CUP leader and the editor of the *İtidal* newspaper, gave speeches. The group then moved to the military station, where an officer addressed the crowd and an emotional speech by the Armenian lawyer Garabed Chalian followed. The procession ended at the Armenian church, where the secretary of the diocese, Kerovpe Papazian Efendi, spoke about freedom and the constitution, followed again by shouts of "Long live the Sultan," "Long live the constitution," and "Long live freedom!"[1]

A wave of gratitude toward the sultan for reinstituting the constitution swept the cities. On the occasion of the enthronement of the sultan, a ceremony took place in front of the government building in Adana with the participation of all government and military figures, religious heads of communities, notables, and the public. İhsan Fikri gave a speech on behalf of the CUP, eliciting a standing ovation and shouts of "Long live our sultan! Long live our nation!" (*Yaşasın pâdişâhımız! Yaşasın millet!*). In his speech, Fikri stated that thirty-three years earlier in 1876, similar cannons had been fired celebrating the enthronement of the sultan. At that time also, the nation had just suffered through a period of despotism, and the sultan had revived the constitution and the principles of freedom, justice, equality, and brotherhood. He continued: "Unfortunately that gift did not last long. As a result of the Russo-Turkish War of 1877–78, the constitution was prorogued, and for 32 years the nation lived under despotism." However, he said, the government had now finally been persuaded of the good intentions of the CUP and bestowed the constitution on the people.[2]

As in other provinces, local deceased revolutionary heroes were also honored in special ceremonies. On August 25, 1909, a requiem service took place in the Armenian Mousheghian-Apkarian School for the soul of the poet Ziya Paşa (1829–80).[3] "Ziya" was the pseudonym of Abdülhamid Ziyaeddin, who was an Ottoman poet, writer, and translator appointed as the vali of Adana in 1878.[4] At the invitation of the Armenian Revolutionary Federation

(ARF), thousands of people participated in the procession. In front stood three young people: one carrying the Ottoman flag, another the ARF emblem, and a third holding a wreath with the words "From the ARF to the Patriotic Hero" in Armenian and Ottoman Turkish.[5] Damar Arıkoğlu, then a young CUP member in Adana, recounted later during the Republican period how he felt that certain Armenian youths who sang the Armenian national anthem while carrying the Armenian flag had detracted from the procession.[6] Nevertheless, after passing through the market and arriving at the CUP club,[7] a reporter for the Armenian newspaper *Arewelk'* described the atmosphere: "The scene was fascinating and captivating, people were crying from happiness. Arm in arm, the Turks and the Armenians went to the tomb of Ziya Paşa."[8] In the front stood the students of the Armenian school, and in the back were the board members of the CUP and thousands of people singing patriotic songs. They passed through the government building and entered the cemetery of the Grand Mosque, where the tomb of Ziya Paşa lay.[9] After prayers and speeches, the procession continued to a Muslim cemetery, where people stood on the grave of Tevfik Nevzat, the Turkish liberal, who, after being sent from İzmir to Adana, was unable to stand the tortures that he suffered during his imprisonment by the ancien régime and threw himself into a well to his death.[10] Two wreaths were laid on his tomb: one from the ARF and the other from the municipality. İhsan Fikri, Artin Arslanian, İzzet Efendi, and others gave speeches. Afterwards, Muslims took oaths on the Quran and Armenians on the Bible vowing to shed their last drop of blood for the constitution.[11] It was decided that a tomb would be built for Nevzat, for which fundraising took place on the spot. Contributors included the CUP of Adana, the ARF, Abdurrahman Bağdadizade (son of Abdülkadir), Garabed Gökderelian, and İhsan Fikri.[12]

In the first few months following the revolution, attempts were made to strengthen the bonds of brotherhood between the different ethno-religious groups in the empire, inspired by the ideals of the revolution and the necessity of working together in harmony to strengthen the fatherland. One aspect of this unity was the confrontation of external threats that endangered the territorial integrity of the empire. For example, when Bulgaria declared its independence on October 5 and Austria-Hungary annexed Bosnia and Herzegovina on October 6, 1908, a large gathering organized by the CUP took place in the Freedom Garden in Adana. Garabed Chalian gave a talk on behalf of the CUP, followed by speeches by İhsan Fikri and the deputy of the prelate of Adana, Fr. Arsen. On behalf of the Greek Orthodox, the vice-metropolitan, Papa Abraham, also gave a talk:

> We have always been Ottoman and will remain Ottoman. We [are] com-
> pletely united after the declaration of the constitution . . . because we will
> live together, we are going to die together. Because our fatherland is one, our
> cemetery is going to be one too. We are going to stand united against that
> [which] threatens the prosperity and the future of the Ottoman.[13]

These talks were followed by speeches by the Armenian Catholic bishop Paul Terzian and İlyas Türkmen. The people responded with shouts of "Protest! Protest!" in all languages against Bulgaria and Austria-Hungary.[14]

Changes in the Dynamics of Power

In addition to this atmosphere of euphoria, which was common to all the provinces of the empire, the revolution and the reinstatement of the constitution also gave rise to significant changes in the dynamics of power in Adana. İhsan Fikri, a self-proclaimed Young Turk, played a major role in the escalation of tensions between the CUP and the local notables. Fikri, whose birth name was Ahmed Tosun, had been a civil servant of the Salonica Agriculture Department. He was later exiled to Diyarbekir, and then to Payas (a town in the district of Dörtyol). After Vali Bahri Paşa interceded with the authorities on his behalf to end his exile, he returned to Adana.[15] Prior to the revolution, he was appointed as the principal of the Industrial School, but was later fired by the vali, who replaced him with Ali Gergerlizade Efendi. After the revolution and the establishment of the CUP branch in Adana under his leadership, Fikri began to persecute his opponents, particularly Gergerlizade. Hence, two groups emerged in Adana: one supporting Fikri and another supporting Gergerlizade.[16] These two opposing groups can best be defined as the CUP and the local notables, respectively.

As shown above, Fikri also played an important part in organizing the festivities in honor of the revolution. He raised funds for this aim, in which Armenians and Turks participated equally.[17] Fikri suggested that the governor should publicly take an oath to preserve the constitution, to which Bahri

Paşa reluctantly agreed. At the end of the festivities, Fikri sent a congratulatory telegram to the CUP branches in Manastır, Salonica, and İstanbul on behalf of the people of Adana. The next day, the CUP Central Committee asked Fikri to establish a CUP branch in Adana. Many of the individuals who became members of the CUP did not have any prior relation with the party; some of them even belonged to the ancien régime. They were motivated to jump on the CUP bandwagon by opportunism and the hope of benefiting from the new order. After one hundred members had joined the branch in Adana, a committee of twelve was elected, composed of seven Turks, three Armenians, one Greek, and one Arab.[18] In reaction, Abdülkadir Bağdadizade, one of the most influential notables of Adana, formed a group called the Agricultural Club (Zirâat Kulübü), composed of Adana notables, people from Idlib, and *softa*s (Muslim students).[19] He also established and edited a weekly paper called *Rehber-i İtidal* to act as the mouthpiece of his party, through which he incited people against the CUP and their Armenian collaborators. The press played an important role in this intra-ethnic struggle. In the postrevolutionary period, five newspapers were published in Adana: *Seyhan*, *Yaşasın Ordu*, *İtidal* (edited by İhsan Fikri), *Rehber-i İtidal* (the anti-*İtidal* paper owned by Ali İlmi Efendi), and *Çukurova*, a weekly newspaper published by Mahmud Celaleddin. *İtidal* was extremely critical of *Rehber-i İtidal* and considered it its enemy.[20]

Thus, the opening of the new public sphere led not only to the escalation of tensions between Armenians and elements of the ancien régime in Adana but also to a fierce struggle between the CUP and the notables of the ancien régime. In this conflict the press played a central role, as both contented and discontented elements used the press to air their satisfaction or dissatisfaction with the new political reality.

The Political Situation Prior to the Massacres

As with the other CUP branches in the provinces, the first task of the committee was to force the local vali, Bahri Paşa, to resign. He duly resigned, and for a period of time the CUP branch administered the province.[21] Upon his resignation, İhsan Fikri described Bahri Paşa in *İtidal* as the "forger who served for twenty to twenty-five years the *mutasarrıflık*s [sub-provincial governorships] of Beyoğlu, Üsküdar, Pristina and the police force of İstanbul. .

. . He is one of the founders of *hafiyelik* [secret police] in the provinces and the master. He even used to boast about this."[22] The CUP also succeeded in removing Police Chief (*Polis Müdürü*) Kâzım Bey and Police Superintendent Zor Ali from their positions.[23] In addition, it began sending delegations to villages, consisting of one Armenian and one Turk, to preach to the masses about the constitution.

When Cevad Bey was appointed vali of Adana, Fikri (on behalf of the CUP) gave a speech welcoming him to the city.[24] Seeing the new vali's weakness, Fikri soon tried to manipulate him into removing Gergerlizade from his position. Gergerlizade, however, gained the vali's favor. This angered Fikri, who began openly attacking the vali in *İtidal*, even calling for his resignation, but to no avail.[25] On January 19, 1909, he wrote a piece in *İtidal* heavily criticizing the vali. He argued that, while in the past, under the despotic regime, nothing had been done regarding the situation in Adana, after the revolution, the hopes of the people were elevated. However, Fikri argued, it had been four months since the vali's arrival, and nothing had been achieved. The complaints of the people were justified: "They have the right. The incompetence of the vali has left the administration in the hands of the previous rulers who are lovers of despotism." He concluded his article by urging the vali to act.[26]

One of İhsan Fikri's main objectives was to bring Ali Gergerlizade to trial by the Administrative Council of the province for his maladministration as the principal of the Industrial School. It seems that due to the close relationship between Gergerlizade and the vali, the latter was reluctant to take any measures against him. As a result, Fikri planned to hold a demonstration against Gergerlizade, during which he also intended to demand the vali's resignation. In reaction, the vali's and Gergerlizade's adherents—who included Abdülkadir Bağdadizade—organized a counterdemonstration in support of the vali. They invited the Armenians to take part and asked them to sign a telegram indicating their satisfaction with the vali. The Political Council of the Armenian Catholicosate, under the leadership of the deputy of the Catholicos, refused to sign.[27] Ali Münif Bey, the deputy of Adana at the time, states in his memoir that Armenians were trying to benefit from this tension.[28] Due to heavy rain, Fikri's demonstration was canceled.[29] It was rescheduled, but then canceled by the police, infuriating Fikri.[30]

Fikri continued attacking Cevad Bey vehemently in his newspaper, *İtidal*. On March 17, 1909, he published an article accusing Cevad Bey of despotism, claiming that government was nonexistent in Adana and that it was people like Abdülkadir Bağdadizade who were truly running the affairs of the country. In this tense atmosphere, Zor Ali, the former police superintendent of Adana who had been dismissed by the CUP, returned to Adana. He declared himself a member of the Fedâkâran-ı Millet (The Martyrs of the Nation), which was a branch of the İttihâd-ı Muhammedî (Mohammedan Union), and called on people of the same mind to join him.[31] Among those who heeded his call was Mehmed Selim Bey, known as Avnullah Kâzımî, who toured the province of Adana making anti-constitutional speeches for which he was arrested and imprisoned in Aleppo.[32] The arrival of these people coincided with that of a reporter for the newspaper *Osmanlı*, Mahmud Fayiz Bey, who was a member of the Liberal Party. During this atmosphere of intra-ethnic tension, news of the counterrevolution reached Adana, further altering the power balance within the provinces.

Prior to the massacres, the relations between the local CUP and the Armenians in Adana seemed to be cordial; after all, the disgruntled elements in the provinces considered Armenians to be the most important allies of the CUP, which had engineered the revolution. İsmail Sefa Özler, an important member of the CUP, wrote an article in the *İtidal* newspaper addressed to the Armenians entitled "To Our Armenian Brothers." Sefa stated that he was happy to see Armenians carrying Turkish Ottoman flags.[33] He argued that Armenians could no longer bear what they had suffered during the previous regime. He also stated that he was confused by rumors that the "Armenians have revolted [and] want their own principality"[34] and asked himself, "I wonder: If Armenians were given [their own] principality, would their condition be much better?"[35] His prediction was that they would be poor and miserable, becoming vulnerable to being swallowed by European countries. He admitted that the ancien régime had poisoned their minds: "It has introduced you [Armenians] as traitors and us as cruel. Cannon, rifle, army, and soldiers have been turned against you. They wanted to erase you altogether." He lamented that obedience is one of the native characteristics of Turks and all the Ottomans and that they had been the pawns of the evil regime for thirty years. He finished his article by saying: "Oh, you Armenians who gave your souls and blood wanted to save the fatherland. Your oppression [in] the past has [been] rendered sacred to all the world's humanity [and] to all the Ottomans, especially the Turks."[36] This article demonstrates the way in which the CUP viewed the Armenians in the postrevolutionary period, and it acknowledges the false manner in which Armenians were represented by the ancien régime as seditious and traitorous.

Armenians in the Public Sphere

The public sphere created after the 1908 Revolution allowed formerly illegal Armenian political parties to become legal and more active in Adana. Prior to the revolution, the Hnchaks were the most influential Armenian political party in Cilicia; after the revolution, the ARF took serious steps to establish a presence in the region. For example, in Sis, ARF party members Harutyun Kalfayan and Zakaria Bzdigian established a club whose membership reached two hundred.[37] In February 1909, they paid a visit to Dörtyol (Chorkmarzban), later sending a letter to the Armenian daily *Arewelk'* arguing that, despite the presence of the Hnchaks and the Ramgavars (Armenian Liberal Democrats) in the city, nothing was achieved there. Bzdigian and Kalfayan were largely successful in their efforts to mobilize people and to convince them that "'federation' and 'action' are synonyms."[38]

The correspondence of the ARF members in the region of Adana provides a rare glimpse into the political situation and the impact of the revolution in Adana. Unlike the Hnchaks, the ARF left behind an archive through which the history of the period can be reconstructed. Less than a month after the revolution, Bzdigian contacted Agnuni (Khachadour Maloumian) to update him about the political situation in Adana.[39] He explained that the ARF was very active in trying to establish different branches in the province and expressed high hopes regarding its success. In another letter to Agnuni, Bzdigian emphasized that they were pursuing a political path of decentralization and that they were working hard to create favor for this idea.[40] He stressed that they remained committed to this principle, even though they were cooperating with the CUP. He continued, "There is a minority among the Turkish elements that believes in the Ottoman Federation State. Of course, there will be people opposing the idea, but we need to use excellent propaganda and convince people like that. In my meetings with the Turks,

I speak about the self-administration of provinces, and I find among them people concurring with the idea."[41]

Like Bzdigian, the Gomideh (local party chapter of the ARF) of Khor Virab in Adana seemed optimistic about the ARF's prospects in the region. In a letter to the Western Bureau of the ARF, it referred to the latest achievement of establishing five groups in Adana and argued that sympathy toward the ARF among the people was rising. It also indicated the "high hopes that they [the ARF] will be able to bring the majority of the people under their flag."[42] However, regarding the Armenian-Turkish relations, the committee admitted that the previous enthusiasm was decreasing in Adana, as nationalistic feelings among the Turks grew day by day. It lamented, "This phenomenon does not inspire happiness in us."[43]

According to a letter by the Gomideh of Adana to the Responsible Body in İstanbul, the formation of the CUP did not imbue confidence. Within the ranks of the committee were counterrevolutionaries and people from the ancien régime. In a different letter, the Gomideh addressed the problem of the Abdal tribe and its leader, Kerim, whose anti-Armenian sentiments and activities had continued after the revolution. The letter argued that Kerim had found protectors within the CUP and the Turkish revolutionary ranks. They asked the ARF center in İstanbul to appeal to the Central Committee of the CUP as well as to the Sublime Porte. Villagers also appealed officially to the ARF.[44] Regarding the agents of the ancien régime, Bzdigian's analysis was that, despite there being sincere people among the Turks, there was a "strong element too who [was] not going to give up the privileges that it had during the ancien régime. Of course, these people [were] not going to look with a friendly eye on the principles of equality and fraternity."[45]

In another letter sent to the İstanbul Responsible Body, the Adana Gomideh concurred:

> Unfortunately, the feelings of a certain element among the Turks are getting bad toward the Armenians [and] there are suspicious behaviors. They could not cut the head of the agents of the ancien régime at the right time. This was one of the worst wrong steps taken by the Young Turks whose repercussions appear today. It seems that the word of order comes from İstanbul. The Turks are ascribing wrong feelings to the Armenians, supposedly that the Arme-

nians are indulging in the idea of the independence of Armenia. The agents of the ancien régime are feeding the Turkish masses with harmful ideas as a result of which the Turks have begun to arm themselves, and the Turks bought two thousand to three thousand gunpowder boxes that arrived in Adana. The officers [regulating] gunpowder are reluctant to give gunpowder to the Armenians.[46]

According to the letter, there were a few influential Turks in Adana who were working tirelessly to bring discord among Armenians; the aims of these figures could be very dangerous, especially when the CUP had lost its direction.[47] The letter provided the following names of these influential people: Abdülkadir Bağdadizade, Hacı Ali Debağzade, Kerim (the head of the Abdal tribe), Bekir Bayrakdar, and their satellites. They argued that this group was infamous for its antagonism toward Armenians and that all of them belonged to the ancien régime. The Gomideh asked the Responsible Body of the ARF to bring this to the attention of the Ottoman cabinet, as the threat was increasing. The Adana diocese also complained to the patriarchate via telegram, but unfortunately the latter did not take any steps in response.[48]

Another major point of disappointment for the Armenians of the empire was the elections. The 1908 parliamentary elections, although falling short of fully democratic standards, were nonetheless competitive elections that revealed much about the social, political, and ideological currents in the empire. The main competition was between the CUP and the Liberal Party, although nondominant groups also played significant roles. The elections also demonstrated the anxiety of the CUP toward the electoral process; their fear was that nondominant groups (especially the Greeks) were going to achieve significant victories and hinder their political objectives. The elections required two-stage balloting: primary and secondary. They were not based on proportional representation but on the numbers specified for a particular electoral district. Gerrymandering and electoral irregularities were reported during these elections by Armenians and Greeks.[49]

As in other provinces, the Armenians of Adana had high expectations for the elections but soon lost hope of electing Armenian members to the parliament. The ARF, which ran an extensive electoral campaign, was especially critical of the process, complaining of irregularities and gerrymandering.[50] Armenians believed that proportional representation was the best way to provide a fair election and give the nondominant groups a voice.[51] Pursuing its usual strategy, the ARF entered into negotiations with the CUP in Adana regarding the election of two Armenians, but to no avail.[52] In a pessimistic letter sent after the elections to the ARF Responsible Body in İstanbul, the Adana Gomideh lamented that the elections were conducted in a disorganized manner. First, the letter argued that because of an incomplete census, many rightful voters had been excluded from the electoral registrar; had the census process not been rushed, they "would have had two representative[s] for (sancak) Adana and one of them would have been an Armenian." Second, only 20 percent of those who registered actually voted, and in a very disorganized manner. Third, in order to neutralize the voting of Armenians, the officials had mixed the Armenian and Turkish neighborhoods together.[53] Armenians saw a hidden agenda behind these electoral irregularities, the overriding aim of which was "to neutralize the Christians and form a parliament only from the Muslim Turkish elements." The Gomideh argued: "They have done the same in all the other districts populated by Armenians. It is always the same Machiavellian means that have been used in all the places."[54] In the end, only one Armenian was elected from the province of Adana: Hampartsoum Boyadjian, the prominent Hnchak leader representing the district of Kozan. Ali Münif Bey (CUP) and Abdullah Faik Efendi were elected for the district of Adana; Mehmet Reşid Efendi for the district of Cebel-i Bereket; Hacı Mahmud Bayram Efendi for the district of İçil and Arif Hikmet and Abdülhalim Bey for the district of Mersin.

Despite the new political activism by the ARF and other parties, Bishop Seropian remained the most influential political figure in the Armenian community—even more so than Catholicos Sahag II. Newspapers in the capital praised his work. One reporter in the Armenian daily *Biwzandion* described Seropian as "courageous by his pen, a bit extreme with his character, but with work he is sharp." The reporter endorsed the bishop's project of building an Armenian high school in Adana and called for support for this initiative,[55] arguing that Cilicia is a country close to the heart of Armenians and the most desirable place in Turkey, with many opportunities for prosperity—a country near the sea, with an attractive location and fertile plains, in which Adana occupies the first place.

Cultural and National Rejuvenation

The new public sphere also allowed Armenians to disseminate their culture, history, and politics using new tools. One of these was the establishment of auditoriums, which aimed to improve the literacy of Armenians and raise their national and political consciousness. The first such auditorium was opened by the ARF, followed by another opened by the Hnchaks. In addition, a nonpartisan auditorium was established in the Mousheghian-Apkarian School called the National Auditory (Azgayin Lesaran), whose aim was "to elevate the people both morally and intellectually through lectures and classes."[56] An opening was held on August 24, 1908, under the auspices of the Armenian Catholicos Sahag II Khabayan. At the event, the organizer Yesayi Sarian Efendi announced that the Armenian schools would be open as salons on Sundays for all the students to come and read newspapers in different languages.[57] Fr. Arsen, the deputy of the prelate of Adana, wrote in a letter to the newly established club that the auditorium was one of the benefits of the constitution.[58]

In the correspondence between the local ARF branches, the Responsible Body in İstanbul, and the *Droshak* (ARF organ) office in Geneva, there was a constant demand for ARF publications such as the *Droshak*, *Pro-Armenia*, *Hairenikʻ*, and *Razmik* newspapers, as well as the constitution and bylaws (*Dzragir ew Kanonagir*) of the ARF, revolutionary brochures and novels, pictures of heroes, postcards, and images of Armenian kings.[59] One of the ARF's biggest challenges was that the local Armenian population was mainly Turkish speaking; as a result, the members of the ARF delivered speeches about the revolution in their auditorium in Turkish.[60] The ARF also established an auditorium in Mersin to spread its ideology. This was undertaken primarily by Dr. G. Keshishian, who wrote to the Responsible Body asking for materials such as books, newspapers, and brochures.[61] The aim was to spread the impact of the party among the different districts of the province of Adana.[62] However, the process of sending these materials was not smooth; most of the time they were delayed.[63]

Expressions that were seen by many Armenian ecclesiastic and political figures and groups as cultural revival were often interpreted by the disgruntled reactionary forces of Adana as preparation for autonomy. Armenians were beginning to publish and perform poetry, odes, and dramas pertaining to their national past—in Z. Duckett Ferriman's words, "doing things which any Constitutional and progressive Regime (rule) permit[s] as a sign of life, mental and moral activity and progress."[64] However, public processions carrying the Armenian coat of arms and other symbols were striking and made the Muslim population uneasy.[65] For example, when CUP members Mehmed Bey, Ali Efendi, and Garabed Gökderelian visited Haçin in order to explain the meaning of constitution and freedom, a large procession took place toward the government building. Besides the Ottoman flag, the Armenians were carrying a flag featuring a large cross. This enraged the senior captain (*kolağası*), who stopped the procession and forced the Armenian carrying the flag to bring it down, resulting in a quarrel between him and Garabed Gökderelian.[66] Ahmed Midhat Efendi, the editor of the daily *Tercümân-ı Hakîkat* (Interpreter of truth), stated, "While we, the educated, understand the meaning of these symbols, the simpleton who constitutes the majority [of the people] will have a different impression, [namely] that Armenians are seeking independence." He argued that reactionary forces would use this excuse to create discord between Armenian and Turks.[67]

Such negative interpretations were endemic to Adana. In an article about Adana published in the Armenian newspaper *Biwzandion*, the Armenian author addressed this problem by saying that he did not agree with the "unrealistic idea" of establishing an independent state. He argued that the Ottoman Constitution guarantees—without discrimination—freedom, equality, and justice, which are "the natural and irrefutable rights of a people, whose violation is the biggest crime." He argued that the duty of Armenians should be to yield to the constitution sincerely by joining hands with all the other elements to work for the prosperity of the country, regardless of race or religion. He continued:

> But that does not mean that we should forget our nationality [*azkutyun*], our racial idiosyncrasies [*inknahatkut'iwn*], our history, our memories, and not pass them to our children, be it in our schools, churches, be it in our

family circles, because it is enough to say that there is no law built on justice [that] can prevent [this]. Because that would simply mean to force someone to forget and disown his father, mother, and fatherland. Thus, we are going to remember and commemorate all of this always. Hence, we are going to remain faithful Ottomans.[68]

Theatrical presentations offered another means of cultural expression. After the revolution, a theatrical company was established by the Muslim youth of Adana called the Freedom Stage Company (Sahne-i Hürriyyet Kumpanyası). The proceeds of these presentations went to different schools. On Monday, January 14, 1909, the company presented a play in one of the Armenian schools entitled *Ermeni Mazlumları yâhut Fedakar bir Türk Zabiti* (Armenian victims; or, a self-sacrificing Turkish officer), written after the revolution by Mehmet İhsan, an Ottoman military officer, promoting the ideas of Ottomanism, brotherhood, and coexistence. The performance drew hundreds of people, and according to *İtidal*, "there was not a place to throw a pin." After the play, İhsan Fikri lectured on the necessity of theater in social life, and Artin Arslanian followed with a speech about the brotherhood between Armenians and Turks.[69] Other plays were also put on by Muslims, such as Abdülhak Hamit Tarhan's *Târık yâhut Endülüs Fethi* (Tariq or the conquest of Andalusia)—first published in İstanbul in 1879—which was performed on November 29, 1908, in the Gazino (Tavern).

While for Armenians, theatrical presentations that dealt with the Armenian past were a form of cultural romanticism, in the post-massacre period they were cited by reactionary forces as "proof" of the Armenian desire for independence.[70] However, these plays took place in the public sphere and were attended by all ethnic groups. Henry Charles Woods rightly notes that, although pictures of the kings of Armenia were shown at some of these performances, this was not intended as a call for autonomy. In fact, local Ottoman Turkish officials were invited to and attended these performances, and no attempt was made to hide these pictures from them.[71]

For example, *İtidal* reported that on Sunday, April 11, 1909, Armenians performed a play in the Gazino of Ziya Paşa in Mersin entitled *Sivas'ın Timurleng Tarafından Harâbiyeti* (The destruction of Sivas by Tamerlane).[72] The play, based on an 1868 work by the noted Armenian poet and playwright

Bedros Tourian (1851–72), had a strong flavor of cultural nationalism.[73] The local mutasarrıf, as well as other officials, were invited to attend. According to the description of the reporter, at the beginning of the play, Tamerlane gives an order to exterminate all the Armenians. A fierce struggle takes place between Tamerlane and an Armenian king. The king, along with his servant and daughter, becomes Tamerlane's prisoner. At the end, the king, hands chained and wearing a thorn crown, sits hopelessly in a cell allocated to him by Tamerlane. Suddenly two spirits appear before the king.[74] An angel tells him:

> Do not feel sorry; thanks to unity the day will come that you will restore your monarchy [kralhğını tasdik edecekler]. You are going to preserve your independence. Be restful, do not detach yourself from unity. Once more in the future you will regain your crown.

İtidal reported that when the curtain closed, the Armenians in the audience began applauding and shouting, "Long live Armenia," "Long live the Armenian Kingdom," and "Long live Armenians!"[75] But at the time, nothing critical was said about these presentations. In his unpublished autobiography, Seropian claims that the play was modified from its original in order to respect the Turkish sensibilities.[76]

Dramatic presentations were not confined to Armenian and Turkish plays. A performance of Hamlet, put on by the Armenian students of St. Paul's College of Tarsus, unintentionally made government officials and the local mufti uneasy. Missionary Helen Davenport (Brown) Gibbons, who taught at the school, gave a detailed description of the play and her role in the production in a letter sent to her mother on April 7, 1909. Gibbons described how, when things began to go badly for Hamlet's stepfather, people stopped fanning. The attending dignitaries became uncomfortable and hunched their shoulders. They kept their eyes glued to the stage. She continued:

> They are not familiar with our great William, and believe, no doubt, that we invented the play as well as the actors' costumes. Horror of horrors! We had forgotten what they might read into the most realistic scene. An Armenian warning for Abdülhamid? The assassins mastered the struggling king. He lay there with his red hair sticking out from his crown, and the muscles of his

neck stiffened as he gasped for breath while his throat was cut with a shiny white letter-opener.[77]

The Relationship of the Armenians with the Local Government

The relationship of the Armenian ecclesiastic leadership with the local government deteriorated after the revolution, especially after the removal of Vali Bahri Paşa. This was especially evident in the government's inconsistent response to reports of impending violence against Armenians. The Catholicos of Sis, Sahag II, sent telegrams to the government and the Armenian Patriarchate in İstanbul, indicating imminent threats of massacres in the area. These telegrams were published in the local Armenian press.[78] The Armenian daily *Biwzandion* printed a telegram reporting that fanatic Turks from the villages around Sis were armed and walking the streets of Sis. They had attacked and looted an Armenian caravan, injuring the people and threatening that on the morning of the Ramadan holiday (*Ramazan Bayramı*), all the "*gavur*s [infidels] are going to be massacred."[79] The *locum tenens* immediately sent a *takrîr* (report) to the grand vizier. "What an irony," the article lamented, "that the government is striving to show that the whole country is in peace by attempting to deny the lamentations of the catastrophe while the Catholicos of Sis is sending such an alarming telegram." The article concluded by saying that the government would claim that these were "nonexistent rumors."[80] The Ottoman Turkish newspapers of İstanbul had already reacted negatively to the telegrams, explicitly stating, "We do not want to believe in the existence of the threat of massacre."[81]

In September of 1908, three Armenians disappeared from Haçin. One was found alive, while the other two were ruthlessly slaughtered and found in a valley. The local kaymakam, who was Greek, worked with self-dedication and found the two perpetrators, who were taken to a prison in Sis. However, Müftüzade Ahmed and Yüzeyir, two influential partisans of the ancien régime who had incited the perpetrators, remained at large. Complaints about them were sent to the CUP and the ARF. Investigators from Sis determined the complicity of Müftüzade but were unable to prosecute him. A letter to *Biwzandion* lamented, "[Müftüzade] is armed and roaming around in Haçin where he is inciting secretly our naïve compatriots to get arms and ammunition and get ready to massacre the Armenians, saying that this freedom is for the Armenians."[82] On January 19, 1909, the British ambassador echoed this in a report to Edward Grey, the British foreign secretary, stating that a *hoca* (preacher) in the town of Haçin had preached a sermon recommending the massacre of Armenians; in this case, the authorities had taken prompt action and put him in prison.[83]

Tensions were high during the Ramadan holiday in October in Adana as rumors circulated that the Muslims were going to attack the Christians.[84] Nonetheless, on Monday, October 13, 1908, the holiday passed in a peaceful manner.[85] From the evening of Sunday until the first and the second day of the holiday, guards patrolled the neighborhoods and markets of the city day and night. Each guard unit consisted of one Muslim and one Armenian notable and one or two soldiers. The police took part in safeguarding the streets; the chief of the gendarmes, Kadir Bey, also roamed from neighborhood to neighborhood.[86] On October 25, the British vice-consul, Doughty-Wylie, wrote to the British ambassador, Gerard Lowther, that direct threats of massacre had been made against the Christians in Adana. He said the new vali of Adana, Cevad Bey, had called troops from Damascus and instructed them to patrol the town.[87] On October 25, Doughty-Wylie wrote again, informing Lowther that the troops had arrived from Beirut and that the holiday passed quietly, "owing to the energetic measures of the Vali." He said that the vali had done all he could but cautioned that the situation in Adana "seems to be marked [by] division between Christian and Moslem, which is useful to the opponents of liberty, fraternity, and equality."[88] However, in the period immediately following the holiday, few murders of Armenians were reported.

Complaints about injustices taking place after the revolution were sent to the Armenian diocese of Adana, which forwarded them to the vali, the Catholicos of Sis, and the government in İstanbul, as well as to the Armenian Patriarchate. In January, Minas Soghomonian Efendi—one of the notables of Kessab—along with thirty-one Armenians sent a signed letter to the prelate, Bishop Seropian, complaining about the injustices committed by a certain Serkoy Muğasi and demanding that the authorities intervene. Seropian responded that he had passed the request to the Catholicos and asked them to make every effort to defend their rights. He continued, "The evil and the traitors cannot last long. Sooner or later the masks of these types of people will be removed and the egoistic people who are hiding behind

them will come out."[89] On January 6, 1909, the prelate of Bahçe, Fr. Vahan
Sdepanian, sent a letter to Seropian complaining about the mufti of Bahçe,
İsmail Efendi, and the judge (*hakim*), demanding their resignation. Seropian responded that the Provincial Administration had sent a telegram to
the Ministry of the Interior and assured him that the mufti would be relieved from his position within a few days.[90] A few days before the holiday,
eighty families of the Abdülkerim tribe were settled on the farms of Nacarlı,
which belonged to Armenians. The Armenians of Nacarlı complained to Seropian, who sent a detailed report to the vali and the Armenian Patriarchate
of İstanbul. Seropian argued in his letter, "The Patriarchate can rest assured
that we are going to follow every lead in order to secure the return of that
and other lands."[91]

The Armenian press in the capital continued to receive distressed letters about the condition of different districts in Cilicia. The Armenian daily
Zhamanak received a letter from Sis arguing that the government was still on
the same path that it had followed during the ancien régime: "The pack that
organized the events [massacres] of 1895–96 [still] want the same [thing], to
subject the Armenians who jumped out of the frying pan into the fire. They
incite the simple people, saying that the Armenians of Zeitun are ready to
revolt."[92] One letter to *Biwzandion* claimed that *hoca*s in Sis were inciting
people against Armenians and that, even though the local authorities and the
CUP knew about it, they had not taken any measures. The letter argued that
although the mutasarrıf was committed to freedom and the new regime, his
leniency on this matter remained incomprehensible.[93] *Dzayn Hayreniats'*, the
organ of the Reformed Hnchakian Party, also published letters from Adana.
Fr. Nerses Tanielian, the prelate of Haçin who was an old Reformed Hnchak,
argued in a letter that the implementation of the constitution and the declaration of freedom "has not brought a real change in the painful life of the
Armenian." He continued, "The Armenian is still suffering under despotism.
The old bribe-taking officials are here and still remain."[94]

Another serious incident took place outside Hamidiye, where an Armenian student from St. Paul's College in Tarsus by the name of Arakel Berberian was brutally murdered.[95] The local officials were not able to find the
killers. On January 20, 1909, Catholicos Sahag II sent a letter to the Armenian patriarch of İstanbul discussing the murder of Berberian.[96] He said that

people need "protection as much as bread." In his appeal, he warned that if the agitators began to form a collective movement, then he was going to stand in person at the head of the self-defense group. He finished his letter by saying, "It is better to die once rather than live with the fear of death."[97] The Armenian patriarch answered by advising him to seek the medium of law in order to find a solution to the situation.[98]

At the time, Bishop Seropian was on a mission in İstanbul. When he returned to Adana, he found that letters warning of imminent threats had accumulated.[99] He appealed to the new vali, who immediately took action.[100] Seropian also sent a pastoral letter to the Armenians of Adana emphasizing the need for harmony among the people and recommending that Armenians behave affably toward the local Turkish people.[101] He warned them that there would be people who "want to fish in troubled waters" and suggested that they pay them no mind. He urged Armenians to show respect for their free Ottoman fatherland and to nurture sincere friendships with their Turkish compatriots. In addition, he encouraged Armenians facing collective or individual injustices to appeal fearlessly to the local government. Seropian also stressed the need to school all uneducated Armenians.[102]

Seropian immediately began to visit the towns and villages around Adana to acquaint himself with their condition. When he visited Cebel-i Bereket, he found that "an anti-constitutional plot was being planned by local ağas and selfish fanatic religious people, whose first victims were going to be the Armenians."[103] Seropian also met with the mutasarrıf of Cebel-i Bereket, Asaf Bey. The situation there made a bad impression on him, and he noted, "Unfortunately, in the whole district there was only one kaymakam who behaved appropriately in accordance with the constitution, whereas the other officials, beginning with the mutasarrıf, instead of preaching harmony among the people, were inciting Turkish fanaticism against the Armenians."[104] The uncertain situation and the rising tension led Seropian to encourage Armenians to buy arms:

> We advise the people, in order to be able to fulfill their duties toward the country and constitution, [that] every person should be armed more or less according to his ability. That readiness should be at the same time somehow a means for self-defense, against an unfortunate attack, until the constitutional government comes to their aid.[105]

When Seropian returned to Adana he submitted a written report to the vali of Adana conveying his concerns.[106] On January 10, he submitted the same report to the grand vizier, the president of the parliament, the Justice Ministry, the Ministry of the Interior, the Armenian Patriarchate of İstanbul, and Armenian and Ottoman Turkish newspapers. He reported that the vali of Adana, instead of forming a special commission to investigate the situation, accused him of making false allegations.[107]

According to a contemporaneous historian, Seropian played an important role in creating fear in the hearts and minds of Armenians of an imminent massacre by the Muslims.[108] Asaf Bey claimed that when Seropian visited his district he had incited the people against him; Asaf Bey denounced Seropian as a dictator and a close confidant of Bahri Paşa.[109] He claimed that Seropian was roaming around the districts of Adana and spreading false rumors that the Muslims were preparing to kill the Armenians.[110] This hostility toward Seropian is dominant in the memoirs of Asaf Bey.[111] On March 4, 1909, Seropian traveled to Egypt in order to raise funds from the Armenian General Benevolent Union (AGBU) and appeal to other wealthy Armenians for the Armenian Rural Economy (*giwghatntesakan*) School, which was going to be built on the Telan property.[112] It was in his absence that the atmosphere in Adana deteriorated dramatically.[113] Most of the Ottoman Turkish sources (newspapers and archival material) claim that Seropian escaped to Egypt after stirring trouble in Adana.[114]

Self-Defense, or Preparation for an Uprising?

During the postrevolutionary period, the idea that Armenians were arming themselves in a frenzied manner for the purpose of establishing an independent Armenia was prevalent in the public discourse of Adana. The issue of Armenians and Muslims arming themselves soon became no longer simply part of a common discourse but moved into the public sphere under the aegis of political parties. After the first round of massacres (April 14–16), this discourse reached new heights and "confirmed" the "theory" perpetuated by the local government and the Muslim population of Adana.

In the postrevolutionary period, arming the Armenians was indeed one of the top priorities of the ARF. However, its aim was to infuse people with the idea of self-defense in order to prepare Armenians for any future confrontations with counterrevolutionary, anti-constitutional, and above all, anti-Armenian activities by the reactionary forces in Adana.[115] The correspondence of the ARF branches of Adana with the Responsible Body in İstanbul on the one hand and with the Western Bureau on the other, revealed here for the first time, attest to this anxiety. For example, in one letter, the ARF Gomideh of Adana asked the Responsible Body to supply it with Mauser rifles at a reasonable price. It also requested explosive ingredients, which were to be used by an explosives expert named Vagharshag Sako.[116] The issue of arming Armenians was especially marked during the Ramadan holiday in October of 1908 as rumors spread in Adana that the Muslims were preparing to massacre Armenians.[117] Despite the fact that the local government had in this case taken the necessary measures, the ARF stressed that "the future looked very dark."[118] The Gomideh asserted that it was ready to transfer weapons sent from the Caucasus to people in Adana.[119]

In addition to fears that reactionary forces might cause a repetition of Hamidian massacres, the ARF's urgent demand to arm Armenians was motivated by the fact that Muslims were doing the same. In October of 1908, Dr. G. Keshishian wrote, "Already the Turkish people of Adana-Tarsus-Mersin have armed themselves. The government is careless and acts slowly. . . . Religious fanaticism is rising here, and we are afraid that in the future there will be a collision." Keshishian asked for the immediate supplying of eighty Mausers.[120] In January 1909, H. Kalfayan complained to the Responsible Body that the arming of Armenians in the region was going very slowly.[121] In the same month, an ARF activist by the name of Bedros wrote to the Western Bureau lamenting that, in Sis, Armenians would not be able to defend themselves because of a decree that all those who owned weapons must hand them in to the government. He continued, "And even if they did not hand in their weapon, the people would be afraid to use them because those who use weapons are going to be tried by the military court."[122]

In none of this correspondence is there any mention of a large plan of uprising or any discussion about the formation of an independent Armenia in the region of Cilicia; rather, the discourse around arming Armenians is focused solely on defense and the aim of averting any mass violence against Armenians. And indeed, during the first phase of the massacres in Adana, it was due to the Armenians' possession of arms that they were able to initially mount a good defense of the Armenian Quarter. However, as we are going to see, once their ammunition ran out, they had to give up.

The Telan Farm Conflict in Postrevolutionary Adana

Another major issue that continued to strain the relationship between Armenians and the local government was the confiscation of the Telan property, which, as discussed in chapter 2, began in the Hamidian period. As mentioned above, the Telan property was confiscated, labeled *mahlûl*, and designated for the resettlement of Muslim Turkish refugees (*muhâcirs*).[123] In January of 1909, the Cilician Catholicos, Sahag II, appealed to the Armenian Patriarchate, demanding that it prevent the wealth of his predecessor, Catholicos Mgrdich, from being taken by Mgrdich's heirs. The Catholicos said that during the days of despotism (the reign of Abdülhamid II), he had been able to settle the question of the ownership of Telan Farm and establish it as the property of the monastery. He lamented that it would be painful if, in this period of freedom and justice, the property were not returned to the Catholicosate—especially given its dire financial situation. He warned that if the Central National Administration were not able to achieve anything on this matter, he would resign.[124] This dispute fed the tension between the Armenians and the Muslims of Adana. As a result, several Turks were killed on the property. The police accused Armenian farmers of committing the crimes, but the Armenians claimed they were being set up by conservative forces in Adana, which hoped to benefit from the deterioration of the situation. When the farmers were arrested, the Catholicos of Sis resigned in protest.

The deputy Catholicos and other Armenian representatives sent telegrams to Armenians throughout Cilicia urging them to organize demonstrations—although Bishop Seropian continued to advocate the law as a means for seeking redress. In a letter to the Armenian Patriarchate on February 7, 1908, Seropian pressed the locum tenens Fr. Ghevond about making appeals on the decision of Telan. He criticized the decision of the Council of State to allocate the property to the refugees, arguing that an important point had been ignored in the decision: the old imperial decree (*irâde*), which gave the land to the monastery. He asked that copies of the documents be made and sent to him. Regarding the demonstrations, he stated that he did not see the necessity of organizing meetings in Adana but that he was going to inform the people about the telegram of protest that he was going to dispatch to İstanbul.[125] His stance created some tensions between him and the Armenian population. According to Seropian, the person behind the demonstrations was Garabed Gökderelian, who "was devoid of national feeling, was a fake revolutionary led by his private interest [and] who starts making accusations against me in the courtyard of the church."[126] Seropian deplored Gökderelian and viewed him as a troublemaker.

The demonstrations for the Telan property were heavily criticized in the Ottoman Turkish newspapers in İstanbul, and the Catholicos was accused of inciting the people. *İkdam* newspaper in İstanbul published a lengthy article criticizing the Catholicosate for advocating protest via telegrams sent to Armenian-populated areas. The newspaper stated:

> From the perspective of the Ottoman interest, we find the path of the Catholicos improper. It could be that the people in Anatolia [are] not understanding the aim of these meetings [and] ascribe a different meaning to them. It is also probable that some ignorant [*câhil*] Armenians in those meetings do unnecessary acts, as a result of which painful fights start among the people. A spiritual leader must take these circumstances into consideration. If there are disagreements on the mentioned lands, there is the court to solve them. It is best to solve them in a legal manner. We are sad that without any reason, where there is no oppression, such an event is organized to incite the people. In the name of the public interest, we urge that these kinds of acts that create discord among people cease.[127]

The Armenian daily *Zhamanak* responded to *İkdam*'s opinion on the demonstrations by criticizing it for concealing the rightful demand of the Armenians under an illegal cover.[128] It lamented:

> What type of logic is this? Why should a church or a monastery that had bought properties for income for its people be denied of it? It is only with such a logic that the Council of State [Şûrâ-yı Devlet] has given such a decision. This is an unjust decision, which threatens the existence of the school and the church, and whoever is the one giving this [decision] is simply destructive. *İkdam* is advising the Catholicos to appeal to the court. Does *İkdam* know how long this matter has been discussed between the state and the

Armenians? Does it know how many *takrîr*s [reports] and requests have been made on this issue? When all these types of petitions and begging have not yielded any result, how should the people make its voice heard? How should it make others understand how its rights are being usurped? . . . Let our colleague not worry. If one million Armenians meet in one place, not a single agitation will take place. It will be enough that the constitution be implemented [and that] rights and equality be respected in any circumstance.[129]

These demonstrations were later represented as the beginning of a movement against the local government.[130]

Despite the heavy criticism of the demonstrations in the Ottoman Turkish press, the local CUP newspaper, *İtidal*, was supportive of them. On Sunday, February 9, 1909, the Armenians of Adana convened a large meeting at the Armenian church. The meeting was on the question of whether to transfer Telan Farm—the property of the late Catholicos—to the church or to abide by the decision of the Council of State to transfer it to Muslim refugees.[131] *İtidal* said that more than five thousand people gathered in the church, where speeches were given by the Armenian prelate of Adana (Seropian), Hajar Babikian, and Garabed Chalian, all of whom considered the move by the government to oppose the Armenian nation. At the end of the meeting, a telegram was sent with the signatures of Bishop Seropian, Manug Shahbazian, Samuel Avedisian, and Garabed Chalian to the deputies of the parliament, the Council of Ministers, and the press in İstanbul. It read: "Today, five thousand protested against the confiscation of the Armenian property belonging to the Sis monastery . . . these are the remnants of the despotic regime . . . and we do not accept the thoughts of the ministerial council that contradict the constitutional administration."[132] *İtidal* was supportive of the Armenians' demand, arguing that just as Muslims object to assaults on the properties of mosques, it too does not consent to the incursion on the church properties of its "Armenian compatriots." However, it also professed a willingness to listen to the opinion of the government and to write in an unbiased manner.[133]

In his appeals regarding the Telan property, the Catholicos of Sis urged the government and the Armenian Patriarchate to intervene in the matter. He further suggested that the Telan property, half of which was cultivable land and half of which was a swamp, was not suitable from a health perspective for the settlement of Muslim refugees.[134] In a letter addressed to Bishop Seropian, Catholicos Sahag II explained the reasons for his resignation and the indifference of the Ottoman government to the crisis. Sahag lamented the situation, writing, "You work on your land and one day suddenly the government with one order confiscates the property and the institution becomes subjected to the government." Furthermore, he said that all the efforts of the Catholicosate in asking the Ottoman government and the House of Deputies for help had yielded no results. He asked Seropian to explain to his flock that the reason for his resignation was the danger threatening the church. In his letter, the Catholicos expressed trepidation about the rising tension, stating, "The premeditated [kankhagushakwads] storm is approaching, the new clouds of terror are accumulating."[135]

Rumors and the Public Sphere

The spreading of false and provocative rumors was not new to the postrevolutionary period; as discussed in the previous chapter, it also occurred during the Hamidian period in response to the revolutionary activities of some Armenians. However, due to the maintenance of the power structure between dominant and nondominant groups and tight state control over a weak public sphere, rumors did not have a major impact in Adana during the Hamidian period. Conversely, in the unrestrained public sphere that emerged after the revolution, rumors became a catalyst for the escalation of ethnic tensions. Reactionary forces made use of them in order to mobilize the disgruntled elements of society against the new regime that had shattered the prerevolutionary status quo. Thus, the potentiality of the press in the new public sphere played an important role in facilitating the spread of rumors during this period, both verbally and through print media. Scholars of ethnic violence argue that the presence of rumors is sufficient in itself for instigating ethnic violence.[136]

Another important repercussion of rumors in the public sphere was the selling and buying of weapons on the open market. While in the past Armenians had occasionally smuggled weapons into Adana, in the postrevolutionary period this shifted to the purchasing of all types of weapons on the open market by Armenians and Muslims alike—a phenomenon that further contributed to the worsening of interethnic relations.[137] According to Arıkoğlu, weapons were sold in the market, street, and store. The most in-demand weapon was the Mauser. He lamented, "The criers were selling arms by shouting and were not being subjected to any prosecution. Because there was freedom."[138] The arms-buying was interpreted by many as part of an Armenian conspiracy to take over the region of Cilicia.

Alongside general rumors, there existed more specific rumors about potential raids by Armenian *fedayees* (freedom fighters) on Muslim villages. In a letter sent from Adana to the *Zhamanak* newspaper of İstanbul, Hagop Terzian notes that on February 22, 1909, rumors began spreading among the Muslims of Adana that "Armenians are going to attack the [arms] depot."[139] The Muslim population immediately began preparing for self-defense in their neighborhoods. Terzian said that this was bewildering: "We Armenians did not have any clue about it. We heard it from the Turks the second day and read it in *İtidal* [on] the third day with astonishment. In order to find out the source of these rumors official investigations are in process in the official circles."[140]

While the rumors discussed by Terzian dealt with the future, another rumor claimed that the Armenians had already invaded the depot and taken all the weapons and ammunitions.[141] As a result, the government secured the depot day and night. İhsan Fikri visited the vali to find out what precautions were being taken by the government; however, the latter claimed that he had no knowledge of the subject. *İtidal* dealt with this topic in its Sunday, March 6, 1909, issue. Fikri urged the government to take the necessary steps to prevent the dissemination of such rumors, which "disrupt the national harmony." He also asked the leaders of the communities to fulfill their duties by advising their constituents to dismiss these rumors. He continued, "Adana remained secure during the atrocities [the Hamidian massacres] against Armenians of the previous regime, [and] during the constitutional period these words should stop."[142]

These rumors were not confined to the city of Adana. They also spread to other districts such as Tarsus, illustrating Bhavnani et al.'s idea of how rumors born in urban areas spread to the peripheries. *İtidal* reported on March 4, 1909, that people had gathered in the animal market in Tarsus, where the sound of gunfire was heard.[143] Rumors arose that Armenians were going to invade the arms depot and that Muslims were going to massacre Armenians.[144] The leaders of both communities were able to disperse their people. *İtidal* asserted that there were people who benefit from creating discord and tension between the groups: "We repeat again that the government is not fulfilling its duties. If it arrests one or two of these low people and punishes them severely, no one else would use such words."[145] Other rumors claimed that Armenians were going to empty the arms depot of ammunition through an underground secret passage, that they had hundreds of cases of guns, and that they were going to proclaim independence.[146]

A major rumor discussed in the local press dealt with an incident at the Ulu Mosque in the city of Adana in early March 1909. According to reports, Armenians were accused of desecrating the doors of the mosque with human feces. After investigation by the local government, several Turks were held responsible for the act, their aim being to incite Muslims against Armenians.[147] A reporter for the Egyptian daily *Al-Muqaṭṭam* called the accusation a horrible act contrary to religious teaching, which had caused terrible agitation among the population. The newspaper reported that the vali had new doors put on the mosque, and he ordered an investigation, which resulted in the arrest of several Turks who were caught near the door of the mosque with a container of feces. According to the report, these people were aligned with the ancien régime and were aiming to create agitation in the city. In response, *İtidal* criticized *Al-Muqaṭṭam* for spreading false news, claiming that no such men were arrested and that the whole story was a fabrication.[148]

Visible leaders played an important role both in the propagation of these rumors and in directing crowds. As mentioned above, agents provocateurs arrived in Adana in early March—among them the *hoca* Musa Kazım, who was a member of the İttihâd-ı Muhammedî (Mohammedan Union). He began preaching in the mosques of Adana against the new regime. Sermons and speeches of this kind agitated the people and deepened the gap between Muslims and Christians, and by the end of March 1909, the situation was highly charged. Prior to the massacres, rumors spread in Adana that five to six hundred Armenian *fedayees*, led by none other than Garabed Gökderelian, were planning to attack the city.[149] The centrality of Gökderelian to these rumors is extremely important not only in Adana but also in the other districts of the province. When Gökderelian returned to Adana after the revolution, the old feuds between him and Bağdadizade were reignited. Bağdadizade and his faction seem to have played an important role in creating the rumor about Gökderelian and the *fedayees*.[150]

Conclusion

The revolution was a turning point in the history of the Ottoman Empire in general and the province of Adana in particular. The weak public sphere of the prerevolutionary period and its counter-publics were transformed. The economic, religious, social, political, and agrarian tensions that were simmering in the prerevolutionary period suddenly boiled over in the period after the revolution. The new public sphere was no longer confined to the dominant elements; counter-publics and subaltern public spheres now took an active part in it. These changes in the dynamics of power had serious repercussions on the political process in Adana. Unlike in other provinces, where the leadership was composed of members of the CUP or elements loyal to the party, in Adana, the new governor and his clique remained loyal to the ideas of the ancien régime. This created great tension between this strong remnant of the ancien régime and the new political force consisting of the CUP, Armenians, and other nondominant groups.

Rumors spread by agents provocateurs bred distrust and played a significant role in heightening tensions in Adana. The local administration and the Muslim elite were perennially suspicious that the Armenians were planning to revolt in order to reestablish the Armenian Kingdom of Cilicia. This suspicion was a remnant of the Hamidian period, when minor revolutionary activities by Armenians (mostly members of the Hnchak party) were used by agents provocateurs to instill fear in the minds and hearts of Muslims in Adana. The wide-ranging activities of Armenians in the public sphere in postrevolutionary Adana—including increased political participation, inflated romanticism of cultural history through odes, poetry, and theater, and the frantic purchasing of weapons—were used by the same agents provocateurs to prophesize the massacre of the entire Muslim population of Adana and, with the aid of European powers, the reestablishment of the Armenian Kingdom.[151] The average Muslim person in Adana—whether local inhabitant, refugee, or migrant worker—sincerely believed in this "prophecy." This illustrates the ways in which rumors play a crucial role in ethnic violence: by solidifying ethno-religious boundaries, heightening emotions, and preparing a group to fight against an imaginary enemy. The frenzied purchasing of weapons by both sides was a manifestation of these rumors.

Another important point is the role of leadership. In the postrevolutionary period, leaders played a primary role in shaping the future political process and directing crowds. In contentious conditions, leaders can defuse or escalate tensions, such as during the Ramadan holiday in Adana in October of 1908. In that situation, despite the threat of massacre and the rise of tensions, peace was maintained due to the close cooperation and coordination between the Muslim and Armenian notables, as well as the role of the local administration in preserving law and order. However, the personal animosities between various figures in the prerevolutionary period eventually took on a new tenor. Cevad Bey, İhsan Fikri, Abdülkadir Bağdadizade, Bishop Seropian, Garabed Gökderelian, Ali Gergerlizade, and Mehmet Asaf, among others, became important actors in the complex political situation of this fragile period.

CHAPTER 4

AN IMAGINED UPRISING

The First Wave of Massacres

A SIGNIFICANT OUTCOME OF THE YOUNG TURK REVOLUTION OF
1908 was the emergence of a political public sphere in which nondominant
groups took an active role in the political process. Thus, the new public sphere
became contested terrain in which elements of society that were disgruntled
by the old order competed for power with those who were in favor of it while
nondominant groups attempted to make their mark on society. This chapter
focuses on the ways in which the public sphere contributed to the deterioration of interethnic relations and the culmination of this process in violence.
The public sphere during this period became not only an arena for political
views, cultural manifestations, or the enactment of identities, as discussed in
the previous chapters, but also a ferment of interethnic tensions. Furthermore, it led to the solidification of religious boundaries. Despite religion not
being the main motive for the perpetration of the massacres, as attested by
the fact that the rioters did not attack all Christians, it did play an important
role in the enactment of violence against the Armenians. To a much lesser
degree, other Christian ethno-religious groups were targeted, such as Syriacs,
Chaldeans, and Greeks, but the majority of those killed were Armenians. The
massacres in the provinces of Adana and Aleppo mostly targeted Armenian
men, although women were also killed. Rape of Armenian women and girls
seems to have been prevalent, as was shown in the verdicts delivered by the

courts-martial in the post-massacre period. In addition to these acts of violence, many Armenian women and girls were abducted. Some were forcefully
converted to Islam while others were taken as concubines.

The keg of violence exploded in an urban setting, and then spread to different parts of the periphery. Armenians in some of these places attempted
to defend themselves, but with limited success. Moreover, the self-defense
of the Armenians was interpreted by the local government and notables, as
well as by the Muslim population in general, as an offensive act aimed at
the fulfillment of the long-awaited prophecy of reestablishing the Kingdom
of Cilicia. Rumors spread orally and in print by the government through
telegrams helped foment the idea of an uprising. Thus, it could be said that
the massacres in the periphery were a reaction to the "Armenian uprising" in
Adana.

Another important factor, largely unexamined in the study of interethnic violence in the Ottoman case, is the role of emotions. As discussed in
this chapter and the following one, emotions played a central role in the
mobilization of mobs. According to Susanne Karstedt, violent situations are
essentially emotional situations.[1] When humans perpetrate acts of violence,
they are "gripped by a high level of confrontational tension and fear. Anger,
grievance, and ideology fade into the background."[2] Affective disposition was
a key factor in the enactment of the massacres. The Muslim population saw
the Armenian population as a seditious element posing an existential threat.
Rumors fueled this predisposition, leading to the eruption of mass violence.

This was not the first time that intergroup tensions in postrevolutionary
Adana were on the verge of spiraling into violence. As we saw in the case
of the Ramadan holiday in October 1908, interethnic tensions were high in
Adana due to the fear of the imminent massacre of Armenians. At that time,
the vali, Cevad Bey, took the necessary precautionary measure of bringing
troops from Beirut to preserve order. Hence, the tensions were contained.
This raises the important question of why certain intergroup tensions subside
after reaching a peak, while others explode. Intergroup tensions have a way of
remaining in balance when there is some equality in the powers contending
against each other. However, when there is a power disparity between the
two groups, these tensions can be brought to a breaking point by the more

powerful group, with the aim of generating violence against the vulnerable group.[3]

Sporadic Violence

As rumors about an Armenian uprising continued to spread in March 1909, ethnic tension began to escalate dramatically.[4] For example, during this month, three Armenian muleteers were killed on their way from Osmaniye to Haçin.[5] Upon their arrest, the murderers confessed that they acted on the orders of a secret organization whose aim was to massacre the Christians.[6] Terzian notes that the murderers declared that the constitution was opposed to the Sharia and that the Armenians, who were the constitution's biggest supporters, should pay the price for its implementation.[7] Later, ostensibly sick, the murderers were transferred to a hospital, from which they eventually escaped.[8] According to Armenian sources, the local government took no effective measures to prevent these sporadic attacks.[9]

Interethnic tensions exploded in the month of April after one important event that became the catalyst precipitating the first wave of the Adana massacres.[10] On April 10, 1909, an Armenian named Ohannes Yapoudji was attacked by a group of Turks led by a man named İsfendiyar.[11] During the ensuing fighting, Ohannes killed İsfendiyar, wounded some of the other attackers, then fled to the Armenian Quarter in Adana and then to Mersin.[12] From there he escaped to Cyprus. In the words of the American missionary in the city of Adana, Daniel Miner Rogers, "The incident caused a great deal of excitement bringing to the point of combustion already heated spirits."[13]

On Sunday, April 11, Armenians as well as other Orthodox groups celebrated Easter in Adana "with all kinds of festivities and reveling but especially 'the shooting of guns' and drinking. The streets were crowded with merrymakers, many of them shooting off firearms, and the drinking places especially were rendezvous for the revelers."[14] The public manifestations of the Easter festivities of Christians in general and Armenians in particular exacerbated the already contentious situation.[15] The killing of İsfendiyar and the arrival of the news of the counterrevolution from the capital unleashed a wave of violence that had not been seen in the modern history of Adana. İsfendiyar's funeral not only attracted those angered by the killing but also much of the element that was dissatisfied with the new order and with the constitution and its Armenian "collaborators." Thousands carried İsfendiyar's body and roamed the neighborhoods of Adana. Infuriated speeches were given at the funeral.[16] American missionary Rev. Thomas Davidson Christie of Tarsus explained the situation in a letter sent to the American Council in Beirut:

> The utmost was made of this incident to excite the Moslems; the body was dragged through the streets for exhibition; inflammatory addresses were made in the mosques; it was proclaimed that the Armenians had risen and were killing true believers and burning their houses; telegrams and runners with the same message were sent to all parts of the province; instructions were received from Constantinople (of this there is abundant proof) to protect the foreigners and "put down the Armenians."[17]

Thus, the funeral solidified religious boundaries and became the impetus for the rapid mobilization of the various disgruntled elements of the city. The heightened emotions of the crowd contributed to its resentment toward Armenians and the demand for vengeance. In the eyes of the Muslim crowd, Ohannes became equated with all the Armenians of Adana. After the funeral, a mob headed to the Şabaniye neighborhood, surrounded Ohannes's house, and demanded that his family turn him in. The mob broke into the house but could not find him.[18] İsfendiyar's family demanded that the vali capture the murderer.[19] The deputy of the Armenian prelate asked the vali for his assurance that there would be no major outbreak of violence. The vali guaranteed that Ohannes's family would not be harmed.[20] A few days later, Rahmi Sundukzade, one of Ohannes's other attackers, died from the wounds inflicted on him during the fighting, elevating the level of anger and excitement among the Muslim population. The funeral of the second victim also attracted an infuriated mob, further heightening tensions.

Seeing the deteriorating interethnic relations, the Canadian missionary in the city of Adana, William Nesbitt Chambers—along with the Armenian Protestant preachers Hampartsoum Ashjian and Dr. Hampartsoumian—visited the vali, Cevad Bey, to call his attention to the strained state of affairs.[21] The vali assured them that he was taking the necessary measures to maintain the peace.[22] Meanwhile, he demanded that the Armenian prelate turn over Ohannes in order to calm the masses.[23] The prelate responded that it was the government's duty to arrest Ohannes, not his.[24] On April 13, İhsan Fikri, the CUP leader, delivered a speech to his Muslim compatriots, inciting them against the Armenians and the heads of the various Christian communities.[25] It is not fully understood why İhsan Fikri suddenly turned against the Armenians by putting the responsibility for an individual incident on Armenians in general. Meanwhile, rumors spread that Ohannes had escaped with the aid of Garabed Gökderelian, a figure who inspired fear in the hearts of the Muslim population, having long been associated in the collective memory with the idea of a so-called Armenian uprising.[26] As the situation intensified, the vali of Adana telegrammed İstanbul, warning of an imminent threat in Adana. Adil Bey, the undersecretary of the minister of the interior, responded, "The financial institutions along with foreign buildings should be protected and public order should be preserved" (*Müessesât-ı mâliye ile emâkin-i ecnebîyyenin muhâfazası ve iâde-i âsâyişe dikkat olunması*).[27] Most of the Armenian sources understand this telegram as an implicit order to massacre the Armenians.[28]

In his memoirs written after the massacres, Bishop Moushegh Seropian chides Adil Bey, stating that it was his and the central government's duty to send urgent orders to the provincial authorities for the prevention of the massacres and to impress on the local authorities what great responsibility they would incur if they did not put an end to the disturbances. Seropian argues that had Adil Bey acted in this way, he would have been in accordance with the constitution, thereby releasing himself from responsibility and justifying himself before public opinion. However, he writes that Adil Bey preferred "to do a completely different thing, by sending the provincial authorities his famous dispatch, conceived in a purely Hamidian spirit and saying in substance: 'Hands off the Europeans.' The murder of non-Europeans, of Armenians, that is to say, was therefore allowed!"[29] Thus, with the arrival of the news about the counterrevolution from İstanbul, the situation exploded.

The First Wave in Adana: April 14–16

Every week on Tuesday, migrant laborers returned from the fields to the city of Adana in order to get paid and arrange new contracts with the landowners for the coming weeks.[30] In Adana, Tuesday was also a market day. Peasants would travel from their villages to Adana in the morning and return in the evening. On Easter Tuesday, April 13, these peasants chose to stay the night in the city.[31] As mentioned in the first chapter, due to seasonal migration, at that time sixty thousand to seventy thousand more Armenian, Kurdish, and Turkish farmworkers were in Adana than at other times of year. The migrant workers came from poor backgrounds and worked under very harsh conditions, usually experiencing a high degree of tension with landowners.[32] They resented the ways in which the modernization of agricultural methods and the introduction of new machinery had negatively affected their work.

During the first day of the massacres, the attacks were sporadic and unorganized. On the morning of April 14, the disturbances began. Armenians opened their shops in the early morning, but in various quarters of the city soon saw groups of Turks, Kurds, Circassians, Cretan Muslims, Muslim refugees, and Başıbozuks (irregular soldiers) wearing white turbans (sarıks) around their fezzes in order to distinguish themselves from the Christians and carrying hatchets, blunt instruments, axes, and swords.[33] This made the Armenians extremely anxious, and they quickly closed their shops.[34] When the Muslims of the city saw that Armenians were closing their shops early, they too became anxious, and a rumor spread that the Armenians were going to attack them. An emergency meeting was convened between the vali and the Political Council of the Armenian Diocese in Adana; the vali told the Armenian delegation that he would take the necessary measures to preserve peace and tranquility, but that it was extremely important that Armenians open their shops in order to defuse the anxiety of the Muslim population.[35]

Tavit Urfalian Efendi—an Armenian notable, the president of the Armenian National Council, and a member of the court of appeals—along with Abdülkadir Bağdadizade and a few other Muslim notables, went to the market to deliver the vali's assurance and persuade the Armenians to open their shops.[36] According to Terzian, on their way to the market, Urfalian was killed in front of Taş Mağaza (Stone Shop) on the orders of Bağdadizade.[37] Terzian's statement is puzzling: If Bağdadizade and Urfalian were working together with the same objective of calming down the situation, why would the former order the murder of the latter? Seeing this, the chief of the gendarmes, Kadir Bey, immediately resigned. Zor Ali, the former police superintendent who had been dismissed by the CUP, was called to the central police station and reinstated as chief to preserve public order. Meanwhile, Armenian self-defense units positioned themselves in various locations, such as by the ARF Club, and in front of the churches and schools; according to Terzian, in total there were 173 Armenian defenders, while the mob consisted of thousands of people. On the first night, the mob began burning the Armenian Quarter.[38]

On the second day, the attacks and clashes intensified. The American deputy consul in Adana contacted the American embassy to say that the situation in Adana was becoming worse and that the town had been partly burned and pillaged. He further noted that thousands had been killed and the calamity was extending to the neighboring towns.[39] The mob's first objective, specifically that of the Başıbozuks, was to empty the depot and attack the inns (han), which housed Armenians who had come from the periphery of the city for work.[40]

The working-class mob, consisting of Turks, Kurds, migrant workers, fellahin, Circassians, Roma, and Cretan Muslim refugees who came from the surrounding villages, divided itself into groups of five to ten and began looting and attacking the center of the town.[41] Some of the regular soldiers also took part in the looting.[42] Most of the Christian shops were looted, but so were some Muslim ones.[43] The participation of these diverse social groups in the looting and massacres for a variety of reasons attests to participatory violence as a salient feature of the massacres.[44]

Zor Ali rallied his troops and besieged the Armenian Quarter of Şabaniye, where "heavy fighting was going on."[45] Meanwhile, Armenians defended the Armenian Quarter and fortified themselves in their houses.[46] Thousands of Armenians found refuge in the Armenian churches Surp Asdvadzadzin (Holy Mother of God) and Surp Step'anos (St. Stephen), the Armenian Catholic Church, the Armenian schools Mousheghian-Apkarian and Ashkhenian, the house of William Nesbitt Chambers, the house and the factory of Trypani, the German cotton factory, the Congregation of the Sisters of Saint Joseph of Lyon, and the Protestant and Jesuit missionary institutions and churches.[47]

Araxi Boyadjian, a survivor of the massacres and the daughter of Samvel Bzdigian, one of the Hnchak leaders, recounts the Adana massacres in her unpublished memoirs. She recalls that after the proclamation of the constitution, her husband, Mihran, bought fifteen Martini rifles and thousands of bullets for self-defense. On the first day of the massacres, she describes how hundreds of Armenians came to their house in the Yenimahalle neighborhood and gathered in the garden looking for shelter.[48] When the mob surrounded the house, Samvel Bzdigian sent a messenger to Commander Mustafa Remzi Paşa asking for his help in protecting the people and sending soldiers to accompany them to their homes. When twelve soldiers appeared in front of the house, Samvel and Mihran went out to thank the soldiers. However, instead of dispersing the mob, the police commissioner ordered the soldiers to fire on the house. The youths who were sheltered in the house fired back at the soldiers and hit two policemen. Many of the people sheltered in the house were killed, including Araxi's mother. The next day, Araxi and her husband escaped to the Régie Company to find shelter, thinking they would be safe because it was a European establishment. Araxi recounts that there were over one thousand Armenians who came there looking for a safe haven. However, the mob began showering the roof of the Régie Company with bullets. Eventually Araxi and her husband were able to escape to Cyprus via Mersin.[49] Her father was imprisoned and endured torture. After she returned to Adana, she went to see him in prison.[50]

The mob's attack was not confined to the Armenian Quarter; it also targeted foreign missionary institutions.[51] Ample eyewitness accounts by the Jesuits testify to this fact.[52] Major Doughty-Wylie, the British vice-consul, arrived in the Armenian Quarter accompanied by thirty soldiers and found that the American missionaries D. Miner Rogers and Henry Maurer had been killed "at the closest range by five Turks who had previously promised to let them alone."[53] The third missionary, Stephen Van R. Trowbridge, managed to escape.[54] In a series of telegrams sent to A. Jeannier, the French consul in Mersin, Lutfik Khoubeserian—the translator of the French consulate and one of the Armenian notables of the city of Adana—discussed the damage that was inflicted on the Armenians and their properties while highlighting the passive position of the government, arguing, "Had they [the local government] killed some of the Turks in the beginning they would have stopped." However, he says, the authorities did the opposite and joined the mob in massacring and looting.[55]

During this period, Vali Cevad Bey was in "state of panic" and did not know how to handle the situation. Observers at the time said that he "had done absolutely nothing" in order to find a remedy to the urgent situation.[56] In his correspondence with the central government, he uses the passive voice in his description of the parties involved in the events in Adana. One does not get precise information as to who is who in the conflict; he uses the nonspecific term "people" (*ahâli*) in referring to all the participants. On April 14, Cevad Bey sent a telegram to the Ministry of the Interior relaying that the previous night, the regular troops (*nizâmiye*), police, and gendarmes were busy roaming different parts of the city. Although the excitement had not subsided, the Armenian shop owners opened their shops the next morning. However, upon receiving the news from the church, they closed their shops. Seeing this, the Muslim shop owners too closed their shops. Consequently, the Muslim notables along with the division commander began to provide the necessary advice to the Muslim population, and the prominent Christian figures did likewise.[57] In his second telegram sent to the Ministry of the Interior, Cevad Bey stated that because the existing regular troop battalion of around four hundred soldiers, along with the police and the gendarmes, was not enough to pacify the uprising, it was communicated to the local military and civil officers that individuals from the reserve battalions of Mersin, Tarsus, Karaisalı, and Sis should immediately be armed and sent to Adana.[58]

On the first day of the massacres, Cevad Bey wrote to the grand vizier stating that disturbances began with fighting and looting in the subdistrict of Hamidiye.[59] In addition to requesting the reserve battalions from Yarpuz (the capital of Cebel-i Bereket), he asked that the notables and the ulemâ advise the people as necessary to calm the agitations.[60] In a different telegram, he informed the grand vizier that disturbances had subsided overnight and as a necessary precaution, the armed reserve battalions of Tarsus and Mersin, numbering 150 people, were on their way to Adana.

On April 15, the grand vizier sent an order to the Ministry of War to send two battalions to Adana to preserve security and order. He specified that all necessary action should be taken to prevent looting and attacks on the financial institutions, as well as to protect foreigners and consulates.[61] In addition, the Council of Ministers gave permission to the Ministry of War to

MAP. 2. The urban geography of Adana prior to the 1909 massacres, with major landmarks and city quarters labeled. An insert shows the city quarters burned during the 1909 violence. The city map is partially based on the *Plan de la ville d'Adana*, produced by the French military in 1918 and made available by the Technische Universität Berlin. The labels on the map reflect the French spellings. Insert showing the burned quarters based on Zadig Khanzadyan's "Planche 16: Carte No. 30: Rade de Mersina," published in his 1924 *Atlas de geographie economique de Turqie*. Map by Patrick T. Hoehne.

immediately arm the Silifke Reserves and to send them by way of Mersin to Adana to help bring the situation under control.[62] However, in the words of Dr. H. Belart (the director of the Adana Railway), the "redif soldiers called to arms aggravated the situation by their indiscipline."[63] In many cases, the *redif*s (reserve soldiers) joined the mob in the pillaging and killing.[64] Because they did not wear military uniforms, Armenians assumed that they were part of the mob. It was only on the last day of the first wave of massacres that the grand vizier sent a telegram to Adana stating that two battalions from Gallipoli and Dedeağaç had been prepared and would be sent to Adana.[65]

On April 15, Commander Mustafa Remzi Paşa described the situation in the city, saying that the fire of "uprising" had spread immediately to the different parts of the province. He complained that the battalions that had been summoned with the aim of defending their neighborhoods were not doing so. According to him, "people" had looted the depots of Yarpuz and Tarsus. Additional battalions were supposed to be sent by the central government. He said that Armenians were dominating the streets. Sheltered in their houses, they were shooting at Muslims and soldiers without differentiation. He said that the decrease of the infantry battalion in the city of Adana and the arrival of soldiers from Sis, Tarsus, İskenderun, and Karaisalı had not helped the situation, as these soldiers were hesitating to use weapons against their coreligionists. According to him, it was discovered that Armenian women were also carrying guns. He said that it was extremely urgent to send two battalions from the nearest location.[66]

On April 16, the ARF leader from Mersin, Dr. Keshishian, sent a letter to the Responsible Body of the ARF in İstanbul saying that Adana was awash in blood and that the massacres had been continuing for three days. According to him, the number of victims was unknown, but the Armenians had put

FIGURE 4. The destruction in the city of Adana, 1909.
Source: George Grantham Bain Collection (Library of Congress).

up a good resistance. He said that the soldiers had united with the mob and begun to attack the Armenians. He finished his letter by writing, "We are in a grave situation and have taken a defensive posture."[67]

By the third day, the mob grew as Turks arrived from Aleppo and Sivas to take part in the pillaging. As a result, the attacks intensified further. Since the Armenians were reaching the end of their ammunition, they asked the government for protection.[68] This was negotiated by Tekelizade Osman Bey, a prominent Turkish figure who lived in the Armenian Quarter.[69] In response, the vali organized a reconciliation meeting between Turkish and Armenian notables.[70] Missionary Chambers, who was present at this meeting, reported that "each side pledged themselves to do all in their power to restrain their respective people."[71] The British vice-council, Major Doughty-Wylie, persuaded the Armenians to turn in their weapons, and a ceasefire was agreed to.[72] By the fourth day the situation had calmed. Garbage carriages from the municipality collected hundreds of bodies from the streets and threw them in the Seyhan River.[73] Chambers describes the spectacle:

> The horrible sights in the streets and ruined houses, mutilated bodies lying in blood, plundered and burnt shops, charred bodies in the ashes and debris . . . the thousands of Armenians in refuge in the various churches, schools, private houses, factories etc, without food, homeless and prostrated show one of the cruelest, most bloodthirsty massacres of modern times.[74]

According to Trowbridge, the vali pretended that the Armenians had revolted and were responsible for everything. While the governor sent telegrams to the other districts of Adana asking them to call in all the reservists and ordering them "to protect foreign subjects,"[75] he also sent a wire to the minister of the interior saying, "The Armenians have attacked us, the Government buildings are besieged by them, the Armenians are all armed and are massacring the defenseless Turks."[76] However, in Trowbridge's words:

> The Turks, even the soldiers and officers, have not discriminated at all, but have cut down or drowned or burned without mercy all Armenians who fell into their pathway. . . . In many homes the mutilated bodies of women and children are being found, and many Christian Girls have been carried off as booty.[77]

FIGURE 5. The Christian Quarter in Adana, 1909.
Source: George Grantham Bain Collection (Library of Congress).

On April 17, the Armenian Catholic prelate of Adana, bishop Paul Terzian, sent a telegram to the Catholic patriarch, Paul Bedros XII Sabbaghian, reading, "The conflagration continues until today. . . . Our farm, which is located three hours away from the city, has been totally destroyed. . . . The same situation is in Tarsus and Sis."[78]

When the massacres began, the Armenian prelate of Adana, Bishop Seropian, was in Egypt, but he soon rushed to Mersin in order to be with his flock. On Wednesday, April 21, he arrived at the port of Mersin on the Khedivial steamer.[79] On the advice of both Turks and some Armenians, Vice-Consul Doughty-Wylie intervened with the local government to prevent Bishop Seropian from disembarking in Mersin. Doughty-Wylie believed that the presence of Seropian would aggravate the situation further and lead to more bloodshed. As mentioned earlier, the Muslim population of Adana, as well as the local government, saw Seropian as the prime agitator of the Armenians and the reason for their armament. In his journal, Seropian lamented the fact that he was not able to be with his flock during their direst situation and was instead forced to return to Alexandria. On April 23, he arrived at the port of Tripoli (in modern-day Lebanon). Of his journey, he wrote: "All the Turks received me with a hellish gaze on the ship, where they pointed me out to each other as the great revolutionary who wanted to be king of Adana."[80] On his way to Beirut, a group of people attempted to kill him on board the ship, after which he was put under protective surveillance. After passing through Jaffa, he arrived in Alexandria, from where he left for Cyprus.[81]

The carnage, looting, and killing in Adana lasted for three days (April 14, 15, and 16). Many Armenians were killed, as were many of the Muslims who attacked the Armenian Quarter. Chambers reported that many of the Armenians "showed good pluck." Had they not mounted a strong defense, "destruction of life and property would have been complete."[82] Trowbridge recounted that in the city of Adana, Armenians did not die unresisting; on the contrary, "they fought desperately in self-defense and in proportion, as they succeeded in slaying the Mahommedans, the fury of Turks increased."[83]

The Situation outside the District of Adana

With the eruption of violence in the city of Adana, the wave of massacres immediately began spreading to all parts of the province and poured into the nearby province of Aleppo. Rumors about Armenians revolting in Adana and killing all the Muslims played a primary role in inciting the masses and contributed to their rapid mobilization against the perceived enemy. According to the Austro-Hungarian consul in Mersin, the pillaging and destruction in the countryside was terrible, where Armenians and other Christians were working in the fields. In most cases these farmers perished; those who managed to escape were pursued across the fields and hunted like wild beasts. The farms of all Christians were indiscriminately burned and plundered, and their cattle were looted.[84] In the interest of conciseness, I will not be able to cover all the cases of violence inflicted on the Armenians in the provinces of Adana and Aleppo; instead, I will discuss select cases from each province in order to demonstrate the anatomy of these massacres.

Tarsus and Mersin

On Friday, April 14, at 10:00 a.m., a mob of four hundred Başıbozuks hijacked a train from Adana and headed to Tarsus, bringing kerosene with which to burn houses.[85] They were joined there by many Afghans who lived in the suburbs of Tarsus.[86] All cried out that the Armenians had slaughtered the Muslims in Adana, and because of this, the Armenians of Tarsus had to be exterminated.[87] A local mob joined with the Başıbozuks and proceeded to burn the Armenian Quarter.[88] The burning was accelerated by the fact that most of the Armenians stored cotton on the ground floor of their homes, and the liberal application of kerosene by the mob led to the utter destruction of these houses.[89] According to Hagopos Varjabedian, an eyewitness from Tarsus, while all 450 of the Armenian houses were burned, no Greeks were harmed.[90]

It is estimated that more than 70 Armenians were killed in the city of Tarsus and 560 in the surroundings. About 800 Armenian-owned buildings were burned.[91] These buildings were mostly homes, since in Tarsus, unlike in Adana, Armenian and Muslim shops were located in the same areas, and the mob could not easily differentiate between them. Woods asserts that the leader of the mob was a well-known Young Turk who was an important member of the local CUP.[92] Rumors spread in Tarsus that Garabed Gök-derelian "was marching on the city at the head of 15,000 Armenian cavalry," leading to more violent backlash.[93] Meanwhile, Armenians found refuge in the Catholic mission.[94] Significantly, in Tarsus, "fifteen Turks are said to have been killed in protecting their Christian brethren."[95] During the height of the events, Esadzade of Kerkütlü—an inhabitant of the Tekke neighbor-hood—gathered more than 30 wounded Armenians from the streets and took them to his house for treatment. Two other Turks followed suit: Muhtar Güvenzade and his friend Memocan.[96] However, St. Paul's College was re-sponsible for saving the most Armenians in Tarsus, as around 4,000 found refuge on the school grounds.[97]

The coastal town of Mersin, which was the residence of the consuls, was spared during the massacres mainly due to the efforts of its mutasarrıf, Esad Rauf Bey. He brought together the local mufti, the mayor, and the Armenian dignitaries and worked to prevent any type of disturbance in Mersin.[98] In a letter sent by the ARF Gomideh of Mersin to the Responsible Body in İstanbul, the author discussed how the massacres that took place in Adana and its surroundings had horrified and saddened the Armenians of Mer-sin—invoking memories of the 1895 massacres—and also confused them, es-pecially when the city began to be ruled by the armed reserves.[99] The letter added that some Turkish notables in this city would have liked to organize a massacre, but that their friends had dissuaded them. He argued that the ARF members had expected the local CUP to be neutral in the conflict but were surprised by its anti-Armenian behavior during the massacres.[100] All sources thus indicate that Esad Rauf Bey should be credited with protecting the city.

Cebel-i Bereket

The worst massacres outside the city of Adana took place in the district of Cebel-i Bereket, composed of the subdistricts of Osmaniye, Bahçe, Yarpuz, Hassa, Payas, and Ceyhan. The mutasarrıf of Cebel-i Bereket, Asaf Bey, played a dominant role in inciting the public about a major Armenian uprising.[101] He sent erratic telegrams to the vali of Adana and the minister of the interior as well as to the other districts, claiming that the Armenians in his district had revolted. He asked for permission to arm civilians, including hundreds of prisoners who were set free from the towns of Erzin and Payas.[102] He sent wires all around his district stating, "Gökderelian is coming with 1,500, 2,000, 3,000 *ghiaours* [infidels]," with the intention of inflaming the minds of the Muslim people.[103]

On April 16, Asaf Bey sent a very urgent telegram to the Ministry of the Interior stating that, according to a telegram from the kaymakam of Bahçe, the houses of Christians were burning and people were killing each other, and if troops were not sent there immediately, all the Muslim people would be in danger and under siege (*umûm kazâ ahâli-i Müslimesinin tehlike ve muhâsara altında olduğu bildirilmiş*). He further argued that the situation in the district was so bad that the government center was under threat of being occupied by Armenians. He stated that the loss of life had already been great and immediate military aid was needed.[104] On the same day, he sent three further telegrams to the Ministry of the Interior spreading false rumors. One of these telegrams read, "Today more than four thousand Armenians equipped with Martini rifles are fortifying around the town . . . Muslims are also gathering on their borders."[105] In another even more incendiary and alarming telegram, he warned the Ministry of the Interior about the deteriorating situation in the region, stating that there were more than five thousand Armenians equipped with Martini rifles in Dörtyol. He claimed that they had fortified the village and were doing the same in other villages. Asaf Bey urged the government to send a battalion to the region.

He concluded his telegram by stating that the kaymakam of Bahçe had notified him that numerous Armenians from Zeitun and Maraş were going to burn Bahçe.[106]

On April 17, Cevad Bey received multiple telegrams from Asaf Bey asking for help in facing the horrible condition in the district. According to Asaf Bey, all the prisons had been emptied. The prisoners were threatening the gendarmes, and if they could not be contained, he asked that weapons be sent from the commandership of İskenderun. He said that the Armenians were increasing their attack, that the district was surrounded by fire, and that troops were needed. In another telegram, he asked that weapons and ammunition be sent to the people of Ocaklı and Özerli near Dörtyol, as their ammunition had run out. Furthermore, he asked that some of the four hundred Mausers that were found in the Osmaniye battalion's depot be sent to Cebel-i Bereket.[107]

On the same day, Asaf Bey sent a telegram to the directorship (*müdür-lük*) of the Payas prison in which he stated that, if it was too difficult to contain the prisoners, they should be released immediately.[108] Asaf Bey sent orders to Osmaniye and Hassa to distribute weapons to the people.[109] In a different telegram on the same day, he reported that the people of Dörtyol were going to attack and asked for the immediate dispatch of four to five hundred troops.[110] Meanwhile, he sent a telegram to the kaymakamlıks (district governors) of Hassa, Bahçe, and İslahiye, ordering them to protect the foreigners.[111] He also sent a telegram to the Ministry of the Interior and the province stating that in the morning, an attack had begun from Dörtyol on the center of the district and the Armenians of Hasanbeyli had besieged the subdistrict of Bahçe; he again demanded assistance.[112] Asaf Bey also sent telegrams to Osmaniye and Bahçe stating that there was an Armenian uprising in Adana.

A major portion of the Armenian population of his district was massacred. This included the Christian populations of Bahçe, Hasanbeyli, and Osmaniye. After leading the massacres of the Armenians of Erzin and Osmaniye, Asaf Bey led his men, some reserve troops, and a civilian mob to the depot of Arğini to rearm, and then headed to Dörtyol. The five hundred Turkish prisoners of Payas, whose release he had ordered, also took part in the massacres.[113]

Such was the panicked condition of Asaf Bey, who instead of bringing the situation under control, contributed immensely to the massacre of Armenians in these regions. He did so primarily by instilling fear and anxiety among the local Muslim population about acts of massacre supposedly being perpetrated by the Armenians.[114]

Osmaniye

According to an Armenian eyewitness account, when Asaf Bey circulated the news about the "Armenian uprising" in Adana, the local Muslim population in Osmaniye became agitated. The local Muslim notables, with the participation of the local government officials, held a meeting at the barracks to discuss the situation. They came to the decision to announce to the villagers and the roaming tribes surrounding the town that they would provide aid. These people immediately poured into Osmaniye, where weapons and ammunition were distributed to them.[115] Seeing this, Armenians panicked and sent a representative to the kaymakam, who deflected their concerns, saying that the issue was the prisoners who had escaped from the prison of Payas and that they were collecting reservists to arrest them.[116] However, on the next day (April 15), the attacks began. Armenians immediately sought refuge in the Armenian churches, but the mob attacked the Armenian Protestant Church, massacring seventeen protestant pastors.[117] These pastors had arrived on the previous day from Aintab and Maraş in order to participate in the Annual Meeting of the Missions, which was to be held in the city of Adana on April 19.[118] Later the mob attacked the Armenian Apostolic Church, which housed hundreds of Armenians,[119] burning it down with the people inside.[120] Missionary Thomas Davidson Christie, president of St. Paul Institute, states that every Armenian house and shop was plundered and then burned to the ground.[121] After destroying the Armenian Quarter, the mob began searching the houses of Turks who they felt might be hiding Armenians. They found one such house in which fifty Armenians were hiding and proceeded to kill them all.[122]

The massacres in Osmaniye lasted from April 14 until April 29, during which hundreds of Armenians were killed.[123] According to one figure, out of the eight hundred Christian residents, only thirty men and two hundred women remained. In the whole quarter, four houses were left standing.[124]

Those Armenians who were able to escape the massacres went to İskenderun and Lebanon. Some of these refugees wrote a letter to the Armenian Patriarchate in İstanbul about "the horrible incidents in Cebel-i Bereket and the role of its mutasarrıf, Asaf Bey in arming about thirty thousand people and attacking and massacring the Christians." The letter ended by thanking the brave Ottoman soldiers of the Second Army who ended the siege.[125]

Bahçe

In Bahçe, a subdistricts of Cebel-i Bereket that contained 128 Armenian houses and 65 Muslim houses, the Mufti İsmail Efendi and his family instigated and directed the mob during its attacks on Armenian shops and residents.[126] When the news of the disturbances arrived in Bahçe, the Turkish and Kurdish villagers surrounding the subdistrict gathered and prepared to attack the town. Seeing this, the German employees of the Baghdad Railway went to the kaymakam to ask him about the cause of these events. After initial reassurances, the kaymakam later told them that the situation was serious—the vali of Adana had informed the kaymakam that disturbances had broken out in Adana and that he was liable for the safety of the foreigners.[127] Dr. Andre Papoutsakis, employed as the physician of the Baghdad Railway, provides more details of this chain of events.[128] On Wednesday, April 14, he went to the mufti's house and overheard the mufti and *hoca*s talking about arming themselves. When he asked for a reason, he was given an evasive reply. He then went to the kaymakam, a friend of his, and asked him if there was any sense to this. The kaymakam replied that he did not know, and they went together to the government house, where they found the mufti. The mufti promised peace, saying that it was against the Sacred Law to massacre, "but that all Armenians deserved to be killed, as they were a filthy nation."

On April 15, the Muslim population of the town joined villagers from the surrounding areas and, according to Papoutsakis, began shooting, clubbing, and stabbing Armenians to death without encountering any signs of resistance.[129] One of the eyewitnesses of these massacres, an Armenian teacher in Bahçe by the name of Krikor Koudoulian, lamented that Armenians had only a few weapons for self-defense: "We had worked the whole year and could not instill the ideal of self-defense in the dead and enslaved hearts of the [Armenian] rich."[130] Led by the mufti of Bahçe, the mob attacked the Armenian church and the residents, looting and killing most of the Armenians.[131] Some Armenians found refuge in the mosque but were later taken out and killed.[132] Those who escaped to the forests were hunted down by the mob.[133]

On April 16, the mutasarrıf of Cebel-i Bereket sent a telegram to the Ministry of the Interior in which he reported that the kaymakam of Bahçe had informed him that the inhabitants were massacring each other and asserted that if troops were not sent immediately, the entire Muslim population would be besieged. The mutasarrıf cautioned people to refrain from any aggression as long as the Armenians did not attack, but otherwise to respond in kind. He also strongly urged the notables of both parties to guard against looting, fires, and senseless murders. Meanwhile, the carnage continued, and Bahçe burned at every turn. According to a report submitted to the German consulate by the Baghdad Railway engineers, "the fact that this finally succeeded . . . allows the conclusion that the whole movement was well planned; another fact contributing to this assumption is that women and children were spared, with only a few exceptions."[134]

The German employees of the Baghdad Railway noted that in Bahçe, the military consistently fraternized with the rebels.[135] The Germans who sheltered Armenians argued that the family of the mufti of Bahçe, who with one word could have prevented all the bloodshed, showed extreme hostility toward them. They described the situation in Bahçe as "complete anarchy, the kaymakam . . . completely powerless and in the hands of the mufti." On April 20, the German engineers left Bahçe. All of their houses were looted.[136] Around 110 houses were burned, and 113 people were killed in the subdistrict.[137]

Sis

When the news of the Adana massacres arrived in Sis, the situation deteriorated there as well. The resigned Catholicos of Cilicia, Sahag II, sent a telegram to the grand vizier reading, "In all parts mass killing, burning, and plundering is continuing; today it is expected that an attack will take place on Sis. The public agitation is alarming. We are requesting that immediate and absolute measures be taken by the government in order to bring stability and peace and to protect the general life."[138] He also sent telegrams to the locum tenens of the Armenian Patriarchate in İstanbul on April 17, stating, "From all sides, general massacres, conflagration, and looting are continuing. The fear and the awe of the people are dreadful. Please ask the government to secure the life of the people and restore tranquility."[139] A mob from Kars, Hamidiye, and Adana, in cooperation with Chechens and Circassians from the district of Sis, looted twenty Armenian farms around Sis and then besieged the city. The governor, in accord with the local commander and Turkish and Armenian notables, decided to defend the city.[140] Armenian groups participated in the defense of the town. After a failed attempt to attack the city on April 18, the mob launched a fierce three-flank attack the next day. Fighting continued until nightfall, but the mob was not able to take over the town.[141] However, the periphery and the villages around the town of Sis suffered immensely.

The Province of Aleppo

The wave of mass violence was not confined to the province of Adana but also spread into the province of Aleppo. Political processes similar to those in Adana had taken place in the province of Aleppo in the postrevolutionary period: euphoria and the festivities of the revolution were followed by intense political competition between the people of the ancien régime and the new order. The agents of the previous order appeared stronger in the province of Aleppo than in Adana; however, the vali of Aleppo, Reşid Paşa, did a better job of restraining the situation than did his counterpart in Adana.[142] Accordinging to Raphael Fontana, the British consul in Aleppo, the vali made every effort to contain the outbreak. Fontana also praised the colonel of the gendarmes, who demonstrated great vigilance in trying to prevent any incident. He argues that an important restraining factor in Aleppo was the intertwinement of the commercial and material interests of the Muslim notables with those of the Christian merchants, meaning that any losses by pillaging and fire would result in equal financial losses for both parties.[143]

Nevertheless, cities such as Maraş, Urfa, Zeitun (Süleymanlı), İskenderun, Enderun, Kessab, and Antioch endured their share of massacres and mass violence.[144] In some places, such as Zeitun and Dörtyol, Armenians put up a good defense. In the case of Zeitun, Reşid Paşa sent an urgent telegram to the Ministry of the Interior on April 19 in which he relayed that the Armenians of Zeitun had blockaded the government building and violated the peace and that the mutasarrıf of Maraş had asked that an army of two

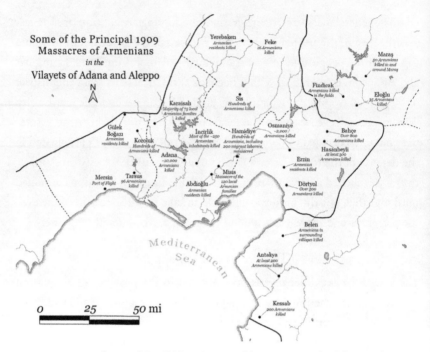

MAP. 3. Some of the 1909 massacres of Armenians in the Adana and Aleppo vilayets. Data sourced from Z. Duckett Ferriman, *The Young Turks and the Truth about the Holocaust at Adana in Asia Minor, during April 1909* (London: [publisher unknown], 1913). Map by Patrick T. Hoehne.

battalions be sent from Aleppo.[145] On the same day, he also notified the Ministry of the Interior that the fighting and disturbances in Antioch (Antakya) had begun in an astonishing manner. Military measures were taken and the commandership of the Fifth Army was notified immediately. On April 20, the Ministry of the Interior replied that it had already notified the Ministry of War and measures were being taken. The minister implored them to use any available means to bring peace, such as using the notables of both the Muslims and the Christians to advise their people, and to protect the foreign institutions and foreigners.[146]

Antioch

Antioch had a population of eight hundred Armenians.[147] During the harvest in the spring, more than five hundred additional laborers—most of them

Armenian—would come to Antioch to work on the farms. When Armenians in the city heard about the massacres in Adana, they closed their shops and hid in their houses. The kaymakam came with his officers to the National Diocese and assured the Armenian notables that there was nothing to fear; he urged that all the shops be reopened.[148] Meanwhile, the local government gathered *redifs* and began distributing weapons to them.[149] On April 19, the Muslim population headed toward the Armenian Quarter of the town and massacred the male Armenian population.[150]

The massacres took place at the instigation of the local ağas.[151] British vice-consul David Douek put the responsibility not only on the local Muslims but also on the authorities, as rifles and ammunition were distributed at the barracks to both the military reserves and the Başıbozuks; when these were exhausted, the barracks renewed them. He stated that, had the local government wished to stop the massacre, they could easily have done so at any moment, as they had enough force at their disposal for that purpose.[152]

The German consular agent in Antioch, M. Missakian, attributed the beginning of the incidents there to the intrigues of influential Muslim notables, who distributed weapons and ammunition to the Muslim population. According to him, the provocations of Avnullah Kâzımî (Mehmed Selim Bey)—the president of the Fedâkâran-ı Millet (The Martyrs of the Nation) of İstanbul—and the mutasarrıf of Karput contributed immensely to the massacre of Armenians. He argued that the incidents lasted until April 25 but that the massacre took place largely in the first two days. According to him, the number of Armenians massacred was around three hundred, most of whom were men. He lamented the local authorities' reluctance to punish anyone who "had the cruelty to deliberately and systematically massacre only the poor Armenians and did nothing to other Christians." Missakian praised the kaymakam of Antioch for attempting to protect the Armenians but reported to Tischendorf, the German consul in Aleppo, that the major (*binbaşı*) and the adjutant (*kolağası*) of the city categorically refused to lend their military assistance.[153] Thus, the kaymakam did not have enough soldiers at his disposal. However, the latter—together with Captain Süleyman Bey and the assistant of the interrogator, Mohammed Bey—did manage to protect the German consulate and the Armenian refugees who found a safe haven there.

On the April 22, Missakian sent another report on the massacre of Armenians in Antioch to Tischendorf.[154] He stated that on April 19, a dispatch
from the province had officially invited the local authorities to send all the
reserves within twenty-four hours. As soon as this news spread, strong indig-
nation and revolt manifested itself among the Muslim population of this city.
He said that the Muslims cried out, "The Armenians have revolted again;
that is why they are sending us."[155] On the next day, the Muslims attacked
the Armenian neighborhoods, massacred the Armenians, and pillaged and
ruined their houses and their church; the bishop and the parish priest were
also killed. Of the Armenians, there remained only ten men who were in the
government building; some women and children were transported either to
mosques or to Muslim houses. Some girls were taken to Muslim homes with
the promise that Muslims would marry them. Missakian reported that fear
and danger reigned everywhere, and reinforcements had not yet arrived from
Aleppo.[156] He argued that while the kaymakam repeatedly asked the major
for help, instead of helping, the latter "had the audacity to arm the *redif*s and
give them ammunition and full freedom to roam the city, which contributed
a great deal to the incident."[157]

Theodor Belfante, the German vice-consul of İskenderun, notified the
Protestant mission in Antioch that massacres had taken place in the village
of Kessab and in the Antioch region. Hundreds of widows and Christian
orphans without support were begging for help.[158] Among the dead were
166 men, 2 eleven-year-old boys, 5 women, 2 vicars, and 2 priests.[159] Another
source estimates the number of victims to be around 350.[160] The organizers of
the massacres were the mutasarrıf—who came from the capital four days before the event—and the Turkish notables Hüsni Ağa, Vahid Ağazade, Rıfat
Bereketzade, and Reşid.[161] The surviving Armenians were saved by the arrival
of a French battleship.[162]

Kessab

Kessab, which stands out upon the Mediterranean seacoast halfway between
İskenderun and Latakia, was a vibrant Armenian town with eight thousand
inhabitants.[163] Its main industry was the production of silk. After the massacres of Antioch, on Thursday, April 22, a mob composed of Turks, fellahin,

Kurds, and Circassians from the neighboring villages and from Antioch, Har, and Cisr eş Şuğur (Jisr al-Shughur) gathered around Kessab preparing for an assault.[164] The nearest government seat was Ordu, whose *müdür* (head)— Hüseyin Hasan Ağa—organized a parley in the village of Esguran and dispatched a telegraph to the governor of Aleppo asking for military protection. He told the Armenian delegation to the meeting that the mob had formed because of fears that the Armenians of Kessab were going to attack Ordu. The leader of Kessab, Serko Ağa, assured Hasan Ağa that no Armenian was going to attack them.[165] Hasan Ağa promised that he would scatter the mob.[166] But this proved to be false, as that evening, he allowed armed mobs from Cisr eş Şuğur, Al-Qusayr, Antioch, and Idlib to enter Ordu.[167] The next morning, he dispatched them to sack Kessab. In addition, he detained eleven gendarmes who were sent by the vali of Aleppo, Reşid Paşa, to protect the foreign institutions in Kessab. Reşid Paşa explained in a ciphered telegram to the Ministry of the Interior in early May that he had done everything in his power to prevent the mob from attacking Kessab. He said that the existing forces in the region were insufficient to deter the mob's momentum, so he sent ulemâ and notables from Cisr eş Şuğur to the villages surrounding Kessab to convince the mob not to attack. However, this did not yield any results.[168]

The mob began its attack on the morning of Friday, April 23.[169] They moved on Kessab from three separate mountain trails: the north, northeast, and east.[170] Around three hundred Armenians attempted to mount a defense; however, unlike the Martini rifles with which the mobs were equipped, the Armenians had only short-range weapons that did not prove effective.[171] Realizing that they were outnumbered, the Armenians resolved to resist as much as they could in order to provide time for the women and children to escape to the mountains and the caves.[172] Missionary P. Sabatino del Gaizo played an important role in assisting this effort.[173] Around noon, the women and children were evacuated to the village of Kaladouran;[174] once they were in a "safer" situation, the men slackened their defense.[175] The mob entered the town, seizing and plundering everything from raw silk—the chief produce of the Armenians of Kessab—to mules, clothing, and rugs. Armenians who were not able to flee were caught and massacred. About 153 Armenians were killed, as were a handful of Turks.[176] By Saturday night, nothing was left to plunder in the town. All of the churches, markets, foreign institutions, and 530 houses were burned to ashes, including provisions, clothing, bedding, farm animals, and pack animals—in a word, everything was lost.[177]After finishing with the looting, the mob began hunting down Armenians in the caves and the mountains.[178]

Among the leaders responsible for the massacre at Kessab and the destruction of Armenian property were Mohammed Kasim, Najib Sekhta, and the ağas of Buçuk and Ordu.[179] Before the attack on Kessab was finished, Reşid Paşa dispatched Selhan Ağa from Cisr eş Şuğur to protect the town of Kessab from the mob. However, instead of arriving in the eight hours necessary to reach Kessab, it took him forty-eight hours. Furthermore, when he arrived, he did not stop the mob but "himself became a plunderer."[180]

On April 22, the French agent in Latakia sent numerous telegrams to Fouques Duparc, the French consul of Beirut, describing the dire situation in Kessab, which lay totally devastated on April 23.[181] Duparc contacted the French consul in Larnaca asking him to send the *Niger* steamer of the French Messageries Maritime company to Latakia. On April 25, the mutasarrıf of Latakia sent about thirty horsemen to Kaladouran, who safely brought a crowd of 500 women and children to Latakia.[182] On the same day, the *Niger* arrived in Kaladouran at the foot of Jebel Aqra (Mt. Cassius) and took 3,000 Armenians on board, heading for Latakia. Later that day, the *Niger* arrived in Ras-el-Bassit and took 2,200 refugees; meanwhile, the French *Jules Ferry* armored cruiser arrived in Beirut on the night of April 24 and continued to Latakia on the twenty-fifth. On April 26 it arrived in Ras-el-Bassit, bringing on board 1,450 refugees and all of the Latin missionaries.[183] On Monday, April 26, it arrived in Latakia, bringing more than 4,000 refugees who were divided among several schools, churches, and the grounds of the American Presbyterian Mission under the care of Dr. James Balph. The total number of Armenians from Kessab who arrived in Latakia was around 6,500.[184] The mutasarrıf of Latakia, Mehmed Ali Bey led the effort to safeguard the wellbeing of the refugees. In Trowbridge's words, "The courageous and kind hearted action of this Turk saved Latakia, and the thousands of Kessab people sheltered there, from the dreadful event of massacre."[185] He even acted as part of the police and patrolled the city at night to prevent any type of mob attack.[186] However, the arrival of the refugees in Latakia caused considerable anxiety among the Muslim population.[187]

The head missionary of Kessab argued that the müdür's "plea that the Kessab people were preparing to attack the Moslem population is sheer nonsense." She argued, "No Moslems living in Kessab and the other villages [were] attacked. [The victims] are entirely Christian, and had none but old fashioned, short range guns, and not enough of those to defend themselves. They had no intention whatever of attacking the Turks. Their barricades and all the fighting they did was only in self-defense."[188]

On May 2 and 3, the Italian *Piemonte* ship together with the French *Jules Michelet* and *Jules Ferry* armored cruisers took the Armenians back to Basit, where they stayed in tents for two months before returning to Kessab.[189]

Dörtyol

Dörtyol (Chorkmarzban), a city in the northern part of İskenderun, was one of the places where Armenians were able to resist the massacres successfully.[190] When the news of the Adana massacres reached Dörtyol on April 15, around 3,500 Armenians from surrounding villages such as Ocaklı and Özerli poured into the town.[191] The Armenians acted preemptively and took over the town's military barracks.[192] This was interpreted by the Muslim population as a clear act of uprising. A telegram sent on April 20, 1909, by the mutasarrıf of Cebel-i Bereket, Asaf Bey, to the president of the Chambers of Deputies stated that the Muslims surrounding Dörtyol were on the defensive and not the offensive, while Armenians were attacking the villages. He asked for the immediate dispatching of soldiers.[193]

The mob that soon surrounded Dörtyol was armed with Mausers and Martinis, which had been distributed by Asaf Bey.[194] For more than twelve days, around ten thousand Armenians were besieged by a mob of seven thousand people composed of Kurdish and Circassian gangs from the interior and Muslim inhabitants from the surrounding villages.[195] More than four hundred of the besiegers were armed and received a steady supply of ammunition from the government. Led by Mihran Der Melkonian, the Armenians were able to resist, but on the second day, the mob grew, even bringing a cannon. On the third day of the siege, Sunday, April 18, the besiegers cut off the water supply to Dörtyol.[196]

On April 21, the British ship *Triumph*, which had arrived at İskenderun
in the morning, carried fifty soldiers, local government officials, and Christian and Muslims notables to Dörtyol with the aim of calming down the
situation.[197] The acting British vice-consul of İskenderun, Joseph Catoni,
along with Rev. H. S. Kennedy, joined the group. A parley was proposed
between the Armenians and the besiegers. Despite the fact that the besiegers
"swore to observe a truce for two days and to allow the water to be turned on
again," they resumed their attack on Friday, April 23, "disregarding their oath
completely."[198] Further peacekeeping attempts did not yield any results.[199]
Belfante, the German vice-consul in İskenderun, attributed the deterioration of the situation "solely to the notorious incompetence of the Ottoman
authorities to ensure the order and security of this unfortunate region."[200]

On Monday, April 26, after hours of negotiations, the regular troops entered Dörtyol and took over the barracks, raising the siege and turning the
water on.[201] Aiding the refugees from the surrounding villages was a major
problem; they had lost all their belongings, and their houses had been looted
and burned down. In May, Dörtyol was put under martial law. The disarming
of Armenians was problematic, as the Kurds, Circassians, and Turkmens who
had been dispersed by the military troops and now surrounded the village
were still armed.[202]

Aintab

Another important place that was spared the massacres in the province of
Aleppo was the city of Aintab. According to the British consul in Aleppo,
agents from İstanbul had been inciting the local Muslim population to massacre the Christians.[203] During the three-week period when the fear of massacres in Aintab was at its height, the kaymakam and the local notables Tahir
Bey and Ahmed Ağa did their utmost to protect the Christians against the
efforts of other notables—such as Abdo Efendi, Nuri Bey, and Arif Bey—
who were inciting the Muslim population of the city.[204] Abdo Efendi gathered six hundred armed peasants from his village, who swaggered about the
Christian quarter looking for a pretext to attack the Armenians. The kaymakam controlled the situation and prevented Abdo from taking further
steps. In addition to this, for nine consecutive nights, he personally patrolled

the streets, along with Tahir Bey and Ahmed Ağa, to prevent any attacks on the Armenian Quarter.

The View from İstanbul

Despite an outpouring of telegrams from Adana to İstanbul, the Ottoman press minimized the massacres. While *Tanin* and its editors were in hiding because of the counterrevolution, the most important Ottoman newspaper, *İkdam*, reported about the massacres in only a cursory manner.[205] The Ottoman press in İstanbul was preoccupied at this time with the counterrevolution and the political turmoil in the capital. However, when the massacres began in Adana, the Armenian leadership in İstanbul began to act immediately.

On April 15, Kamer Shirinian Efendi, the agent of the Armenian patriarch, appealed to Adil Bey, the undersecretary of the minister of the interior, for clarification regarding telegrams that had appeared in the daily *Osmanlı* newspaper.[206] Adil Bey confirmed that telegrams about the massacres had arrived from the province of Adana. Shirinian was particularly troubled by Adil Bey's telegram to the province instructing the authorities to protect the lives of the foreigners. He asked: "Is it possible that the order was given to massacre the Armenians?" Adil Bey replied that no such order was given, but rather the opposite: a telegram was sent to the governorate of Adana demanding that immediate precautionary measures be taken in order to protect the lives, property, and dignity of all Christians.[207] However, the Armenian daily *Arewelk'* reprinted and criticized Adil Bey's telegram, arguing that the only concern of the Ministry of the Interior was to protect the banks and the foreigners.

On Saturday, April 17, a debate ensued regarding the conflict in Adana. The locum tenens, together with Shirinian and the Armenian National Assembly deputy Aristages Kasparian, went to the Sublime Porte, where the Council of Ministers was convening. They were received by Grand Vizier Tevfik Paşa, together with Şeyhülislam Mehmed Ziyaeddin Efendi, Minister of Education Kapriel Noradoungian Efendi, and Adil Bey.[208] The locum tenens raised the issue of the massacres and conflagration in Adana and emphasized the necessity of taking effective measures.[209] The grand vizier answered that the necessary measures had been taken. Adil Bey interjected that the conflict had been initiated by the Armenians, who were armed and "massacring Muslims" and who had "besieged the government building."[210] He said that the Turks were unarmed and that the vali was terrified and asking for help. Kasparian answered that this was impossible to accept:

> If the people are armed it is necessary to accept that both populations are armed. How is it possible to believe that the Armenians are massacring the Turks? . . . For years the Turks and the Armenians have lived together in peace, and even during the great massacres nothing happened there.

Noradoungian noted that as a native of Adana, Kasparian's view carried weight and that whatever was being ascribed to the Armenians was not logical. Adil Bey retorted that he also knew Adana intimately. He said that the agitations had increased in Bahçe in the district of Cebel-i Bereket:

> Armenians come hours away from villages and attack the Turkish villages; Armenians are armed, whereas the Turks are obliged to defend themselves with canes! The armed Armenians have even besieged the center of the district of Cebel-i Bereket and the terrified mutasarrıf is continuously asking for help. The person who shot the British council in Adana is also Armenian![211]

Kasparian responded that this information was false and that it was impossible for Armenians to come from villages hours away in order to attack. He added that he knew the British consul and that it was equally impossible that an Armenian had shot him. Adil Bey answered that such arguments were "manifestations of our emotions," whereas every day telegrams were coming to the Sublime Porte that officially confirmed his views, one of which he furnished as proof of their veracity. The Armenian delegation responded that official information should be received with reservations until the truth became clear, since such statements reflected the antagonism and vindictiveness that had lately arisen between the prelate bishop, Seropian, and the vali, Cevad Bey. It argued that, while importance is due to official information, had the ruler or the governor who was informing them not been incompetent, these painful events would not have spread. The Armenian delegation contended that these provincial officials were themselves mostly responsible for the events and stressed that they should be held accountable.[212]

Adil Bey confirmed that Adana had been subjected to state of siege (*idâre-i örfiyye*) and that orders had been given to send troops from the surrounding area. The locum tenens noted that there were thousands of people contributing to the unrest and that the mob had definitely taken part in the agitation.

It was decided that the locum tenens would send a telegram to the diocese of Adana through the Ministry of the Interior advising the people to calm down. It was also decided that the şeyhülislam would send a telegram to Adana to calm the Muslim people.[213] The telegram written by the locum tenens was given to Adil Bey, who made ample corrections. Initially, the locum tenens did not accept these corrections, but after one and a half hours of negotiation, with great difficulty the following version was accepted:

> With pain it is understood that in the subdistrict of Bahçe, too, the massacre is still continuing. For the purpose of calming down the event, please reply immediately to the telegrams that I have sent yesterday and the day before through the vali. In this period of freedom, the reasons for these events, which are contrary to constitutionalism and patriotism, are incomprehensible. The necessary advice has been given by the şeyhülislam to the Muslim population.[214]

Biwzandion reacted with astonishment that the locum tenens in his telegram mentioned the massacre of Bahçe, while the patriarchate had not received any news from Adana and its surroundings. Apparently, Adil Bey had made it a precondition that the telegram should begin in this way. It was also astonishing, the writer contended, that the locum tenens was preaching to the Armenians to calm down when they were the victims. *Biwzandion* criticized the compromise made by the locum tenens, writing:

> This would have happened in the previous orders . . . now the people of Adana will think that this is the honest opinion of the Armenian national administration and would not believe that this is the result of one and a half hours of bargaining. Adil Bey's heroism is not with this telegram alone. He is an expert on special telegrams during the massacres.[215]

Biwzandion was referring to the initial telegram sent by Adil Bey to the vali of Adana that had asked him to "pay specific attention not to harm the foreign religious institutions and embassies."[216] Armenians generally understood this important telegram as a green light for Muslims to massacre Armenians, exactly "as with the massacres that took place thirteen to fourteen years ago."[217] In a letter of complaint sent by Bishop Seropian after the massacres to the grand vizier, the president of the Chambers of Notables, the deputies of the Ottoman Parliament, and the locum tenens of the Armenian Patriarchate, Seropian criticized the behavior of Adil Bey during this meeting:

> Indeed, Adil Bey has put pressure on the locum tenens and urged him to telegram the Armenians of Adana, imploring them to cease hostilities, thus implicitly attributing to them the origin and responsibility of the massacres. He would otherwise have formally refused his support to the şeyhülislam to obtain from him an exhortation addressed to the Muslim population.[218]

Takvim-i Vekayi, the official gazette of the government, vehemently attacked *Biwzandion*'s statement, saying that it was based on an idea of dissension.[219] It reprinted Adil Bey's original telegram instructing the vali of Adana to prevent riots and looting. The telegram also stated that preparations were being made to dispatch troops to the province from a nearby location to bring peace and order. After ordering the vali to prevent people from attacking each other, it instructed him to "never allow an attack on the consulates and the financial institutions."

After the massacres, on May 1, 1909, Adil Bey was invited to the sixty-third session of the parliament for an interpellation regarding his infamous telegram sent to the vali of Adana on April 14, 1909. Adil provided an explanation and defended his actions. He said that two telegrams were sent from Adana—one to the Ministry of Police and the other to the Ministry of the Interior. The former was sent on April 13 and the latter on April 14. He provided a copy of his response to the telegrams, in which he expressed extreme regret (*şâyân-ı teessüf*) for the disturbances and stated that it was important to suppress them. He stated that sufficient troops were needed and that all necessary measures should be taken to prevent the people from transgressing against each other, and especially to prevent any attacks on the consulates and the financial and foreign institutions (*husûsen konsolatolarla müessesât-ı mâliyeye ve ecânibe taarruz etmelerine zinhâr meydan verilmemesi ve peyderpey mâlûmât îtâsı mütemennâdır*).[220] Adil clarified the telegram, saying that since foreigners were neutral, any attack on them would have led to foreign intervention and political crisis. According to him, the statement regarding foreigners mentioned in the newspaper had been misinterpreted; the orders sent from the ministry were sincere, and protecting the foreigners did not imply killing the Christians:

> This is sad. This is not true at all. We denied this. Our first sentence began with "We are sorry." We said that troops should be sent immediately . . . we were saying that measures should be taken to prevent the killing of one another, and [the order] to especially prevent any attack on the consulate and the financial and foreign institutions is natural. This is the duty of the government . . . the government fulfilled its task.[221]

On Monday, April 19, the mixed (religious and civil) council of the Armenian National Assembly convened an extraordinary session in İstanbul regarding Adana, with the presence of the Armenian Catholicos Madteos II Izmirlian and religious and lay representatives from the Armenian Catholic and Protestant communities. They appealed to the grand vizier for immediate and effective orders to help the needy, to stop the spread of the massacres, and to preserve tranquility.[222] A memorandum was sent to the grand vizier and Şevket Paşa, the commander of the Action Army, in which it was argued that, since the revolution, Armenians had invested the most in freedom and the constitution and hence were a target of the reactionary forces. The memorandum lamented the path taken by Adil Bey, which had led to despotism and allowed the crime to take place.[223] Despite the denials of *Takvim-i Vekayi*, "Adil Bey, totally contrary to the raison d'état [*hikmet-i hükümet*], with this action has opened the way to the catastrophe that struck Adana." The memorandum claimed that the violence in Adana was organized by the palace (Sultan Abdülhamid II), as evidenced by the fact that it took place at the same time in different places.[224]

The memorandum provided the background of the Adana massacres. It justified Ohannes's shooting of two Turks as an act of self-defense. When the mob gathered around the house of Ohannes, instead of restraining it, the local government was satisfied with dispersing it. It even distributed weapons to the mob. The memorandum argued that the local government, instead of taking precautions, ordered Armenians to open their shops and "abided by the orders that were given via telegraph by the undersecretary of the Ministry of the Interior to protect the foreign institutions." The memorandum highlighted the similarities of the Adana massacres to the 1895 Hamidian massacres. It stressed that, in addition to the Circassians and the Kurds, the Ottoman soldiers participated in the killing and looting, as was attested by witnesses.[225]

The memorandum asked that the following measures be taken:[226]

Formation of a court-martial, to be sent to Aleppo and Adana in order to try the culprits.

Due to their negligence, handing of the vali of Adana and the undersecretary of the Ministry of the Interior, Adil Bey, to the court-martial.

Immediate communication to the provinces of Adana and Aleppo regarding the formation and dispatching of the court-martial and the trial of the vali and Adil Bey.

Formation and dispatching of a commission to investigate the physical and material damage. The investigation commission should be composed of supporters of the constitution and should include at least one, if not two, members from the patriarchate.

Removal of the vali and the commander Mustafa Remzi Paşa and their replacement with figures loyal to the constitution.

Recovery of properties and monies that have been looted and their reinstatement to their owners.

Allocation of aid from the State Treasury to the hungry and injured.

In order to rebuild the destroyed houses and revive agriculture, supplying of necessary agricultural implements.

The memorandum concluded with the point that if those responsible for these crimes were not punished, it would be impossible to prevent their repetition.[227]

A delegation from the Armenian National Assembly and representatives of the Catholic and Protestant communities went to see Grand Vizier Tevfik Paşa to ask him to take all necessary preventive measures to establish and preserve the peace. The grand vizier told the delegation that the vali of Adana had been dismissed and that the dispatch of five infantry battalions had been ordered.[228] After receiving satisfactory answers from the grand vizier, the locum tenens sent the following telegram to the Catholicos of Sis and the prelates of Adana, Tarsus, Cebel-i Bereket, and Mersin:

> As a result of the painful events that took place in Adana and its appendages [*mülhakâtı*], a special committee composed of all three religious representatives [Apostolic, Catholic, and Protestant] and members of the parliament went to the grand vizierate and obtained assurances from the vizierate about the reinstatement of peace and assistance for the needy. We are taking the necessary measures; please let us know about the current condition.[229]

The Armenian National Assembly decided to provide 500 GL (Gold Lira) and to immediately establish a fundraising committee. In addition, it continued to appeal to the government to take the necessary peacekeeping measures.[230] On April 19, the patriarchate sent a request to the grand vizier for the formation of a special committee consisting of Fr. Kevork Aslanian and Sarkis Suyn Efendi to take care of the injured, homeless, hungry, and needy and to distribute aid and food to the Armenians of Adana. The grand vizier immediately instructed the province of Adana to provide this committee with all manner of help and to facilitate its work, especially with regard to the women and children whose husbands or fathers were killed.[231]

On April 20, the mixed council convened a meeting on Adana. The political council read the orders that were given to the delegation.[232] The delegation traveled first to İzmir to hold a fundraiser for the victims, after which it headed toward Mersin.[233]

The Armenian National Assembly continued to debate the Adana massacres. On April 24, 1909, a lengthy discussion took place. After a long debate, a new memorandum was accepted by the assembly to be presented to the sultan and the parliament, as well as to the commander of the Action Army. The memorandum dealt with the return of women and children who were taken and converted by force. It emphasized that the court-martial should try the real perpetrators instead of blaming Armenians, the looted materials should be returned to their owners, 30,000 GL should be distributed to the victims through a special committee, and finally, those government officials who saved the lives of Armenians should be rewarded.[234]

Conclusion

Around two thousand people were killed in the city of Adana during the first wave of the massacres, and a large number of bodies were dumped in the river.[235] Around six hundred of these were Muslims killed while attacking the Armenian Quarter.[236] The number of victims in the province of Adana exceeded fifteen thousand; in the other districts of Adana and in the province of Aleppo, most of those killed were Armenians.[237] The British vice-consul Doughty-Wylie estimated the number of those who perished to be between fifteen thousand and twenty-five thousand.[238] Many Armenians fled to Cyprus and Beirut.[239] Around one thousand Armenian refugees arrived in Larnaca on board an Austrian ship.[240]

The damage inflicted on Armenian shops, businesses, and institutions was enormous. In addition, many farms and their agricultural implements were burned. Migrant workers played a particularly important role in destroying agricultural tools, both those belonging to Armenians and those of foreign companies.[241] This was a direct attack on the tools of modernity that were crucial in diminishing the importance of migrant workers in the agricultural field.

The first wave of the Adana massacres did not happen in a vacuum. The massacres were the result of tensions that had accumulated in the region for decades and that had intensified dramatically after the revolution. This intensification was the result of the disruption of the power equilibrium that had existed prior to the revolution. The dissatisfied Muslim element, which constituted an influential part of the population, viewed cultural nationalism among Armenians and the arms race as an existential threat. Affective disposition played an important part in this development. The massacres seem to have been an emotional reaction to a genuine belief in an imaginary plan by Armenians to revive the Armenian Kingdom of Cilicia. In this context, rumors that were fomented within the new public sphere by Muslim elites, as well as by some government officials of Adana and Aleppo, were instrumental in instilling fear and anxiety among the Muslim population. Other agents provocateurs, whose sole aim was to initiate an anti-constitutional reaction, succeeded in their task of mobilizing the masses. While the Armenians engaged in the conflict with a motto of self-defense, the motives of the Muslim population were much more complex. They did not represent a unified front with one objective. Circassians, Afghans, Cretan Muslim refugees, Turkmens, Turks, and seasonal laborers were motivated by a host of factors, ranging from looting and plundering to diminishing Armenian economic power in the region and waging a genuine war against the "Armenian threat" of massacring the Muslims, among other motives.

With a few notable exceptions, the local governments were either incompetent or unwilling to deal with the situation. The correspondence between the different local and central government agencies does not always reflect the reality on the ground but rather tends to reflect the points of view of the provincial administrators. In many cases, these officials were themselves complicit in the massacres or participated actively by disseminating false rumors with the aim of arming and mobilizing the population against the Armenians. Many of the armed soldiers and reserves joined the mob because this was the first time in recent history that Ottoman soldiers were ordered to clamp down on Muslim citizens who were threatening Armenians. While some soldiers implemented these orders, many did not and instead joined their coreligionists in killing and looting.

The first wave of massacres in the city of Adana appears minor when compared to the second wave, which is discussed in the following chapter. Doughty-Wylie argued at the time that, even "among the best of the Turks, both civil and religious, there exists still a unanimous distrust, and even hatred of the Armenians." He notes that, despite the fact that they deplored massacre, they continued to believe in the idea of an armed Armenian revolution.[242] After the first wave of massacres, regiments arrived from Dedeağaç, as did troops and cavalry from Syria, under the command of Osman Paşa, who commanded the Fifth Army Corps. Doughty-Wylie suggested that it was "necessary to make a military parade through certain districts to restore order."[243]

CHAPTER 5

FALSE PROTECTION

The Second Wave of Massacres

DESPITE CONSTANT FEARS OF A RESURGENCE OF VIOLENCE, THE period from April 17 to April 25 saw a fragile peace in the city of Adana. On Saturday, April 18, a group of *hoca*s and notables informed British vice-consul Doughty-Wylie that peace had been made.[1] On April 19, one hundred regular troops arrived in Adana from Beirut.[2] Martial law was declared, and news spread that three battalions from Dedeağaç and Gallipoli were coming to preserve peace and security in the city. This gave immense hope to the Armenians and to some extent assured them that there was no possibility that the massacres would resume. A telegram sent by Vali Cevad Bey to the grand vizier argued that there was a shortage of troops in the province and that the way to keep them in order was to pay their salaries.[3] Consequently, on April 18, the grand vizier replied that the Council of State had agreed to send two months' worth of salaries.[4] Two days later, Cevad sent a telegram to the grand vizier stating that peace and order had prevailed in the city of Adana for four days. Shops were reopened and shopkeepers were again occupied with their work. He indicated that in order to maintain this situation, the military forces were taking all types of action, and mixed committees were advising the people. In addition, declarations were made according to the Sharia and the constitution that the rights of all people from all classes would be protected.[5] On April 21, Cevad sent another telegram to the grand vizier stating that a battalion from Tekirdağ (a city on the Sea of Marmara), which was ready and on its way to Adana, should not wait for the two other battalions from Gallipoli and Dedeağaç but should come separately to Adana. He argued, "Due to the current situation the fast arrival of the soldiers is extremely important to the safety of the fatherland, and if they are even one minute late it will result in a grave regret (*teessüfât-ı vahîme*)."[6]

While calm prevailed in the city of Adana, the massacres in the other parts of the province of Adana and in the province of Aleppo continued. No one in the city of Adana imagined that the massacres would resume. This chapter analyzes the reasons for the ensuing second wave of massacres. It discusses how, after the first wave of massacres, the unrestrained public sphere contributed to the enactment of the second wave. Print media played a central role in "confirming" the rumors circulating heretofore of the so-called Armenian uprising to reestablish the Kingdom of Cilicia. Hence, there was no doubt in the minds and hearts of the local state officials, the notables, and the Muslim population that the Armenians had indeed attempted a failed uprising.

Medical and Humanitarian Aid

While arrangements were being made for the arrival of the additional battalions, relief work began in the city of Adana. The government began distributing wheat to the people. Financial aid was sent through the Armenian Patriarchate and from Armenian communities outside the empire to Adana and Aleppo, totaling 2,530 GL.[7] Four hospitals were established in Adana to receive the wounded, one of which was set up by the wife of the British vice-consul, Lilian Doughty-Wylie. According to the assessment of an American missionary, there was a dire need for two large orphanages to care for the hundreds of orphaned children. He also stated that the relief commissions estimated that £200 per day were needed for bread alone.[8] Even the well-to-do Armenian merchants were not able to help due to the fact that they had lost everything during the first phase of the massacres. It is impossible to accurately assess the number of casualties. Hundreds of wounded Armenians were taken to the Mousheghian-Apkarian Armenian School, which was turned into a hospital. Thousands of other Armenians also found refuge there. Around five hundred wounded Armenians were taken to be treated at the Armenian girls' school in the courtyard of the Surp Step'anos

Church.[9] Many Armenians moved to Mersin, while others left for Cyprus. Father Rigal, a Jesuit priest in Adana, estimated that about twenty thousand Armenians found shelter in the Armenian and Catholic churches.[10]

On April 21—seven days after the first massacres—the British ship *Swiftsure* arrived in Mersin. Dr. Richard Connell, the surgeon from the *Swiftsure*, went to the city of Adana and obtained vital information about the conditions of the injured after the first massacres.[11] Carrying medical supplies, Dr. Connell visited the wounded in the American Mission, the French nuns' school, the French Jesuits' school, the Armenian churches, and the hospital established by Lilian Doughty-Wylie. He reported that they treated all ages and both sexes. He observed that nearly all the children suffered from bullet wounds fired from above at close quarters. He estimated that 50–60 percent of the patients' wounds were caused by Martini rifle bullets; 15–20 percent by swords and other sharp instruments; 15 percent by clubs and sharp sticks; 10–15 percent by Mauser and revolver bullets; 5 percent by bayonets; and 3–6 percent by revolver and short-gun wounds. The figures provided by Connell show the superiority of the Martini rifles in causing bodily harm.[12] This could help to explain the high number of fatalities during both phases of the massacres in light of the frantic buying of Martini rifles and ammunition in the postrevolutionary period.

The French missionaries also played an important role in aiding the Armenians.[13] According to Fr. Sabatier, French sisters treated 120 patients on a daily basis at their dispensary. Two doctors and five sisters devoted themselves to treating the wounds of the victims. Sabatier describes the scene: "Without knowing the profession of nursing, I would have liked to lend my assistance in the bandages, but the sight of these heads so horribly mutilated, these beating wounds, those crushed arms, increased my heart rate and made me lose my senses."[14]

The Marist Fathers aided the doctors in taking care of the wounded.[15] Their testimonies provide grim insight into the types of wounds inflicted on the victims. Fr. Marc described some of the wounds that had been inflicted on minors: "The first is a young Armenian Catholic, 15–16 years of age. His left arm is pierced with a bullet; the bone is bare; the nerves hang down. The wound is so wide that the doctor passes over it several times." He describes another patient whose head had been stabbed. In another case, the chest of a twelve-year-old girl had been pierced: "Put your hand behind the shoulders, to the wound, you will feel the breath that escapes outside." The girl died a day later and was buried in the college courtyard.[16] At the other end of the courtyard, Fr. Louis-Xavier dressed a baby in his mother's arms: "Horror! He has his left arm stabbed with knives; five wide wounds, bones broken in three places; the hand is pierced, and the fingers are at the ends. After being amputated, he began to smile at his mother and caress her with the hand that he had left."[17] Based on the types of the injuries, we can note the extensive use of both live ammunition and blunt instruments in the course of the massacres.

The arrival on the coast of Mersin of five foreign ships (British, French, Italian, German, and Russian) brought confidence to the Armenians, who hoped that within a few days the situation in Adana would improve. However, according to the Austro-Hungarian consul, all of a sudden, the Salonican troops that had arrived to instate order "completed the work of destruction."[18]

The Public Sphere and Violent Discourse: The *İtidal* Newspaper

Although calm prevailed in the city of Adana for eight days after the first wave of massacres, this period was crucial in fomenting the larger second wave that was subsequently unleashed for three days on the Armenians of the city. According to all sources, the *İtidal* newspaper and its editor, İhsan Fikri, the CUP leader, along with his comrades, were instrumental in shaping public opinion and convincing the masses that Armenians had initiated a failed revolt in an attempt to reestablish their kingdom.

The role of Fikri during the first phase of massacres is not clear. Why would he have joined Abdülkadir Bağdadizade's group in attacking the Armenians? One eyewitness account indicates that the mob sought to assassinate Fikri because of his vehement attacks on the vali.[19] Could it be that his inclusion as a culprit in the historiography of the first wave of massacres is actually due to the erratic articles he wrote during the period *between* the two massacres, which in turn instigated the second massacres? Based on events in İstanbul, where reactionary forces were hunting down CUP leaders, one could assume that a similar situation would arise in Adana with regard to İhsan Fikri, as the leading CUP member there. On the other hand, Ferriman claims that Fikri—wearing a white turban for the occasion and brandishing a rifle—stood at his window encouraging the mob. Ferriman adds that Fikri and Bosnian Selim were seen "leading the mob of assassins and directing the work of the massacres."[20]

Most of the Armenian and European sources agree on the culpability of Fikri and *İtidal* in inciting the masses to carry out the second wave of the massacres.[21] As discussed in chapter 7, the investigations of the Ottoman court-martial also attest to this fact. This raises important questions regarding the role of violent discourse in the exacerbation of unstable conditions. Even though a state of emergency was declared in Adana, *İtidal* continued to be published. Thus, the public sphere in the inter-massacre period became a vehicle for inciting the masses to enact more violence toward the Armenians. The rumors that had circulated for months about the potential Armenian uprising in Adana were now "verified" in written form by *İtidal*. The so-called prophecy of the Armenian uprising was finally fulfilled. The newspaper became a fountain of "truth" for the confused and anxious masses of Adana. The local government, instead of cracking down on outlets that could harm the fragile situation, resorted to superficial statements about coexistence and harmony. During riots, revolts, massacres, and ethnic strife, it is the duty of local governments to restrain the phenomenon of the public sphere until the situation calms down in order to restrict any provocation from the parties in conflict. In the case of Adana, no such attempt was made; the public sphere was not restrained, nor did the local government take the necessary steps to suppress provocative statements by reactionary groups. Hence, Fikri was able to attack the Armenians in print, using extraordinarily violent language, and to convince the masses that the Armenians had indeed attempted a revolt. In doing so he cleared the uncertainty that had been lingering for decades in the minds and hearts of the people about the main objective of the Armenians of Adana. His verbal violence played an important role in heightening the emotional level of the Muslim populations to the breaking point. As Sémelin writes, this was an "advance killing with words."[22]

On April 20, 1909, thousands of free copies of issue number 33 of *İtidal* were distributed in the streets of Adana. In this issue, Fikri, along with colleagues such as İsmail Sefa and Burhan Nuri, vehemently attacked the

Armenians. According to Terzian, the Armenians in Adana had hoped that Fikri would condemn the massacres, but instead he viciously condemned the Armenians, portraying them as a rebellious element trying to initiate an uprising.[23] In an article entitled "Müthiş Bir İsyân" (A terrible uprising), Fikri's colleague İsmail Sefa stated that a wave of boiling rage and independence was destroying the country.[24] He argued that Armenians, like the Turks, had been oppressed for thirty-three years by the despotic regime. Then they united with the Turks and applauded their "holy revolution." However, Sefa claimed that Armenians soon began preparing themselves for the ensuing uprising. Hence, they began stockpiling weapons. The phenomenon of Armenian *fedayees* with Mausers roaming the streets alarmed the Muslims.[25] According to Sefa, once the Armenians possessed weapons, their rhetoric changed:

> After preparing the fighting weapons, tongues lost their old softness, and instead of exclaiming, "Until death we are together" [*ölünceye kadar beraberiz*], they exclaimed, "Whenever possible we are going to massacre the Muslims, we are not going to be afraid; the old wounds are still bleeding."

İtidal's version of the incidents began with Armenians cursing Muslims and threatening to kill them.[26] According to Sefa, the first signs of agitation were on Friday when two Muslim youths were killed in the Armenian neighborhood of Şabaniye. He was referring to the murder of İsfendiyar. Although the incident was apolitical, Sefa claimed that the Armenians wanted it to appear otherwise. İsfendiyar and Rahmi Sundukzade were walking by a coffee shop with two friends when an Armenian began cursing at them and then shot at Sundukzade. In an ensuing struggle for the gun, the Armenian shot İsfendiyar and then fled. İsfendiyar died two days later. When İsfendiyar's relatives asked the local government to arrest the criminal, they were notified that he had escaped with the aid of Garabed Gökderelian, and the issue ceased to be a simple crime. Gökderelian had said, "Let the Muslims surrender the Arab Mahmoud to us, and we will turn over [the Armenian]." From this, it appeared that the Armenians were protecting the criminal, despite the assurances of the vali that he would capture the murderer and restore order. For Sefa, this was nothing less than a rebellion in itself.[27] This angered the

Turks, who began demonstrating, forcing the government to send in soldiers to preserve public order. These agitations were increased by another rumor: that Armenians had killed a Muslim woman and her son.

Sefa described the Armenians closing their shops on Wednesday, April 14, and their fortification of churches and tall buildings. Muslim ulemâ and notables advised the Armenians to open their shops so as not to cause any incidents. On the same day, the police discovered an Armenian cart in Keçeci market carrying twelve Martini rifles and a huge number of explosives. *İtidal* also claimed that the first shot was fired by an Armenian from the Armenian Quarter. In addition, while most of the Armenians were armed, the Muslims did not have any firearms. According to Sefa, when the guns were roaring, they "understood with fear and astonishment our living in tragic numbness." Armenians fired constantly from their houses, churches, shops, and clubs, while Muslims, particularly the working class and the poor, remained in the street, running helplessly with hatchets in their hands. The government declared a state of emergency, but because it did not have a sufficient number of troops on the ground, this proved ineffective. Muslims, seeing that Armenians were killing their brethren, burned all the Armenian shops. As the violence escalated, Muslims attacked the markets and streets, slaughtering any Armenian they encountered with hatchets, axes, and bayonets. When the Armenian *fedayees* saw this, they burned down Balcıoğlu Han (an inn). The article said that although Muslims who attacked Armenian houses were careful not to harm Armenian women and children, the Armenians were seen "barbarically killing Muslim women and children."[28] Sefa concluded that when the Armenians, "after all this catastrophe and crime," saw the profusion of soldiers and people pouring in from the villages and understood that they were not going to reach their objective, they stopped their attacks.[29] This article in *İtidal* enraged public opinion in Adana after the first wave of massacres.

In the same issue, an article by Burhan Nuri posed the rhetorical question, Can the Armenians establish a state?[30] Nuri answered that even the residents of a mental asylum (*bîmârhâne sükkânının*) would not believe that Armenians, numbering less than two million and scattered throughout the empire, could defeat the Ottoman Empire and establish an independent country.[31] Burhan also attacked the European powers in his article, saying that no European power could impose the establishment of an Armenian state in Cilicia on the Ottoman Empire. Burhan concluded:

> If the Armenians intend to form a state, the land for that state should not be in the Ottoman Empire; rather they should look for it in the poles, in the sand deserts of Africa, and immigrate there. Otherwise, they cannot reach their goal, scattered [as they are] in İstanbul, Adana, Aleppo, Diyarbekir, Bitlis, and Van.[32]

In the section of *İtidal* on news from the provinces, Fikri lamented that Adana, which had escaped the Armenian disturbances that destroyed all of Asia Minor, would be witness to such a catastrophe.[33] The editorial argued that while the Turks were striving to live with the Armenians in happiness, the Armenians, by organizing an uprising, had been creating a calamity. The editorial explained how Armenians began their plans by populating Adana with Armenians:

> Armenians who were encouraged by the agitations of the Bulgarians, Serbs, Montenegrins, and Greeks during the last half century, and understanding after five to ten bitter attempts that the geographical position of the places where they live and their subjected status was not suitable for a similar agitation, decided to gather in a place that would invite European intervention when needed, in the biggest center of the Armenian ecclesiastic Sees, in Cilicia. Prior to the incidents of Adana, they had gathered group-by-group in Adana and had formed a dreadful plurality in these places.[34]

Armenians, according to the editorial, had arrived in Adana from Maraş, Haçin, Harput, Diyarbekir, and the Armenian-populated provinces of Anatolia. In addition, five to ten families began settling in houses that had previously been inhabited by a single family. The article argued that by forming a majority in the area, Armenians hoped to create agitation and demand autonomy. They were encouraged in this by the success of the Austrians and the Bulgarians, the demands of Serbia and Montenegro, and the question of Crete. For this purpose, they hoped to provoke the intervention of the European powers. The article concluded, "Looking at the painful situation, there is no doubt that they [the Armenians] were the reasons for the destruction of themselves, the Muslims, and of the country."[35]

The articles published by *İtidal* were reprinted in the Arabic-language newspaper *Al-Ittiḥād al-'Uthmānī* (Ottoman unity), published in Beirut.[36] In addition, *Al-Ittiḥād al-'Uthmānī* sent a reporter, Ahmad Adil Arslan, to Adana to report on the incidents. Adil followed Fikri's line, claiming that the main reason for the incidents was the Armenian desire to reestablish a kingdom.[37] The government investigation commission to Adana later discovered that Arslan had been sent to Adana specifically to write articles against the Armenians and to attribute responsibility for the events to them. For this, he was paid one Turkish pound per day.[38]

The editorial board of *İtidal* thus provided its own version of the causes and reasons for the deterioration of interethnic relationships and their culmination in the massacres. Regardless of the veracity of the claims made by *İtidal*, they were vital in shaping public opinion in Adana, particularly the belief in an Armenian conspiracy. This played an important role in heightening the emotions of the Muslims of the city of Adana, who saw themselves as victims. There is no doubt that *İtidal* presented the Armenians as being the main perpetrators of the crime.

The Second Wave: April 25–27

When Armenians heard that additional troops were coming to Adana from Mersin to help preserve order, they were elated.[39] Ostensibly aiming to pacify the situation in the province, three out of the four battalions that were sent from Rumeli arrived in Mersin on Friday, April 23, 1909. On the morning of Sunday, April 25, these three battalions from the Second Army continued to Adana on a special train.[40] One of the battalions was placed in the area of the old military division, while the other two other set up camp in the center of the barracks. A day after their arrival, the second wave of the massacres began. The troops actively participated in attacking and burning the Armenian schools that housed the injured and the refugees from the first wave of the massacres and perpetrated attacks on the Armenian Quarter. This occurred while the ships—with their commanding officers—were in Mersin, and no one interfered. Some observers blame the extent of the atrocity on the British and the French consuls for having convinced the Armenians to hand in their weapons, thus stripping from them any means of self-defense.[41]

FIGURE 6. Destroyed buildings in the city of Adana, 1909.
Source: Ernst Jackh Papers, Rare Book & Manuscript Library,
Columbia University in the City of New York.

Hagop Terzian, an eyewitness to the massacres, reported that during the
turmoil, a mob told the newly arrived soldiers, "The Armenian *fedayees* have
attacked the Turkish neighborhood, and our Muslims are being massacred—
quick, come to aid!"[42] Without verifying the truth of this news, the Rumelian
soldiers attacked the Armenian Quarter. Terzian and his family found refuge
in the Surp Step'anos Church, which was packed with Armenians. Armenians who survived the first round of massacres were at the Gregorian Armenian, Armenian Catholic, Armenian Protestant, Jesuit, Syriac, and Chaldean
churches. Those Armenian villagers who were in the Mousheghian-Apkarian
School were all burned alive.[43] Surp Step'anos Church was besieged and set
on fire. The people inside were able to escape to the nearby Syriac Church,
where the Syriacs were hiding, but the mob soon broke into the churchyard and started killing. Armenians and Syriacs had no choice but to return to Surp Step'anos Church.[44] Terzian describes how, when they were
under attack in the church and had lost any hope of survival, Marist Antoine

Ressicaud from the Jesuit church suddenly appeared in the company of an Ottoman officer, saving them from certain massacre.[45] At the same time, the Christians found in the other churches were taken to the government building by the British vice-consul. The Ottoman officer ordered the mob to disperse under threat of arms and called an additional fifty soldiers to the scene.[46] Under the protection of the soldiers, thousands of Christians moved to the Jesuit church. Terzian provides a vivid image of what he saw on his way to the church:

> Stepping barefoot on the piles of embers which blocked the streets, we were running for our life, with the aim of arriving to the Jesuit church as soon as possible. Not far away we saw hundreds of bodies in front of the Mousheghian-Apkarian School, which were burned during their escape and were hit mercilessly, and some, half-naked, were rendering their souls with roaring agony.[47]

The group arrived at the Jesuit church. The church, school, and court-yard were empty, as the thousands of Christians who had been there were transferred with the aid of the British vice-consul of Adana, Doughty-Wylie, to the large garden near the government palace. The Jesuit church was sur-rounded with fire. The group was then taken under the protection of the army to the government palace. According to Terzian, there were twenty thousand people in the government courtyard who had survived the first and the second massacres. Escorted by the soldiers, the people were brought outside the city and housed in the Trypani factory and the German factory near the train station.[48] According to Boghos Marakarian, a survivor of the massacre, on the next day, Ali Gergerlizade notified the people that Sultan Abdülhamid II had been dethroned. Gergerlizade said: "From now on, this new young government, by granting Armenians absolute freedom and safety, [has assured that] all of us Muslims and non-Muslims will live together in harmony and brotherhood."[49]

The information furnished by Terzian indicates that not all soldiers par-ticipated in the massacres and looting. It was thanks to some of these soldiers that thousands of Armenians were saved from the clutches of the infuriated mob. However, the question remains as to why many in the Rumelian army did participate in the massacres and looting; were they given orders by the

CUP to eliminate Armenians, as the traditional Armenian historiography attests?

Multiple explanations have been provided by contemporaneous eyewitness accounts. One contends that after the Rumelian regiments set up camp in Adana, shots were fired at their tents and a rumor immediately spread that the Armenians had opened fire on the troops from a church tower in town.[50] Another argued that rumors spread that Armenians had attacked the Salcılar neighborhood and killed all the Muslims; without validating these rumors, this prompted the military commander of Adana, Mustafa Remzi Paşa, to order the attack on the Mousheghian-Apkarian School, which housed the injured from the first wave of the massacres.[51] Regular soldiers, reserve soldiers, and mobs, along with the Başıbozuks, then attacked the Armenian Quarter, burning down churches and the schools,[52] and on April 27 the gendarmes destroyed the Triumphal Arch that was erected during the festivities for the reinstatement of the constitution.[53] Another explanation had it that when the Rumelian battalions arrived in Adana, they demanded that the Armenians of the Armenian Quarter hand in their weapons, to which the Armenians responded by shooting five soldiers, precipitating the second wave of the massacres.[54]

Yet another explanation, reported secondhand by Doughty-Wylie, was that the event was caused by a small band of Hnchak revolutionaries who "wished to bring about foreign interference, and who killed 16 Rumelian Soldiers, who were on picket in the Armenian Quarter"; Doughty-Wylie added parenthetically, "I do not know if this is true or not."[55] Doughty-Wylie initially accepted this account and refuted the participation of the Rumelian army in the massacres, saying, "We will deny [this] by every means in our power."[56] However, a few days later he said that he had received a new explanation, according to which the shots were fired by Turks, "either with the wish to bring about a quarrel between the different sorts of soldiers or to raise more hope to rush the hated Armenian quarter."[57] Doughty-Wylie concluded, "[The] uncomfortable feeling resting on Roumeliot officers for this most unfortunate occurrence is something to do with their eagerness to prove the existence of a revolutionary plot among the Armenians, and I give this explanation for what it is worth."[58]

Another report is provided by Missionary Trowbridge, according to whom "some wild Armenian young men had fired from those windows of the Armenian School at the Turks." The school housed three thousand Armenian refugees, and an emergency hospital had been opened under the care of the missionaries. However, he stressed that "the mass of the people were wholly innocent of any insurrection." Trowbridge explains:

> Sunday night [April 25] a furious attack was made upon the school by the Turkish mob. Shortly the building was set on fire. There was only one entrance to the street, by a gate at the end of the cul de sac. As the people, driven by the smoke and flames, sought to escape through the alley to the street they were shot down in heaps. Many of the wounded who lay in the hospital inside could not move and perished.[59]

Trainee Hammann, the dragoman of the German consulate in Aleppo, visited Adana after the second wave of massacres and observed:

> Around three thousand well-armed soldiers, aided by an eager, fanatical crowd, rushed into the district where the Armenians had entrenched themselves in their solid stone houses. The tactics of the attackers was to starve the Armenians gradually and decimate by stubborn bombardment. The few Mohammedan houses in this district were marked by the word "Islam" painted in chalk over the door and thus protected from the ravages of the raiders. After two days, the Turks headed for the final storm. Where the resistance was too persistent, fire was put into the roof from the windward side. The inmates, who tried to save themselves on the street, were beaten to death and the stolen property was dragged by cart to safety. Eyewitnesses report indescribable atrocities in which the rabble reveled. The sight of the corpses and pools of blood is said to have infuriated the soldiers and the raw instincts of the mob in an ecstatic intoxication. In this way, the disproportionate number of people killed—in Adana and the surrounding area, it may be six thousand to seven thousand—is explained by the small number of wounded.[60]

According to the report sent by the Austro-Hungarian consul of Mersin to Marquis von Pallavicini, the ambassador in İstanbul, in the afternoon of Sunday, April 25, under the pretext of forcing the Armenians of the Armenian Quarter to surrender, the soldiers attacked the quarter and reduced it to ashes.[61] The consul lamented that the officers of the warships were silent witnesses to "this last catastrophe"; the soldiers looted, burned, and massacred before their eyes. He condemned the "barbarous and ignorant conduct" of the Salonican troops. He argued that the government was trying to attribute this disaster to the Armenians, whom it accused of having set fire to their own neighborhood with the aim of reviving a revolutionary movement, but that the reality was contrary to this; the commanders of the foreign vessels unanimously declared that this was "a general massacre organized against the Christians and later limited to the Armenians." The consul criticized the British vice-consul for having claimed that the troops from Salonica carried out their duty. However, he admits that the British vice-consul changed his position in the face of the declarations made to him by the commanders of foreign ships, later recognizing that these troops completed the destruction of the city and brought the utmost misery. In a letter to the Responsible Body of the ARF in İstanbul, Simon Zavarian, one of the founders of the ARF, contended that the Rumelian soldiers were most probably deceived by the local inhabitants. He noted in his letter that in all places, there were individuals among the Muslims who helped Armenians.[62]

The vali of Adana, Cevad Bey, endorsed the version of events that began with Armenian *fedayees* firing on the Rumelian soldiers camping nearby. On April 26, he sent a telegram to the grand vizierate stating that on the evening of Sunday, April 25, gunfire was heard in the Armenian Quarter, causing great agitation among the Muslim population. As a result, the government dispatched a military force, which took control of the areas from which guns were fired and learned that a few Armenian *fedayees* were responsible.[63] He further reported that at night, fires began in two places in the city that were very difficult to put out due to a shortage of fire extinguishers. He noted that, with the arrival of some infantry battalions, all kinds of military measures were successfully taken in calming down the situation. He also noted that soldiers had been able to protect the foreign population, shops, institutions, and other places.[64]

Cevad's telegram does not reflect what really transpired. While thousands of Armenians were massacred, his primary concern seems to have been the protection of foreign people and institutions. Most of the missionary eyewitnesses attribute responsibility to the vali, who in Trowbridge's words "had it in his power to suppress the lawlessness and massacre and <u>deliberately</u> <u>refrained from doing so, saying</u> . . . 'We are not responsible.'" Trowbridge continues: "Such a Governor out to be hung! We mean this literally."[65]

On the April 27, the grand vizierate sent a telegram to the province of Adana regarding the renewal of disturbances (*iğtişâş*) in the center of the province. It demanded to know in which areas clashes continued and the number of the existing troops in those regions. It ordered that troops stationed in calmer areas be sent immediately to the troubled areas and emphasized the importance of the advisory role of religious leaders and powerful figures in putting an end to the clashes.[66] On the same day, the grand vizierate sent a telegram to the Ministry of War ordering of the dispatch of four battalions from the Second Army to Mersin and İskenderun.[67]

The conflagration in the city of Adana continued until Tuesday morning and destroyed the entire Armenian residential quarter, as well as most of the houses in the outlying districts that were inhabited by Christians.[68] During these attacks, kerosene was used liberally to ignite the houses. An important factor that contributed to the acceleration of the fire was the manner in which the houses in Adana were constructed. Most of the houses and the shops in the city of Adana were built with wooden planks that were inserted horizontally into the walls. When these wooden planks burned, the walls and the roofs collapsed. Therefore, most of the houses were razed completely. The wind also played a significant role in spreading the fire.

Regardless of the true reasons for the second wave of massacres, all sources indicate that many of the Rumelian soldiers participated in the massacres and looting along with the mob.[69] It is probable that rumors instilled fear in the minds of the Rumelian soldiers that Armenians were preparing for another "uprising." It could be that they arrived with preconceived notions that the first round of "riots" or "revolt" was indeed instigated by Armenians in order to reestablish the Kingdom of Cilicia; after all, most of the Muslim population in Adana sincerely believed in this "prophecy." Another motive could have been material gain, as many of the Rumelian soldiers were seen looting Armenian houses and foreign businesses.[70]

There is no doubt that the local CUP members were complicit in the massacres and played a primary role in instigating the Muslim population of Adana against the Armenians through their violent discourse, as in the

İtidal newspaper. Based on the available documents consulted for this study, the Central Committee of the CUP does not seem to have played any role in the massacres in Adana.[71] However, since the CUP Central Committee met secretly, we do not have records of its meetings.

The Aftermath

A day after the second wave of massacres, *İtidal* resumed its verbal attack on the Armenians. An article by İsmail Sefa scolded the Armenians of the city and claimed that the Muslims had no inherent hostility toward Armenians. If they did, "they would have filled their shops, factories, and the sanctuaries with Martinis, Mausers, powder-magazines, dynamite, and bombs, and when the agitations took place they would not have been bewildered in the streets, carrying only bayonets in their hands."[72] Sefa argued that Armenians had treacherously fortified themselves on rooftops and smuggled Armenian *fedayees* into Adana from Zeitun, Harput, and Haçin. He further claimed that the Armenians had betrayed the temporary armistice agreed upon after the first wave of massacres, since they never put down their weapons.[73] He railed, "The Armenian Kingdom that has been embodied in the imagination of some mischievous and traitorous Armenians, let them be sure, will never be incarnated and found."[74] Sefa concluded his article by suggesting that European powers may have been involved in the agitations.

In another issue of *İtidal*, İhsan Fikri explained how the second wave of disturbances began.[75] He argued that the arrival of the three battalions from Rumeli had comforted the Muslim population of the city. Since they believed the army would restore order, they no longer felt it necessary to carry arms on the streets. According to him, on the night of April 25, gunfire and the sound of bombs were heard coming from the direction of Kale Kapısı. Muslims who were gathered in coffeehouses suddenly began running to the Muslim Quarter and yelling, "Armenians have struck" (*Ermeniler basdılar*). Sounds of bullets were also coming from the Armenian market in Tepebağ. He lamented that Muslims once more fell victim to the bullets of the Armenians. As to the Rumelian battalions, Fikri stated that while they were having breakfast in their camp in Kale Kapısı, shots were fired on them from the direction of Tepebağ, and they immediately rushed there, where clashes began with the Armenians. He claimed that, according to their investigation,

FIGURE 7. Destroyed buildings in the city of Adana, 1909.
Source: Ernst Jackh Papers, Rare Book & Manuscript Library,
Columbia University in the City of New York.

the attackers in Kale Kapısı were four Armenian *fedayees*. However, he says
that due to the abundance of troops, aid from the Muslim population in
fighting against the Armenians was not needed, and all the fighting was
done by the troops. Sefa also criticized Armenians for their failed attempt
and chided them for spreading false news about the event. Fikri finished his
article by challenging Armenians: "Let us see whether humanity will bleed
for your charlatanism, or [if it will] listen to our words, which are based one
by one on documents."[76]

The second wave of the massacres was larger in scale and more violent
than the first. While the massacres in the city of Adana were taking place,
rumors spread throughout the provinces that Armenians had revolted in
Adana, killed all the Muslims, and were going to destroy the villages. This
caused extreme anxiety and provoked retaliatory attacks by the Muslims on
Armenian villages. However, in this case, the massacres in Adana and in the
provinces took place at the same time.

Around twenty thousand Armenians were killed in Adana.[77] The Armenian survivors were moved to camps where tents were erected for them. Around twenty to thirty people died on a daily basis in this period due to epidemics. After the end of the second wave of massacres, arrests of Armenians and Turks began. More than one hundred Armenians were imprisoned and tortured and accused of being wholly responsible for the massacres.[78]

The physical destruction in the city of Adana was unimaginable. More than one thousand houses were burned, and others were looted. All the public buildings belonging to Christians were burned. The Catholic missionaries lost their church, residence, college, and the Jesuit school. The Sisters of St. Joseph lost their chapel, boarding school, day school, and dispensary. The Armenian Catholicos lost its bishop's residence, presbytery, and the boys' and the girls' schools. The Chaldeans lost their church and presbytery. The Gregorian Armenians lost one church and two colleges. The Syriacs and the Protestants lost their church. Numerous houses of Muslims were burned.

Most of the mills and the bakeries were also burned, making the task of supplying bread more difficult. There was a great need for rice, underclothing, and cooking utensils. A relief committee was established in Adana, with Doughty-Wylie as chairman and William Nesbitt Chambers as secretary. According to one estimate, 4,823 houses were burned, in addition to churches, schools, and public edifices.[79]

Conclusion

When the first wave of massacres ended, no one thought that a second wave would start only eight days later. The unrestricted public sphere in the inter-massacre period—as manifested in the *İtidal* newspaper—was used by the opponents of Armenians to incite the masses in Adana by pushing their version of events, which included a failed Armenian "revolt." Affective disposition remained a crucial factor in this period. The potent images of Armenian *fedayees* and European warships were used by agents provocateurs to manipulate the emotions of the Muslim population. They insinuated that the presence of European warships in Mersin, used by European powers as a deterrent against conflict, was connected to a larger plan of an Armenian uprising, whereby European military intervention would lead to the reestablishment

of the Kingdom of Cilicia. However, no military intervention, humanitarian
or otherwise, took place.

Of course, mobs are motivated by ideological beliefs as well as by financial gain, which plays a significant role during massacres. The masses that
took part in the massacres of Adana and Aleppo were composed not only of
city denizens but also of villagers, tribes, and immigrants. Kurds, Circassians,
Turkmens, Cretan Muslims, Arabs, Ansariyeh, fellahin, and seasonal laborers
were motivated to take part in the massacres by the prospect of plundering
and looting Christian properties in general and those of Armenians in particular. They were well aware of the relative wealth of the Armenians in the
region of Adana and Aleppo and generally viewed the disparity with disdain.
The crisis in the region presented the ultimate opportunity to strike back in
order to restore the equilibrium that had existed prior to the economic and
political rise of Armenians. While Armenians' economic ascent had taken
place decades prior to the Young Turk Revolution of 1908, their political ascent had happened more abruptly. Ideas of constitutionalism, equality, liberty,
and fraternity that were heralded in the public sphere—especially by Armenians—were viewed unfavorably by the majority of the Muslim population
and considered an abrogation of the Sharia. This led to deep dissatisfaction
in the region among a major section of society with regard to non-Muslims.

CHAPTER 6

AFTER THE FACT

Humanitarian Aid and Reactions to the Massacres

ALTHOUGH HUMANITARIAN RELIEF BEGAN IMMEDIATELY AFTER the first wave of massacres, the second wave of massacres in Adana elevated the catastrophe and brought the demand for aid to a new level of urgency. Armenian organizations and other ethno-religious groups of the empire, American and European organizations and missionaries, as well as the Ottoman state, all contributed to alleviating the suffering of the survivors of the two massacres. The most pressing issues were providing food and medical aid. Humanitarian aid was not confined to the city and the province of Adana but also extended to the province of Aleppo. The tasks of aid organizations included treating the wounded, providing food, supporting the widows and the orphans, rebuilding destroyed houses, rehabilitating the refugees, and providing agricultural implements.[1] In addition to the delivery of humanitarian aid, the Adana massacres inspired public uproar on both the national and international levels. While today these massacres are largely forgotten, at the time they were covered extensively by the press.

The Adana case demonstrates the limitations of humanitarianism and humanitarian intervention. Except for British vice-consul Doughty-Wylie, no representative of a European power intervened during the massacres on humanitarian grounds. It seems that none of them wanted to destabilize the international system. They confined themselves to direct and indirect humanitarian aid in response to the crisis. In Davide Rodogno's words:

The European powers' nonintervention in favor of the Ottoman Armenians is important, for it reveals that despite the extent and incontrovertible evidence of massacre, atrocity, and extermination, the nature of the international system prevented intervention from taking place. The horror that these massacres aroused in "civilized" Europe was not enough to trigger a humanitarian intervention. Saving strangers, even Christian coreligionists, was an international practice subordinated to the maintenance of peace and the security of Europe.[2]

That said, many relief efforts were made on the local, regional, and international levels. The postrevolutionary public sphere facilitated this humanitarian relief. Local as well as international press outlets were used to disseminate information about the condition of the refugees and the need for financial aid. Furthermore, Armenian organizations and prominent Armenian figures, both at the forefront of the relief efforts, were able to air their dissatisfaction with "the culturally effacing effects of international humanitarianism."[3] While in the period of the Hamidian massacres Armenians were prevented from becoming involved in relief work, in the postrevolutionary period Armenian activities toward this end were tolerated.[4] Even criticism of the government's handling of the relief work was common.

The Adana massacres were covered extensively in the European press. This was vital in raising awareness about the suffering of the Armenians and the need for humanitarian aid. In this international public sphere, professional journalists writing from a humanitarian perspective for major European newspapers reported freely from the ground about the horrors of the massacres in Adana. However, most of these newspapers did not cover the Muslim refugees or those who were killed while attacking the Armenian neighborhoods. As Watenpaugh argues, this lack of response to Muslim suffering "colored the way modern humanitarianism was encountered in the late Ottoman period."[5]

The Immediate Response: Food, Shelter, and Medical Help

After the conclusion of the second wave of massacres, thousands of Armenians were sheltered in the churchyard, public garden, and streets near the railway station in the city of Adana. Many of them had come from the suburbs and villages seeking safe haven.[6] The British, American, and German consulates aided the refugees, and the government supplied eight-hundred pounds of bread on a daily basis. In order to facilitate the distribution of bread, thirteen thousand refugees crammed into the Greek Trypani factory and were divided into thirty groups.[7] Lists show that the German cotton factory supported five thousand refugees, out of which one hundred were seriously injured. The few German employees of the factory had only the bare necessities to live on; they did not have the funds to buy flour and rice to feed the refugees. Thus, for fifteen straight days, the director of the factory, Richard Stöckel, fed five thousand people.[8]

There was an urgent need for doctors, nurses, bandages, and sanitation items. Hence, the German command SMS *Hamburg* dispatched its chief doctor, Dr. Bockelberg, to treat the severely injured in Adana.[9] According to reports, Bockelberg "performed his task with great circumspection and with expert skill under the most difficult circumstances. In tropical heat, working tirelessly from morning to night, he [did] extraordinary work in the hospital he . . . set up, with only a minimum of personal and material resources."[10]

The American Red Cross (ARC) was among the first organizations to respond to the massacres.[11] It had established a center in Beirut to distribute supplies to the survivors. Its first task was to send doctors and nurses, along with medical supplies, to Adana. On April 28, they sent an Armenian physician, Dr. Armadouni; however, upon arriving in Mersin, he was not able to proceed due to the government's restrictions on Armenians.

Captain Cecil Thursby, of the HMS *Swiftsure* at Mersin, notified the vali of the formation of a relief committee (the Adana Relief Committee) and showed him the list of members. It consisted of Thursby as president; Mr. R. R. Chambers of the American mission; Richard Stöckel of the German factory; a delegate from the French priests; three Muslims; M. Costi Trypani; and a representative from each of the three Armenian churches.[12] The vali informed Thursby that he had received a credit of 30,000 GL (equivalent to around $11 million today) from İstanbul for relief purposes. This was to be administered by Abdülkadir Bağdadizade, who was appointed by the vali as president of a local relief committee and later served as the president of the local investigation commission into the massacres. This information shocked Thursby: "I confessed this information startled me. This man has been [a] notorious robber for many years, is a bitter fanatic, and [has been] freely accused of having started the massacres."[13]

On April 30, the Adana Relief Committee sent out an urgent call for medical aid. They stated that "smallpox" had broken out in Adana and that there was an urgent need for medical supplies such as cotton wool, iodoform powder and chloride gauze, phenic and crude boric acid, disinfectants, and quinine, among other supplies.[14] Thursby himself sent a telegram to the ARC asking for the immediate dispatching of medical supplies and communicated that doctors were very urgently required for the smallpox outbreak at the Trypani factory.[15] In response, the ARC of Beirut dispatched a medical team, which arrived in Adana on May 12.[16] At this time there were also around ten marines and a doctor from the HMS *Swiftsure* working under the direction of Lilian Doughty-Wylie.[17]

As a result of epidemics spreading among the refugees, they were taken from the Trypani and German cotton factories to an open space. The work of the transfer was managed by Commandant Carver of the *Swiftsure* and by the Canadian missionary William Nesbitt Chambers.[18] An eyewitness account recounts the miserable condition of the refugees in the Trypani factory:

> In the Greek factory the thirteen thousand [people] filled all available space. The buildings were packed, with people sitting everywhere on the floor; many crawled under the machinery to find a place to lie. Out in the yard of the factory the latecomers were jammed together tightly, so that for many there was actually "standing room only." Among the refugees here few were wounded, but many sick. There had been an epidemic of measles in the town before the trouble began, and in the crowding of refugees from the first massacre there had been a thorough spread of infection. The two weeks that had elapsed since the beginning of the first massacre gave time for the incubation period, and now many children broke out with the rash of measles.[19]

The combined epidemics of dysentery, typhoid, fever, and measles took over fifty lives daily, but the arrival of doctors kept this calamity in check.[20] The Armenian Patriarchate Relief Commission reported that during the first month, two thousand children died of measles and diarrhea alone.[21]

The commander gave orders for the erection of tents. Missionary Elizabeth Webb and her sister Mary spent the whole afternoon sewing tent covers, with seventy women under their direction. By night about sixty tents had been finished. Missionary Stephen Van R. Trowbridge described the scene:

The procession of weary and wretched refugees which moved along the high-
way from the big cotton mill into the country fields was an unforgettable
sight. The march lasted all the morning. The multitude was streaming past
the consul's headquarters for four hours. "Dragging past" would perhaps describe the movement better. Haggard and forlorn the poor people moved
slowly along, some carrying their houses! There was no weeping and wailing
but an awful despair had settled down upon all. We hope the tents and the
open air will furnish some refreshment and restoration. Christian women
and children keep coming in from the villages. The men have all been killed.[22]

Due to the damage that was inflicted on the mills and factories, it was
difficult to obtain flour in order to feed the refugees. It was estimated that a
sum of £200 per day was required to prevent starvation.[23] The ARC sent five
hundred blankets and one hundred quilts from Beirut for the most destitute
people in the Yenimahalle camp, where the British fed 13,425 people.[24] On
May 4, the German factory was also emptied, except for around forty of the
most seriously wounded, and its refugees were relocated a half-mile from the
Yenimahalle camp. The people from the German factory were fed by German funds, and the place came to be known as the "German camp." On May
11, around 22,000 refugees were fed in Adana. All the Christian refugees in
the camps were aided by the International Committee at Adana under the
presidency of the British vice-consul. The British vice-consul estimated that
£300 per day was necessary for general relief, excluding hospital costs.

In the city of Adana there were three hospitals, which housed 375
wounded people under the care of foreigners. The number of the wounded
after the second massacres was not larger than after the first wave, because in
the second instance the majority had been killed. Much assistance was given
by Dr. Connell of the *Swiftsure*, Dr. Bouthillier of the French cruiser *Victor
Hugo*, and Dr. Bockelberg of the German cruiser *Hamburg*, together with a
number of sailors and marines.[25] Local Armenian doctors also rendered their
services. Despite the presence of the *Victor Hugo*, the French were relatively
reserved, although significant French property—the Jesuit convent and the
nursing home—had been destroyed in Adana. Admiral Pivet, who arrived in
Mersin with the armored cruiser *Jules Ferry* on May 14, was indignant with
the French consul of Adana for his inaction.[26]

FIGURE 8. A refugee camp in Adana, 1909.
Source: Ernst Jäckh Papers, Rare Book & Manuscript Library,
Columbia University in the City of New York.

On May 15, the American armored cruiser *North Carolina* arrived in
Mersin.[27] Despite the assurance of the vali, the Armenians under the protec-
tion of the American mission were shot. As a result, the commander of the
North Carolina threatened the vali that he would send five hundred men to
Adana.[28] Of the other nations, Russia was represented by the gunboat *Ura-
letzt*, Austria by the cruiser *Zenta*, and Italy by a torpedo boat destroyer.[29]
Aid also arrived from London, Boston, Paris, New York, Manchester, Chi-
cago, and Washington.[30]

Two houses were rented near the railway station, and a dispensary and
small hospital were soon reopened. On May 29, one of the French sisters as-
sessed the situation:

> At the dispensary we are able to attend daily to some 100 to 150 wounded,
> and we give relief to more than 1,500 people. A dreadful feature is the num-
> ber of those out of their minds; one of our women invalids was hiding two

whole days down in a well with seven corpses around her ... is it to be wondered at that her mind gave way?[31]

The wife of the British consul called upon two of the sisters to help her at an infirmary that she had erected.[32] The missionaries and nuns began forming plans of education pending the reconstruction of the colleges; the nuns also worked on erecting an orphanage but, lacking the necessary means, were unable to do so.

According to Trowbridge, the doctors estimated the sick and wounded to number around 1,600, only 8 percent of whom were Muslim. He said, "This shows how one sided the struggle has been. It shows that a massacre has taken place, not an Armenian insurrection. If an insurrection had taken place a very different percentage of Moslems wounded would have resulted."[33] Muslims who were injured during the massacres were treated in the government hospital outside the city. Around 50 were inpatients and 150 were outpatients. In addition, 40 wounded were treated in the Turkish military hospital. Around 50–60 other wounded were admitted in different places and treated by Armenian doctors, and the rest were treated in their homes.[34]

Aid to the Periphery

Aiding the victims outside the city of Adana proved to be a more difficult task. M. Roque Ferrier, the French consul general of Aleppo, created a relief caravan in Adana in order to bring aid to the victims of the massacres in the districts between Adana and Aleppo.[35] Rev. Etienne (prior of the Trappists of Shekle), the Jesuit priest Father Rigal, the mother superior with two of the Sisters of St. Joseph, and an adequate escort of Ottoman Turkish soldiers also joined the caravan.[36] On May 27, the caravan began its journey. It was accompanied by seven wagonloads of provisions and medical stores, a large part of which was generously furnished by Admiral Pivet. The caravan visited the villages and districts of Hristiyan-Köy, İncirlik, Ağzıbüyük, Misis, Hamidiye, Osmaniye, and Hasanbeyli, among others.[37] Father Rigal provides information about the numbers of people killed, houses burned, and survivors from these regions. In the subdistrict of Bahçe, around 80 percent of the Armenian population was massacred. After the completion of his mission, Ferrier returned to Aleppo, where he died. The Catholic missionaries scattered in the

different districts played an important role in aiding the victims: the Trappists and Lazarists at Akbeş, the Capuchins at Tarsus and Antioch, the Fran-
ciscans at İskenderun and Kassab, and the Carmelite fathers at İskenderun
and Beylan.[38]

The ARC did not confine its activities to the province of Adana but also
supplied aid to afflicted areas in the province of Aleppo, such as Antioch,
Kessab, Latakia, İskenderun, and Maraş.[39] The ARC used local missionaries to facilitate the task of distributing relief supplies. The field agents in the
provinces of Adana and Aleppo were Rev. Chambers (Adana), Rev. Dodds
(Mersin), Rev. Kennedy (İskenderun), Dr. Balph (Latakia), Rev. Maccal-
lum (Maraş), and Rev. Trowbridge, who assisted immensely with the work
of the ARC. The ARC sent financial aid through the American embassy in
İstanbul, which forwarded the amounts to Adana and Aleppo. In May, the
ARC dispatched $5,000 for relief in the Aleppo and Adana districts of Tur-
key, raising its total amount of assistance to $20,000 (equivalent to around
$620,000 in 2021 dollars).[40] It continued its work throughout the summer,
extending through the winter of 1909. When the American ambassador at
İstanbul, Mr. Oscar S. Straus, appealed to the ARC on behalf of the six thousand widows and orphans at or near Adana, the ARC contributed $1,000.[41]
The ARC also sent provisions to Tarsus, İskenderun, Kessab, Antioch, and
Maraş.[42] For example, on July 3, in response to an appeal from E. Chambers, the American missionary at Kessab, for financial aid to buy shoes, cotton cloth, and wheat, as well as additional aid to rebuild destroyed houses,
the ARC immediately dispatched the sum to cover the shoes and the cloth.
However, due to its commitments to other areas in the provinces of Adana
and Aleppo, it was not able to assist in the rehousing.[43]

Other organizations aiding the survivors included various Armenian
organizations, the International Relief Committee established in İstanbul
and presided over by Sultan Mehmet V, and the International Committee
at Adana chaired by Doughty-Wylie. Nearly sixty thousand persons received
aid from American, French, German, Armenian, and Turkish relief committees or officials at Adana; twenty-two thousand at Maraş; fourteen thousand
at Haçin; two thousand at Mersin; two thousand at Latakia; four thousand
at Tarsus; and comparatively large numbers at Aintab and İskenderun.[44]
Friends of Armenia of London—an organization established in 1897 to help

the widows and orphans of the Hamidian massacres—also played a significant role in aiding the victims. Friends of Armenia collected funds for the
relief work in Adana through advertisements in English newspapers.[45]

Relief Organizations in the Capital

On May 4, the International Relief Committee was established in İstanbul
under the honorary presidency of Sultan Mehmet V.[46] Its members included
prominent figures such as Said Paşa, the president of the Chamber of Notables; Talat Bey, the vice president of the Chamber of Deputies; all the leading members of the Armenian community; the leading Greek and Jewish
bankers; and the heads of all the financial establishments in İstanbul, most
prominently the Imperial Ottoman Bank. The committee held its first meeting on May 25, at which 1,000 GL were pledged.[47] The committee was divided into two groups: one would collect from outside the empire and the
other would deal with the distribution of the aid. Appeals were made asking
for additional subscriptions.

Over a period of eight months, the committee collected around 16,000 GL
(equivalent to around $5,900,000 in 2021 dollars) locally, in addition to approxi-
mately 27,000 GL from different parts of the world: 20,877 GL from American
sources and 6,418 GL from the committee's Beirut branch.[48] The International
Relief Committee dispatched these funds to Adana.[49] On September 9, the
American consul of Adana, Edward Nathan, reported that the relief work in
Adana was progressing well. According to him, the International Relief Committee paid out 3,000 GL for tools to one thousand people representing about
sixty trades, and it paid additional sums for the repair of houses. While the
former enabled many families to become self-sufficient, the latter expenditure
assisted families that had been living in tents to gain proper shelter.

On December 4, the vali of Adana, Cemal Paşa, sent a telegram to W.
N. Chambers, president of the Commission of Industries in Adana, telling
him that an aid commission had been formed under his presidency with a
capital of 4,000 GL taken from a 100,000 GL sum allocated by the government for food, shelter, and other necessary provisions for the families who
suffered during the recent disturbances. According to him, this commission
was to provide for the future of the destitute people and incidentally to revive
the oriental handweaving and needlework of the women of the city and the

FIGURE 9. Armenian refugees in the city of Adana, 1909.
Source: Ernst Jäckh Papers, Rare Book & Manuscript Library,
Columbia University in the City of New York.

adjacent districts. George Lütfullah Efendi, Gergerli Efendi, Dikran Ashi-
kian Efendi, and George Keshishian Efendi were elected as members of the
commission.[50]

Armenian Relief Organizations

Several Armenian relief organizations also rendered help to the victims of the
massacres. The Armenian Relief Committee (Npastits'-Hants'nazhoghov)
established by the Political Assembly of the Central National Administration in November 1908 played a notable part in the relief work. This committee sent 1,000 GL to Adana for food and appealed to Armenian, Turkish,
and foreign benefactors of İstanbul and Europe for aid.[51] The commission
dispatched a delegation to Adana, which was followed by doctors, nurses,
pharmacists, surgical tools, and medicines, as well as other necessities such as
flour, clothes, and blankets.[52]

The Armenian Relief Committee supported 6,000 souls by national sub-scriptions.[53] The patriarchate collected 17,000 GL to this end, of which 2,053 GL was given to the International Relief Committee and 15,000 GL directly to the Adana Relief Committee. When survivors of the first wave of massacres came to the capital, the Armenian Relief Committee provided financial assistance to help many of them return to their homes.[54] When one hundred orphans were brought to İstanbul from Adana by the Armenian Ladies Union, the committee covered half of the expenses of the orphanage while also supporting an artisan workshop that aimed to train orphaned youths. In Antioch, the committee funded a carpet-weaving factory in the interest of ensuring the townspeople's livelihood.[55]

Other Armenian organizations that contributed to the relief work included the Armenian General Benevolent Union of Egypt, which—together with local Christians and missionaries—provided for one thousand homeless people in Mersin.[56] The Armenian General Benevolent Union (AGBU) sent 5,000 Egyptian pounds for the purpose of providing aid to the people who were left homeless in Adana, Dörtyol, Haçin, Mersin, and Tarsus.[57] An Armenian from France by the name of Dikran Khan Kelegian contributed 20,000 francs. Besides the above-quoted sources and the government funds, nearly 63,000 GL was pledged to Adana relief work.[58]

The Armenian Revolutionary Federation (ARF) of İstanbul organized the Red Cross Group and sent it to Adana, where it established a hospital and a pharmacy. The ARF relief activities also extended to the surrounding villages. Other Armenian organizations, such as Azganvēr Hayuheats' Ěnkerut'ean (The Society of Women Dedicated to the Nation), helped Adana in terms of education.[59] The prelate of Adana, Bishop Seropian, contributed to the effort by issuing an appeal from Cairo on May 25 for the aid of the Cilician victims.[60] The Armenian patriarch of Jerusalem contributed 60 GL to aid the victims of Adana.[61]

Response of the Ottoman Government

As mentioned earlier, the Ottoman Parliament initially voted to allocate 30,000 GL to Adana in order to aid the survivors of the massacres.[62] On May 6, the grand vizierate sent a telegram to the Ministry of Finance requesting an additional 15,000 GL from the local Agricultural Bank of Adana for necessary aid as well as urging the expediting of the amount ratified by parliament.[63] Despite a willingness to help the refugees, the slow actions of the Ottoman state drew the criticism of some observers. In May, a military report from the SMS *Lübeck* complained that the Turkish government had not yet delivered a penny of the agreed-upon funds. On May 9, a telegraph was sent to the German embassy in İstanbul asking the Turkish government for the immediate payment of at least £5,000 of the approved £20,000 to the local relief committee.[64]

Despite this delayed response, the government supplied necessary assistance not only to Adana but also to the other parts of the afflicted provinces. For example, on May 2, the vali of Aleppo, Reşid Bey, wrote to the Ministry of the Interior saying that sixty widows and their children had arrived in İskenderun and were situated in the Protestant school;[65] on May 4, the Ministry of the Interior sent a telegraph to the province of Aleppo, ordering it to instruct the authorities of İskenderun to house and feed the women and children.[66] In the case of Latakia, Mehmed Ferid Paşa, the minister of the interior, sent an urgent telegram to the grand vizier requesting aid and shelter for five thousand refugees who had arrived in Latakia on the French cruiser and Messageries ship. On May 4, the grand vizierate wrote to the Ministry of War, asking that three hundred tents be sent to Latakia;[67] on May 9, the Ministry of the Interior also ordered the Ministry of Finance to send funds that had been requested by the district governorship of Latakia to aid the Armenians. Two days later the Ministry of the Interior sent a telegram to the province of Adana announcing the return of the Armenians of Kessab and the surrounding areas of Latakia to their homes while also notifying the Ministry of War in order to guarantee the refugees' recovery and safe passage.[68]

Further information on the government's assistance of the victims of Adana was provided by an investigation commission that was sent from the capital after the massacres. The commission wrote a report from Adana to the grand vizier detailing the prevailing conditions. It stated that the people in need in Adana and the appendages were receiving aid from the government and the International Relief Committee. Due to the horrible condition of the refugees, an aid commission was established. According to this commission, based on an investigation that was done in the periphery, the types of aid required were as follows:

Finding refuge for displaced persons
Caring for orphans
Aiding widows and their children
Providing machines to artisans to allow them to earn their livelihoods
Providing loans for farmers and for the rebuilding of mosques, churches, and
schools

According to the report, the present need surpassed the allocated 30,000 GL, and the financial loss from the destruction of buildings was in the thousands. The commission demanded a loan of an additional 150,000 GL, to be provided either by the Ottoman Bank or the Agricultural Bank of Adana.[69]

Mustafa Zihni, who had replaced Cevad Bey as vali of Adana, also sent a telegram to the Sublime Porte on June 23 affirming the statement of the mixed investigation commission that 150,000 GL was needed by the aid commission to aid the people most in need, rebuild houses, and help the artisans and farmers.[70] A request was sent to the parliament to allocate 100,000 GL to Adana and 20,000 GL to Aleppo, which the parliament ratified. On July 26, 1909, the grand vizier sent an order to the Ministry of Finance ordering it to dispatch the amount.[71]

Widows and Orphans

Another monumental task undertaken by the relief organizations in general and the Armenian ones in particular was aiding the widows and orphans of the massacres.[72] Widows and orphans existed in Adana, Tarsus, Dörtyol, Ocaklı, Özerli, Hamidiye, Osmaniye, Bahçe, Hasanbeyli, Misis, İncirli, Abdioğlu, Şeyhmurat, Bahçe, Arpalı, Abidin Paşa, and other places.[73] As a result of appeals by the patriarchate and the resignation of Patriarch Tourian in protest of the government's response to the massacres, the government promised to provide 20,000 GL over five years to the patriarchate to administer care to the orphans and widows of the massacres. However, the promised 20,000 GL was reduced to an insufficient 1,000 GL. As a result, the Central National Administration decided to detach the issue of the

FIGURE 10. Armenian widows in Adana, 1909.
Source: George Grantham Bain Collection (Library of Congress).

widows from that of the orphans and established a separate Commission for the Care of Widows (Ayriyakhnam Hants'nazhoghov). Individuals from the Armenian Protestant and Catholic communities were invited to join this commission,[74] which established workrooms for weaving carpets and socks in places such as Haçin, Adana, and Tarsus and provided aid to the widows of Kessab, Aleppo, Aintab, Maraş, and Zeitun.[75] According to a report of the commission, there were 3,285 Armenian widows in Adana and 787 in Aleppo, thereby totaling over 4,000 in the two provinces.[76] In addition, there were 143 Syriac, Syrian Catholic, and Chaldean widows.

After the massacres, the combined number of orphans in Adana and Aleppo was 4,296 boys and 3,910 girls, totaling around 8,200 children.[77] A small number of those orphans comprised Syrian Catholic, Syriac, and Chaldean children. A few of the orphans found refuge with relatives, but the majority remained homeless. The Political Assembly of the Central National Administration thus established the Armenian Patriarchate Orphanage Committee (APOC) (Vorbakhnam Hants'nazhoghov). Khachadur Kruzian was elected to head the commission and was dispatched to Adana; he went first to Mersin, where an orphanage had already been opened under the supervision of the prominent Armenian writer Zabel Yesayan.[78] An appeal was made to help establish more orphanages for the Cilician orphans. In June 1909, Yesayan, who was also the director of APOC, was sent to Adana to alleviate the suffering of the victims of the massacres in general and the orphans in particular. She and her counterparts, Arshagouhi Teotig and Satenik Ohandjanian, played a central role in sheltering the Armenian orphans.[79]

Orphanages were established in Adana, Haçin, Maraş, Aintab, Dörtyol, and Hasanbeyli, most of them in or after August of 1909.[80] The Adana orphanage was initiated by Yesayan on August 1–15, 1909; it began with 100 boys and girls and steadily increased in size.[81] The Haçin orphanage was established under the supervision of Fr. Nerses. Around 1,940 orphans were cared for by Ottoman and European missionaries.[82] Some of these were sent away: 25 to Rodosto, 43 to İstanbul under the care of the patriarch, and 26 to the German orphanage at İzmir. Nazan Maksudyan argues that the integration of a certain number of Armenian orphans into the establishments of American, German, French, Swiss, and Danish missionaries created a feeling among the Armenians that "the nation's survival was under threat, since children's education in a foreign culture and in a non-Armenian institution was regarded as the ultimate destruction of the Armenian historical community."[83] Yesayan herself resisted the placement of the Armenian orphans in European institutions.[84]

In one of his reports on the Adana Relief Committee, Doughty-Wylie discusses the difficulties that arose regarding the orphanages. He said that delegates from the Armenian Patriarchate were sent to Adana so as to not "allow Armenian children to be sent to foreign institutions or out of their own districts." Doughty-Wylie said that the delegates asked for their help with money and advice but demanded that instruction and education generally remain in the hands of the patriarchate.[85]

Ottoman Greeks and Jews Come to Aid

The Greeks of Beirut formed a relief committee to fundraise for the victims of Cilicia,[86] while the Jewish community of İstanbul—headed by its notables Elyas Tsakhki Bey and Senior Bakhor Elis Alfandari—took the initiative of opening a subscription to aid the families who had suffered during the events in Adana. They solicited the support of Grand Rabbi Haim Nahum, who "approved this generous idea and congratulated the gentleman to have come up with this initiative." He promised to ask some members of the community to donate: "We hope the Jewish families will respond to this and help the destitute families and those who have suffered and alleviate their pain."[87] In Salonica, a concert was held by the Jews for the benefit of Adana's victims. The *Journal de Salonique* promoted and covered the event in detail.[88] At the request of the Honorable Garabet Efendi, municipal physician, three illustrious musicians from İstanbul—Kazım Bey (violinist), Cemil Bey (cellist), and maestro Silvelli (pianist)—participated in the event. A commission was formed for the event and began collecting donations; the Société La Bienfaisance Israelite donated 10 GL;[89] Mr. Spaidel, concessionaire of the mines of Thasos, also donated; and the Central Committee of the CUP contributed a sum of 50 GL. The total amount collected after the concert was 915 GL.

Despite the aid that was given to Adana, many Armenians began to leave the city. In June, the vali of Adana informed the Sublime Porte that 258 trip permits (*mürûr tezkiresi*) had been granted to people aiming to go to İstanbul, İzmir, Beirut, and Cyprus. He reported that the desire to leave was increasing day by day and that, according to the investigation of the police, most of those who received permits were not going to their stated destination but rather to Egypt or America. He argued that there were several reasons for the emigration of Armenians—chief among these were the lack of jobs and the idea that the verdicts handed down by the courts-martial were based on false testimonies. For his part, the vali refuted the idea of false testimonies.[90]

The Reaction of the Press and the International Community

The massacres of Adana were covered extensively in both the national and international press and were widely condemned by the international community. In this section, I discuss in detail the press coverage in order to demonstrate the breadth of reactions to the massacres and to determine how this coverage promoted the participation of various communities and countries in relief and fundraising efforts.

The reaction of the Arabic press in the Ottoman Empire and in Egypt was mixed. *Lisān al-Ḥāl* (The mouthpiece), published in Lebanon, covered the massacres primarily by presenting the positive work undertaken by the government to aid the refugees.[91] The newspaper called on its readers to put their full confidence in the government to remedy the situation.[92] It was critical of Adana's *İtidal* newspaper for spreading false news about the responsibility of the Armenians in the massacres and refuted this assertion.[93] However, it criticized both the Armenians and the Europeans for exaggerating the number of victims and for attributing the killing solely to the Muslims, arguing that eyewitness accounts in Adana and Mersin demonstrated that Christians were also involved.[94] *Lisān al-Ḥāl* argued that the events had spread due to insufficient military presence and the late arrival of troops. However, it defended the government, claiming that it had done everything it could and had fulfilled its duties. In addition, it lauded the parliament's allocation of 30,000 GL to help the victims without regard to religion or race. It reported that the grand vizier had stated that the Adana "events" (*ḥawādith*) were the result of corruption stemming from the Yıldız Palace.[95]

Al-Muqtabas (The outlet), published in Damascus, had somewhat more nuanced coverage of the events. It mentioned the Armenian refugees who had gone to Lebanon during the massacres, fearing an outbreak in Aleppo similar to that in Adana, despite the assurances of the vali of Aleppo that he would protect the Armenians and other Christians.[96] The newspaper was one of the only periodicals in Arabic that used the word "massacres" (*madhābeḥ*) in referring to Adana.[97] *Ṣada Bābel* (The echo of Babil), published in Baghdad, had an openly positive attitude toward the Armenians. In one of its issues, it discussed the attempts of the Armenian Patriarchate to urge the government to officially exonerate the Armenians from the events that took place in Adana.[98] When the government did announce that the Armenians were not responsible for the Adana events and that they did not have any separatist tendencies, *Ṣada Bābel* hailed the announcement: "We would like to congratulate our Armenian brothers on the appearance of this truth and we hope that they continue their service to the Ottoman Empire, which they have performed for many years."[99]

The most negative coverage of the Adana massacres was published by *Al-Ittiḥād al-'Uthmānī* (The Ottoman union) of Beirut, which reprinted articles from Adana's *İtidal* newspaper. In all of its issues on the topic, it blamed Armenians for starting the strife in Adana.[100] In one of his letters, *Al-Ittiḥād* al-'Uthmāni's correspondent Adil argued that the Adana massacres were not the result of religious strife between the Muslims and Armenians but were a political sedition (*fitnah*) based on the principles of revolution and built on the pillars of independence. He argued that the corrupters (read: Armenians) were encouraged by the independence of the Bulgarians, and he accused the Armenians of preparing for the uprising.[101] Adil repeated the motifs used in *İtidal*: Armenians buying weapons, the theatrical presentation in Mersin, notebooks and tobacco papers with images of Armenian kings, Armenians wearing military attire, underground tunnels, and the activities of Armenian *fedayees*.[102] He claimed that, while Kurds were busy looting, Armenians exceeded all other groups in killing people, especially in killing women. The newspaper also blamed the Russians for inciting the Armenians of Adana.[103] Adil criticized Syrian and Egyptian newspapers, which argued that the event was religious in nature, as spreading rhetoric that was harmful to the Ottoman Union.[104] *Al-Ittiḥād al-'Uthmāni* also accused the Armenian prelate of Adana, Bishop Seropian, of agitating the uprising, arguing that his aim was to elicit foreign intervention.[105]

The reaction of the Hebrew language press within the empire was more sympathetic toward the plight of the Armenians. The Zionist newspaper *Ha-Po'el ha-Tza'ir* (The young worker), published in Palestine, argued that the Armenians occupied a position in the region analogous to the Jews in Russia. It reported that general massacres (*ṭevaḥ klali*) had been perpetrated by the Kurds and the Turks against the Armenians and estimated the number of victims to be between ten thousand to fifteen thousand.[106] A few months after the massacres, *Ha-Zvi* (The gazelle), published in Jerusalem, printed an open letter by a famous Armenian poet addressed to the Turkish newspapers. The letter dealt with the condition of the Armenians in Adana and demanded that the CUP announce once and for all that Armenians did not have any desire to reestablish a kingdom.[107]

Ha-'Olam (The world), the central organ of the World Zionist Organization, discussed a visit by the ministers of the interior and justice to the new Armenian patriarch. At the meeting, the patriarch brought the ministers' attention to the barrage of complaints from the Armenians of Adana about the illegal nature of the courts-martial. The two ministers promised to conduct an investigation and to put an end to the reasons for the complaints. The article also lamented the extensive emigration that was taking place from Adana.[108]

Ha-Herut (Freedom), published in Jerusalem, reported that the Council of Ministers had ordered Cevad Bey, the former governor of Adana, to return to Adana in order to be tried by the court-martial for his role in the massacres.[109] *Ha-Herut* estimated the number of dead to be 17,000 Armenians and 1,900 Muslims and stated that in the city of Adana, 99 Greeks had been killed. It reported on the abject condition of the survivors as well as on the aid that was arriving from many sources. The article described the city as resembling a cemetery.[110]

The Jewish newspaper *Journal de Salonique*, published in Salonica, reported extensively on the massacres with a pro-government tone. When the French parliamentarian Denys Cochin interpellated the French government on intervening on behalf of the Armenians with the Sublime Porte, the journal observed critically that, when it came to defending the unfortunate and the oppressed, the eloquence of French deputies was invariably exercised at the expense of the Ottoman Empire:

> When tens of thousands of Israelites [Jews] were barbarously massacred in Kishinev or Odessa, when women, children, [and] old men were horribly mutilated in Romania, simply because they were Jews, no official voice of protest was raised to stigmatize this work of systematic extermination. Mr. Denys Cochin was silent at this time. Is it because he felt it was not worth raising his voice in favor of a sect that did not belong to the Christian religion, or because he understood that France would not have listened if it had been a question of officially protesting to the cabinets of St. Petersburg and Bucharest?[111]

The newspaper praised the new Turkey, saying that the French deputy would be mistaken to believe he was still in the presence of an absolutist and autocratic government like the Hamidian regime. It defended the Ottoman Parliament, saying that it alone had the right to control the affairs of the government and further argued that any intervention by the French government was unjustified, since from the first hour the parliament had taken all the necessary measures. In a surprising statement, the newspaper also argued that Cochin seemed to forget that there were more deaths in Adana among the Turks than among the Christians.[112] *Journal de Salonique* touted the government's stance regarding the Adana massacres.

In a different article, *Journal de Salonique* published a list of accusations that had been put forward against the vali of Adana. It listed various circumstances to which the vali had been indifferent.[113] One of these episodes dealt with the two sons of the ex-mufti of Haçin who encouraged by other leaders, roamed the district and excited the population with the following words: "We cannot unite with the Giaours [infidels] they cannot be our brothers; therefore, [there will be] no equality between us . . . it is our duty to get rid of the Christians and to slaughter them all." The vali did not take any measures to prosecute them. In a similar instance, when the editors of the *İtidal* newspaper, İhsan Fikri and İsmail Sefa, gave lectures in various localities exhorting the Muslim population to take revenge on the Armenians, no measures were taken against them.[114] These episodes demonstrated that the vali was both aware of and unconcerned with the reactionary forces.

The tone of European and American newspapers was much more critical of the Ottoman government and more sympathetic to the Armenians. The Viennese newspaper *Neue Freie Presse* represented the events in Adana as a conflict between Armenians and Muslims that led to a catastrophe. According to the newspaper, Armenians were slaughtered as in the great massacres fourteen years ago, this time not on higher orders but simply because the news of the counterrevolution from İstanbul sparked the passion of the Muslim people.[115] The German newspaper *Pester Lloyd*, published in Budapest, reported on the massacres with daily short news pieces on Adana; a similar type of reportage appeared in the Polish newspaper *Kurjer Lwowski*, published in Lviv, Ukraine.[116] It seems that European press outlets often copied the news from one another; for example, both *Pester Lloyd* and the Austrian newspaper *Wiener Zeitung* reported on the complicity of troops arriving from Dedeağaç in the massacres.[117] *Wiener Zeitung* estimated the number of victims to be around twenty thousand.[118]

The Greek press also covered the massacres. *Proodos*, published in İstanbul, provided detailed information on the Adana massacres.[119] One eyewitness account described the destruction of the city and blamed the vali for failing to deploy troops to the Adana bridges to prevent the criminals from invading the city. The person also lamented the massacres that took place in the villages surrounding Adana.[120] *Proodos* reported that two hundred Greeks were killed in Adana and that the damages inflicted upon Greeks amounted to 20,000 GL.[121] On April 24, 1909, *Proodos* published an editorial on its front page entitled "The Adana Massacres," most probably written by the editor, Konstantinos Spanoudis.[122] After the describing the disaster in Adana, it drew a connection to the reign of Abdülhamid II, stating, "The flames of Adana were the candles that illuminated the dead of a bad past." The editorial argued that instead of crying and mourning, action should be taken as soon as possible. It argued that the aid that the parliament had agreed to send to Adana was insufficient. Regarding the punishing of the culprits, it said:

> All government officials, from the prefect to the last Müdür, must be held accountable for what happened, to clear things up and put an end to this situation which on the one hand damages the state due to the colossal disasters and on the other hand shakes the reputation of the state and causes international complications due to some "well wishers."

In Athens, the *Skrip* newspaper ran telegrams that it received from other news agencies about the massacres of Adana.[123]

Empros, also published in Athens, covered the massacres almost on a daily basis and provided detailed information about the reasons behind them.[124] *Empros* lamented the deaths of thirty Greeks who were killed at the beginning of the massacres and chastised the Greek government for failing to provide information about the victims.[125] It provided the testimony of a Greek engineer, Mr. Gianopoulos, who recounted, "Bodies were falling, their houses were on fire, women and children were asking for mercy. Afterwards, looters disregarding the danger were looting the stores and taking sewing machines, bags of merchandise and anything else they could find."[126] On May 3, 1909, *Empros* covered the second massacres, describing how the army sent from Dedeağaç assisted the mob in systematically killing Armenians. It argued that what little was saved from the first massacres was destroyed completely by the second wave.[127] It also republished lengthy pieces about Adana from European newspapers such as *Le matin*.[128] It estimated the number of the Armenians killed to be thirty-five thousand.[129]

Some of the most detailed coverage of the Adana massacres appeared on the pages of the German newspaper *Berliner Tageblatt*, published in Berlin.

After the second wave of massacres, the paper began to feature eyewitness accounts. One of these, which appeared on the front page of the newspaper, was by a German engineer and businessman named Walter Siehe, who resided in Adana.[130] Siehe explained the ways in which the revolution had changed the situation in Adana. He said that provocations made by Armenians—whether through writing or drawing images of the Armenian empire—caused great fear among the Muslims. In addition, he said that the government was responsible for allowing large quantities of revolvers and Gras rifles, as well as ammunition, to pass freely.[131] He recounted that when he arrived in Adana, he saw laborers armed with clubs. After witnessing the killing of Armenians, Siehe traveled to Mersin with great hardship; he praised the governor of Mersin for his work. He related the destruction of Adana, highlighting that the movement was directed against the Armenians and not the Greeks. He lamented the material losses of the German-Levantine Cotton Company, which amounted to millions of marks. Siehe also praised the British vice-consul for his heroic work and accused the palace and the sultan of being behind the massacres.

In order to provide more detailed information about the situation, *Berliner Tageblatt* commissioned a special correspondent, Edward Mygind, to travel to Adana to report on the situation.[132] As acknowledged by Mygind in a lengthy front-page piece on May 16, this coverage was motivated in part by the German economic interest in the region.[133] Mygind elaborated on the activities of Armenian revolutionaries in Adana and their desire for independence. He argued that, through their parades and other activities, they created a reactionary backlash amid the local population. This negative sentiment targeted not only the Armenians but extended to the Germans. Mygind attributed much responsibility to İzzet Paşa, the former secretary of Sultan Abdülhamid II, who was residing in Egypt at the time, for engineering the movement.[134]

In an article sent to *Berliner Tageblatt* on May 25 for publication on June 15, Mygind raised the question of whether the agitations could have been prevented. He argued that the vali knew of the Armenian activities, such as in "Armenian political clubs . . . in which the question of Armenia's self-government or even independence was discussed" and where flags inscribed with the words "Kingdom of Armenia" were made. However, he asserted that the vali rightly refrained from reporting this to the center on the grounds that "the new constitution guaranteed special freedom and the right of assembly." Likewise, the vali took no stance against the agitations organized by the sultan or İzzet Paşa "as long as they did not preach openly against the new government and [the] principle of equality between races and religions." Mygind maintained that, in this regard, the vali's behavior was completely correct prior to the massacres. However, he was to blame for his actions after the first shots were fired; he argued that if the vali were a true, energetic, and self-confident leader, he could have prevented the horror. In order to make his point, Mygind provided the eyewitness account of an American missionary—who happened to be in the government palace with the vali when the massacres began—which portrays the vali as cowardly and unprepared to handle the situation.[135] He also criticized the European consuls of Mersin, who he refers to sarcastically as the "the seven wise men of Mersin," for not being able to stop the massacres. However, he praised the efforts of the British vice-consul, thanks to whom thousands were saved. After providing details of the damage that was inflicted on German businesses in the region, Mygind criticized the German government for not intervening on behalf of its nationals.

The French newspaper *Le temps*, which covered the massacres in detail as they unfolded, reported on discussions of the massacres within France. As mentioned earlier, the issue of the Adana massacres was raised in the French National Assembly by Denys Cochin, who criticized the French government for its inaction in protecting the Armenians.[136] Stéphane Pichon, the minister of foreign affairs, provided a rebuttal in *Le temps* to Cochin's interpellation.[137] He recounted the ways in which the French had taken part in alleviating the suffering of the Armenians, such as by providing financial aid and sending the armored cruisers *Jules Michelet* and *Jules Ferry* to aid the Armenian refugees.[138] He acknowledged Cochin's assertion that the cruisers could have taken more energetic action but argued that the result of such action could have been even more disastrous for the Armenians. He laid the responsibility for the massacres on the vali and the civilians of Adana, as well as on part of the garrison. He sympathized with the difficult position of the Young Turks, saying that their "authority [was] insecure, and they [were] not masters of their instruments."[139]

Upon publishing articles on the Armenian Question, *Le temps* received many letters from prominent Armenians in the francophone world. The Armenian Droshak committee in Geneva sent an inflammatory letter to *Le temps* in response to comments in the newspaper made by the Ottoman ambassador in Geneva, who claimed that Muslims and Armenians shared the responsibility for the Adana massacres. The letter argued:

> It is truly incredible that after so many testimonies, even from the representatives of the new regime, noting unanimously that the massacres were prepared and organized before the April 13 coup by Hamidian officials, the current government seeks to [include] Armenians among the instigators of this horrible butchery. . . . We cannot remain indifferent when after so many hecatombs and the ruin of entire provinces, after unspeakable atrocities committed by the populace and the soldiers commanded by stupid officials, we now come to incriminate the victims and crack down on them. Our own responsibility obliges us to impress these facts on the European opinion.[140]

Another letter was sent by Arshag Tchobanian, editor of the Armenian journal *Anahit* and secretary of the Armenian Union of Paris.[141] Tchobanian denied any culpability of his compatriots in the massacres, arguing that the Armenians acted only in self-defense. He complained that the real culprits— the vali and the military commander—had received paltry punishments.

For its part, *Le temps* chided the Armenians for their high expectations and their criticism of the Young Turks:

> Let there be no doubt that the Turkish element's responsibility in the massacres of Adana is preponderant. There is no need for evidence to assure this: history is enough. But let the Armenians allow us to tell them: it is not in their interest to charge the Young Turk party with responsibilities which have their roots in the past. One of our co-correspondents from Armenia writes to us: Do you take the Young Turks for angels? Certainly not, and we have sometimes blamed them to the point of being displeased. They are not angels who govern in Constantinople. They are men, fallible men who are harassed by difficulties. We sincerely believe in their goodwill.[142]

The article agreed with the Armenians that some culprits should have been punished more rigorously but argued that the Young Turks could not do everything at once. It expressed confidence in the Young Turks to resolve the situation if given sufficient time.[143]

The French daily newspaper *Le matin* also provided extensive coverage of the massacres. Its correspondent Antonio Scarfoglio composed detailed and mesmerizing accounts of the massacres and their aftermath.[144] Upon arriving in Adana he wrote:

> It is the horror of Messina and Reggio [referring to the earthquake of 1908 in Sicily], an entire city lying in the fields, killed with a stroke of the sword of destiny, suffocated in fifteen seconds, the same horror of gutted, raped houses, which show naked shreds of privacy . . . streets cluttered with debris, sewing machines, old watches, women's hats, ribbons, letters. The same horror and the same, terrible landscape. Here the same silence, the same impression of the collective, complete, final death of an entire city; this mathematical certainty that nothing more lives, that nothing more will be renewed, that everything, everything is dead, except the memory, but even more horrible perhaps than in Messina![145]

In a different article, Scarfoglio narrated with graphic detail the account of an Armenian woman who saw her husband smeared with petroleum and burned in front of her, her two sons flayed alive, her daughter raped and gutted, her house burned, and her happiness and life destroyed.[146] This woman recounted the horrors of the massacres, telling the story of the Burdukian family, who owned a farm. Scarfoglio used his writing skills to paint a shocking image of the suffering, emphasizing the sadistic ritual quality and the anti-Christian symbolism of the killing.

The Swiss newspapers also covered the massacres. On May 5, *Gazette de Lausanne* published two eyewitness accounts of the massacres on its front page.[147] The first was from a Swiss woman named Lucie Borel, who worked as a teacher in the American girls' school in Adana, and the second was by Mr. Chambers, the American director of the school. Borel described the scenery after the massacres:

> The city seems to be calm now, terribly calm, because the factories and the traffic of a city of 100,000 locals make Adana in ordinary times a very lively city. All is calm but I don't know if peace is returned to the hearts of this

unhappy Armenian population that has been tracked down in recent days as
wild beasts.

The newspaper made a call to aid the Armenians of Adana and Tarsus
at risk of famine and destitution, invoking the details of the eyewitness accounts to demonstrate the urgency of the situation.[148] Appeals were made by
the delegates of the Swiss rescue committees on behalf of the Armenians.
The delegates gathered in a conference at Bern. Committees from Zurich,
Bern, Basel, Geneva, Lausanne, Neuchâtel, and Bernese Jura were represented. It was found that these committees collectively had at their disposal
about 35,000 francs, apart from sums already sent to İstanbul. In addition, the
Geneva committee had twenty commitments from people who each pledged
to pay 150 francs per year for the support of a child in an orphanage.[149] *Journal de Geneve* made similar appeals for subscriptions to assist displaced families in the province of Adana, urging its readers to send aid without delay.
The sums collected were sent via the headquarters of the American missions
in İstanbul.[150]

In an editorial, *Journal de Geneve* inveighed against the Turkish government's policy toward the Armenians. It discussed a lecture that was given by
a Swiss national, Henry Imer, who was a professor at the American college of
St. Paul of Tarsus.[151] Imer told the audience that, as in the past, the Ottoman
Turkish government was making efforts to veil the truth; it invented absurd
stories of brawls and Armenian provocations while continuing to contend
that in Adana, the number of Muslims killed exceeded that of Christians.
The editorial continued, "This is all a lie. As in 1889, in 1894, in 1895, in 1896,
the massacres of April 1909 were accomplished under the inspiration and
with the complicity of the Ottoman authorities. And the troops sent to restore order participated [in this] monstrous crime." It argued that Sultan
Abdülhamid II had massacred Christians whenever the word "reform" was
uttered and accused him of being behind the recent massacres. It contended
that the sultan sought to justify himself in the eyes of Islam by restoring
the old order of things, supposedly in order to better resist attacks directed
against his throne and against the religion of Muhammad.

Journal de Geneve also criticized the new regime, saying that it merely carried out vague investigations and pronounced scant punishments. Probably

out of fear of displeasing Muslims and the dominant reactionary populations of the province, the government of İstanbul adopted on its account all of the lies of the old regime. In short, the new government, which had hanged so many unhappy soldiers found guilty of being seduced by the promises of Ab-dülhamid II, did not show any desire to achieve justice for Armenia.

The British press also provided thorough coverage of the massacres. On May 8, the left-wing *Manchester Guardian* printed an appeal by Kevork Utudjian, the Armenian bishop of Manchester. After describing the hor-rendous situation of the Armenians of Adana, Utudjian spoke about a meet-ing that he had presided over at the Midland Hotel, where an immediate subscription was opened among British Christians amounting to the sum of 811 pounds. He asked for further donations to be forwarded to the Wil-liams Deacon's Bank Ltd. in Manchester.[152] An appeal was also made from İstanbul by Sir Edwin Pears to "the British public for aid." He urged British citizens to send funds to the largest relief organization that had been estab-lished in İstanbul.[153]

Many articles about the massacres also appeared in the American press, including the *Washington Post* and the *New York Times*.[154] The *Washington Post* reported in detail on the death of two American missionaries, Rogers and Maurer,[155] referring to the former as "Martyr Rogers" in an obituary.[156] Dur-ing the massacres, the newspaper also published appeals made by Armenian-Americans to President William Howard Taft. For example, on April 18, it printed a letter by Rev. M. G. Papazian, the pastor of the Armenian Protes-tant Church of New York, which read:

> The pastor and people of the Armenian Protestant Church in New York, as-
> sembled for public worship on this Sabbath morning, and hearing with deep
> sorrow of fresh outbreaks amid massacres in Asia Minor, respectfully beg of
> you to exert your great influence and power to effectually suppress another
> season of human slaughter.[157]

The newspaper covered on its front pages the alarming news of the large number of people killed in the massacres and urged the government to send additional cruisers to the area.[158] It also covered peripheral areas such as Maraş, Latakia, and even the village of Kozolook.[159] When the vali of Adana, Cevad Bey, put the blame for the massacres on the Armenians, claiming that more Muslims than Armenians were killed, the *Washington Post* fired back, "This statement by the vali is considered here to be an obvious and monstrous misrepresentation, made with the object of throwing the responsibility on the Armenians and of justifying the numerous arrests of Christians."[160]

To afford all possible protection to American citizens and their families in the Ottoman Empire, the US administration decided to dispatch two armored cruisers, the *North Carolina* and the *Montana*, which had been docked at Guantanamo Bay in Cuba under the command of Captains Marshall and Reynolds, respectively.[161] Their immediate destination would be İskenderun on the Mediterranean coast of Turkey, in close proximity to Tarsus and Adana.[162]

The *New York Times* provided ample coverage of the massacres. On April 25, it reported that thirty thousand people had been killed, presenting the figure as a conservative estimate.[163] It also gave an account of an April 29 meeting of prominent churchmen and citizens in the Presbyterian Board of Missions at 157 Fifth Avenue in Manhattan, at which a provisional memorial was drafted, to be submitted to Philander Chase Knox, secretary of state. The memorial was read and a committee of five was nominated to revise it, after which hundreds of New York's most prominent citizens signed it. Among those known to be in sympathy with the movement were Bishop David H. Greer, former mayor Seth Low, and Nicholas Murray Butler, president of Columbia University. The memorial stated that the signers "did not allege that forceful intervention was within the powers of the United States" but argued that "earnest remonstrance and the highest possible exertion of moral influence were certainly within the government's prerogatives." It urged Secretary Knox to forward memorials to England and the other signatories of the Berlin Treaty, asking them to use their power to end the massacres.[164]

New York Times special correspondent William Bayard Hale covered the massacres. On July 11, 1909, he provided a detailed account of the missionary Rev. Herbert A. Gibbons's personal experience during the massacres.[165] The newspaper also printed the investigations of the massacres carried out by the well-known journalist James Creelman, whose stated purpose was "to learn the underlying causes of such horrors and to place the responsibility."[166] Creelman's articles also appeared in the *Sunday Times* and *Pearson's*

Magazine. In these articles, Creelman did not shy away from placing responsibility on the local government, saying: "It is beyond question that the
piteous massacre and pillage, which began with the attack on the defenseless
Armenian school, was deliberate barbarism in which the Turkish provincial
Government was directly involved."[167] In his journey through the destroyed
villages, Creelman asked Turks to explain

> how it came that in a single day the people of a prosperous farming country
> could change into wild beasts. The answer invariably was that the Armenians
> intended to rise in arms and establish an independent kingdom, and that
> it was only fair that loyal Turks should defend themselves. Here and there
> a Moslem spoke of photographs representing Armenians dressed as Kings,
> princes, or armed warriors.[168]

Conclusion

As in the case of the Hamidian massacres, no humanitarian intervention
took place to stop the Adana massacres, confirming once more the unwill-
ingness among the European powers to interfere. Their excuse was that, by
intervening, they might exacerbate the already dire condition. However, the
real reason for not intervening was to avoid destabilizing the international
system. As Rodogno puts it, "The irony that the warships of seven nations—
Britain, France, Italy, Austria-Hungary, Russia, Germany, and the United
States—were stationed just miles away off the coast and did not intervene
only highlighted their failure."[169] European powers confined themselves to
rendering direct and indirect aid to victims of the massacres.

This chapter discussed the local, regional, and international humanitarian
aid efforts that were rendered to the victims of Adana. In this new public
sphere where humanitarian agency was available to Armenians, Armenians
no longer considered themselves passive victims unable to take care of their
brothers and sisters; they became active participants in the relief work. Multiple Armenian organizations were established and leading Armenian figures
and political parties participated in it. European consuls and missionaries
also worked intensively to assuage the suffering of the Armenians. Appeals
for aid were issued throughout the world, and international, national, and

local organizations raised significant funds on behalf of the Armenians. Despite a relatively slow response, the Ottoman government also participated in the aid effort.

Although these massacres have fallen into obscurity, the international press at the time covered them extensively. This coverage raised awareness about the plight of the Armenians of Adana and their urgent need for medical and material aid. We see in the international newspapers a great sympathy toward the suffering of the Armenians, in addition to detailed accounts of the massacres themselves. Through their reporting, these newspapers facilitated and accelerated the fundraising efforts. However, they generally failed to discuss the fate of the Muslim refugees.

In assessing the reactions of the international press, one can see a consensus that Sultan Abdülhamid II and his reactionary forces were behind the massacres. The newspapers also ascribed responsibility to the local government, which many accused of being complicit in the massacres. We can also note a certain sympathy toward the Young Turks, who themselves suffered a counterrevolution that could have wiped out their existence were it not for the Action Army, which arrived from Salonica to quell the counterrevolution. Once back in power, the Young Turks took drastic measures through courts-martial to try those responsible for the counterrevolution in the capital. While they were successful in prosecuting the authors of the counterrevolution, the same could not be said in the case of the Adana massacres—an outcome that cast doubt on their sincerity and ability in bringing the real culprits of the massacres to justice. The next chapter discusses in detail the ways in which these courts-martial acted. It also dwells on the commissions that were sent to investigate the massacres and explains why the courts-martial failed to render justice to the Armenians.

CHAPTER 7

JUSTICE ON TRIAL

The Courts-Martial and Investigation Commissions

ON MAY 4, 1909, THE MINISTER OF THE INTERIOR, FERID PAŞA, announced a state of siege in the province of Adana to restore peace and public safety.[1] In order to try those accused of crimes, a local preliminary court was established, made up largely of local officials.[2] According to the British vice-consul Charles Doughty-Wylie, this court had "the worst reputation."[3] Some sources say that the court and its attached bodies were composed of the organizers of the massacres.[4] Abdülkadir Bağdadizade, the prominent notable of Adana who was involved in the massacres, was appointed the president of a local commission of investigation.[5] The court began working through suggestions of this commission, upon which arrests were made. The preliminary court generally accused Armenians of being behind the disturbances.[6] The Armenian Patriarchate responded by demanding that the government declare the preliminary examinations of the local court null and void because they were conducted by government officials at Adana, some of whom were involved in the massacres.

The local court's first action was to search all the Armenian houses for arms, reflecting the attitude of the locals that the massacres had been instigated by the Armenians (although Muslim houses were also inadvertently searched). Many Armenians and Muslims were arrested.[7] Hagop Terzian, one of the people arrested at the time, explains in detail how confessions were forcefully extracted from the Armenians; he concentrates specifically on the role of a vicious interrogator named Zülfü in torturing the Armenian prisoners.[8] According to him, after the second wave of massacres, prominent Armenian figures in Adana were arrested and taken to the military barracks near the train station. Armenian prisoners were also brought from Mersin, Tarsus, Sis, and Haçin.[9] Ferid Djemil, a Dashnak activist from Sis, wrote a letter to ARF leader Agnuni (Khachadour Maloumian) about the court-martial that was established in the city, which imprisoned more than 150 Armenians. He complained that while important Armenian figures were imprisoned, the Turks who were imprisoned were only looters and regular citizens.[10] Another testimony about the prison comes from Artin Arslanian, a Hnchak activist who was imprisoned and tortured in the prison of Adana.[11] He recounts how interrogators put a hot iron rod on the face and ears of a certain Mgrdich Dökmeci and forced him to write down how he made dynamite.[12] Arslanian was himself forced to give a false statement in which he claimed that Bishop Seropian was planning to establish the Armenian Kingdom of Cilicia and make Adana the center.[13]

The new vali, Mustafa Zihni Paşa, seeing the inability of the local court to work properly, demanded that a court-martial be dispatched immediately from İstanbul. He argued that the investigators and interrogators were incapable of conducting proper inquiries due to powerlessness and fear. He said that the new court-martial should interrogate all the government officials and employees without exception.[14] Furthermore, he complained about the negative influence of the former commander of Adana, Mustafa Remzi Paşa, on the court-martial's workings in Mersin.[15] Despite this, the British vice-consul at Mersin lamented that Zihni was "acting with marked hostility and partiality against the Armenians, but . . . hoped that the special court-martial, and the Civil Commission, which, after all, [was] to be dispatched to the spot by Parliament, [would] rectify his action, and [would] specially amend the composition of the Relief Committee."[16] The subsequent courts-martial that arrived in Adana were nevertheless influenced by the findings of the commission of inquiry formed by the former vali, Cevad Bey.[17]

This chapter analyzes the modi operandi of the various courts-martial and the investigation commissions that were sent to Adana. It discusses the workings of the courts-martial and the reactions of both the Muslim and the Christian populations, as well as the local and central governments. This chapter demonstrates how irregularities in the workings of the courts-martial resulted in a miscarriage of justice. Despite a willingness to investigate and try the culprits of the massacres, the courts-martial suffered from procedural discrepancies. Significant among these was the fact that the second court-martial sent from İstanbul did not start the investigation process afresh but rather relied on the findings of the local court-martial, which were tainted by a bias against Armenians. I consider how partial justice was nonetheless achieved due to extensive Armenian lobbying in the capital, the active role of the press, the efforts of MP Hagop Babigian (a CUP member and one of the members of the investigation commission), and the efforts of the CUP to satisfy local and international pressure. I say "partial justice" due to the fact that the most significant culprits of the massacres did not receive their deserved punishments.

The Court-Martial from İstanbul

When the news of the local court's verdict arrived in İstanbul, the Armenian patriarch protested to the government about the injustice and demanded the dispatch of a court-martial from İstanbul.[18] The government dispatched a court-martial on May 8, 1909, under the presidency of Major General (*Mîr-livâ*) Kenan Paşa. The members of the court-martial lodged in the CUP administrative office in Adana. According to Terzian, upon its arrival, the new court-martial inspired much hope among the prisoners. The procedures took place in the state high school of Adana, which was allocated to the court-martial.[19] Most of the Armenians were released from the prison. However, the court-martial was prejudiced by the report that had been drawn by the local court. It did not start a new investigation from scratch but rather took over the prisoners and the investigation reports submitted by the investigation commission formed by the former vali, Cevad Bey. Hence, some of the decisions of the new court-martial in Adana were influenced by the opinion of the local court. As a reaction to this, the Armenian patriarch of İstanbul submitted his resignation—which he later withdrew in February 1910, after the newly appointed grand vizier, İbrahim Hakkı Paşa, promised him a satisfactory solution to some of his complaints.[20]

As the massacres had spilled over into Maraş and Antioch (Antakya), thus increasing the number of people involved in them, the court-martial established in Adana was incapable of dealing with all the incidents in other parts of the province. Another court-martial with separate inquiry commissions was therefore established.[21] This court-martial, under the presidency of Eyüb Bey, was sent to Erzin in the district of Cebel-i Bereket.[22] In addition to this, a third court-martial was established under the presidency of Staff Colonel Reşhid Bey.[23]

Upon the arrival of the court-martial from İstanbul, the religious heads of the different Christian groups in Adana sent a letter to the court describing in detail the events that took place in Adana.[24] The letter explained the massacres in fifteen points. It discussed the premeditated nature of the massacres, the pillaging and violence that lasted three days, the second massacres that began on April 25 and lasted until April 27, the role of agents provocateurs in inciting the Muslim populations, the imprisonment of and false accusations against the Christians, the connection between the events in İstanbul and the massacres in Adana, and the destruction of agricultural implements and the massacring of the seasonal laborers who came to work in the fields, among other important points. The letter concluded with the hope that the necessary steps would be taken to erase this blot from the name of Ottomanism.[25]

The Austro-Hungarian consul in Mersin complained about the course of the court-martial, arguing that the court demonstrated no intent to punish the primary culprits. He said that those who testified against Muslims—mostly widows of massacred Armenians—were received very poorly by the court-martial. The Armenian Catholic bishop Paul Terzian, who presented a list of the victims of the massacres from among his flock, also indicated the names of those who committed massacres; he was treated by the court as a liar and impostor. The consul lamented, "Under these conditions no Christian dares to appear there [at the court] anymore. The main culprits continue to enjoy their freedom, and some of them were even appointed members of the Commission charged to distribute the relief voted by the Chamber."[26] Meanwhile, the British vice-consul argued that some of the witnesses who testified on behalf the Muslims were unreliable.

During the house searches at the time of the massacres, some Armenian activists found refuge in the British consulate; among them were Garabed Chalian and Zakaria Bzdigian, heads of the Hnchak and Dashnak political parties, respectively. On June 6, the minister of foreign affairs wrote to the grand vizier saying that those who were responsible for the Adana riots were hiding in the British consulate and should be handed to the court-martial; in order to demonstrate their guilt, he requested that all types of proof and written documents be handed to the British consulate and the embassy.[27] The minister of war, Rıfat Paşa, provided the British ambassador, Sir. G. Lowther, with a translation of minutes drawn up by the court-martial of Adana. The minutes accused the above-mentioned of being members of the Adana revolutionary committee, based on statements made by the former dragoman of the province Avedis Efendi and a teacher in training named Ohannes Semekian, among others.[28] With the intervention of the British vice-consul, the Armenians sheltered in the British consulate were thus handed to the court-martial, after which some were released.[29] However, the British vice-consul expressed strong reservations about the witnesses, calling Avedis Efendi "a notorious spy" and Ohannes Semekian "a man of no character" who had been ejected from the local CUP for selling secrets to reactionaries.[30]

Besides the court-martial, two other official bodies were dispatched to Adana on May 12 with the task of investigating the massacres. Faik Bey, the president of the Court of the First Instance of the Council of State, and Haroutyun Mosditchian, the Armenian judicial inspector of Salonica Province, were chosen by the Ministry of Justice to investigate on behalf of the government, while Hagop Babigian, the Armenian deputy of Tekirdağ, and Yusuf Kemal Bey, the deputy of Kastamonu, were sent by the parliament. Both of these commissions conducted their investigations in Adana and were supposed to send their official reports to their respective bodies. The investigation commission that was sent by the parliament visited Dörtyol, Hamidiye, Osmaniye, Hasanbeyli, Bahçe, and other places, collected eyewitness accounts, and conducted hearings. However, as is discussed later, no official statement as to the opinion of the parliamentary investigation commission has ever been published.

On June 6, 1909, the president of the court-martial, Major General Kenan Paşa, sent a ciphered telegram to the Ministry of War complaining about the attempts of the parliamentary investigation commission to delay the decision of the court-martial. The telegram specifically discussed Babigian's efforts to delay the sentence of an Armenian from Tarsus. He said that Babigian was accusing the court of bias, and that if such interferences were to continue, the court-martial would not be able to fulfill its duties and achieve the desired peace in the province.[31] After finishing his investigation, Babigian returned to Adana, while Kemal Bey stayed an additional twenty-two days.[32] According to M. Barre de Lancy, the vice-consul of France in Mersin, there were tensions between Kemal Bey and Babigian, which could have been the reason for Babigian's early return.[33]

On June 7, Babigian wrote to the grand vizier asking for the adjournment of the sanction of sentences. He said that his advice, alluded to above, had not been taken into consideration by the court; despite the fact that the grand vizier had ordered that his request be followed up, the order was not carried out.[34] He said he had also told the court that sentences should be enforced without delay on Bağdadizade, Bosnian Salih, İhsan Fikri, and their acolytes in Adana, and on Said Ağa, Haci Halil, and Hasan Ağa in Bahçe, as well as on other scoundrels of the same category in Osmaniye and İslahiye, so that order could be restored. But instead of proceeding with this, he argued, the court-martial had striven for two months to discover an Armenian revolt. It devoted all its activity to punishing the poor survivors, whose only crime was to have defended their lives. He concluded his letter by saying that, unless serious measures were taken to prevent the court-martial from molesting the Armenians who escaped the disaster, incurable wounds would be opened.[35]

As a result of the activities of the court-martial of Adana, 130 Muslims and 95 Christians were arrested.[36] By June, the number had increased to 427 Muslims and 174 Christians.[37] Some of the stolen properties were collected and returned to their owners, and houses were searched for weapons.[38] On June 10, the first court-martial sentenced six Armenians and nine Muslims to capital punishment by hanging.[39] In order to set an example, they were hanged at different points within the city.[40]

On June 16, the head of the Christian religious leaders of Adana sent a letter of protest to the court-martial, Vali Mustafa Zihni Paşa, the investigation commission, the Central Committee of the CUP, and the grand vizier. The letter emphasized that the Christians of Adana had been faithful to the constitution, and as true Ottomans, their desire was to assure its continuity and prosperity. The letter protested against the imaginary uprising that was attributed to them.[41] On June 17, the religious leaders sent another telegram to the Imperial Palace, the Sublime Porte, the Chamber of Notables, the

FIGURE 11. Armenians on the gallows in the city of Adana, 1909.
Source: Ernst Jäckh Papers, Rare Book & Manuscript Library,
Columbia University in the City of New York.

presidency of the Chamber of Deputies, the Ministry of War, the Ministry of
Justice, and the patriarchs, protesting that instead of trying the real culprits
of the massacres, the court-martial was mainly concerned with prosecuting
common people who had only followed orders. It said that innocent citizens among the Christians were condemned on the false testimonies of witnesses and sentenced to death for legitimate self-defense and claimed that
the court-martial was predisposed to finding Christians guilty.[42]

Conversely, on June 30, the Ministry of the Interior sent a ciphered telegram to the provinces of Adana and Aleppo affirming the court-martial's
conclusion that the disturbances in Adana and its surroundings had been
prepared by the Armenians for political aims and ordering that copies of all
the supporting documents acquired by the court-martial be sent to Adana,
Aleppo, and the Ministry of War.[43]

On July 7, the president of the first court-martial, Kenan Bey, sent a detailed report to the minister of war, Salih Hulusi, about the reasons for the

"tragic events."[44] He discussed the procedures taken to try the people responsible for the events and refuted the allegations made against the court-
martial. He explained the political aspirations of the Armenians during the
ancien régime and their influx into the province of Adana due to its geographic advantage, economic importance, and location on the route of the
Bagdad Railway. He said that after the revolution, the activities of the Armenian parties (Hnchaks and Dashnaks) in Adana raised the suspicion of
the Muslims. Kenan Bey's report concentrated on the buying of weapons by
Armenians. He stated that the weakness and inability of the new vali, Cevad
Bey, to deal with the tensions led to the incidents. He also noted the role of
Bishop Seropian, who through his sermons spread the idea of establishing
an Armenian state. Kenan Bey then discussed in detail the strife between
İhsan Fikri and the notables of Adana (Gergerlizade and Bağdadizade) and
Cevad Bey. Kenan argued that the local government alienated the Muslim
population by not paying attention to its grievances and by taking the side of
the non-Muslims. He presented Armenians as being on the offensive instead
of the defensive, arguing that when the "uprising" began, Armenians killed
Muslim residents of the Armenian Quarter and began advancing toward the
Muslim neighborhoods. However, he admits that the actions of reservists
who were called to Adana turned the situation into a catastrophe and escalated the disturbances. He thus presented the events in Adana as an equal
strife between Armenians and Muslims.

The report accused Cevad Bey of arresting both guilty and innocent parties after the end of the massacres. Kenan Bey said that when Armenians
were found guilty, they invariably blamed Muslims of being the real culprits.
In the final section of the report, he dealt with the preparation of the Armenians for the uprising and discussed how the court-martial acted in an
unbiased manner, without exception.[45]

The decisions of the court-martial caused immense anger among the Armenians. The patriarchate and the Armenian National Assembly complained
to the government about the unjust course of the court-martial in Adana.[46]
They demanded that the people primarily responsible for the massacres, such
as Cevad Bey and the military commander Mustafa Remzi Paşa, be subjected to trial.

On December 31, 1909, the resigned Armenian patriarch of İstanbul, Yeghishe Tourian, sent a lengthy letter to the Armenian Catholicos of Ech-miadzin stating that the dispatching of the court-martial to Adana, the rein-statement of peace, and the trial of the people responsible for the massacres had at first given hope to the Armenians. However, he was astonished to see the number of letters pouring in from Adana lamenting that the majority of the criminals were left unpunished. After İsmail Fazıl Paşa had been ap-pointed the new president of the court-martial, he had visited the Armenian Patriarchate on August 23 and informed the patriarch of the types of punish-ments that would be given to Mustafa Remzi Paşa, İhsan Fikri, Bağdadizade, and others. Tourian said that he was shocked with the mildness of these sentences and resigned in protest. In his letter, Tourian expressed deep disap-pointment with the course of the court-martial.[47]

The Report of the Government Investigation Commission

The official report of the government investigation commission from the Ministry of Justice was submitted on July 10, 1909, by Faik Bey and Ha-routyun Mosditchian.[48] The report was informed by their personal visits to the districts of Dörtyol, Osmaniye, Bahçe, Hamidiye, and Tarsus, and the vil-lages of Hasanbeyli and Kharnı, as well as by correspondence obtained from the districts of Hassa, İslahiye, and Haçin. The report outlined the political situation in Adana, explaining how after the arrival of Vali Cevad Bey, two parties were formed in Adana: one with the vali, formed around Ali Gerger-lizade, and another opposed to the vali, headed by İhsan Fikri. The latter did all in his power to get rid of the vali. Meanwhile, rumors spread that Armenians were going to massacre Muslims, and vice versa. According to the report, the authorities acted very slowly in punishing the inventors of these rumors. The report then recounted the events of the first wave of massacres, demonstrating at every step how false rumors led to an escalation of violence.

The report continued by categorically limiting and designating the de-gree of responsibility and culpability of the organizers of the massacre. It indicated that the mutasarrıf of Cebel-i Bereket, Asaf Bey, was the only ir-refutably guilty person, having freely allowed assassinations, pillages, and in-cendiarism in his district. Mosditchian included in the report the telegrams that Asaf Bey sent to the surrounding districts, as well as to the governor and the Ministry of the Interior, the various commandants of the reserves, and the director of the Payas prison, in which he incited the masses against the Armenians. His actions against Armenians in Dörtyol and Ocaklı, and his telegrams to the governors of Maraş and Aleppo stating that the whole of Cebel-i Bereket was under the fire of revolt, had exacerbated the situation. The report provided extensive proof from Asaf Bey's telegrams about his malicious intentions. The report also indicated that, even though other telegrams and letters from all parts of the province, as well as from Cebel-i Bereket, arrived to Cevad describing the deplorable situation, the vali took no effective measures to prevent the disaster. Along with the military commander of Adana, the vali instead attached greater importance to the telegrams of Asaf Bey, whose claims were unfounded. One of them stated, "Gökderelian was marching on our village, in our town, with 1,500, 2000, 3000 mounted men; he attacked our town, the losses are enormous."

The report also discussed the second wave of massacres. It said that the Ottoman soldiers who arrived in Adana on April 25 with the object of ensuring tranquility were induced by the local government and military commander to believe that the Armenians had fired on the military camp from the top of their church belfry, provoking a second wave of massacres "more terrible still than the preceding." After a long examination of the belfry of the church, they found that it was impossible to fire on the soldiers' camp because the Muslim Quarter was obstructing it. They concluded that this was a rumor spread with evil intent. The report also accused the *İtidal* newspaper and its editors of inciting the masses. It praised the work that was carried out by the former Gendarmerie Regimental commander in Adana, Hüseyin Daim Bey, who alone protected his quarter and saved lives; this was offered as proof that the vali and the military commandant could have prevented troubles had they so desired. It denounced the provocations made by Abdülkadir Bağdadizade and the work of the correspondent Adil Arslan Bey from *Al-Ittiḥād al-'Uthmānī*, who was brought to Adana in order to write articles against Armenians.

The committee estimated the number of people killed in Adana Province to be 5,683, of which 1,487 were Muslim and 4,196 were Christian. The report indicated that it was impossible to give a precise figure of the total deaths because there were many unregistered people and foreigners in the province, but it is believed that the number of deaths in the broader area was around 15,000 Muslims and Christians combined. Around 30,000 women, children, and infants remained homeless and hungry. The number of houses, shops, places of worship, and schools that were burned amounted to 4,823, of which 386 belonged to Muslims and the rest to Christians.

The report advised the government to provide aid to the victims and to help the agriculturalists. It asked that, in addition to the 30,000 GL already pledged, another 100,000 GL be sent. On top of that, it recommended that another 50,000 GL be allocated to the tradesmen through the Agricultural Bank. In order to prevent the repetition of such events, the report suggested appointing a capable person to assume this responsibility; forming a fundamental judicial body for Adana and its environs; increasing the number of commissaries and police agents; keeping regular soldiers at specific locations to be indicated by civil and military authorities; creating a *corps de garde* and commissariats of police in a number of towns, villages, and other places; and turning Dörtyol into a central town of the district. The report also advised that instead of punishing ignorant individuals who were inclined to follow any current without discernment, the three or four people chiefly responsible for fomenting the massacres should be punished as an example to others.

Upon receiving this report, the cabinet of Grand Vizier Hüseyin Hilmi Paşa ordered the arrest of the former vali Cevad Bey, the military commander Mustafa Remzi Paşa, İhsan Fikri, Abdülkadir Bağdadizade, Asaf Bey, and their accomplices. On July 27, Cevad Bey was arrested. The vali of Adana, Mustafa Zihni Paşa, refused to obey the cabinet's decision. The court-martial protested against the government interference that was prompted by the investigation report and threatened to resign, which it did soon after.[49]

Hagop Babigian and the Adana Massacres

Hagop Babigian, the head of the parliamentary investigation commission and a staunch CUP member, was the deputy of Tekirdağ (Edirne) in the Ottoman Parliament.[50] Upon his return to İstanbul, the subject of Babigian and his report became the center of attention in the Armenian, Ottoman, and international press and political circles.[51] At this time, Babigian gave an interview of great significance to *Yeni Tasvir-i Efkar* that caused uproar within

Ottoman Turkish circles and led to the resignation of the court-martial under the presidency of Kenan Bey.[52] In the interview, Babigian attributed the massacres of Adana to two factors: reactionary forces and despotism. He said that based on the official investigations and examinations, it was evident that the massacres were carried out by reactionary figures due to the frustration of their personal aims and benefits under the constitutional government. With the aim of undermining the new order, these figures agitated ignorant people and appealed to their religious feelings, thus using them for their own purposes. He dismissed the assertion that rebellious Armenians were the reason for the disturbances and claimed to have evidence to the contrary. He said that investigations disproved the allegations that Armenians were going to declare an independent Cilicia, and he criticized the court-martial for using "spy interrogators seeking the destruction of our country." Babigian exonerated Bishop Seropian from any role in the massacres, pointing out that on the contrary, Seropian's complaints to the vali about potential disturbances and the need for precautionary measures had been dismissed as exaggerations. He said that, in total, around 20,000 people were killed, of which 620 were Muslims and the rest Christians. He also raised alarm that many of the Armenians of Adana were trying to travel to the US due to the dire situation.[53]

On July 11, Cevad Bey sent a letter to *Yeni Tasvir-i Efkar* discussing his alleged disregard of Seropian's complaints.[54] Cevad said that he was not going to discuss Seropian's involvement in the massacres, or the lack thereof, as he left that decision to the court-martial. However, pertaining to the report that was submitted to him by Seropian upon his return from Cebel-i Bereket—which advocated for the removal and banishment of some people and the necessity of replacing the kaymakam and the mutasarrıf—Cevad asserted that he had duly forwarded the report to the Ministry of the Interior. In his rebuttal, Cevad also included a telegram that he sent to the Ministry of the Interior dated January 27, in which he refuted the allegations that were made in the fifteen-page report sent to him by Seropian.

The Babigian interview caused much agitation in Adana.[55] The president of the court-martial in Adana reacted vehemently against the statements made by Babigian and refuted the assertion about the bias of the court. He argued that the allegations were baseless and that by putting all the blame

FIGURE 12. Armenian deputy Hagop Babigian.
Source: Dr. Sylvie Merian's private collection.

on the Muslims, covering up the misdeeds of Seropian, and presenting the crimes perpetrated by Armenians purely as self-defense, Babigian had merely demonstrated his own bias.[56] The court-martial resigned on the same day as a sign of protest against Babigian's interview.[57]

The mufti of Adana and some of the local ulemâ and notables complained to the vali about the interview and asked him to notify the Sublime Port as soon as possible.[58] They argued that Babigian's interview had directly caused the court-martial's resignation, and they protested the decision of the Council of Ministers, which was influenced by the statements of Babigian, to retry the former vali, the military commander, and the mutasarrıf of Cebel-i Bereket. Furthermore, they said that they were astonished by the intervention of the Council of Ministers in the decisions given by the court-martial, which was an extraordinary court. *Yeni Tasvir-i Efkar* responded by rejecting responsibility for the resignation of the court-martial and reaffirming the duty of the newspaper to publish the truth.[59]

Yeni Tasvir-i Efkar also interviewed Faik Bey, a member of the government investigation commission.[60] In his interview, Faik Bey disagreed with Babigian's assertion that twenty thousand people had been killed.[61] He maintained that six thousand people (Christians and Muslims) had been killed in Adana but said that it was impossible to know the exact number of laborers killed. He also said that Babigian had not given him such a figure. As to the truth about the origins of the incident, Faik Bey said:

> This work was not done by the reactionaries; the reason for this is the ignorance of the people, both Muslims and Christians, which resulted in the tension. Hence, the reasons for this event in Adana are first ignorance, second ignorance, and third ignorance again. The remedy for this should first be school, second school, and third also school.[62]

As for Babigian's criticism of the court-martial, Faik Bey argued that this was an extraordinary court and that it was beyond the investigators' duty to analyze or criticize its functions, although he affirmed that the court-martial had fulfilled its duties. He contended that Babigian's opinions were his own and did not represent the thoughts of the investigation commission. Regarding the previous vali, Cevad Bey, Faik said that his actions did not reflect any intent of inciting the Muslims against the Armenians but were rather a manifestation of his ineptness.[63]

After the turmoil caused by his initial interview, Babigian provided a clarification in *Yeni Tasvir-i Efkar*.[64] He said that upon reading his interview he found many mistakes, but that he was extremely tired and had not been able to correct them until now. He said that he did not at any time "accuse the honorable court-martial of bias," yet maintained that many people were given wrong sentences, the reasons for which he showed in detail. He discussed the case of an Armenian man named Kiragos, who, together with bank employees, was trapped in the Ottoman Bank in Adana at the time Kiragos allegedly committed crimes. However, he contended that evil people, such as Abdülkadir Bağdadizade, and spies of the old regime, such as Avedis Sislian, who were under Bağdadizade's control, gave false statements leading to Kiragos's conviction and execution. Babigian also raised the question of how a person can be found guilty of a crime when he is defending his house from the attacks of a mob. He said that the decision to try the vali, the commander, and others was taken by the Council of Ministers in accordance with the sublime will of the sultan. On June 22, the grand vizier sent a telegram to the province of Adana regarding the issue raised by Babigian of Armenians emigrating from Adana—which was supported by the investigation commission—and in order to preserve peace and security in Adana, requested to be informed as to who and how many people were emigrating.[65]

Babigian's report did not appear at the time because three days prior to his testimony in the parliament he died under mysterious circumstances.[66] The original Ottoman version of his report has never been found. While the French version appeared first in 1913, the Armenian version appeared in 1919.[67] However, a contemporaneous author believes that despite the fact that the parliamentary commission's report was not published, the government circular addressed to the provinces that exonerated the Armenians was largely based on the parliamentary report.[68]

At the beginning of his report, which was completed on June 25, 1909, Babigian explains that when the commission left İstanbul he believed the news of the Adana events was highly exaggerated, but now he only wishes it were so.[69] He says that the only way to prevent the occurrence of such incidents is to talk about the truth without any reservations.[70] Babigian provides the reader with heart-rending eyewitness accounts of the massacres.[71] He argues that the evidence indicates that the massacres of Adana were not only directed at the Armenians but toward all the Christians of the area, as well as toward the constitution itself.[72] Babigian provides an important analysis of the number of the victims. He explains that there existed an incredible difference between the official reports and other findings; while Armenian and foreign journalists estimated the number of deaths to be between thirty thousand to thirty-five thousand, the official estimate of the government, which was based on the city administration's records and some eyewitness accounts of *muhtar*s (headmen), estimated the number of dead to be only six thousand. Babigian argues that the government's estimate did not take into account the large number of peasants who came to the city for the season and were not registered. The number of these workers, who came from Anatolia and as far as Mosul, was no less than forty thousand; at least half of this group was composed of Armenians, a large portion of which was massacred.[73] Hence, he estimates that the number of those killed was around twenty thousand.

The two main figures that Babigian accuses in his report are Cevad Bey (the governor) and Asaf Bey (the kaymakam of Cebel-i Bereket), who he argues are "entirely responsible for the *organization and implementation of the massacres.*"[74] He disagrees with the opinion of his colleague from the parliamentary commission, Yusuf Kemal, that the second round of massacres was initiated by Armenians firing from their houses on the soldiers' camp. As to the bearing of arms and the killings perpetrated by Armenians, he writes:

> No one is claiming that the Armenians did not use weapons. No one wants to deny that soldiers and other Muslims were killed by Armenian bullets. But . . . it is important to raise the question of whether it is right to punish the use of weapons in these circumstances [of self-defense]. Here is the problem that the court-martial remains unwilling to solve.[75]

He argues that if Armenians were really instigating an uprising, one could not explain the fact that it was the Muslims who attacked the Armenian neighborhood. He writes that Armenians did nothing but defend themselves, and self-defense is a natural right.[76] Babigian criticizes vehemently the actions of the local government in arresting people arbitrarily after the massacres[77] and attacks the court-martial as being unequal to its task:

> [In light of] the fact that the architects of the crimes committed in and around Adana were not bothered by the court, whose jurisdiction was the scene of awful atrocities that can only be characterized as a national crisis, and that instead innocent Armenians were tried . . . whose only crime was self-defence and the escape from death, I cannot help but think to myself that this is but a repeat of the massacres committed during the Hamidian regime.[78]

Babigian concludes his report by saying that CUP party members participated in the tragic and barbarous events that took place in Adana (he does not differentiate between the local CUP branch and the Central Committee of the CUP).[79] According to him, their participation is attested by many elements in the province, including consuls, American missionaries, and Latin priests.[80] However, it is important to mention that although local CUP members did take part in the agitations and the massacres, there is no proof that the Central Committee of the CUP was involved.[81]

Babigian's death on August 1, 1909, raised suspicions in Armenian circles that he was poisoned by the CUP because he was going to disclose secret information about the CUP's involvement in the massacres.[82] In an interview conducted with his daughter Alice (Babikian) Maremetdjian in Pittsburgh, Pennsylvania, in May 1980 by her daughter-in-law Simone Merian and granddaughter Sylvie Merian, she stated that two or three Turks (members of the parliament) had come, "supposedly to help [her] father write the report for the next day. He was supposed to read his report [the] next day." She says that they offered him a poisoned cigarette, which he smoked, resulting in his death at the age of fifty-two. According to her, the family immediately contacted the Armenian Patriarchate, who sent a few people to photograph the whole report and bring it back to the patriarchate.[83] More than a dozen doctors who did the autopsy on Babigian's body concluded that Babigian died from heart disease.[84]

On August 4, Babigian's funeral took place in the Surp Asdvadzadzin Church in Kumkapı, presided over by Patriarch Yeghishe Tourian and with a crowd of around twenty thousand.[85] Many people gave speeches, including

Babigian's fellow member of the investigation commission Yusuf Kemal Bey;[86] Kozmidi Efendi, who spoke on behalf of the Greek deputies; and Krikor Zohrab Efendi of the Armenian deputies, who said that before the opening of the parliament, Babigian was a virtually unknown personality in Armenian circles:

> When he was elected as a deputy there was the conviction that he was not a nation-loving [*azgaser*] Armenian. Alas, in order to know him, the Adana catastrophe had to happen. . . . Babigian Efendi did not go to revive these victims, [but] rather as a final victim. . . . His death became a general mourning for the nation.[87]

The last speech was given by the Ramgavar (Armenian Democratic Liberal Party) member Mihran Damadian. He compared the catastrophe of Adana and the accusations made against Armenians to the Dreyfus Affair and Hagop Babigian to Émile Zola. Babigian's body was taken from the Surp Asdvadzadzin Church to San Stefano to be buried in the courtyard of the Armenian Church.

The Second Court-Martial Sent from İstanbul

The complaints against the decisions of the first court-martial led the government of Hüseyin Hilmi Paşa to form a new court-martial and dispatch it to Adana.[88] İsmail Fazıl Paşa, the military commander of İzmir, assumed the presidency of this court, which took on the task of trying the former vali, Cevad Bey; the military commander, Mustafa Remzi Paşa; Abdülkadir Bağdadizade; the mutasarrıf of Cebel-i Bereket, Asaf Bey; and İhsan Fikri, among others.[89] According to M. Barre de Lancy, vice-consul of France in Mersin, the court extended the waiting period for Armenians accused of crimes to appear before the court and even gave assurance to some that they would be acquitted; this was the case with the five political refugees at the British consulate.[90]

The decision of the Council of Ministers to try Cevad Bey, Mustafa Remzi Paşa, and Asaf Bey made an excellent impression on the Christian population.[91] The measure was extended to all civil and military officials and all those believed to be editors of the newspaper *İtidal*, including its director, İhsan Fikri, who, although president of the CUP, was designated by public rumor as the main instigator of the second wave of massacres. De Lancy attributed the implementation of these measures to the reports presented by Babigian, Mosditchian, and even the Turkish delegate Faik Bey. In any case, they produced real relief among the Armenians and raised hope that justice would finally be served. However, the decision disturbed the Muslim population of Adana.[92]

On July 21, the Christian religious leaders of Adana sent a report to İsmail Fazıl Paşa providing detailed information about the course of events.[93] The report focused on how the indifference of Cevad Bey and Mustafa Remzi Paşa emboldened the mob during the first wave of massacres and how false rumors that Christians had killed soldiers in the Salcılar neighborhood led Mustafa Remzi Paşa to attack the Armenians during the second wave. They argued that if the court-martial were to put pressure on those who carried out the massacres, they would undoubtedly admit from whom they received their orders, and then the truth would come forth and justice would prevail.

On August 12, the Council of Ministers officially exonerated the Armenians in Adana of an attempted uprising. On August 13, the government sent a circular to the provincial authorities stating that the past agitations of Armenians were not blameworthy, since they had aimed at removing the oppression of the government (meaning the Hamidian regime);[94] Armenians had proven their sincere attachment to the Ottoman fatherland by assisting the nation in obtaining the constitution and thereafter by working in harmony for the nation's wellbeing. It refuted the idea that Armenians were entertaining separatist political designs. It argued that the complaints of Armenians about the oppression that continued after the constitution had been wrongly interpreted by simple folk. It acknowledged that the activities of the Armenian parties had provoked erroneous interpretations that led to mutual distrust and misunderstanding but blamed the local administration for not suppressing this mistrust. The circular asserted that the real instigators of the massacres, as well as the functionaries who failed in their duties, were going to be punished. It asked the provincial authorities to decree all measures necessary to bring about good feelings among all Ottoman subjects, without distinction of race, and to strive to strengthen allegiance to the constitution.[95]

On August 20, the mufti of Adana, Mehmed Lütfi Efendi, on behalf of the notables and the ulemâ of the city, sent a telegram to the grand vizierate expressing astonishment at the government's statement. He argued that the statement totally contradicted the report of the investigation commission and trampled on the explicit rights of the innocent Muslim population:

> We Muslims do not have any benefits by creating this event . . . it is the Armenians who have a stake in this event, to reach their political goal of independence. . . . We maintain that Muslims are innocent and uninvolved in this painful event. This bad and cursed event has totally destroyed our country and fortune. It has been three months that, based on the incriminations of the Armenians, more than three hundred [Muslims] have been imprisoned and denied participation in commerce and agriculture.[96]

The letter reinforced the belief of the Muslim population that the events had been planned for quite a long time by the "Armenian seditious people" (*Ermeni erbâb-ı fesâdının*) and concluded that it is the Muslims' right to not remain silent when Armenians are presented as innocent.[97]

On August 23, a ciphered telegram was sent to the province of Adana from the Ministry of the Interior, responding that the aim of the government statement was not to accuse the Muslims but rather to move on from the past and to protect the national as well as the Islamic interest and that it was from this perspective that the statement needed to be accepted. It stressed that the statement aimed to prevent misunderstanding between the two elements and that it was the task of the mufti and others in positions of authority to educate people and give effective advice in order to achieve this end.[98]

On August 27, the president of the new court-martial, İsmail Fazıl, sent an official report to the government entitled "A Concise Memorandum on the Adana Events."[99] He began this memorandum by discussing how painful the event was and by referencing many things that were being said, written, and published about the event. He wrote that some were attributing the event to the Armenians who had armed themselves with the desire of independence, while others blamed reactionary forces or the fanaticism of Muslims who attacked the Armenians like wild beasts. He refuted all of these claims and instead imputed the events to the ignorance of the population of Adana and its surroundings, irrespective of race or religion. He said the arrival of forty-five thousand seasonal laborers from Diyarbekir, Harput, and Bitlis and from among the tribes increased the magnitude of this ignorance.

He argued that living under despotism for thirty years had blinded people to the virtue of morality (*fazîlet-i ahlâkiye*) and that the arrival of freedom had emboldened the lower classes to act in whatever way they wanted. Certain narrow-minded people among the Armenians, thinking themselves "in the middle of France," had armed themselves, putting together theatrical presentations and carrying Armenian symbols and placards, with the aim of establishing independence and an Armenian kingdom. He said that tensions before the massacres were so high that "it was sufficient for a fly to fly in order to bring a tragic event." According to him, the killing of some Muslims by an Armenian ignited the conflict, and the inability of city administrators to take the necessary preventative measures resulted in the death of two thousand Muslims and four thousand Christians, the widowing or orphaning of thousands of women and children, and the destruction of many houses.

Fazıl provided a summary of the sentences given by the first court-martial: 43 Armenians and Muslims received death sentences, 129 received between three to fifteen years of hard labor, and 93 received one month of prison time. He also provided a list of sentences given by his court-martial: Cevad Bey was expelled for six years and barred from assuming an administrative position; Mustafa Remzi Paşa was sentenced to three months in prison and forced to retire in some place outside Adana; Abdülkadir Bağdadizade was exiled for two years to Hijaz; İhsan Fikri was banished for two years; İsmail Efendi, another editor of *İtidal*, was sentenced to one month in prison; Major Selim Bey received forty-five days in prison; Osman Efendi, the captain of the 4th Battalion of the 38th Regiment, received three months; and the captain of the 4th Division of the 4th Battalion of Karaisalı received two months. The six people convicted of attacking the depot of Adana were sentenced to five to seven years of confinement in a fortress, and the three Muslims guilty of the massacres in Karataş were sentenced to death. Four Muslims were sentenced to fifteen years of hard labor and fifteen others from three to fifteen years. These sentences do not include the people who were sentenced by the Erzin and Maraş courts-martial.

Fazıl attested that the sentences given by the court-martial were unbiased and argued that they should be implemented both in order to institute justice and as a lesson to the people. In his report he also provided a list of extraordinary measures that should be implemented in Adana immediately: the regulation and reform of the police force and the judiciary, the reconstruction of houses to relieve the destitute, the establishment of unity among the different elements of the population, the reemployment of the injured, the relocation and settling of the above-mentioned tribes, and the evaluation of the condition and character of laborers who came from outside of Adana. On November 6, the new minister of the interior, Talat Paşa, notified the grand vizier of the memorandum that was sent by İsmail Fazıl Paşa regarding the events of Adana. He provided detailed descriptions of these recommendations and urged that they should be implemented.[100]

Conclusion

Trying thousands of perpetrators of acts of massacres and mass violence is a major challenge, especially if the process is reliant on the legal system. In the context of world history, different societies have taken various measures to achieve this goal. Although most have resorted to courts-martial, others have employed different systems, such as the Gacaca court system in the aftermath of the Rwandan genocide. In the case of Adana, the legal process was carried out in a few stages. Immediately after the massacres, a clearly biased investigation commission and a court—both of which were formed by people who had vested interests in the massacres—were established to try the culprits of the "disturbances." This was an unfair and disorganized procedure in which hundreds of Armenians were imprisoned. Under torture, Armenian prisoners provided false statements that confirmed what the local government wanted to hear: that the Armenians had been preparing an uprising to reestablish the Kingdom of Cilicia. After complaints made by the Armenians, the central government decided to dispatch a court-martial, under the presidency of Kenan Bey, to Adana. However, this court-martial did not start the legal procedure afresh; rather, it used the statements and accounts that were gathered by the local inquiry commission and thus failed to separate itself from the tainted judicial process. Although the parliament and the government sent their own investigation commissions to Adana together with the court-martial, these bodies did not have any authority within the workings of the court-martial. Despite this, some members of these commissions—in particular, Babigian—discovered the biased manner in which Kenan's court-martial was acting. Babigian argued that the real culprits of

the massacres—certain notable figures from within the local Muslim community—were escaping justice while the court-martial was preoccupied with
trying Muslim peasants and Armenians, some of whom were innocent. There
is no doubt that Babigian's stance on the matter influenced the resignation of
Kenan's court-martial and the dispatch of a new court-martial from İstanbul
under the presidency of Fazıl Paşa, whose task was to try the figures who
stood behind the massacres. This begs the metaphorical question of who was
to blame—the bullet, or the one who pulled the trigger? The peasants, tribe
members, refugees, and laborers who took part in the massacres, whom I
refer to collectively as the "mob," had various objectives in doing so. However, they were generally encouraged and sometimes instigated to perpetrate the killings and lootings by powerful individuals. In cases of massacres, looting, and rampaging, people are more likely to commit crimes if they
know that a higher authority has given them approval. They are emboldened
by the sense that taking part in these acts will not expose them to any legal
recourse.

However, the sentencing of the primary culprits of the Adana massacres
was not carried out in a just manner. Almost all of them received very light
sentences and most were pardoned eventually. The reason for this is multifaceted. It is important to understand that even though the revolution had taken
place in July 1908, major elements of the ancien régime still had unlimited
power in some provinces, including Adana. Bağdadizade and his acolytes
had immense influence within the province, and any serious attempt to crack
down on them could have been counterproductive. It seems that the CUP
was aware of its weakness in such places; it was easier for them to send some
Muslim peasants to the gallows than to go after influential figures whose
culpability was more significant. The decision to hang the six Armenians
was also given by Kenan's court. According to primary sources, including the
influential opinion of Babigian, some of the Armenians who were hanged
were innocent. There are two ways of understanding why: one is that Kenan's
overzealousness in sentencing Armenians to death was based on the biased
evidence of the local court-martial in spite of Babigian's appeals to delay the
executions; the other is that hanging only Muslims might have angered the
Muslim population, and hence, to defuse the tension, Armenians also had to
be sent to the gallows.

The government's commitment to seeking justice in Adana is questionable. The chaotic situation in the capital, the instability in the provinces, and the uncertainty of the CUP's future were all factors that impeded the course of justice in the Adana massacres. However, due to local and international pressure, some sort of legal recourse had to be taken—although it would be dubious to assert that the legal procedure ultimately pursued by the central and the local authorities was the best one possible. How were the trials conducted? What types of crimes were perpetrated during the massacres? What was the legal basis for trying the convicts? The next chapter discusses these questions and assesses the legal measures taken to try the convicts.

CHAPTER 8

THE FORM OF JUSTICE

The Courts-Martial and the Imperial Ottoman Penal Code

EVEN THOUGH THOUSANDS PARTICIPATED IN THE MASSACRES
and looting in Adana, the courts-martial were able to convict only a few hundred people. Those convicted were tried according to the Imperial Ottoman
Penal Code (*Cezâ Kânûnnâme-yi Hümâyunu*), or the IOPC. This chapter
provides a more detailed analysis of the workings of the courts and assesses
whether justice was carried out. It examines the legal system and the types
of crimes that were committed. Furthermore, it discusses the sentencing of
the important figures complicit in the Adana massacres and the various reactions of the Armenians and Muslims to the verdicts of the courts-martial.
The chapter demonstrates that, as with other massacres and genocides in
the course of history, justice in Adana was achieved nominally.[1] Beset by
maladministration, bias, extrajudicial interference, and political consider-
ations, the courts-martial sent from İstanbul nonetheless did pass sentences
and executed more than thirty Muslims as well as six Armenians. Hundreds
received sentences ranging from three years to life in prison. It was important
for the CUP regime to demonstrate its adherence to law and legality even if
it meant executing its own coreligionists. This distinguished the CUP from
the Hamidian regime; while the latter was reluctant and defensive about ac-
knowledging the massacres perpetrated against the Armenians of the eastern
provinces, the former was willing to institute some sort of justice. In the
postrevolutionary period, institutions and sources of justice were essential in

establishing the legitimacy of the new regime and in renouncing any connection with the ancien régime. In addition, in this new era consecrated by the mottos of justice, freedom, liberty, and brotherhood, the CUP felt accountable to the international community and thus needed to demonstrate that it adhered to the rule of law. However, while the CUP felt comfortable in executing uninfluential Muslim people, some of whom were even innocent, it was reluctant to pass harsh sentences on the real culprits of the massacres despite the abundant circumstantial evidence against them. In addition, the CUP used imperial pardoning as a tool to contain the pressure from the Muslim population of Adana. Eventually, most of the convicts were released during World War I to serve in the army.

With the appointment of Cemal Paşa as the new vali of Adana, a new phase began. Public order was restored, and an attempt was made at reconciliation between the parties. Through his strong persona, Cemal improved the situation in Adana by managing the humanitarian work and building houses for the Armenian refugees. However, although he accused the local government of ineptness, he nevertheless blamed Armenians for instigating the massacres.[2]

The Imperial Ottoman Penal Code

Since the courts-martial sent to Adana used the IOPC in delivering its sentences, it is important here to briefly discuss the evolution of the IOPC. The code was first promulgated in 1840 as part and parcel of the Tanzimat Reforms.[3] In 1851, Ottoman legal reformers promulgated the New Penal Code (*Kânûn-ı Cedîd*). In 1858, with the efforts of Sultan Abdülmecid and Mustafa Reşid Paşa, the 1851 penal code was replaced with the IOPC.[4] Although parts of the IOPC included adaptations of the 1810 French Criminal Code, it was not based purely on Western norms, as it was heavily infused with Islamic principles. The aim of the code was to centralize, reform, and rationalize the Ottoman judicial system.[5] After 1858, the IOPC went through a continuous process of revision. It was republished with amendments in 1863 and duly appeared in the *Düstur* (The Ottoman Code of Public Laws) in 1873.[6] In June 1911, the Ottoman Parliament modified the IOPC.[7]

By 1911, the IOPC was divided into four chapters.[8] The preliminary chapter consisted of 47 articles detailing legal procedures, punishments, and guidelines for determining criminal culpability.[9] Chapter 1, consisting of 121 articles, dealt with crimes against the security of the empire that carried the death sentence. Other offences dealt with in this chapter included bribery, abuse of office, and negligence of duty.[10] Chapter 2, of particular interest here, contained 86 articles concerned with crimes such as homicide, bodily injury, threats, abortion, rape, kidnapping, theft, and the destruction of property.[11] These crimes were punishable by incarceration, fines, or death, depending on the severity of the crime. The final chapter of the IOPC dealt with minor offences.[12]

The Sentences of the Courts-Martial

According to a list from December 23, 1910, a total of 347 people were convicted by the first, second, and third courts-martial, the majority of whom were Muslims.[13] The sentences were based on the type of crime and ranged from fifteen days to life imprisonment or from temporary exile to total banishment, in addition to death sentences. The first court-martial, which also delivered all the death sentences, sentenced 273 men. The second court-martial sentenced 26, and the third court-martial sentenced 50. Of the 347 convicted, 322 were Muslims and 25 were Christians. Of the 25 Christians, 23 were Armenians, 6 of whom received death sentences and were hanged on June 10, 1909. Of the 322 Muslims, 41 received death sentences by hanging. The first 9 were hanged on June 10; 28 more were hanged in the period from August 3 to December 11, 1909, and 4 escaped.[14]

Capital punishment of both Muslims and Christians was carried out by hanging (*salb*) in the open air where people could watch.[15] Hence, the public sphere was used to demonstrate the legitimacy of the new regime to the people. Prior to the act of hanging, the order of the sultan and a verse from the Quran surah al-Baqarah was read: "And there is for you in legal retribution [saving of] life, O you [people] of understanding, that you may become righteous."[16] The process took place either at night or in the early morning. Before being taken to the location of execution, permission was given to the person for ablution and praying, and an imam even preached to him. Dressed in white and with hands tied behind his back, the convict stood on a stool and a noose was put around his neck. Depending on the religion of the person, it was prohibited to execute during certain holidays.

After the body had been displayed for a time, it was handed to the family of the executed. The offense and the penalty were written in large letters on a sheet and hung on the body. Announcements were made about those who were executed.

Of the 281 Muslims who received noncapital sentences, 137 received imperial pardoning. This means that only 144 continued their sentences. Most of those who were pardoned had been accused of murder, assistance or involvement in murder, looting, or involvement in the massacres of Misis and Abdioğlu;[17] the terms of these sentences ranged from three to fifteen years.

Armenians found the manner in which the courts-martial were conducted to be unsatisfactory. After the massacres, Simon Zavarian visited Adana in order to assess the situation. He sent a series of letters to the Responsible Body in İstanbul. One of these letters, sent from Bahçe, dealt with the workings of the courts-martial inquiry commissions in different places in the province.[18] Zavarian found many procedural errors. He argued that the investigations were done in centers of towns and villages, which prevented 90 percent of the people who lived in the surrounding areas from going to the investigation commission to complain, as they were afraid to travel for half a day or more. He contended that the investigation commission should not only investigate the reported cases but rather should seek out "all [the] barbarism that has been done." He argued that the investigation commissions should deal with the thousands of cases of Armenian and Syriac harvesters in the same manner as those of the locals. He suggested that Christians should also participate in the investigation commission, even as secretaries, advisors, and lawyers; otherwise, they would accuse the military of bias. Zavarian reported that 90 percent of the Armenians did not have houses and that all their possessions had been looted. In some places, stolen cattle were returned upon the orders of the military, but the same could not be said about household items. He highlighted an important point, namely that the lootings were not the result of fanaticism but of the pursuit of financial gain. Thus, he suggested that the investigation of the killings and lootings should be combined and that the size of the investigation should be increased with the addition of Christian experts. He also asserted that it was important to punish the *aşiret*s (tribes) who, even after sedentarization, followed the orders of their leaders in the process of massacres. He complained that the criminal officials from Tarsus to Adana, Mersin, Hamidiye, Osmaniye, Dörtyol, and even Kars and Hassa were still in their positions—a fact that did not correspond to justice. He suggested that the weapons that were distributed to the reserve soldiers (*redifs*) and others during the massacres should be retrieved. He said that the most able-bodied Armenians had been massacred; Haçin alone lost three thousand to four thousand Armenian men, while the total number of workers killed was fifteen thousand. Hence, fifteen thousand Armenian families were deprived of income. He therefore proposed that these families be supported financially for a period of ten years by the government or be compensated. He recommended that orphanages and industrial schools be established in Haçin and Hasanbeyli and that the rest of the orphans be transferred to Bahçecik (Bardizag) and Adapazarı in İstanbul. Finally, he urged that priests be sent from Armash and Jerusalem to Adana, as the local priests had been killed.

Overall, 25 percent of the Armenians convicted received the death sentence and were hanged, whereas 11 percent of the Muslims convicted were hanged; 20 percent of the Armenians received pardoning as opposed to 42.5 percent of the Muslims. Furthermore, five Armenians were sentenced to life in prison.[19] Armenians were extremely angry about these decisions and protested the injustice, proclaiming the innocence of the six Armenians who were executed.[20] Articles and booklets were written denouncing the decisions of the courts. *Kasap* (butcher) Missak, one of the Armenians who was hanged, became a symbol of this injustice for Armenians, some of whom even represented him as the Armenian Dreyfus.[21] Armenian sources indicated that some of the Turkish peasants who were hanged were also innocent. The real culprits of the Adana massacre thus appear to have escaped justice.

Types of Perpetrated Crimes

In order to better understand the ways in which these sentences worked, it is worthwhile to examine a few cases. During the massacres, Cin Ahmed, the son of Muhtar İbrahim of Ayas, was found guilty by the first court-martial of killing six Armenians during the second week of April and was sentenced to death according to articles 56 and 170 of the IOPC.[22] He was hanged on August 3, 1909.[23] Article 56 reads:

Whosoever dares, by making the people of the Ottoman dominions arm themselves against each other, to instigate or incite them to engage in mutual slaughter, or to bring about acts of raping, pillage, devastation of country or homicide in diverse places is, if the matter of disorder comes into effect entirely or if a commencement of the matter of the disorder has been made, likewise put to death.[24]

Berber (barber) Yusuf, son of Osman, was sentenced according to article 180 to fifteen years in prison for killing and extortion. Article 180 reads:

If in a killing taken place during a quarrel, or in an injury to a member, or in a death from the effects of wounding, or in the perpetration of the acts of beating or wounding, several persons have participated and it has not been determined who the [actual] perpetrator is, the punishment prescribed by law for the act with respect to each one of such persons is awarded by being reduced from one-third to one-half; and in acts rendering necessary the punishments of death or *kyurek* [labor] in perpetuity, the punishment of *kyurek* for not less than ten years is prescribed.[25]

The previous head of the municipality of Ayas, Ahmed Bican Mikdadzâde, son of Osman, was sentenced to ten years in prison for killing and extortion based on article 175 of the IOPC. Article 175 reads: "The person who is an auxiliary to a killer is put in *kyurek* temporarily."[26]

On August 5, the Ministry of the Interior notified the province of Adana that an Armenian by the name of Rupen, son of Haço and grandson of Garabed, from the Tepebağ neighborhood, who on the first Wednesday and the second Thursday of April was involved in the murder of fifty Muslims in Tarsus and was at large, had been sentenced according to article 57 of the IOPC to fifteen years in prison with hard labor.[27] Article 57 reads:

If a gang of ruffians jointly carry out or attempt to carry out any of the riotous acts set forth in the above written Arts. 55 and 56, those from among the persons included in such [a] band of ruffians who are the actual chief ruffians or the agitators of disturbance are put to death wherever they are caught; and such from among the others who are taken and seized at the place of the *jinayet* [crime] are placed in *kyurek* perpetually or temporarily according to the degree of their *jinayet* or complicity in the matter of the disorder which may become manifest.[28]

During the massacres of Adana there were numerous cases of rape. Most of those who violated minors, girls, or women were sentenced to three years in prison with hard labor. For example, an Armenian woman named Takuhi, who had come to Adana on Friday, April 17, fearing for her life, was raped by a Muslim man named Halil, son of İbrahim. Based on IOPC article 198, the latter was sentenced to three years of hard labor,[29] yet he was pardoned on August 3, 1910.[30] In another case, a Cretan Muslim refugee, who during the massacres of Abdioğlu on the third Friday of April had abducted and raped a thirteen-year-old Armenian girl by the name of Lusaper, was sentenced to three years of hard labor according to articles 198 and 200 of the IOPC and was ordered to pay her ten GL as compensation for loss of virginity (*zımân-ı bikr olarak*).[31] Article 198 reads: "If a man does the abominable act to a person, that is to say violates her honour by force, he is placed in *kyurek* temporarily."[32] Article 200 reads: "If such abominable act by force takes place with regard to a girl who has not yet been married to a man, the person who has dared to do this further becomes liable to pay compensation in addition to such punishment of *kyurek*."[33] In another case, Kerim Mustafa from the Sondeyi (Sokdeği) neighborhood of Adana raped the daughter of the Armenian Kiragos and the wife of Oskanian from the Yenimahalle neighborhood and also took the virginity of Oskanian's daughter Baydzar. He was similarly sentenced under article 198.[34] Another case included multiple men convicted of raping Aygül, the daughter of Gayane,[35] and a case involving *Çoban* (shepherd) Ali, son of Muhammad, from a village in Adıyaman, who was convicted of raping of Makide, the daughter of an Armenian Catholic.[36]

The Sentencing of Important Figures

Asaf Bey, who had been exonerated by the Erzin court-martial in Cebel-i Bereket, was convicted by the court-martial under the presidency of İsmail Fazıl Paşa. On August 3, the minister of war, Salih Hulusi, wrote to the grand vizier asking for clarification regarding this case and inquiring how a decision by one court-martial could overrule the decision of another.[37] On

November 29, the grand vizierate informed the Ministry of War that it sided with the decision that was taken by the Adana court-martial presided over by İsmail Fazıl Paşa. It argued that when Asaf Bey was found innocent by the Erzin court-martial, his correspondence of April 17 had not been used in the verdict; given this correspondence, which agitated the local population and gave orders for the distribution of weapons, the sentencing of the Adana court-martial made sense.[38] On January 26, 1910, Asaf Bey was tried again by the second court-martial and found guilty of agitating the population; he was expelled from his position for four years and barred from assuming any administrative positions.[39] Thus, Asaf Bey, who was tried and condemned twice, was in effect allowed to go free.

Abdülkadir Bağdadizade, who played a central role in inciting and leading the Muslim population against the Armenians and who had planned the attacks on the Armenian bazaars and the quarter, also essentially escaped punishment. On October 4, Senior Colonel Mehmed Ali, commander of the Composite Forces, sent a telegram to the Ministry of War reporting that the court-martial had found Abdülkadir Bağdadizade innocent, but that due to Bağdadizade's potentially dangerous influence, he was sentenced to banishment for two years in Hijaz. However, Bağdadizade was later pardoned and, after having been found in İstanbul, received permission to return to his hometown of Adana.[40]

Cevad Bey, the former vali of Adana, was debarred from service in any official position for a period of six to seven years. Woods comments on this:

> Whether the lenient treatment which was meted out to this official was due (as it as rumored to have been) to the threat of Cevad Bey, that if he were punished by the Central Government he would produce documents which would compromise officials holding positions in the employment of the state, [has] long remained a mystery.[41]

Mustafa Remzi Paşa, the commander of Adana who had failed to take any measures to suppress the disturbances in Adana, was sentenced to three months of detention in Mersin.

On June 11, 1909, by an order from the Ministry of the Interior, the İtidal newspaper was shut down.[42] On October 10, the grand vizier informed the Ministry of the Interior that with the sublime will of the sultan, the court-martial had passed sentence on İhsan Fikri to be banished for two years outside Adana. However, Fikri escaped after being banished to Ankara;[43] wanting to go to Beirut, he claimed that due to illness he had to stay near a coastal town, as he was unable to deal with the cold weather of Konya.[44] He was later found roaming in Egypt. His colleague İsmail Sefa was sentenced to one month in prison for publishing an article in *İtidal* on April 20 with the title "Müthiş bir İsyân" (A terrible uprising).[45]

The former mufti of Bahçe, İsmail Efendi, and his brother Yusuf Efendi played important roles in the massacres of Bahçe, as was attested by the investigation commissions. On July 10, after an inquiry by the Ministry of the Interior, the vali of Adana, Mustafa Zihni Paşa, informed the ministry that İsmail and Yusuf had been arrested and handed over to the court-martial.[46] The newspaper *Tanin* covered this case in detail and argued that the measures taken by the government were finally satisfactory.[47] İsmail was among a group of twenty-five Muslims hanged in December 1909.

Garabed Gökderelian was found guilty by the Erzin court-martial of agitation and sentenced to permanent exile in Benghazi. His sentence was later reduced to three years in Rodosto.[48] According to Terzian, Gökderelian was able to save himself due to his writing ability and eloquence of speech.

The first court-martial of Adana found Bishop Seropian guilty of aspiring to separate a section of the country and creating unrest among the two elements, and based on article 57 of the IOPC, decided to arrest and try him.[49] The court-martial demanded that he appear for his sentencing; upon failing to do so, the court-martial sentenced him to capital punishment in absentia according to articles 56 and 66 of the IOPC. On November 17, 1909, Seropian sent a letter to the Council of Ministers in which he asked for justice and exoneration.[50] He said that for four years he had been seeking the economic, moral, and educational advancement of his people and he did not deserve the sentence that was given to him. He said that he wanted justice not for the sake of personal gain. He did not want to be another Dreyfus. He raised a few important points: that he was tried in absentia, that the government did not pay attention to his complaints prior to the massacres, and that the interrogators extracted false statements through the imprisonment and torture of Armenian witnesses. One of these witnesses was Artin Arslanian from Aintab, who after arriving to Alexandria by boat and obtaining a guarantee of his safety, sent a detailed letter to Adana on August 5 recounting how his statement was given under threats and harassment. Seropian argued that the testimonies gathered against him were not valid.[51] Toward the end of his letter, Seropian requested that he be tried again because of the illegal sentence that he had received.

Reactions to the Verdicts

Many Muslims wrote letters of complaint about the verdicts. For instance, on September 21, prisoners İbrahim Efendizade Hamza and İsmail Kibarzade from Adana sent a telegram to the grand vizier, complaining that they were living in a miserable prison due to baseless accusations and that "Armenian compatriots [had] drenched Anatolia with blood." They said that the Adana tragedy was unleashed by a few Armenian revolutionaries and that by not punishing them, the government "was transgressing the rights of the Muslims." They wrote that there were poor people in prison who after three months were not aware of the reasons as to why they were there, and that, if the constitutional government did not release the peasants from prison in time for the harvest, thousands of Muslims would remain hungry and destitute.[52] Another telegram sent by Hamza, along with fifteen of his friends, to the Ministry of War argued that, while the Muslims of Adana were preoccupied with agriculture and did not have any seditious ideas, the Armenians, who caused the tragedy, blamed the Muslims. He accused the investigation commissions and courts of bias.[53]

The court-martial's lenient treatment of the main figures responsible for the Adana massacres caused a great deal of discontent among the Armenians in Adana. On August 20, the heads of the Christian denominations sent a report to the patriarchates at İstanbul arguing that the court had striven to hide the criminal events and was attempting to exonerate former vali Cevad Bey and Commander Mustafa Remzi Paşa. The report expressed anger at the sentences received by these two men, which consisted merely of banning them from government positions for a few years, and went so far as to hold them responsible for the expansion of the criminal movement to other parts of the province. They accused Cevad Bey and Mustafa Remzi of both instigating and ending the massacres. The report stated that while the court-martial indulged those who were guilty, it acted with violence and contempt toward the victims. It described the mistreatment of the Christian eyewitnesses and said that by basing its judgments on the reports of the initial commission of inquiry and the false evidence given by spies, the court-martial had rendered itself incapable of establishing justice. The report said that although the innocence of the Armenians was clear and affirmed by the central government, they remain accused. It argued that the court-martial neglected to conduct a thorough examination due to the fear that the truth would come out. The letter concluded by demanding justice in the name of the salvation of the fatherland.[54] As a sign of protest, the Armenian patriarch later resigned his post, declaring that he would only return when justice was completely executed. The Catholicos of Sis also resigned from his post.

. On November 25, the Christian religious leaders of Adana sent a protest letter to the Ottoman Parliament.[55] The letter said that the massacres were against the constitutional regime and argued that the idea of a Christian revolt was entirely fallacious. It expressed the hope that the "deputies of the nation will . . . establish the real motives for the Adana massacres." The letter provided the following observations pertaining to this question:

Local authorities coordinated with the Muslim notables.

Enemies of the people dispatched telegrams about Armenians to the central government.

The events of İstanbul (i.e., the counterrevolution) and Adana were connected.

Authorities were in favor of the pillagers and the general massacres.

The events must have been organized, since they began at the same time in different places.

The second round of massacres was mostly committed by soldiers.

Local authorities did nothing to recover stolen goods.

The court-martial showed itself to be incapable and unjust by not punishing the culprits.

Functionaries who protected Christians have been dismissed.

Nothing of this sort could happen in Adana without the support of a higher authority.

The letter asserted that the courts-martial formed in Adana were imperfect and incapable; these courts busied themselves with ordinary assassins without focusing on the principal fomenters of the events and lightly punished or acquitted the real culprits. It said that this outcome would only encourage the Muslims' audacity, to the detriment of the despairing Christian population; the only way to make the Christians forget the consequences of this grievous event was through the broad application of justice and mercy. The letter argued that justice in Adana would have a beneficial effect on the whole of the empire, while allowing injustice to stand would serve to corrupt and ruin the future of all Ottomans. It raised other points, such as compensating the victims, providing aid, and creating a law that would condemn to death those who failed in their duties and would suppress Cevad Bey. In conclusion, the letter thanked the chamber for the financial assistance it had already given and asked for additional amounts for the reconstruction of churches and schools.

As previously discussed, the Armenian patriarch of İstanbul also resigned in protest over the light sentences given to the key culprits of the massacres. In the same letter to the Armenian Catholicos, Archbishop Madteos II Izmirlian, in which he described his reaction to these sentences, the patriarch indicated that the Central National Administration had expressed satisfaction with the current vali of Adana (Cemal Bey).[56]

Pardoning and Reducing of Sentences

In many cases, death sentences were changed to lifetime hard labor sentences.[57] This could have been in the interest of preventing disturbances, since the death sentences of about twenty-five Muslims had resulted in agitations among the Muslim populations.[58] Ali Münif Bey, the deputy of Adana, mentions in his memoir how the decision to hang thirty-six Muslims agitated the Muslim population of Adana. He recounts how he attempted to prevent the implementation of these sentences.[59] He claims that Grand Vizier Hüseyin Hilmi Paşa had personally assured him that the thirty-six men would not be hanged and that the decision to go ahead with the executions left him in shock. He expresses his feelings of disappointment with the grand vizier, even describing how his eyes were swollen from crying all night. In response to the executions, Ali Münif Bey claims that he proposed the resignation of the government, causing Hilmi Paşa to resign one day later.[60]

On January 8, 1910, the minister of war informed the grand vizier that due to the Muslim holiday, the sultan had ordered the court-martial to change the sentences of ten Muslims from death to life in prison.[61] By the time of the enthronement holiday (*cülûs-u hümâyun*) of the sultan in 1910, many more Muslims as well as Armenians had received full pardons; most of these people received three-year sentences.[62] On April 28, 1910, the vali of Adana wrote to the Ministry of the Interior reporting that those who were convicted by the court-martial of Erzin would be released on the occasion of the imperial enthronement.[63]

On November 24, 1909, the grand vizierate notified the Ministry of War that Samuel Avedissian, a member of the appeals court who had been sentenced to three years of hard labor by the local court-martial, had been pardoned by the sultan.[64] On April 25, 1910, the grand vizier wrote to the Ministry of the Interior about the further pardoning of Muslim and Armenian prisoners who were involved in the Adana incident. According to him this would lighten the mood and help repair the situation in Adana.[65] On May 23, 1911, the grand vizierate submitted a list of those who would receive imperial pardon by the decision of the Council of Ministers.[66] On May 7, 1912, the minister of war wrote to the Ministry of the Interior saying that on account of the imperial enthronement, sentences by the courts-martial of ten years or more had been reduced.[67]

Cemal Bey

On August 4, 1909, the minister of the interior called the vali of Adana, Zihni Paşa, to İstanbul to question him about the situation in Adana and replaced him by imperial order with Ahmed Cemal Bey, the mutasarrıf of Üsküdar.[68] Upon arriving in Mersin, Cemal was received by the authorities but not by the Muslim notables of Adana, despite it being their custom to greet a newly arriving vali.[69] The French vice-consul in Mersin wondered if this demonstrated the irritation of the Muslims of Adana at recent declarations made in İstanbul in favor of the Armenians or if it was simply a consequence of the new liberal regime, which made it more difficult to foment intrigues by capturing the confidence of an incoming vali. In either case, he reported that Cemal Bey made a strong impression on the general population and expressed the hope that Cemal would succeed in bringing calm and appeasement to this region, where Christians and Muslims needed to work together to develop trade to its full potential.[70]

Upon arrival in Adana, Cemal Bey's first project was to remove the camps of Armenians that had been set up after the events, which presented a striking sight upon entering the city.[71] He managed to do so by sheltering the refugees in houses repaired with relief funds while waiting for the construction of new neighborhoods. Cemal also went to Tarsus for the same purpose. He ordered the kaymakam to rent houses for a few months to shelter people—although he met resistance there from owners who, according to custom, preferred to make contracts for the entire year.

On August 24, Cemal Bey sent a ciphered telegram to the Sublime Porte with an update on the situation. Upon his arrival in Adana he united the Aid Distribution Commission and the International Relief Committee and added a few people to the mixed commission. He took the necessary measures to rebuild the burned houses in the environs and in the villages and formed building commissions in each subdistrict, as well as commissions for reemployment and for hospitals.[72] The tasks of these commissions were duly performed. During this period, 550 Armenian refugees who had escaped to Cyprus during the massacres returned to Adana.[73]

Cemal Bey's other principal aim was to repair relations between the Armenians and the Muslims. He gathered about 250–300 people in the club of the CUP and for two hours explained to them the condition and problems of the government. Cemal also explained to them the government's statement regarding the Adana events. Many said that they had not understood the statement at first but now did and would write letters of thanks to the government. That evening Cemal also spoke at length with the Armenian religious leaders. On August 28, the Ministry of the Interior informed the grand vizier about the measures being taken by Cemal.[74] He concluded his telegram by stating: "Day in day out, opinions are being calmed down."[75]

On October 30, Cemal sent a telegram to the Ministry of the Interior discussing in detail his work in Adana, including construction, job creation, and the sedentarization of tribes. He also elaborated on the expenses for these projects and the projected government aid required.[76] In his memoirs published in 1922, Cemal boasts about his achievements in Adana:

Thanks to the steps I took, four months after my arrival all the Armenian houses in the vilayet had been rebuilt and in the provisional capital there was not a single small family house which had not been finished. In brief, within five or six months the Armenians had freely resumed their trade, agriculture, and industry, and between Turks and Armenians there was no trace, at any rate superficially, of the previous hatreds.[77]

Cemal also recounted how Armenians as well as Europeans had recognized and congratulated him on his efforts to restore the property of Armenians.[78]

During this period, telegrams were sent to the government with the aim of restarting the animosities among the different elements of the population and discrediting the court-martial. Cemal asked the police to investigate who was behind the telegrams, as a result of which he was threatened by a petition signed by two hundred people. Recognizing that the aim of such machinations was to make the investigations and prosecutions unproductive, he further deepened the investigation. He discovered that the letter was written by İsmail Sefa, who had been sentenced to one month in prison by the court-martial for publishing harmful articles in the *İtidal* newspaper. Cemal Bey submitted the investigation papers to the court-martial. He also decided to send İhsan Fikri, Bağdadizade, and İsmail Sefa to İstanbul, where Sefa awaited trial. He argued that their presence inside the province was causing much harm.[79]

Cemal's most important project was to build an orphanage for the Armenian orphans. The construction of the Ottoman Orphanage (Dârü'l-Eytâm-ı Osmânî) was completed in 1911. Maksudyan asserts that during the early period of his appointment, Cemal was praised by the European inhabitants of the city as "admirably gifted, a man of will, with intelligence and activity."[80] Armenians, however, were not happy with the fact that no religion and only Turkish would be taught in the Ottoman Orphanage. Cemal's attempts to implement his own version of Ottomanism in the orphanage were perceived by Armenians as deliberate attempts at the Turkification of the Armenian orphans.[81] These conditions were unacceptable to the Armenian authorities.[82] The Armenian literary figure Zabel Yesayan argued on numerous occasions with Cemal on his policy. It is regrettable that this is the same Cemal who just six year later would become one of the architects of the Armenian Genocide.

Conclusion

Although cases of lone wolves exist in the course of history, massacres are generally perpetrated by multiple actors within a society, ranging from workers, peasants, and ruffians to local and/or central government officials. In these cases, addressing the motives and the perpetration of massacres on the individual level is difficult. This chapter has supplied examples from the trials and the verdicts that were given by the courts-martial. While most of those convicted were punished in accordance with the IOPC based on the types of crimes they were shown to have committed, the real instigators and other figures responsible for the massacres (whether through complicity, ineptness, or negligence) received very light sentences. While hundreds of Muslims were punished for physical crimes with sentences ranging from death to a few months in prison, the people who fomented an atmosphere of agitation and violent discourse, and were thus truly responsible for the massacres, received the lightest sentences. One wonders why the Young Turks had such a lenient approach to these key figures. Woods attempts to answer this question, arguing that it is possible to draw two conclusions from the attitude of the Young Turks toward the massacres: either that the central government at İstanbul was itself complicit in the massacre or that it was afraid of the potential local and general repercussions of punishing these men in an adequate way.[83] While refuting the former reason, Woods accepts the latter conclusion. He also rightly contends that, although certain important Turks were unfairly exonerated by the courts-martial in Adana, it must not be forgotten that many Muslims were hanged for murdering Christians. Some of them belonged to the wealthy class of the population, while others were religious leaders or men who held high political positions in their respective communities.

However, most of those who were punished were simple people who were driven by the emotions of hate, fear, anger, and resentment, as well as by financial gain. The crucial question the courts had to answer was, Who were the key figures that directly or indirectly played essential roles in inciting the population to perpetrate these heinous crimes? At the end of the day, massacres are not random events: they are a rational type of behavior carried out by individual architects and actors. Given the gravity of these crimes and

their consequences, the main culprits should have received harsher punishments according to the IOPC in order to send the clear message that fomenting and inciting violence would not be tolerated. However, in general,
no such verdicts were given. The most significant culprits escaped justice.
The impunity with which these men were allowed to act reverberated in the
years to come. The failure to punish the true perpetrators of the massacres
emboldened the inner clique of the CUP to commit a larger crime against
the Armenians during World War I: the Armenian Genocide.

CONCLUSION

IN THE SUMMER OF 1909, ZABEL YESAYAN, THE PROMINENT
Armenian novelist and activist from İstanbul, traveled with an Armenian
delegation to the region of Adana to aid in the relief efforts for the Armenian survivors. Upon arriving, she painted a vivid image of the scene:

> The destroyed city spreads under the magnanimous and dazzling sun like an
> endless cemetery. Ruins all over. Nothing has been spared. All the churches,
> all the schools, and all the houses have been turned into piles of shapeless and
> scorched heaps of stone, through which the skeletons of buildings are erected
> here and there. From the east to the west and from the north to the south,
> until the farthest borders of the Turkish neighborhoods the unforgivable and
> cruel hatred have burnt down and destroyed everything. And through this
> deadly solitude, through the vast heaps of ashes stand up two imperishable
> minarets with audacity.[1]

Yesayan's literary description of the human and material suffering of the city,
published two years later under the title *Awéraknerun Méj* (*In the Ruins*), is
a testimony of the Adana massacres of 1909.[2] Like many of her contempo-
raries, Yesayan was shocked by the horrors she saw in Adana. In an era in
which the Armenians of the empire thought that they had been relieved of
the shackles of Hamidian despotism, the Adana massacres came to prove
otherwise. Armenians were unable to comprehend the catastrophe and its

magnitude. Their dream of living in harmony with their Turkish brothers after the revolution was shattered. After the courts-martial failed to the deliver justice to the victims of the massacres, their trust in the Young Turk regime diminished, as many believed that the CUP was involved in the massacres.

The ARF was the only Armenian political party that continued its cooperation with the Young Turks. Immediately after the massacres, negotiations began between the ARF and the CUP that resulted in an agreement of cooperation on August 3, 1909. The terms of the accord included defending the constitution, countering reactionary movements, dispelling the false statement that the Armenians were seeking independence, and extending provincial rights.[3] This cooperation was conditional on the government taking the necessary actions on vital issues arising from the Adana massacres. Thus, despite all criticisms, the ARF decided to make a final attempt to cooperate with the CUP for the sake of preserving the constitution and pursuing land restitution and reform, the two bastions of its policy with the Young Turks. Although according to one historian "one cannot rule out a degree of self-interest in the decision [to cooperate with the CUP],"[4] the Dashnaks always adhered to their primary goal of land restitution and reform in the eastern provinces.[5] However, the reluctance of the CUP to pursue these goals would be a crippling blow to ARF-CUP cooperation in the years to come.[6]

The Balkan Wars of 1912–13 created an opportunity for the revival of the Armenian Question. Armenian leadership, aided by European powers, pressed the Ottoman government to improve the condition of the Armenians in the eastern provinces. Known as the Armenian Reforms, this international initiative is considered one of the last attempts by Armenians, Europeans, and the Ottoman government to find a "solution" to the Armenian Question.[7] The European interest in reforming the provinces should also be seen as part of the competition between the European powers (Italy, Britain, and France) and Russia on the one hand and Germany on the other. The Armenian Reforms were prepared in İstanbul by André Mandelstam (the dragoman of the Russian embassy) and the representatives of the Armenian National Assembly at a meeting that also included the ambassadors of France, Britain, and Italy. However, the reform project, signed in February 1914, was abolished by the Ottomans on December 16, 1914, after the

Ottoman Empire joined the war on the side of the Central Powers (Germany, Austria-Hungary, and initially, Italy) against the Triple Entente (Great Britain, France, and Russia).

The Armenian Genocide, which was perpetrated by the inner clique of the CUP during World War I, led to the extermination of the Armenians of the eastern provinces.[8] I do not adhere to the continuum approach in interpreting the Armenian Genocide—which argues that the previous phases of violence culminated in genocide—but one thing seems undeniable: the level of ethno-religious tensions in the empire was so high by the beginning of the twentieth century that any crisis, whether due to internal or external factors, had the potential to explode in a cataclysmic spiral of violence.[9] Unlike the counterrevolution of 1909, the crisis of World War I unleashed a series of massacres on the Armenians that spread throughout the empire.

On the eve of World War I in July 1914, 80,000 Armenians lived in the province of Adana according to one estimate; the city of Adana had a population of 26,000 Armenians.[10] In 1915–16, Talat Paşa, the chief architect of the Armenian Genocide, entered the remaining Armenian population of the province of Adana in his notebook at 12,263 out of what had been 51,723 in 1914 according to his estimates.[11] Prior to the war, the political situation in Adana was tense. The Young Turk leader İsmail Sefa (Özler) had begun to advocate for the elimination of the capitulations and the nationalization of the economy, leading to bitterness on the part of the Armenian and Greek entrepreneurial middle classes.[12] As in other provinces, the authorities began arresting Armenian leaders and professionals. On May 20, 1915, deportations of Armenians from Adana began; the first convoy consisted of four thousand Armenians. Talat Paşa sent Ali Münif Bey—the Adana MP and his second in command in the Ministry of the Interior, as well as a member of the Special Commission on Deportation—to the city to oversee the process of deporting Armenians from Adana, Tarsus, and Mersin. Consequently, the authorities arrested around one hundred Armenians, including Garabed Gökderelian and the lawyer Garabed Chalian, all of whom were deported to Aleppo. Muslim refugees (*muhâcir*s) were settled in the Armenians' places.[13] These details fail to appear in Münif's memoirs. From early September until late October of 1915, Münif supervised the deportation of five thousand Armenian families. The deportees were taken to concentration camps in İntilli and Katma, and then to the transit center at Karlık located near the Aleppo railroad station. The only Armenians who were allowed to remain in Adana were the craftsmen and specialists who "catered" to the needs of the Ottoman army. The Armenians of the port city of Mersin and of other districts and subdistricts of Adana met a similar fate.

After the Armistice of Mudros (October 30, 1918), which ended World War I, France occupied Cilicia. In December 1918, France sent four battalions of the Armenian Legion to take over and oversee the repatriation of more than 170,000 Armenians to Cilicia.[14] According to a statistic produced in 1919 by the Armenian Patriarchate Information Bureau (Teghekatu Divan), 47,075 Armenians—more than half of the original population—managed to return to the province of Adana.[15] However, the French occupation of Cilicia, which provided some hope for Armenians, was cut short by the incursion of Kemalist troops. While some Armenians resisted the Kemalist troops, thousands were massacred. The remaining Armenians retreated with the French forces. On October 21, 1921, France signed the Ankara Agreement with the Kemalists and relinquished Cilicia.[16] This was a shock to the Armenians. By January 1922 the region was completely under Kemalist control.[17]

Unlike the massacres of Adana in 1909, which were locally organized and implemented by various interest groups, the Armenian Genocide during World War I was centrally planned by the state through multiple mechanisms. The bureaucratic apparatus and the cooperation of local elites as well as paramilitary organizations proved to be crucial in coordinating and executing the genocide throughout the eastern provinces. During the genocide, the CUP was motivated by a grandiose detrimental ideology of solving once and for all the Armenian Question. Such an ideological motivation was not present among the perpetrators of the Adana massacres. On the contrary, in 1909 the CUP itself was more concerned with threats of its own existence as a result of the counterrevolution. It would not be an exaggeration to assert that the CUP's attitudes toward Armenians changed drastically in the subsequent five years.

In his memoirs written in Berlin and published posthumously, Talat Paşa accused the Armenians of inciting the Adana massacres in order to bring about foreign intervention with the goal of recreating the Armenian Kingdom of Cilicia. However, he added, "By saying this I do not want to exclude the participation of the Muslims in the massacres; my intention is to prove that these incitements and provocations were used by Armenians and Bulgarians for political purposes."[18] After the massacres, Talat Paşa became the minister of the interior. Despite accusing the Armenians, he stated that his desire and goal was to unite the various nationalities, especially Armenians and Turks, in a bond of friendship.[19] He claimed that, despite his political views, he still wanted justice to prevail:

> On this issue, as an unbiased government person forgetting my political goal, I wanted the perpetrators of the massacres, be they Muslims or Armenians, to be punished. I insisted that in these events the mufti who has incited people to massacre, as well as the other Muslims, be punished. As a result, the court sentenced the mufti and his partners to death. And I was the one who ensured the approval of the Ministerial Council's decision.[20]

This was the same Talat Paşa who, six years later, would become the main architect of the second genocide of the twentieth century.

The feeling of existential threat, heightened emotions, and suspicions regarding the intentions of the Armenians, as well as geostrategic calculations, became important factors in finding a final solution to the Armenian Question. Faced with external enemies as well as (imaginary) internal ones, the members of the inner clique of the CUP decided the fate of the Armenians through an orchestrated genocide. The architects of the Armenian Genocide were some of the same CUP members who had demonstrated sympathy to the Armenians in 1909. As argued in this book, given the appropriate conditions and political stresses, ordinary men can turn into brutal murderers.

Going beyond essentializations, this book has unpacked the factors that led to the massacres of Adana. These factors were rooted in both long-term and short-term developments. The former consisted of major transformations that took place in the province as a result of global economic changes, reforms, the sedentarization of nomadic tribes, migrations, and immigration in the nineteenth century. Adana's geographic location and its fertility for cotton production transformed it into a major economic hub that attracted Armenians from the surrounding provinces, migrant workers, and Muslim refugees. However, while modernization in the second half of the nineteenth century led to an acceleration in the pace of cotton production, it also caused severe anxiety among the workers who supported their families by itinerant labor in the fields. Uneven economic development in the region led to the growing resentment of the migrant workers—as well as of the Muslim lower and lower-middle classes—toward the Armenians, whom they saw as the chief beneficiaries of Adana's incorporation into the global economic system. The sedentarization of tribes in the region of Cilicia and the resettlement of Muslim refugees from Crimea and the Caucasus led to a dramatic rise in the competition over resources. The land question in Anatolia, which became the crux of the Armenian Question in the second half of the nineteenth century, also resonated in Adana. The expropriation of Armenian lands in Adana during the Hamidian period and their reallocation to Muslim refugees and roaming tribes became one of the most significant sources of ethno-religious tension in the region.

The short-term developments fall into three processes: The Young Turk Revolution of 1908, the emergence of opposing public spheres in the empire, and the counterrevolution of 1909. The revolution affected changes in the dynamics of power in the empire that had serious repercussions on political processes, which played out differently in each province based on local exigencies. In Adana, a power struggle developed between the ancien régime, represented by strong local notables, and the new order, represented by the weak elements of the Young Turks as well as locals who appropriated the CUP name and clubs for their own purposes. The result was predictable: remnants of the ancien régime, embodied by the governor and his allies, maintained control in Adana. However, during the counterrevolutionary crisis, both contesting groups turned against the Armenians.

Another important outcome of the revolution was the emergence of a strong public sphere and its subaltern counter-publics. The extensive activities in the postrevolutionary public sphere of Armenians and Armenian revolutionary parties—once considered seditious elements threatening to revolt in order to reestablish the Kingdom of Cilicia—alarmed the notables as well as the Young Turks of Adana. The inflated romanticism of the Armenians toward their historical past, expressed through poetry, theatrical presentations, and odes, combined with their frenzied purchasing of weapons for self-defense purposes, sent the wrong message. For the disgruntled elements in Adana, this provided the ultimate proof of the prophecy of an Armenian

Kingdom. Indeed, agents provocateurs presented the Armenians' behavior as an existential threat and succeeded in creating an atmosphere of "us versus them."

Analyzing the massacres through the themes of the public sphere, emotions, and rumors contributes to our understanding of the escalation of interethnic tensions and its culmination in the massacres. In the postrevolutionary public sphere, subaltern counter-publics invented and circulated counter-discourses that led to oppositional interpretations of their position in the new political milieu. These groups' increased activities after the revolution represented a change in the status quo. This led to the intensification of the dominant group's affective disposition toward the nondominant group, the Armenians. The emotional spectrum of fear, hatred, resentment, and rage became the lens through which they viewed the socioeconomic and political activities of the Armenians. In this world of affective disposition, rumors played a critical role in the solidification of the ethno-religious identity of the dominant group, giving it a sense of bonding and preparing the ground for a violent backlash against the perceived enemy. Thus, rumors elevated preexisting negative emotions and justified the brutality toward the Armenians.

The counterrevolution of 1909 reverberated strongly through Adana; the events in İstanbul and the massacres of Adana were not merely a coincidence. The cocktail of underlying socioeconomic and political anxieties at a crucial time in which thousands of migrant workers were present in Adana was a recipe for disaster. A few days before the massacres, an altercation between an Armenian and a few Muslims resulted in the death of two of the Muslims and became a precipitating event. During this tense period, rumors fueled the fires. In the period after the first wave of massacres, the public sphere became instrumental in the initiation of the second wave; the *İtidal* newspaper was allowed to publicly confirm the "prophecy" regarding the seditious plans of the Armenians to kill the Muslims of Adana and erect the Kingdom of Cilicia.

The twin massacres in Adana resulted in the deaths of more than twenty thousand Armenians and two thousand Muslims. The disproportionate number of deaths clearly suggest that the Armenians were victims, not instigators. The massacres also inflicted tremendous damage on Armenian properties; Armenian farms and their modern tools of production were burned and destroyed. Many of the villagers, tribes, and immigrants who took part in the massacres were motivated not by ideology but by the prospect of plunder, as well as by economic resentment toward the Armenians. For them, this was a unique opportunity for personal gain and satisfaction.

While today the Adana massacres do not appear in most books of Ottoman and Middle East studies, at the time they were covered internationally. From Omaha to New York and from Geneva to Cairo, the international press appealed for aid to alleviate the suffering of the Armenians. However, as with the Hamidian massacres, humanitarian intervention did not take place on behalf of the Armenians. This book argues that the Europeans did not intervene on behalf of the Armenians because doing so would have risked destabilizing the finely tuned international system. Thus, the Ottoman fear that the warships of the major powers, docked near the city port of Mersin, would deploy their forces to Adana—culminating in the so-called Armenian uprising and the recreation of the Kingdom of Cilicia—did not materialize. What actually transpired was the offering of selective humanitarian aid to alleviate the suffering of the Armenians. In this context, the international press played an important role in raising awareness about the condition of Armenians in Adana. It also acted as a medium to facilitate the fundraising efforts for the destitute of Adana. Most of these newspapers placed the responsibility for the massacres on Sultan Abdülhamid II and showed sympathy toward the plight of the Young Turks.

After the counterrevolution was quelled by the Action Army, the Young Turks took drastic measures to return to power. However, while they were successful in trying those responsible for the counterrevolution in İstanbul, they failed to charge the real culprits of the Adana massacres with serious crimes, contenting themselves with pursuing the "bullets" rather than those who "pulled the trigger." Most of the primary culprits of the Adana massacres received very light sentences, and many of them were later pardoned. It seems that the CUP preferred to execute Muslim peasants, even some who were innocent, than to prosecute influential figures and risk destabilizing the recently restored political balance. Were it not for the Armenian deputy Hagop Babigian's complaints and the appeals of the Armenian administration, these prominent figures would not even have received their light sentences. Despite the fact that the government to some extent adhered to legal standards in trying the culprits of the massacres, Armenians believed that justice was not carried out. The role of the Central Committee of the CUP in the massacres is questionable. Based on the documents consulted for this book, I have not found any strong proof implicating the Central Committee in the massacres. This might be one of the reasons that the Dashnaks continued their cooperation with the CUP. Nevertheless, members of the local CUP were clearly involved in the massacres in various ways.

What transpired in the provinces of Adana and Aleppo is not exceptional in the course of history. Many similar massacres have taken place in different societies and geographic regions in the twentieth century. Despite the fact that each and every act of violence of such magnitude is unique, they share common features in terms of triggers, agents provocateurs, participants, interest groups, the role of the military and the police, modes of perpetration, and the trying of culprits. The themes of the public sphere, emotions, and rumors are not unique to Adana; they also appear in other, similar phases of massacres in the modern period. For the sake of comparison, I have arbitrarily chosen two cases of massacres that took place in different time periods and geographic areas in the twentieth century: the Odessa pogroms of 1905 and the Sikh massacres of 1984. While many other massacres could be compared to those of Adana, my intention here is to demonstrate that massacres share common themes. This demonstrates the global parallelism in the structures of massacres and emphasizes the fact that violence is not inherent to a specific religion or culture. As demonstrated in this book, given particular circumstances and societal stressors, even ordinary men can become perpetrators.

Odessa, a port city on the Black Sea, was similar to Adana in possessing a multiethnic population, in this case composed of Greeks, Jews, Italians, Russians, and Ukrainians, among other communities.[21] In the period between October 18 and 22, 1905, ethnic Russians, Ukrainians, and Greeks killed over four hundred Jews and damaged or destroyed over 1,600 Jewish properties (although these official figures do not reflect the true numbers).[22] The 1905 pogrom of Odessa was the worst in a series of anti-Jewish pogroms in the city that also included pogroms in 1821, 1859, 1871, 1881, and 1900.[23] Although in the earlier phases these pogroms were perpetrated by Greeks, beginning in 1871 Russians also participated in them. Economic competition between the Jews and Greeks as well as religious friction played important roles in the pogroms. In the period after 1871, pogroms were often perpetrated with the tacit approval of the Tsarist authorities. Reminiscent of the spread of rumors prior to the massacres in Adana, every year during the Orthodox Holy Week, rumors of pogroms circulated among Jews of the city.[24] Other rumors, such as rumors about Jews vandalizing the Greek church, helped lead to the pogroms of 1871.

Like the Adana massacres, the 1905 Odessa pogroms resulted from a host of factors, including economic competition, the Russo-Japanese War (1904–5), the Russian Revolution of 1905, the October Manifesto, and anti-Semitism. A contributing factor in the growth of anti-Semitism was the economic advancement of Jews in the city. Their success in the trade of the city and their desire to hire only Jewish workers, coupled with the spread of rumors of Jewish plans to harm the Greeks, contributed to the escalation of tensions.[25] Similar to the Turks' suspicions regarding the influx of Armenians to Adana, Russians felt jealousy toward the dramatic growth of the Jewish population of Odessa and were convinced that the Jews were amassing great wealth and power in the city. However, as Robert Weinberg argues, Jews neither dominated Odessa's economy nor had control of its politics; the majority of the wealth in the city belonged to non-Jews.[26]

The relation between the Russians and Jews began to worsen as a result of the Russo-Japanese War (1904–5). When some Jews were reluctant to support the war with Japan, Russians immediately decried their lack of patriotism and their disloyalty. When the Jews realized the rising potential of a pogrom against them, in a manner similar to the Armenian self-defense movement, the National Committee of Jewish Self-Defense urged Jews to arm themselves in order to protect their property.[27] As in Adana, this was immediately interpreted as preparation for offensive action. The fears of pogroms were heightened when the Jews were blamed for instigating shootings and fires at the port of Odessa, where strikes, disorder, and the arrival of the mutinied *Potemkin* ship led to the death of more than one thousand people in June of 1905. A few days after this outbreak of violence, an anonymous anti-Semitic pamphlet titled *Odesskīe dni* (Odessan days) appeared—analogous to İhsan Fikri's *İtidal* issue no. 33—blaming the Jews and in particular the National Committee of Jewish Self-Defense for the recent disorder. It demanded that the members of the committee pay for the damages inflicted, that they be disarmed, and that their apartments be searched.[28] According to Weinberg, the appearance of the pamphlet "graphically illustrates how in times of social unrest and political uncertainty anti-Semitism could come to the fore."[29]

When Tsar Nicholas II issued the October Manifesto on October 17 of the same year, promising to create an elected assembly and award civil liberties, the population of Odessa was elated and began celebrating in the streets. Within this newly created public sphere, the Jews hoped that the manifesto would lead to greater freedom and civil liberties and a decrease in anti-Semitism. However, as with the reaction of the Adana notables to the constitution, the conservative elements in Odessa considered the manifesto to be a threat to their own interests, as well as to the autocracy and the Russian Empire itself. Peaceful celebrations of the October Manifesto on October 18 quickly turned violent when participants began chanting anti-regime propaganda and carrying red flags.[30] In the afternoon of the same day, armed confrontations between Russians and Jews took place near the Jewish district of Moldavanka.[31] Skirmishes took place between supporters and opponents of the October Manifesto. The latter directed their anger toward the Jews, claiming that they were the real root of Russia's troubles.[32] What began as a conflict between opposing political views soon turned into anti-Jewish violence. The same phenomenon transpired in Adana, when a power struggle between opposing factions (the notables and the CUP) was consolidated into anti-Armenian violence.

The pogroms against the Jews began on October 19 and ended on October 21. Loyal elements joined with right-wing organizations such as the Black Hundreds and began targeting Jews. Non-Jewish day laborers composed the majority of the crowd. Unskilled laborers, dockworkers, and vagrants joined the mobs in attacking Jewish property.[33] As in Adana, instead of protecting the Jews, the local police participated in the massacre.[34] Despite suffering hundreds of deaths, the Jewish self-defense forces defended some of the Jewish houses and neighborhoods. Jewish men, women, and children were brutally beaten, mutilated, and murdered. It was only on October 21, after much of the violence had ended, that the governor of Odessa, Dimitri Neidhardt, and the commander of Odessa's military garrison, A.V. Kaulbars, appeared on the streets, telling the rioters to return home. The relative inaction of both of these top figures drew criticism, leading to the resignation of Neidhardt.

In the aftermath of the pogroms an official government inquiry was established under the leadership of Senator Aleksandr Kuzminskii. Kuzminskii reprimanded Neidhardt for withdrawing all police from their posts in the early afternoon of October 18, an action he believed warranted criminal investigation.[35] He concluded that Neidhardt was guilty of negligence of duty by not ordering the police to take strict action to prevent trouble and suppress the disorder. Kuzminskii also decided that while Neidhardt was responsible for keeping law and order, Kaulbars was justified in waiting for orders from the governor.[36]

Like many government officials, Kuzminskii believed that the Odessa pogrom was a spontaneous display of outrage against the Jews, whose political activity had elicited the pogromist response. This brings to mind the report of Kenan Paşa, the president of the court-martial sent from İstanbul. Blaming victims for their suffering is not a novelty in the pages of Russian history; it dates back to the 1880s, when government apologists blamed the Jews for the anti-Jewish disturbances of 1881–82. Despite his criticism of Neidhardt, Kuzminskii concurred with the authorities in Odessa in blaming the pogrom on its victims, citing the visible role played by Jews in the revolutionary movement and the events of 1905.[37]

Hundreds of Jews were killed and around five thousand injured, while thousands of businesses were ruined. The Odessa Jewish Central Committee to Aid the Victims of the Pogroms of 1905 was established immediately and collected 672,833 rubles from Jews in Odessa and abroad to aid those hurt by the pogrom. The pogrom resulted in the emigration of many Jews from Odessa and Ukraine to Western Europe and the United States.

The details of the Odessa pogrom resemble those of the Adana massacres in many respects. In both cases, the dominant group targeted a nondominant group that was seen as an existential threat. Thus, affective disposition played an important role here as well. The events that triggered each of these massacres were not inherently ethno-religious in nature, but the violence soon assumed an ethno-religious aspect due to underlying socioeconomic and political anxieties. In both cases, competition over resources was a significant factor in motivating the behavior of the perpetrators, many of whom had no conscious political purpose but were driven simply by the lure of looting. The way in which the Kuzminskii report blamed the victims for their own misfortune resembles the conclusions of the Adana investigation reports, but with one major difference: after months of deliberations and lobbying by Armenian groups, the Ottoman government released a statement exonerating the Armenians of the events of Adana; such an exoneration did not transpire with regard to the Jews of Odessa.

The violence in Adana and Odessa also greatly resembles incidents of ethnic violence in India, both between Muslims and Hindus and between Sikhs and Hindus. Two examples of these violent encounters are the Sikh massacres of 1984 and the Gujarat massacres of 2002.[38] Due to the limited scope of this study, I will concentrate here on the Sikh massacres.

The 1984 Sikh massacres, labeled by the Indian government and the media as the anti-Sikh riots, took place in response to the assassination of the Indian prime minister Indira Ghandi by her Sikh bodyguards on October 31, 1984. In a period of four days, between eight thousand to seventeen thousand Sikhs were killed. Members of the Indian National Congress (INC) and the New Delhi police were complicit in the massacres. Ghandi's assassination was the result of political tensions that had simmered for years in the region of Punjab, where the Sikhs hold a majority. As with the Adana massacres, in order to understand these massacres, we need to understand the underlying tensions between the Hindus and the Sikhs and especially the development of a militant secessionist movement in Punjab.

In 1973, the Sikh political party Akali Dal put forward the Anandpur Sahib Resolution, demanding the recognition of Sikhism as a religion separate from Hinduism, the devolution of power from central to state government, and more autonomy for the Punjab region.[39] Despite the fact that most Akalis denied that the resolution had separatist intentions, the INC immediately rejected the document, considering it a secessionist move.[40] Jarnail Singh Bhindranwale, a messianic and charismatic leader who was the head of a fundamentalist center of Sikh learning, joined the Akali Dal in 1982 in order to revive and implement the Anandpur Sahib Resolution.[41] He is credited with creating Sikh militancy in Punjab.

According to Virginia Van Dyke, Ghandi initially supported the rise of Bhindranwale as a "tool with which to divide the more moderate Sikh leadership" and "allowed the growing tension to simmer rather than dealing decisively with the issues in contention in order to cultivate the Hindu vote."[42] It was only after Bhindranwale began directing a campaign of terror against both Hindus and Sikhs from the Golden Temple Complex in Armitsar[43] that Ghandi ordered the army to launch Operation Blue Star in order to remove him and his followers from the Sikh sacred site.[44] From June 1 to June 8, clashes took place between the militants and the government forces. While Indian government figures say that four hundred people were killed, including eighty-seven soldiers, Sikh groups claim that one thousand innocent pilgrims were killed during the operation.[45] The action caused anger among the Sikhs and increased the support for the separatist Khalistan movement. A month after Operation Blue Star, the government published *White Paper on the Punjab Agitation*, in which it presented its version of the events.[46] According to Khushwant Singh, *White Paper* put the entire responsibility for Bhindranwale's misdeeds on the Akalis, without mentioning the government's role in building him up.[47] In the aftermath of the operation, Sikhs were harassed and discriminated against. The police began arresting them without warrants and held them in detention without trial.[48]

Four months after Operation Blue Star, Ghandi was assassinated by two of her Sikh bodyguards. Similar to the case of Adana, the ethno-religious background of the assassins was highlighted, and the act was interpreted in terms of Sikhs versus Hindus. In the words of Giorgio Shani, the assassination resulted in a further "communalization of Indian politics by allowing the INC . . . to juxtapose a Hindu/Indian 'Self' against a Sikh 'Other,' with tragic consequences for the Sikhs of Delhi."[49] The assassination led to a series of massacres targeting the Sikh population that aimed to teach the Sikhs "a lesson they would not easily forget."[50]

As in Adana, the massacres were organized by local political officials with the complicity of the police.[51] Leaders of the congress instructed the police not to intervene. On the night of Ghandi's assassination and the next morning, congressional party leaders met with supporters and distributed money and weapons, even supplying voter lists, school registration forms, and ration lists to facilitate the targeting of Sikh homes and businesses.[52] The mob entered the Sikh neighborhood of New Delhi on November 1 carrying blunt instruments and combustible materials, committing massacres and destroying shops and residences. Mobs humiliated and raped surviving Sikh women.[53] The Delhi police aided the perpetrators, who were directed by congressional politicians such as Jagdish Tytler and Hari Krishan Lal Bhagat in a role reminiscent of the notables in Adana. Like the Payas prisoners in the Adana massacres, prisoners were released to take part in the violence. Congressional party members commissioned trucks to bring villagers and armed them with blunt instruments and gasoline. In addition, Gujjars and lower-caste Hindus were mobilized to take part in the violence. Similar to many of the participants in the Adana and Odessa massacres, these actors were motivated primarily by the promise of looting. As one historian claimed, "They showed neither anger nor grief at the slaying of the Prime Minister."[54] On November 2, a curfew was announced in Delhi but not enforced. With complete impunity, mobs ignored orders and continued rampaging and killing. It was only on November 3 that the violence subsided.

As in Adana and Odessa, rumors played an essential role in inciting the mob.[55] Throughout the four days of violence, rumors were deliberately floated that Sikhs were dancing, setting off firecrackers, and distributing sweets in celebration of the assassination.[56] Other rumors spread by the police claimed that "the Sikhs had poisoned the water supply and that a train from Punjab had arrived full of dead Hindus."[57] The media also took part in inciting the population; state-controlled television continually aired the display of Gandhi lying in state, where crowds could be clearly heard yelling the inflammatory slogan "Khun ka badla, Khun se lenge" (Blood for blood). In addition, the media helped to destabilize the situation by constantly emphasizing the ethnicity of the assassins.[58]

Evoking the "ancient hatreds" rationale, the INC officials and their acolytes explained the massacres as a communal riot based on popular sentiments. Such discourse, as with the Adana massacres, aims to absolve the politicians who instigated violent acts and to blame the individuals who perpetrated them. Attributing the violence to the religiosity of the people provides politicians with an easy shield.[59]

Situating the Adana massacres in the global context of violence inflicted on other nondominant groups provides us with a better understanding of what transpired in Adana. In violence inflicted on nondominant groups in post-despotic regimes, the public sphere and its subaltern counter-publics play essential roles in the intensification and solidification of ethnic tensions. Preexisting affective dispositions and underlying socioeconomic and political tensions resurface with great intensity. In intergroup hostility, rumors about machinations by nondominant groups against dominant groups add fuel to the fire by confirming the "theories" of the ruling elite about the sinister intentions of the targeted group. The ultimate result is a descent into a spiral of violence, whereby the dominant group resorts to massacres in order to "protect" itself from the nondominant group. It is my hope that this study will not only provide material for further research of ethno-religious violence in the context of the Middle East but will also be understood in a global context. The crimes perpetrated in the twentieth century have demonstrated that no society in the world is immune to mass violence. To prevent the occurrence of such violent episodes, it is imperative that we understand why and how past acts of massacres and genocides took place. More importantly, it is necessary to confront the conundrum of how and why ordinary people can become perpetrators of violence in a very short period of time.

BIBLIOGRAPHY OF PRIMARY SOURCES

Archival Sources

Başkanlık Osmanlı Arşivi (BOA), İstanbul, Turkey
Bâb-ı Âlî Evrak Odası
(BEO)
Dâhiliye Emniyet-i Umûmiye Muhaberât ve Tensîkât Müdüriyeti Evrakı
(DH.EU.MTK)
Dâhiliye Nezâreti, Mektûbî Kalemi
(DH.MKT)
Dâhiliye Nezâreti, Mektûbî Kalemi Perakende Evrakı
(DH.MKT.PRK)
Dâhiliye Nezâreti, Muhaberât-ı Umûmiye İdaresi Evrakı
(DH.MUİ)
Dâhiliye Nezâreti, Şifre Evrakı
(DH.ŞFR)
Dâhiliye Nezâreti, Siyâsî Kısım Evrakı
(DH.SYS)
Dâhiliye Nezâreti, Tesrî-i Muamelât ve Islâhât Komisyonu
(DH.TMIK.M)
Sadâret Mektûbî Mühimme Kalemi Evrakı
(A.MKT.MHM)
Yıldız Mütennevî Marûzâtı
(Y.MTV)

Armenian

Archives of the Armenian Diocese of Adana (AADA), Madenataran Library, Yerevan, Armenia

Archives of the Armenian Patriarchate of Jerusalem (AAPJ), Jerusalem

Armenian National Archives (ANA), Yerevan, Armenia

Armenian Revolutionary Federation (ARF) Archives, Watertown, MA

Izmirlian Archives (IA), Madenataran Library, Yerevan, Armenia

French

Archives jésuites (AJV), Vanves, Paris

Ministère de l'Europe et des Affaires étrangères, Centre des Archives diplomatiques de La Courneuve (CADC)

Ministère de l'Europe et des Affaires étrangères, Centre des Archives diplomatiques de Nantes (CADN)

British

British Foreign Office Documents (FO)

The National Archives, UK (TNA)

American

American Board of Commissioners for Foreign Missions (ABCFM) Archives, Cambridge, MA

Ernst Jäckh Papers, Columbia University, New York, NY

Minnesota Historical Society (MHS) Archives, St. Paul, MN

United States National Archives and Records Administration (USNA), College Park, MD

Published Archival Material

Armenian Patriarchate. *La situation des Arméniens en Turquie exposée par des documents 1908–1912*, vol. 3. Constantinople: [publisher not identified], [1913?].

Chorley, Emily, Wolfgang Gust, George Shirinian, ed. "Adana 1909." *The Armenian Genocide*. Documents from the German and British Foreign Office. http://www.armenocide.net/armenocide/armgende.nsf/WebStart-En?Open Frameset.

Further Correspondence respecting the Affairs of Asiatic Turkey and Arabia, April–June 1909. Foreign Office (FO), Public Record Office (PRO). Confidential Print. London, Great Britain.

Further Correspondence respecting the Affairs of Asiatic Turkey and Arabia, January–March 1909. Foreign Office (FO), Public Record Office (PRO). Confidential Print. London, Great Britain.

Further Correspondence respecting the Affairs of Asiatic Turkey and Arabia, July–September 1909. Foreign Office (FO), Public Record Office (PRO). Confidential Print. London, Great Britain.

Further Correspondence respecting the Affairs of Asiatic Turkey and Arabia, October–December 1909. Foreign Office (FO), Public Record Office (PRO). Confidential Print. London, Great Britain.

Herkelean, Varuzhan, ed. *Atanayi vkanerĕ ew Surb Stepʻanos vkayaranĕ, 1909, Laṛnaga.* Nicosia: [publisher not identified], 2010.

Karakacaya, Recep et al., eds. *Osmanlı belgelerinde 1909 Adana olayları,* vols. 1 and 2. Ankara: T. C. Başbakanlık Devlet Arşivleri Genel Müdürlüğü, 2010.

Ohandjanian, Artem. *Österreich—Armenien: 1872–1936 Faksimilesammlung Diplomatischer Aktenstücke.* Vol. 4, *1897–1909.* Wien: Ohandjanian, 1995.

Pamboukian, Yervant. *Niwtʻer Hay heghapʻokhakan dashnaktsʻutʻean patmutʻean hamar,* vol. 6. Peyrutʻ: Hamazgayini Vahē Sētʻean Tparan, 2010.

Politisches Archiv des Auswärtiges Amt (DE/PA-AA/R). Berlin, Germany.

Ruyssen, Georges-Henri, ed. *La Questione Armena.* Vol. 3, *1908–1925, documenti dell'archivio della congregazione per le Chiese Orientali* (ACO). Roma: Ed. Orientalia Christiana, 2014.

Society for the Propagation of Faith. *The Adana Massacres and the Catholic Missionaries: Account of Eye-Witnesses.* New York: Society for the Propagation of Faith, 1910.

Periodicals

Armenian

Aragadz
Arewelkʻ
Azatamart
Biwrakn
Biwzandion
Droshak
Dzayn Hayreniatsʻ
Horizon
Kilikia
Kohak
Mshak
Zhamanak

Arabic

Al-Ittiḥād al-ʻUthmānī

Al-Muqaṭṭam
Al-Muqtabas
Lisān al-Ḥāl
Ṣaḍa Bābel

English
American Red Cross Bulletin
Levant Herald and Eastern Express
Manchester Guardian
New York Times
Olive Tree: A Monthly Journal Devoted to Missionary Work in the Reformed Presbyterian Church, U. S. A.
Pearson's Magazine
Pro-Armenia
Spectator
Sunday Times
The Times
Washington Post

French
Gazette de Lausanne
Journal de Geneve
Journal de Salonique
Le matin
Les missions catholiques
Le temps
Pour les peuples d'Orient

German
Berliner Tageblatt
Neue Freie Presse
Wiener Zeitung

Greek
Empros
Proodos
Skrip

Hebrew
Ha-Ḥerut

Ha-ʿOlam
Ha-Poʿel ha-Tzaʿir
Ha-Zvi

Ladino
El-Tiempo

Ottoman Turkish
İkdam
İtidal
Meşveret
Serbesti
Şura-yı Ümmet
Takvim-i Vekayi
Tanin
Tasvir-i Efkâr
Tercümân-ı Hakikat
Yeni Tasvir-i Efkar

Polish
Kurjer Lwowski

Memoirs

"Araxi (Bzdigian) Boyadjian's Memoir." Larnaca. Unpublished manuscript, 1948.

Arıkoğlu, Damar. *Hâtıralarım*. İstanbul: Tan Gazetesi ve Matbaası, 1961.

Arslanian, Artin. *Adana'da adalet nasıl mahkûm oldu*. Le Caire: [publisher not identified], 1909.

Asaf, Mehmed. *1909 Adana Ermeni olayları ve anılarım*, edited by İsmet Parmaksızoğlu. Ankara: Türk Tarih Kurumu Basımevi, 2002.

Ashjian, Hampartsoum H. *Atanayi eghehẹrnĕ ew Gonyayi husher*. New York: Kochnak Dbaran, 1950.

Bartevian, Suren. *Kilikean arhawirkʿĕ*. G. Polis: Nishan-Babigian Press, 1909.

Çalyan, Karabet. *Adana vak'ası ve mesulleri*. Dersaadet: Artin Asadourian Matbaası, 1909 [Hijri date: 1325].

Djemal Pasha, Ahmed. *Memories of a Turkish Statesman, 1913–1919*. London: Hutchinson & Co., 1922.

Khabrig, Minas. *Etʿĕ Chʿorkʿ-Marzpanĕ intsi het khôsēr*. Pēyrutʿ: Hratarakutʿiwn Chʿorkʿ-Marzpani Hayrenaktsʿakan Miutʿean, 1983.

Koudoulian, Krikor G. *Hay lẹṛĕ: Karmir drwakner Kilikioy aghētēn*. İzmir: Tpagr. Mamurean, 1913.

Markarian, Boghos. *Ink'nakensagrut'iwn Pŏghos Margareani: Ew ziwr ĕntanik'i andamots' patmakann.* Pĕrkĕnfilt, Niw Chērzi: [publisher not identified], 1951.

Papazian, Vahan. *Im husherĕ,* vol. 2. Beirut: Hamazgayin, 1952.

Seropian, Moushegh. *Atanayi jardĕ ew pataskhanatunerĕ.* Gahire: Tparan Ararat-S. Darbinean, 1909.

Seropian, Moushegh. *Ink'nakensagrut'iwn,* vols. 2 and 3. Unpublished manuscript, n. d.

Seropian, Moushegh. *Les vêpres ciliciennes: Les responsabilités, faits et documents.* Alexandrie: Typo-Lithographie Centrale I. Della Rocca, 1909.

Talât Paşa, Mehmed. *Talât Paşa'nın hâtıraları.* İstanbul: Cumhuriyet, 1998.

Tengirşenk, Yusuf Kemal. *Vatan hizmetinde.* İstanbul: Bahar Matbaası, 1967.

Teotig, Arshagouhi. *Amis mĕ i Kilikia.* K. Polis: V. ew H. Tēr-Nersēsean, 1910.

Toros, Taha. *Ali Münif Bey'in hâtıraları.* İstanbul: İsis, 1996.

Yesayan, Zabel. *Aweraknerun mēj.* K. Polis: Hayots' Hratarakch'akan Ēnkerut'iwn, 1911.

Interviews

Interview with Alice (Babikian) Maremetdjian (daughter of Ottoman deputy Hagop Babigian), on May 25–26, 1980. Conducted by daughter-in-law Simone Merian and granddaughter Sylvie Merian.

Salnâmes

Salnâme-i vilâyet-i Adana 1308 (1890). Adana: Vilâyet Matbaası, 1890.

Salnâme-i vilâyet-i Adana 1321(1903). Adana: Vilâyet Matbaası, 1903.

Other Primary Sources

Adossidès, A. *Arméniens et Jeunes-Turcs: Les massacres de Cilicie.* Paris: P. V. Stock, 1910.

Alichan, Ghevond. *Sissouan ou Arméno-Cilicie.* Venice: Mekhitarist Press, 1899.

Araks, Madenashar. *Kilikia: P'ordz ashkharhagrut'ean ardi Kilikioy.* Peterburg: Tparan I. Libermani, 1894.

Azkayin ĕndhanur zhoghov. Armenian National Assembly Minutes, 1909.

Babigian, Hagop. *Atanayi egheṛnĕ: Niwt'er Hay martirosagrut'ean patmut'ean.* Translated by Hagop Sarkissian. İstanbul: Artsakank Press, 1919.

Bardakçı, Murat. *Talât Paşa'nın evrak-ı metrûkesi: Sadrazam Talât Paşa'nın özel arşivinde bulunan Ermeni tehciri konusundaki belgeler ve hususî yazışmalar.* İstanbul: Everest Yayınları, 2013.

Beaufort, Francis. *Karamania; or, a Brief Description of the South Coast of Asia-Minor and of the Remains of Antiquity. With Pans, Views, Etc.* London: R. Hunter, 1817.

Bucknill, John Alexander Strachey, and Haig Apisoghom Sdepan Utidjian. *The Imperial Ottoman Penal Code: A Translation from the Turkish Text, with Latest Additions and Amendments, Together with Annotations and Explanatory Commentaries upon the Text and Containing an Appendix Dealing with the Special Amendments in Force in Cyprus and the Judicial Decisions of the Cyprus Courts.* Oxford: Oxford University Press, 1913.

Bždigian, Zakaria. *Kilikean kskidzner, 1903–1915.* Beirut: Hraztan Press, 1927.

Cevdet, Ahmed. *Tezâkir,* vol. 3, edited by Cavid Baysun. Ankara: Türk Tarih Kurumu Basımevi, 1953.

Cuinet, Vital. *La Turquie d'Asie: Géographie administrative, statistique, descriptive et raisonnée de chaque province de l'Asie-Mineure,* vol. 2. Paris: E. Leroux, 1891.

d'Annezay, Jean. *Au pays des massacres: Saignée arménienne de 1909.* Paris: Bloud, 1910.

Der Melkonian, Bedros Archbishop. *Patmut'iwn azatut'eann hachěnoy i tserats' K'özaneants'.* K. Polis: Tp. Aramean, 1871.

Ferriman, Z. Duckett. *The Young Turks and the Truth about the Holocaust at Adana in Asia Minor, during April, 1909.* London: [publisher not identified], 1913.

Fitzner, Rudolf. *Aus Kleinasien und Syrien.* Rostock: C. J. E. Volckmann, 1904.

Fraser, David. *The Short Cut to India: The Record of a Journey along the Route of the Baghdad Railway.* Edinburgh: Blackwood, 1909.

Gibbons, Helen Davenport (Brown). *The Red Rugs of Tarsus: A Women's Record of the Armenian Massacre of 1909.* New York: The Century Company, 1917.

Heyd, Wilhelm. *Histoire du commerce du Levant au moyen-âge.* Leipzig, O. Harrassowitz, 1885.

Karakoç, Sarkis. *Arâzi kânunu ve tapu nizamnâmesi.* İstanbul: Kitabhane-i Cihan, 1923 [Hijri date: 1342].

Kilikioy Orbakhnam Kedronakan Handznazhoghov. *Teghekagir 1909 Ōgostos 7–1910 Dektember 31.* K. Polis: Tparan ew Kazmatun Ō. Arzuman, 1911.

Konstandnupolsoy Patriark'ut'iwn. *Deghekakirk' kawarakan harstaharut'eants'.* G. Bolis: Tpagrut'iwn Aramyan, 1876.

Konstandnupolsoy Patriark'ut'iwn. *Hoghayin grawmmants' handznazhoghov, teghekagir hoghayin grawmants' handznazhoghovoy,* vols. 1–4. K. Polis: Tpagr. T. Tōghramachean, 1910–12.

Konstandnupolsoy Patriark'ut'iwn. *Npastits' handznazhoghov: Hashuets'uts'ak ew teghekagir, 1897–1908.* K. Polis: Tpagrut'iwn "Shant'," 1911.

Lambert, Rose. *Hadjin and the Armenian Massacres.* New York; Chicago: Flemming H. Revell Company, 1911.

Les massacres d'Adana: Avril 1909. Bruxelles: Joseph Polleunis Editeur, 1909.

Les massacre d'Adana et nos missionaries: Recit de temoins. Lyons: Imprimerie Vve Paquet, 1909.

Russegger, Joseph. *Reisen in Europa, Asien, und Afrika: Mit Besonderer Rücksicht auf Die Naturwissenschaftlichen Verhältnisse der Betreffenden Länder; Unternommen in den Jahren 1835 bis 1841.* Stuttgart: E. Schweizerbart'sche Verlagshandlung, 1841–48.

Sâmî, Şemseddin. *Kâmûsu'l-a'lâm: Tarih ve coğrafya lûgatı ve tabir-i esahhiyle kâffe-yi esmâ-yi hassa-yi câmidir.* İstanbul: Mihran Matbaası, 1889.

Sayabalian, P. Zhak. *Teghekagir ayriakhnam handznazhoghovi: 1910 Sept. 11–1912 Sept. 11.* Ghalat'ia: Tparan "Shant'," 1912.

Şeref, Abdurrahman, ed. *Son vak'anüvis Abdurrahman Şeref Efendi tarihi.* Vol. 2, *Meşrutiyet olayları, 1908–1909,* edited by Bayram Kodaman and Mehmet Ali Ünal. Ankara: Türk Tarih Kurumu Basımevi, 1996.

Terzian, Hagop. *Atanayi kiank'ě.* K. Polis: Tpagrut'iwn Z. N. Pērpērean, 1909.

Terzian, Hagop. *Kilikioy aghetě: Akanatesi nkaragrut'iwnner, vawerat'ught'er, pashtonakan teghekagirner, t'ght'akts'ut'iwnner, vichakagrut'iwnner, amenēn karewor patkernerov.* İstanbul: [publisher not identified], 1912.

Tourian, Bedros. *Erkeri zhoghovatsu.* Erevan: Haykakan SSH GA Hratarakch'ut'yun, 1971–72.

Woods, Henry Charles. *The Danger Zone of Europe: Changes and Problems in the Near East.* Boston: Little, Brown, 1911.

Z., S. *Adanskie chernye dni.* Baku: Baku, Electric Printing House of the Newspaper Baku, 1909.

Zion, Po'alei, *Odesskiĭ pogrom i samooborona.* Paris: Libr. A. Schulz, 1906.

NOTES

Introduction

1. "Syrian Shops Attacked in Turkey," *Middle East Eye*, September 23, 2019, https://www.middleeasteye.net/fr/node/143936.

2. Omer Faruk Gorcen, "As Turks Clash with Syrians, a Dangerous Spark Is Lit in Istanbul," *Middle East Eye*, July 2, 2019, https://www.middleeasteye.net/news/turks-clash-syrians-dangerous-spark-lit-istanbul.

3. Jacques Sémelin, *Purify and Destroy: The Political Uses of Massacre and Genocide* (New York: Columbia University Press, 2007), 5.

4. Bedross Der Matossian, "From Bloodless Revolution to a Bloody Counterrevolution: The Adana Massacres of 1909," *Genocide Studies and Prevention: An International Journal* 6, no. 2 (Summer 2011): 152–73.

5. See, for example, William L. Cleveland and Martin Bunton, *A History of the Modern Middle East*, 5th ed. (Boulder.: Westview Press, 2013); James L. Gelvin, *The Modern Middle East: A History*, 5th ed. (New York: Oxford University Press, 2015); M. Şükrü Hanioğlu, *A Brief History of the Late Ottoman Empire* (New York: Oxford University Press, 1995); and Donald Quataert, *The Ottoman Empire, 1700–1922*, 2nd ed. (Cambridge: Cambridge University Press, 2005).

6. For example, see Vahakn N. Dadrian, "The Circumstances Surrounding the 1909 Adana Holocaust," *Armenian Review* 41, no. 4 (1988): 1–16. In the historiography written in Armenian, the continuum approach is much more prevalent. For example, see Hrachik Simonyan, *Hayeri zangvadzayin kotoradznerě Kilikiayum: (1909 t'. April)* (Erevan: EPH Hrat., 2009). The book appeared in English in 2012; see Hrachik Simonyan, *The Destruction of Armenians in Cilicia, April 1909*, trans. Melissa Brown and Alexander Arzoumanian (London: Gomidas Institute, 2012). See also the special issues of *Hask:*

Hayagitakan taregirk', vol. 12 (2010) and *Ts'eghaspanagitakan handes* 1, no. 1 (2013). For the Turkish narrative, see Esat Uras, *Tarihte Ermeniler ve Ermeni Meselesi* (Ankara: Yeni Press, 1950); Salahi Sonyel, *İngiliz gizli belgelerine göre Adana'da vuku bulan Türk-Ermeni olayları (Temmuz 1908–Aralık 1909)* (Ankara: Türk Tarih Kurumu Basımevi, 1988); Cezmi Yurtsever, *Ermeni terör merkezi Kilikya kilisesi* (İstanbul: C. Yurtsever, 1983); Kemal Çiçek, *1909 Adana olayları /makaleler-The Adana Incidents of 1909 Revisited* (Ankara: Türk Tarih Kurumu, 2011); and Yusuf Sarınay and Recep Karacakaya, *1909 Adana Ermeni olayları* (İstanbul: İdeal Kültür Yayıncılık, 2012). Turkish diplomat Yücel Güçlü recently published a book promoting the narrative of the Armenian uprising; see Yücel Güçlü, *The Armenian Events of Adana in 1909: Cemal Paşa and Beyond* (Lanham: Hamilton Books, 2018). For more nuanced approaches, see Ronald Grigor Suny, *"They Can Live in the Desert but Nowhere Else": A History of the Armenian Genocide* (Princeton, NJ: Princeton University Press, 2015), 194–200; Michelle Elizabeth Tusan, *The British Empire and the Armenian Genocide: Humanitarianism and the Politics of Empire from Gladstone to Churchill* (London: I. B. Tauris, 2016), 94–118; Raymond H. Kévorkian, with the collaboration of Paul B. Paboudjian, "Les massacres de Cilicie d'avril 1909," in "La Cilicie (1909–1921): Des massacres d'Adana au mandat français," ed. Raymond H. Kévorkian, special issue, *Revue d'Histoire Arménienne Contemporaine* 3 (Paris: La Bibliotheque Nubar, 1993): 7–248; Raymond H. Kévorkian, *The Armenian Genocide: A Complete History* (London: I. B. Tauris, 2011), 71–118; Aram Arkun, "Les relations arméno-turques et les massacres de cilicie de 1909," in *L'Actualité du genocide des Arméniens: Actes du colloque organisé par le Comité de Défense de la Cause Arménienne à Paris-Sorbonne les 16, 17 et 18 avril 1998*, ed. Hrayr Henry Ayvazian et al. (Paris: Eidpol, 1999). In Turkish, see Meltem Toksöz, "Adana Ermenileri ve 1909 'İğtişaşı,'" in *Tarih ve Toplum, Yeni Yaklaşımlar* 5 (Spring 2007): 147–57. See also Matthias Bjørnlund, "Adana and Beyond: Revolution and Massacre in the Ottoman Empire Seen through Danish Eyes, 1908/9," *Haikazean Hayagitakan handēs* 30 (2010): 125–55.

7. Dadrian, "The Circumstances Surrounding the 1909 Adana Holocaust."

8. Kévorkian, *The Armenian Genocide*, 113.

9. Jacques Sémelin, "In Consideration of Massacres," *Journal of Genocide Research* 3, no. 3 (2001), 381.

10. Vahakn N. Dadrian, *The History of the Armenian Genocide: Ethnic Conflict from the Balkans to Anatolia to the Caucasus* (New York: Berghahn Books, 1995), 121–27.

11. Christopher R. Browning, *Ordinary Men: Reserve Police Battalion 101 and the Final Solution in Poland*, rev. ed. (New York: Harper Perennial, 2017) and James Waller, *Becoming Evil: How Ordinary People Commit Genocide and Mass Murder* (New York; Oxford: Oxford University Press, 2007).

12. See Edip Gölbaşı, "The Official Conceptualization of the Anti-Armenian Riots of 1895–1897," *Études Arméniennes contemporaines* 10 (2018): 33–62. Samples of denialist literature include Edward J. Erickson, *Ottomans and Armenians: A Study in*

Counterinsurgency (New York: Palgrave Macmillan, 2013); Michael Gunter, *Armenian History and the Question of Genocide* (New York: Palgrave, 2011); Justin McCarthy, *The Armenian Rebellion at Van* (Salt Lake City: University of Utah Press, 2006); and Guenter Lewy, *The Armenian Massacres in Ottoman Turkey: A Disputed Genocide* (Salt Lake City: University of Utah Press, 2005). For an extensive study of denial in Turkey, see Fatma Müge Göçek, *Denial of Violence: Ottoman Past, Turkish Present, and Collective Violence against the Armenians, 1789–2009* (New York: Oxford University Press, 2015).

13. The provocation thesis has been debunked by Robert Melson, who sees provocation by Armenian revolutionary groups as "merely one aspect of a more generalized threat that the government imputed to its Armenian population." Melson also argues that the provocation thesis falls short of "being a credible explanation for the massacres because it neither convincingly demonstrates that the revolutionary parties were a serious threat nor does it address itself to the question of why they were seen as a threat." See Robert Melson, "A Theoretical Inquiry into the Armenian Massacres of 1894–1896," *Comparative Studies in Society and History* 24, no. 3 (July 1982): 486, 494.

14. Paul Brass, ed., *Riots and Pogroms* (London: Macmillan, 1996), 34.

15. Sémelin, *Purify and Destroy*, 167.

16. Johne D. Klier, "The Pogrom Paradigm in Russian History," in *Pogroms: Anti-Jewish Violence in Modern Russian History*, ed. John D. Klier and Shlomo Lambroza (Cambridge: Cambridge University Press, 2007), 34.

17. Ibid., 13.

18. Davide Rodogno, *Against Massacre: Humanitarian Interventions in the Ottoman Empire, 1815–1914* (Princeton, NJ: Princeton University Press, 2012), 31.

19. Ibid., 31–38.

20. Philip G. Dwyer and Lyndall Ryan, eds., *Theaters of Violence: Massacre, Mass Killing and Atrocity throughout History* (New York: Berghahn Books, 2012), xv.

21. Ibid.

22. Jacques Sémelin, "In Consideration of 'Massacre,'" *Journal of Genocide Research* 3 (2001): 378.

23. Ibid.

24. Melson, "A Theoretical Inquiry," 484.

25. Sémelin, "In Consideration of 'Massacre,'" 379.

26. Melson, "A Theoretical Inquiry," 484.

27. On the reform period, see Roderic H. Davison, *Reform in the Ottoman Empire, 1856–1876* (Princeton, NJ: Princeton University Press, 1963); Moshe Ma'oz, *Ottoman Reform in Syria and Palestine, 1840–1861: The Impact of the Tanzimat on Politics and Society* (Oxford: Clarendon Press, 1968); Selim Deringil, *The Well-Protected Domains: Ideology and the Legitimation of Power in the Ottoman Empire, 1876–1909* (London: I. B. Tauris, 1998); Selçuk Akşin Somel, *The Modernization of Public Education in the Ottoman Empire, 1839–1908: Islamization, Autocracy, and Discipline* (Leiden: Brill, 2001);

Kemal H. Karpat, *The Politicization of Islam: Reconstructing Identity, State, Faith, and Community in the Late Ottoman State* (New York: Oxford University Press, 2001); Benjamin C. Fortna, *The Imperial Classroom: Islam, the State, and Education in the Late Ottoman Empire* (Oxford: Oxford University Press, 2002); and Itzchak Weismann and Fruma Zachs, eds., *Ottoman Reform and Muslim Regeneration* (London: I. B. Tauris, 2005).

28. Ussama Samir Makdisi, *The Culture of Sectarianism: Community, History, and Violence in Nineteenth-Century Ottoman Lebanon* (Berkeley: University of California Press, 2000).

29. İpek Yosmaoğlu, *Blood Ties: Religion, Violence, and the Politics of Nationhood in Ottoman Macedonia, 1878–1908* (Ithaca, NY: Cornell University Press, 2013).

30. Leila Fawaz, *An Occasion for War: Civil Conflict in Lebanon and Damascus in 1860* (Berkeley: University of California Press; London: I. B. Tauris, 1994).

31. See Stephan H. Astourian and Raymond H. Kévorkian, eds., *Collective and State Violence in Turkey: The Construction of a National Identity from Empire to Nation-State* (New York: Berghahn Books, 2021) and Ümit Kurt, *The Armenians of Aintab: The Economics of Genocide in an Ottoman Province* (Cambridge, MA: Harvard University Press, 2021).

32. Craig Calhoun argues that Habermas does not mean to suggest that what made the public sphere bourgeois was its class composition. Rather, he asserts, society itself was bourgeois, and therefore produced a certain form of public sphere. See Craig Calhoun, ed., *Habermas and the Public Sphere* (Cambridge, MA: MIT Press, 1992), 7.

33. Jürgen Habermas, "A Philosophico-Political Profile," interview by Perry Anderson and Peter Dews, *New Left Review* 151 (May–June 1985): 104, cited in Fawwaz Tarablousi, "Commentary: Public Spheres and Urban Spaces: A Critical Comparative Approach," *New Political Science* 27, no. 4 (December 2005): 529–541.

34. For critiques of Habermas's public sphere, see the articles by Geoff Eley, Nancy Fraser, Craig Calhoun, and Mary Ryan in Calhoun, *Habermas and the Public Sphere*.

35. Mary Ryan, "Gender and Public Access: Women's Politics in Nineteenth-Century America," in Calhoun, *Habermas and the Public Sphere*, 265; and Geoff Eley, "Nations, Publics, and Political Cultures: Placing Habermas in the Nineteenth Century," in Calhoun, *Habermas and the Public Sphere*, 306.

36. Eley, "Nations, Publics, and Political Cultures," 326.

37. Nancy Fraser, "Rethinking the Public Sphere: A Contribution to the Critique of Actually Existing Democracy," in Calhoun, *Habermas and the Public Sphere*, 123.

38. Craig Calhoun, "Nationalism and the Public Sphere," in *Public and Private in Thought and Practice: Perspectives on a Grand Dichotomy*, ed. Jeff Weintraub and Krishan Kumar (Chicago: University of Chicago Press, 1997), 88.

39. Ibid., 100.

40. One of the best existing studies is Miriam Hoexter, Shmuel N. Eisenstadt, and Nehemia Levtzion, eds., *The Public Sphere in Muslim Societies* (Albany, NY: State University of New York Press; Jerusalem: Van Leer Jerusalem Institution, 2002). See also Dale F. Eickelman and Armando Salvatore, "The Public Sphere and Muslim Identities," *European Journal of Sociology* 43, no. 1 (2002): 92–115 and Srirupa Roy, "Seeing a State: National Commemorations and the Public Sphere in India and Turkey," *Comparative Studies in Society and History* 1, no. 48 (2006): 200–232.

41. Haim Gerber, "The Public Sphere and Civil Society in the Ottoman Empire," in Hoexter, Eisenstadt, and Levtzion, *The Public Sphere in Muslim Societies*, 75.

42. Selma A. Özkoçak, "Coffeehouses: Rethinking the Public and Private in Early Modern İstanbul," *Journal of Urban History* 33, no. 6 (2007): 965–86.

43. Ibid.

44. See Ami Ayalon, *The Press in the Arab Middle East* (New York: Oxford University Press, 1995).

45. In the Armenian case, the newspapers *Masis* and *Meghu*, among others, played an important role in the intra-ethnic political discourse of the mid-nineteenth century onward.

46. However, it is important to note that the emergence of the political public sphere did not take place simultaneously for all ethnic groups.

47. The *Pro-Armenia, Meşveret, Şura-yı Ümmet*, and *Al-Muqaṭṭam* newspapers are the best examples of such tools.

48. For the best study on the postrevolutionary press, see Palmira Brummett, *Image and Imperialism in the Ottoman Revolutionary Press, 1908–1911* (Albany, NY: State University of New York Press, 2000).

49. For example, during the first two years after the revolution, approximately eighty new Armenian newspapers were published in the Ottoman Empire: forty-nine in İstanbul, eight in Van, six in İzmir, and the rest in Diyarbekir, Erzincan, Trabzon, Erzurum, and Sivas. See Amalya Kirakosyan, *Hay parberakan mamuli matenagrut'iwn (1794–1967)* (Yerevan, 1970), 488–89.

50. Warren A. Peterson and Noel P. Gist, "Rumor and Public Opinion," *American Journal of Sociology* 57, no. 2 (September 1951): 159–67.

51. Ravi Bhavnani, Michael G. Findley, and James H. Kuklinski, "Rumor Dynamics in Ethnic Violence," *Journal of Politics* 71, no. 3 (July 2009): 877.

52. Ibid., 878.

53. Sémelin, *Purify and Destroy*, 295.

54. Thomas Brudholm and Johannes Lang, eds., *Emotions and Mass Atrocity: Philosophical and Theoretical Explorations* (Cambridge: Cambridge University Press, 2018), 8.

55. Roger D. Petersen, *Understanding Ethnic Violence: Fear, Hatred, and Resentment in Twentieth-Century Eastern Europe* (Cambridge: Cambridge University Press, 2006), 2.

56. Suny, *"They Can Live in the Desert,"* 121, 133–34, 172–73.

57. Sémelin, *Purify and Destroy*, 10–53.

58. Ibid., 73.

59. On the origins of humanitarian intervention, see Gary Jonathan Bass, *Freedom's Battle: The Origins of Humanitarian Intervention* (New York: Vintage, 2009).

60. Rodogno, *Against Massacre*, 2. See also Charlie Laderman, *Sharing the Burden: The Armenian Question, Humanitarian Intervention, and Anglo-American Visions of Global Order* (Oxford: Oxford University Press, 2019).

61. Rodogno, *Against Massacre*, 10.

62. Ibid., 255.

63. Keith David Watenpaugh, *Bread from Stones: The Middle East and the Making of Modern Humanitarianism* (Oakland, CA: University of California Press, 2016), 12.

64. Ibid., 59.

65. Tusan, *The British Empire*, 16.

66. Ibid., 4.

67. Ibid., 14.

68. Ibid., 27.

69. Ibid., 56.

70. Between 1889 and 1896 there were ten different Blue Books published on the situation of Armenians in the Ottoman Empire. These official volumes contained hundreds of pages of information.

71. Tusan, *The British Empire*, 60.

72. Ibid., 71.

73. Watenpaugh, *Bread from Stones*, 70.

74. Ibid., 70–71.

75. Tusan, *The British Empire*, 244.

76. See Şerif Mardin, *The Genesis of Young Ottoman Thought: A Study in the Modernization of Turkish Political Ideas* (Syracuse, NY: Syracuse University Press, 2000) and Nazan Çiçek, *The Young Ottomans: Turkish Critics of the Eastern Question in the Late Nineteenth Century* (London: I. B. Tauris, 2010).

77. See Robert Devereux, *The First Ottoman Constitutional Period: A Study of the Midhat Constitution and Parliament* (Baltimore: Johns Hopkins University Press, 1963). See also Aylin Koçunyan, *Negotiating the Ottoman Constitution 1839–1876* (Leuven: Peeters, 2018).

78. Gustave Rolin-Jaequemyns, *Armenia, the Armenians, and the Treaties* (Manchester: John Heywood, 1891), 34.

79. Jacob Hurewitz, *Diplomacy in the Near and Middle East: A Documentary Record 1535–1956*, vol. 1 (Princeton, NJ: Van Nostrand, 1956), 190.

80. For more information about the activities of the Armenakan Party, see Ardag Tarpinian, *Hay azatagrakan sharzhman ōrerēn: Husher 1890ēn 1940* (Paris: Publication of the Armenian National Fund, 1947).

81. On the platform of the party, see "Sōts'ialistakan dēmokratakan hnch'akean kusakts'ut'iwn," in *Tsragir Hnch'akean kusakts'ut'ean*, 3rd ed. (London: Hunchak Press, 1897). For further information about the party, see Anahit Ter Minassian, *Nationalism and Socialism in the Armenian Revolutionary Movement* (Cambridge, MA: Zoryan Institute, 1984); and Ter Minassian, "The Role of the Armenian Community in the Foundation and Development of the Socialist Movement in the Ottoman Empire and Turkey, 1876–1923," in *Socialism and Nationalism in the Ottoman Empire 1876–1923*, ed. Mete Tunçay and Erik Jan Zürcher (London: I. B. Tauris, 1994), 109–156.

82. For an in-depth discussion of the ARF, its ideology, and revolutionary activities, see Houri Berberian, *Roving Revolutionaries: Armenians and the Connected Revolutions in the Russian, Iranian, and Ottoman Worlds* (Berkley: University of California Press, 2019) and Ter Minassian, *Nationalism and Socialism*.

83. See Janet Klein, *The Margins of Empire: Kurdish Militias in the Ottoman Tribal Zone* (Stanford: Stanford University Press, 2011), 1–94. For the latest literature on the Hamidian massacres, see "Les massacres de l'époque hamidienne (I): récits globaux, approches locales," special issue, *Études Arméniennes contemporaines* 10 (2018); and "Les massacres de l'époque hamidienne (II): représentations et perspectives," special issue, *Études Arméniennes contemporaines* 11 (2018).

84. Mark Levene argues, "Massacres have deep meaning, they are part of people's consciousness, even their 'folk' memory." See Mark Levene, introduction to *The Massacre in History*, ed. Mark Levene and Penny Roberts (Providence: Berghahn Books, 1999), 3.

85. Bedross Der Matossian, *Shattered Dreams of Revolution: From Liberty to Violence in the Late Ottoman Empire* (Stanford: Stanford University Press, 2014), 23–38.

86. *Levant Herald and Eastern Express*, August 13, 1908, 2. On the manifestations of the constitution in Adana, see Kudret Emiroğlu, *Anadolu'da devrim günleri: II. Meşrutiyet'in ilanı, Temmuz-Ağustos 1908* (Ankara: İmge Kitabevi, 1999), 188–93.

87. Nader Sohrabi, *Revolution and Constitutionalism in the Ottoman Empire and Iran* (New York: Cambridge University Press, 2011), 226–236.

88. Der Matossian, *Shattered Dreams of Revolution*, 149–72.

89. Sohrabi, *Revolution and Constitutionalism*, 225.

90. From the Responsible Body to the Western Bureau, April 29, 1909, Armenian Revolutionary Federation (ARF) Archives, C/193–80/.

91. In his study on communal violence in South Asia, Stanley Tambiah argues, "Spreaders of rumors, shouters of slogans, instigator[s] of violence among the public . . . were a critical element in the rapid sparking and spread of violence at key junctions of the city [Delhi]." The same could be argued in the case of the Adana massacres.

See Stanley J. Tambiah, "Address: Reflections on Communal Violence in South Asia," *Journal of Asian Studies* 49, no. 4 (November 1990): 747. According to Parvis Ghassem-Fachandi, "rumor derives its power from the fact that it accesses a level of consciousness in which everyone can participate, even those skeptical of the rumor's content." See Parvis Ghassem-Fachandi, *Pogrom in Gujarat: Hindu Nationalism and Anti-Muslim Violence in India* (Princeton, NJ: Princeton University Press, 2012), 82.

92. Sémelin, "In Consideration of Massacres," 384.

93. Babigian's family always spelled their name "Babikian" when writing in French or English. I am using the Armenian pronunciation.

Chapter 1: A Frayed Tapestry

1. See Claude Mutafian, *La Cilicie au carrefour des empires*, vols. 1 and 2 (Paris: Les Belles Lettres, 1988).

2. Ali Cevad, *Memâlik-i Osmaniyenin tarih ve coğrafya lûgatı* (Dersaadet, İstanbul: Kasbar Matbaası, 1314 [1897]), 11.

3. Madenashar Araks, *Kilikia: P'ordz ashkharhagrut'ean ardi Kilikioy* (Peterburg: Tparan I. Libermani, 1894), 16–18.

4. O. J. Campbell, "Document 85, Report on the Vilayet of Adana," United States National Archives and Records Administration (USNA) Inquiry Documents: Special Reports and Studies, 1917–1919, 6.

5. Araks, *Kilikia: P'ordz ashkharhagrut'ean ardi Kilikioy*, 25–30.

6. Campbell, "Document 85," 8.

7. See Puzant Yeghiayan, *Atanayi Hayots' patmut'iwn* (Beirut: Atanayi Hayrenakts'akan Miut'yan Varch'ut'iwn, 1970); Vital Cuinet, *La Turquie d'Asie: Géographie administrative, statistique, descriptive et raisonnée de chaque province de l'Asie-Mineure*, vol. 2 (Paris: E. Leroux, 1891), 12; and Araks, *Kilikia: P'ordz ashkharhagrut'ean ardi Kilikioy*, 34–35. For a detailed study of the ecology and climate of Cilicia, see Christopher Gratien, "The Mountains Are Ours: Ecology and Settlement in Late Ottoman and Early Republican Cilicia, 1856–1956," (PhD diss., Georgetown University, 2015).

8. Francis Beaufort, *Karamania; or, a Brief Description of the South Coast of Asia-Minor and of the Remains of Antiquity. With Pans, Views, Etc.* (London: R. Hunter, 1817), v–vi. This material was collected during a survey under the orders of the Lords Commissioners of the Admiralty in 1811 and 1812.

9. Mutafian, *La Cilicie au carrefour* 1:185–94.

10. On Byzantine and Seljuk relations before the Battle of Manzikert in 1071, see Joseph Laurent, *Byzance et les Turcs Seldjoucides dans l'Asie occidentale jusqu'en 1081* (Paris: Berger-Levrault, 1913). See also A. C. S. Peacock and Sara Nur Yıldız, eds., *The Seljuks of Anatolia: Court and Society in the Medieval Middle East* (London; New York: I. B. Tauris, 2015).

11. See Alexei Sukyasyan, *Kilikiayi Haykakan petowt'ean ev iravownk'i patmut'iwn: XI-XIV darer* (Erevan: Erevani Hamalsarani Hratarakch'ut'iwn, 1978); Ghevond Alichan, *Sissouan ou Arméno-Cilicie* (Venice: Mekhitarist Press, 1899); Mutafian, *La Cilicie au carrefour* 1:345–403; and Mutafian, *Le Royaume Arménien de Cilicie: XIIe-XIVe Siècle* (Paris: CNRS Editions, 1993).

12. On Cilician literature, see, for example, Hiranth Thorossian, *Histoire de la littérature arménienne, des origines jusqu'à nos jours* (Paris: Imprimerie Araxes, 1951); Manuk Abeghyan, *Erker*, vol. 4 (Erevan: Armenian Academy of Sciences, 1966–85); James Etmekjian, *History of Armenian Literature* (New York: St. Vartan Press, 1985); Srbouhi P. Hairapetian, *Hayots' hin ew mijnadarian grakanut'ean patmut'iwn* (Ant'ilias, Libanan: Tparan Kilikioy Kat'oghikosut'ean, 1988); and Agop J. Hacikyan, ed., *The Heritage of Armenian Literature*, vol. 2, *From the Sixth to the Eighteenth Century* (Detroit: Wayne State University Press, 2002). On the art of Cilician Armenia, see Sirarpie Der Nersessian, *L'Art arménien* (Paris: Arts et Métiers Graphiques, 1977), 123–62; Hermann Göltz and Klause E. Göltz, *Rescued Armenian Treasures from Cilicia* (Wiesbaden: Ludwig Reichert, 2000); Mutafian, *Le Royaume*, 2:127; and Mutafian, *La Cilicie au carrefour*, 1:441–56.

13. On commerce, see Wilhelm Heyd, *Histoire du commerce du Levant au moyen-âge* (Leipzig: Otto Harrassowitz, 1885), 365–72.

14. On Sis, see Araks, *Kilikia: P'ordz ashkharhagrut'ean ardi Kilikioy*, 125–55.

15. See Amine Jules Iskandar, *La nouvelle Cilicie: Les arméniens du Liban* (Antelias: Catholicosate of Cilicia, 1999). See also Seta B. Dadoyan, *The Armenian Catholicosate from Cilicia to Antelias: An Introduction* (Antelias: Armenian Catholicosate of Cilicia, 2003).

16. See Dickran Kouymjian, "Cilicia and Its Catholicosate from the Fall of the Kingdom to 1915," in *Armenian Cilicia*, ed. Richard G. Hovannisian and Simon Payaslian (Costa Mesa: Mazda Publishers, 2008), 297–307.

17. The Armenian Apostolic Church is an eastern church. It was established by two of the apostles, Bartholomew and Thaddeus. The church has four major divisions. After the collapse of the Armenian Kingdom of Cilicia in 1375, two Catholicosates emerged: one was located in Sis, in the Ottoman province of Adana, until World War I, and the other was located in Echmiadzin, in today's Armenia. While the latter (also called the Catholicos of All Armenia) has not moved since the collapse of the Armenian Kingdom, the former moved after the Armenian Genocide to Antelias, a suburb of Beirut. There are also two other patriarchates: one in Jerusalem and the other in İstanbul. For more information, see Maghakia Ormanian, *The Church of Armenia*, trans. G. Marcar Gregory (London: A. R. Mowbray & Co, 1912; 3rd rev. ed., New York: St. Vartan Press, 1988); and Hratch Thilingirian, "The Catholicos and the Hierarchical Sees of the Armenian Church" in *Eastern Christianity: Studies in Modern History, Religion and Politics*, ed.

Anthony O'Mahony (London: Melisende, 2004), 140–59. There were also Catholic and Protestant Armenian church hierarchies in the Ottoman Empire.

18. Yeghiayan, *Atanayi Hayots' patmut'iwn*, 664–68. In 1866, Bishop Kapriel Kechechyan and Fr. Marcellino formed the Armenian Catholic community in Sis and built a small church and a school.

19. Ibid., 660.

20. Vahakn Keshishian et al., *Ermeni kültür varlıklarıyla Adana* [Adana with its Armenian cultural heritage] (İstanbul: HDV Yayınları, 2018), 19.

21. Ramazan Bey, of the Yüreğir clan of Oğuz Turks, founded the Ramadanid Principality (*Ramazanoğulları Beyliği*; 1352–1608) and made Elbistan the capital.

22. For a list of beys from 1353 to 1608, see *Yurt ansiklopedisi*, vol. 1 (İstanbul: Anadolu Yayıncılık, 1981), s.v. "Adana," 25.

23. Kasim Ener, *Tarih boyunca Adana ovasına bir bakış* (İstanbul: Berksoy Matbaası, 1964), 292–305.

24. Suavi Aydın, "Adana," in *Encyclopedia of Islam*, vol. 3, ed. Kate Fleet, Gudrun Krämer, Denis Matringe, John Nawas, and Everett Rowson, accessed August 17, 2018.

25. On the Kozanoğulları, see Misak Keleshian, *Sis-Matean: Patmakan, banasirakan, teghekagrakan, azgagrakan ew harakits' baraganer* (Pēyrut': Tparan "Hay Chemarani," 1949), 91–110.

26. Andrew G. Gould, "Lords or Bandits? The Derebeys of Cilicia," *International Journal of Middle East Studies* 7, no. 4 (1976): 494.

27. H. P. Boghosian, *Hachēni ēndhanur patmut'iwnē: Ew shrjakay Gōzan-Taghi Hay giwgherē* (Los Angeles: Bozart Press, 1942), 518–19.

28. Papken Giuleserian, *Patmut'iwn Kat'oghikosats' Kilikioy: 1441-ēn minch'ew mer ōrerē* (Ant'ilias, Libanan: Tparan Dprevanuts' Kat'oghikosut'ean Kilikioy, 1939), 500.

29. The most important of these tribes included the Avşar, Varsak, Reyhanlı, Sırkıntılı, Tecirli, and Cerit tribes. The most important *derebey*s belonged to the following families: Kozanoğulları, Küçükalioğulları, Kokuluoğulları, Menemencioğulları, and Karsantioğulları.

30. The Turcoman Avşars were one of the most powerful tribes of Cilicia.

31. Stephan Astourian, "Testing World-System Theory, Cilicia (1830's-1890's): Armenian-Turkish Polarization and the Ideology of Modern Ottoman Historiography" (PhD diss., University of California, Los Angeles, 1996), 77.

32. Ibid., 73.

33. Yonca Köksal, "Coercion and Mediation: Centralization and Sedentarization of Tribes in the Ottoman Empire," *Middle Eastern Studies* 42, no. 3 (2006): 474.

34. Virginia Aksan, *Ottoman Wars, 1700–1870: An Empire Besieged* (London: Routledge, 2014), 364.

35. See Fawaz, *An Occasion for War*.

36. Russegger wrote a travelogue called *Reisen in Europa, Asien, und Afrika: Mit Besonderer Rücksicht auf Die Naturwissenschaftlichen Verhältnisse der Betreffenden Länder; Unternommen in den Jahren 1835 bis 1841* (Stuttgart: E. Schweizerbart'sche Verlagshandlung, 1841–48).

37. William Burckhardt Barker, *Lares and Penates: Or, Cilicia and its Governors* (London: Ingram, Cooke, 1853), 90–91.

38. Meltem Toksöz, *Nomads, Migrants and Cotton in the Eastern Mediterranean: The Making of the Adana-Mersin Region, 1850–1908* (Leiden: Brill, 2010), 42.

39. See Vahé Tachjian, "La période d'occupation égyptienne en Cilicie (1832–1840): Changements économiques et démographiques," *Chronos: Revue d'Histoire de l'Université de Balamand* 11 (2005): 103–41.

40. Toksöz, *Nomads, Migrants and Cotton*, 46.

41. Ehud Toledano argues that the fellahin were not brought from Egypt by İbrahim Paşa but instead were Alawis from northern Syria. See Ehud Toledano, "Where Have All the Egyptian Fellahin Gone? Labor in Mersin and Çukurova (Second Half of the Nineteenth Century)," in *Eastern Mediterranean Port Cities: A Study of Mersin, Turkey—From Antiquity to Modernity*, ed. Filiz Yenişehirlioğlu, Eyüp Özveren, and Tülin Selvi Ünlü (Cham: Springer, 2019), 126–42.

42. On the Ottoman demographic policies in Cilicia, see Hilmar Kaiser, "Baghdad Railway Politics and the Socio-economic Transformation of the Çukurova (Cilicia)" (PhD diss., European University Institute, 2001), 24–34.

43. Astourian, "Testing World-System Theory," 128.

44. Ener, *Tarih boyunca Adana ovasına bir bakış*, 307; Barker, *Lares and Penates*, 81.

45. *Yurt ansiklopedisi*, vol. 1, s.v. "Adana," 29.

46. Araks, *Kilikia: P'ordz ashkharhagrut'ean ardi Kilikioy*, 78–85.

47. Ahmet Cevdet, *Tezâkir*, ed. Cavid Baysun, vol. 3, *Tezkire* no. 31 (Ankara: Türk Tarih Kurumu Basımevi, 1953).

48. Cevdet, *Tezâkir*, Tezkire no. 36, 223–24.

49. In accordance with the Vilâyet Law, each of these districts included subdistricts, as follows: the districts of Adana included the subdistricts of Adana, Karaisalı, and Hamidiye; the district of Mersin included the subdistricts of Tarsus; the district of İçil included the subdistricts of Silifke, Ermenak, Mut, Gülnar, and Anamur; the district of Kozan included the subdistricts of Sis (Kozan), Kadirli (Kars), Haçin (Saimbeyli), and Feke; and the district of Cebel-i Bereket contained the subdistricts of Yarpuz, Osmaniye, İslahiye, Hassa, Bahçe (Bulanık), and Payas.

50. The *Salnâme*s (yearbooks) of the province of Adana provided detailed information. See, for example, the *Salnâme-i vilâyet-i Adana 1308 (1890)* (Adana: Vilâyet Matbaası, 1890), 38–68. For a more detailed account, see *Salnâme-i vilâyet-i Adana 1321 (1903)* (Adana: Vilâyet Matbaası, 1903), 105–237.

51. *Yurt ansiklopedisi*, vol. 1, s.v. "Adana," 113.

52. Ibid., 66.

53. Mesrob Krikorian, *Armenians in the Service of the Ottoman Empire, 1860–1908* (Boston: Routledge and Kegan Paul, 1978), 65.

54. Ibid., 67–68.

55. See Huri İslamoğlu-İnan, *The Ottoman Empire and the World-Economy* (Cambridge: Cambridge University Press, 2004); and Şevket Pamuk, *The Ottoman Empire and European Capitalism, 1820–1913* (Cambridge: Cambridge University Press, 1987), 19–21. On the consequences of the treaty, see Roger Owen, "The 1838 Anglo-Turkish Convention: An Overview," *New Perspectives on Turkey* 7 (Spring 1992): 7–14.

56. On economic development in Cilicia, see Kaiser, "Baghdad Railway Politics," 35–46.

57. Toksöz, *Nomads, Migrants and Cotton*, 55–56.

58. Araks, *Kilikia: P'ordz ashkharhagrut'ean ardi Kilikioy*, 218–38.

59. Meltem Toksöz, "Ottoman Mersin: The Making of an Eastern Mediterranean Port-town," *New Perspectives on Turkey* 31 (Fall 2004): 71–89.

60. Naval Intelligence Division (UK), *A Handbook of Asia Minor*, vol. 4, part 2 (London: Naval Staff, Intelligence Dept., 1919), 46.

61. On the different types of seasonal laborers, see Kaiser, "Baghdad Railway Politics," 49–53; and Yeghiayan, *Atanayi Hayots' patmut'iwn*, 162. See S. M. Dzotsigian, *Arewmtahay ashkharh* (New York: Hratarakut'iwn S. M. Tsots'ikean Hobelianakan Handznakhumbi, 1947), 86–87. Dzotsigian puts the number of migrant workers arriving at seventy-five thousand. See also Gratien, "The Mountains Are Ours," 235–45. A representative report sent from Adana to the Ministry of the Interior in July of 1894 estimated the number of Armenian migrant workers that year to be between sixty and seventy thousand. See BOA, DH.MKT 288/78 (27 Rebîülevvel 1312/28 September 1894). I would like to thank David Gutman for providing me with this document.

62. Astourian, "Testing World-System Theory," 233–34.

63. David Fraser, *The Short Cut to India: The Record of a Journey along the Route of the Baghdad Railway* (Edinburgh: Blackwood, 1909), 80.

64. Toksöz, *Nomads, Migrants and Cotton*, 136.

65. Kaiser, "Baghdad Railway Politics," 38.

66. See Sven Beckert, *Empire of Cotton: A Global History* (New York, NY: Vintage, 2015), 242–73.

67. *Kilikia*, May 1, 1863, no. 9, 201–9.

68. Ani Vosganyan, *Atanayi nahangi Hayeri tntesakan vijakě 1909 t', unezrkum* (Yerevan: H. H. GAA "Gitut'iwn" Hratarakch'ut'win), 35.

69. Toksöz, *Nomads, Migrants and Cotton*, 173.

70. See *Yurt ansiklopedisi*, vol., 1 s.v. "Adana," 34.

71. Toksöz, *Nomads, Migrants and Cotton*, 184. On the Mavromatis family, see Meltem Toksöz, "Family and Migration: The Mavromatis' Enterprises and Networks," *Cahiers de la Méditerranée* 82 (2011): 359–82.

72. Toksöz, *Nomads, Migrants and Cotton*, 184.

73. Fraser, *The Short Cut to India*, 77.

74. Ibid., 80.

75. Ibid.

76. See Kaiser, "Baghdad Railway Politics," 54–71.

77. Giuseppe Carpa, "Il Vilajet di Adana: L'antica Cilicia," *Bolletino Della Reale Societa Geografica*, series 5, vol. 14, no. 7 (July 1, 1915): 784.

78. On the mechanization of the cotton industry, see Zafer Toprak, "20. yüzyılın ilk çeyreğinde Çukurova'da emek ve sermaye," *Toplumsal Tarih* 191 (November 2009): 70–76.

79. On the Deutsche-Levantine Baumwolle-Gesellschaft (Delebage), see Kaiser, "Baghdad Railway Politics" and Toksöz, *Nomads, Migrants and Cotton*, 185–86.

80. Toksöz, "Ottoman Mersin," 83.

81. Fraser, *The Short Cut to India*, 78.

82. *Biwrakn*, January 27, 1907, nos. 9–10, 238.

83. Imports included zinc, copper, coal, shot, tin, iron wire, iron pipes, nails, window glass, beer, sugar, coffee, margarine, tea, belting, drugs, printing material, lubricating oils, cotton-separating machines, sewing machines (a German rival of the Singer machine had just emerged), guns, cotton yarn, wool yarn, wool stuff, cotton stuff, and *basma* cloth, among others. See G. H. M. Doughty-Wylie, "Report on the Trade of the Province of Adana for the Year 1908 by Major G. H. M. Doughty-Wylie, His Majesty's Acting Vice-Consul in Diplomatic and Consular Reports," in *Report on the Trade of the Province of Adana*, ed. Foreign Office and Board of Trade, Annual Series, no. 4235, 18–23.

84. Ibid., 23–24.

85. See Cuinet, *La Turquie d'Asie*, 18–21.

86. Naval Intelligence Division (UK), *A Handbook of Asia Minor*, vol. 4, part 2, 48. One of the best studies on the Baghdad Railway is that of Hilmar Kaiser. See Kaiser, "Baghdad Railway Politics."

87. United States Department of Commerce and Labor, Bureau of Manufactures, *Daily Consular Reports and Trade Reports*, Monday, January 25, 1909, no. 3389, 1–2.

88. Doughty-Wylie, "Report on the Province of Adana," 6. See also Fitzner, *Aus Kleinasien und Syrien*, 119.

89. Naval Intelligence Division (UK), *A Handbook of Asia Minor*, vol. 4, part 2, 48.

90. Vosganyan, *Atanayi nahangi Hayeri tntesakan vijakě 1909 t', unezrkum*, 53. On other Armenian merchants of Adana and Mersin, see *Biwrakn*, June 3, 1906, no. 19, 454.

91. *Biwrakn*, January 27, 1907, nos. 9–10, 237.

92. Yeghiayan, *Atanayi Hayots' patmut'iwn*, 160.

93. Ibid., 160. These were all looted and burned during the 1909 massacres.

94. Vosganyan, *Atanayi nahangi Hayeri tntesakan vijakë 1909 t'*, unezrkum, 57.

95. Araks, *Kilikia: P'ordz ashkharhagrut'ean ardi Kilikioy*, 222.

96. Yeghiayan, *Atanayi Hayots' patmut'iwn*, 164.

97. Boghosian, *Hachëni ëndhanur patmut'iwnë*, 179.

98. Uğur Ümit Üngör and Mehmet Polatel, *Confiscation and Destruction: The Young Turk Seizure of Armenian Property* (London: Bloomsbury, 2013), 12.

99. Minas Khabrig, *Et'ë Ch'ork'-Marzpanë intsi het khösër* (Pëyrut': Hratarakut'iwn Ch'ork'-Marzpani Hayrenakts'akan Miut'ean, 1983), 22.

100. Ibid., 23.

101. See Cengiz Orhonlu, *Osmanlı imparatorluğunda aşiretlerin iskanı* (İstanbul: Eren Yayıncılık, 1987). On the Crimean War, see Candan Badem, *The Ottoman Crimean War (1853–1856)* (Leiden: Brill, 2010). See also Köksal, "Coercion and Mediation," 469–91.

102. Gratien, "The Mountains Are Ours," 96–149.

103. Cevdet, *Tezâkir, Tezkire* no. 26, 107.

104. Ibid., 109. See also Yusuf Halaçoğlu, "Fırka-ı ıslâhiye ve yapmış olduğu iskân," *İstanbul Üniversitesi Edebiyat Fakültesi Tarih Dergisi* 37 (1973): 1–20. In regions such as Kozan, located in the province of Adana, there were many unsettled tribes. The most important of these were the Avşar, Sırkıntılı, Varsak, Tecirli, and Cerit tribes, which were under the control of the Kozanoğulları.

105. On the Reform Committee memorandum written by Ahmed Cevdet Paşa, see Saim Yörük, *Fırka-i ıslâhıye: Cevdet Paşa—Kozan ve gâvur dağı ahvâline dâir lâyiha* (İstanbul: İdeal Kültür Yayıncılık, 2017).

106. Cevdet, *Tezâkir, Tezkire* no. 27, 108.

107. For a detailed description of the campaign, see Ahmet Cevdet Paşa, *Ma'ruzât*, ed. Yusuf Halaçoğlu (İstanbul: Çağrı Yayınları, 1980), 131–72.

108. Gratien, "The Mountains Are Ours," 37–38.

109. Cevdet, *Tezâkir, Tezkire* no. 27, 135.

110. Cevdet Paşa, *Ma'ruzât*, 117.

111. On the settling of the tribes, see Orhonlu, *Osmanlı imparatorluğunda aşiretlerin iskânı*.

112. Cevdet, *Tezâkir, Tezkire*, no. 27, 108.

113. Cevdet, *Tezâkir, Tezkire*, no. 28, 137–39.

114. Bedros Archbishop Der Melkonian, *Patmut'iwn azatut'eann Hachënoy i dserats' K'özaneants'* (K. Polis: Tp. Aramean, 1871).

115. Ibid., 11.

116. Ibid.

117. Ibid., 18

118. Halaçoğlu, "Fırka-ı İslâhiye," 16. The Avşars were one of nomadic Oğuz tribes who moved from Central Asia to Eastern Turkey and Iranian Azerbaijan.

119. Reşat Kasaba, "Do States Always Favor Stasis? The Changing Status of Tribes in the Ottoman Empire," in *Boundaries and Belonging*, ed. Joel Migdal (Cambridge: Cambridge University Press, 2004), 38–39.

120. Cuinet, *La Turquie d'Asie*, 6.

121. Ibid.

122. For a general study about this wave of immigration, see Kemal H. Karpat, *Ottoman Population: Demographic and Social Characteristics* (Wisconsin: University of Wisconsin Press, 1985), 61–77. See also Isa Blumi, *Ottoman Refugees, 1878–1939: Migration in a Post-Imperial World* (London: Bloomsbury Academic, 2013).

123. Stephan H. Astourian, "The Silence of the Land: Agrarian Relations, Ethnicity, and Power," in *A Question of Genocide: Armenians and Turks at the End of the Ottoman Empire*, ed. Ronald G. Suny, Norman M. Naimark, and Fatma M. Göçek (New York: Oxford University Press, 2011), 58.

124. On the Crimean refugees, see Ethem Feyzi Gözaydın, *Kırım: Kırım Türklerinin yerleşme ve göçmeleri* (İstanbul: Vakit Matbaası, 1948), 63–100. See also Ahmet Cevat Eren, *Türkiye'de göç ve göçmen meseleleri: Tanzimat devri, ilk kurulan göçmen komisyonu, çıkarılan tüzükler* (İstanbul: Nurgök Matbaası, 1966), 96–113.

125. Bedri Habiçoğlu, *Kafkasya'dan Anadolu'ya göçler ve iskanları* (İstanbul: Nart Yayıncılık, 1993), 74–75.

126. Nedim İpek, *Rumeli'den Anadolu'ya Türk göçleri, 1877–1890* (Ankara: Türk Tarih Kurumu, 1994), 288.

127. The Nogays were a Turkic ethnic group who lived mainly in the North Caucasus region.

128. On the formation of the Refugee Commission, see Eren, *Türkiye'de göç ve göçmen meseleleri*, 39–61. On the constitution of the commission, see ibid., 96–113. See also David Cameron Cuthell Jr., "The Muhacirin Komisyonu: An Agent in the Transformation of the Ottoman Anatolia (1860–1866)" (PhD diss., Columbia University, 2005).

129. Cevdet, *Tezâkir, Tezkire* no. 27, 124.

130. Hilmi Bayraktar, "Kırım ve Kafkasya'dan Adana vilayeti'ne yapılan göç ve iskânlar (1869–1907)," *Türkiyat Araştırmaları Dergisi* 2 (2007): 409.

131. Ibid., 410.

132. Ibid., 411–12.

133. Ibid., 412. On the Telan property and farm, see Keleshian, *Sis-Matean*, 271.

134. Keleshian, *Sis-Matean*, 277. On Khabayan, see ibid., 261–87.

135. On the number of refugees from the Caucasus, see Habiçoğlu, *Kafkasya'dan Anadolu'ya göçler ve iskanları*, 70–73. See also Karpat, *Ottoman Population*, 65–70.

136. Bayraktar, "Kırım ve Kafkasya'dan," 414.

137. Ibid.

138. Karpat, *Ottoman Population*, 69.

139. Ibid., 415. On the Georgian Muslim refugees who arrived in Trabzon, see Oktay Özel, "Muhacirler, yerliler ve gayrimüslimler: Osmanlı'nın son devrinde orta Karadeniz'de toplumsal uyumun sınırları üzerine bazı gözlemler," *Tarih ve Toplum, Yeni Yaklaşımlar* 5 (Spring 2007): 93–112. See also Oktay Özel, "Migration and Power Politics: The Settlement of Georgian Immigrants in Turkey (1878–1908)," *Middle Eastern Studies* 46, no. 4 (2010): 477–96.

140. Murat Bardakçı, *Talât Paşa'nın evrak-ı metrûkesi: Sadrazam Talât Paşa'nın özel arşivinde bulunan Ermeni tehciri konusundaki belgeler ve hususî yazışmalar* (İstanbul: Everest Yayınları, 2013), 35.

141. Ibid., 39.

142. Bayraktar, "Kırım ve Kafkasya'dan," 416.

143. Ibid.

144. Ibid.

145. Ibid.

146. Ibid., 418. Other villages established via refugee settlement during this period include Ahmediye, Haliliye, Hilmiye, Mahmudiye, Saidiye, Salihiye, and Sıddıkiye in the subdistrict of Hamidiye; Şerefiye in the subdistrict of Misis; Bahriye, Hüseyniye, Kızlarçalı, and Kuyuluk ve Ümran in the subdistrict of Payas; Hamidülasar, Mecidiye, Orhaniye, and Osmaniye in the subdistrict of Sis.

147. Ibid., 422.

148. Ibid., 423.

149. On the complaints of the refugees, see Georgi Chochiev, "XIX. yüzyılın ikinci yarısında Osmanlı İmparatorluğu'nda Kuzey Kafkas göçmenlerinin toplumsal uyarlanmasına dair bazı görüşler (göçmenlerin otoriteye başvuruları)," *Kebikeç* 23 (2007): 407–56. On the impact of malaria on the forced settlements, see Gratien, "The Mountains Are Ours," 168–214.

150. Bayraktar, "Kırım ve Kafkasya'dan," 431. For example, there are forty-eight refugee villages in the region of Ceyhan and Yumurtalık today, consisting of twenty-four villages from Bulgaria, twenty-one from the Caucasus, and three from Crete. See İpek, *Rumeli'den Anadolu'ya Türk göçleri, 1877–1890*, 288.

151. Astourian, "The Silence of the Land," 62.

152. The fellahin are Turkified Arabs who are the descendants of the Egyptian fellahin that were brought to work in the cotton fields of Cilicia.

153. The Ansariyeh (or al-Nusariyeh) is a branch of Shiism. Their name is derived from Nusair Abu Shu'ayb Muhammad ibn Nusayr (d. 868). In the second half of the nineteenth century, some Ansariyeh emigrated from the Syrian mountains to the Cilician plain.

154. See Araks, *Kilikia: P'ordz ashkharhagrut'ean ardi Kilikioy*, 39–49.

155. Justin McCarthy, *Muslims and Minorities: The Population of Ottoman Anatolia and the End of the Empire* (New York: New York University Press, 1983), 54.

156. Cuinet, *La Turquie d'Asie*, 9. On the Maronites of Mersin, see Şerife Yorulmaz, "Maronites in Mersin through Its Process of Becoming an Important Port City (the Nineteenth and the Twentieth Century)," in Yenişehirlioğlu, Özveren, and Ünlü, *Eastern Mediterranean Port Cities*, 93–110.

157. According to Cuinet, in 1880, Armenians in the province of Adana numbered 97,450 people with the following religious breakdowns: 69,300 Armenian Apostolics, 11,550 Armenian Catholics, and 16,600 Armenian Protestants. See Cuinet, *La Turquie d'Asie*, 4–5. In 1889, Şemseddin Sâmî estimated the population of Adana to be 350,000 Christians, Turks, Kurds, and Arabs, with most of the Christians being Armenians. See Şemseddin Sâmî, *Kâmûsu'l-a'lâm: Tarih ve coğrafya lûgatı ve tabir-i esahhiyle kâffe-yi esmâ-yi hassa-yi câmidir* (İstanbul: Mihran Matbaası, 1889), 217. According to the 1890 Salnâme of Adana, there were 341,376 Muslim residents, 6,262 Greek residents, 22,815 Armenian residents, 1,653 Catholic residents, 2,144 Protestant residents, and 115 Syriac residents, making a total of 374,365 residents. See *Salnâme-i vilâyet-i Adana 1308 (1890)*. An Armenian book published in 1894 on Cilicia estimated the Christian population of Adana to be 168,990. Of these, 97,450 were Armenians; of those Armenians, it was supposed 69,300 were Apostolic, 11,550 Catholic, and 16,600 Protestant. Muslims constituted 162,400 residents, including Ottomans, Kurds, Turkmens, Circassians, Persians, and Syrians. The remaining 72,050 of the estimated 403,440 total were followers of other religions and denominations, including 50,000 fellahin and members of nomadic tribes (Nusayri) and 16,050 Romani. See Araks, *Kilikia: P'ordz ashkharhagrut'ean ardi Kilikioy*, 39–40. In 1910, Ormanian estimated the number of Armenians (Apostolic, Catholic, and Protestant), based on the dioceses of Sis, Adana, Haçin, and Payas, to be 88,600, with the greatest number of Armenians—37,900—living in Adana, followed by 22,200 Armenians living in Haçin. See Ormanian, *The Church of Armenian*, 207. Justin McCarthy puts the number of Armenians at 74,930 and the Muslim population at 573,256. See McCarthy, *Muslims and Minorities*, 110. McCarthy's methodology, described in appendix 4 of his study, has been challenged by Marashlian. See Levon Marashlian, *Politics and Demography: Armenians, Turks, and Kurds in the Ottoman Empire* (Cambridge, MA: Zoryan Institute, 1991).

158. Astourian, "Testing World-System Theory," 111. For a detailed discussion of the topic, see Fuat Dündar, *Crime of Numbers: The Role of Statistics in the Armenian Question (1878–1918)* (New Brunswick, NJ.: Transaction Publishers, 2010).

159. For a critique of the Ottoman figures, see Marashlian, *Politics and Demography*.

160. Ibid., 172, 184.

161. Kévorkian, *The Armenian Genocide*, 276.

162. Mehmet Polatel, "Armenians and the Land Question in the Ottoman Empire, 1870–1914" (PhD diss., Boğaziçi University, 2017), 64. See also Üngör and Polatel, *Confiscation and Destruction*.

163. Ibid.

164. Sarkis Karakoç, *Arâzi kânunu ve tapu nizamnâmesi* (İstanbul: Kitabhane-i Cihan, 1342 [1923]), 175–254. For the English version, see *The Ottoman Land Code*, trans. F. Ongley (London: W. Clowes and Sons, 1892).

165. Kaiser, "Baghdad Railway Politics," 6.

166. Astourian, "The Silence of the Land," 56.

167. Ibid.

168. For the Armenian version of the report, see Konstandnupolsoy Patriark'ut'iwn, "Deghekagir kawaṛakan harstaharut'eants' nerkayatsyal aṛ duṛn hanoun azgayin zhogho-voy i 11 April 1872," in *Deghekakirk' kawaṛakan harstaharut'eants'* (G. Bolis: Tpagrut'iwn Aramyan, 1876). The second report is in the same book. See "B. Deghekagir kawaṛakan harstaharut'eants' i khorhrdanakan handznakhmbē aṛ azgayin zhoghovn," 9–44. For the English version, see "First Report on Provincial Oppressions Submitted to the Sublime Porte in the Name of the Armenian National Assembly April 11, 1872," in *Reports on Provincial Oppressions* (London: Gilbert and Rivington, 1877), 1–8. For the second report in English, see "Second Report on the Oppression of the Armenians and Other Provinces of Asiatic Turkey Presented to the Armenian National Assembly on the 17th of September, 1876 by the Commission Appointed for that Purpose," in *Reports on Provincial Oppressions*, 9–57.

169. Astourian, "The Silence of the Land," 57.

170. Ibid., 56.

171. Ibid., 62.

172. Ibid., 65.

173. See Konstandnupolsoy Patriark'ut'iwn, Hoghayin Grawmants' Handznazhoghov, *Teghekagir hoghayin grawmants' handznazhoghovoy*, vols. 1–4 (K. Polis: Tpagr. T. Tōghramachean, 1910–12).

174. Astourian, "The Silence of the Land," 65.

175. Konstandnupolsoy Patriark'ut'iwn, *Teghekagir hoghayin grawmants' handznazhoghovoy* 1:10–11.

176. Konstandnupolsoy Patriark'ut'iwn, *Teghekagir hoghayin grawmants' handznazhoghovoy* 2:5.

177. Ibid.

178. Konstandnupolsoy Patriark'ut'iwn, *Teghekagir hoghayin grawmants' handznazhoghovoy* 3:5.

179. Ibid.

180. Ibid., 5–6.

181. On these events, see Yeghiayan, *Atanayi Hayots' patmut'iwn*, 174–210.

182. The relative safety of Adana's Armenians was due to the efforts of Vali Bahri Paşa.

183. Christopher Clay, "Labour Migration and Economic Conditions in Nineteenth Century," in "Turkey before and after Atatürk: Internal and External Affairs," special issue, *Middle Eastern Studies* 34, no. 4 (October 1998): 26.

Chapter 2: Agitation and Paranoia

1. The grand vizier was the de facto prime minister of the sultan in the Ottoman Empire.

2. BOA, A.MKT.MHM 502/67 (17 Teşrîn-i Sânî 1307/29 November 1891).

3. BOA, BEO 2/137 (19 Mayıs 1308/31 May 1892).

4. BOA, A.MKT.MHM 617/7 (31 Temmuz 1312/12 August 1896). Two days prior, a ciphered telegram on this topic had been sent by the vali of Adana, Faik Bey, to the Ministry of the Interior. See BOA, DH.ŞFR 196/21 (29 Temmuz 1312/10 August 1896).

5. BOA, A.MKT.MHM 541/30 (16 Kânûn-ı Evvel 1313/28 December 1897).

6. BOA, A.MKT.MHM 541/30 (8 Kânûn-ı Evvel 1313/20 December 1897).

7. BOA, MKT. MHM 551/2 (28 Ağustos 1322 /10 September 1906).

8. BOA, DH.TMIK.M 267/35 (3 Nisan 1324/16 April 1908).

9. See, for example, the case of Ohannes Cherchiyan and his brothers in Mersin. Seditious material was found in their house and shop. BOA, BEO 94/7017 (11 Teşrîn-i Evvel 1308/23 October 1892); and BOA, BEO 116/8631 (18 Teşrîn-i Sânî 1308/30 November 1892).

10. *Biwzandion*, October 14, 1908, no. 3653, 1.

11. *İtidal*, April 7, 1909, no. 33, 2. See also Damar Arıkoğlu, *Hâtıralarım* (İstanbul: Tan Gazetesi ve Matbaası, 1961), 44.

12. According to reports that arrived on that day, 170 houses in the empty lands of Burnaz in the district of Cebel-i Bereket were considered suitable for refugee settlement, as were another 25 houses in the Bulanık district. The report also stated that the mutasarrıf of Kozan was directed to settle twenty thousand to thirty thousand refugees in that area. BOA, DH.MKT 2006/33 (15 Eylül 1308/27 September 1892).

13. BOA, BEO 3521/264057 (12 Mart 1325/25 March 1909).

14. Arıkoğlu, *Hâtıralarım*, 42.

15. Bahri Paşa was a member of the Reform Legislation Department of the Council of State (*Şûrâ-yı Devlet Tanzimat Dâiresi*) and was appointed vali of Adana on March 11, 1898. See BOA, BEO 1089/81675 (26 Şubat 1313/10 March 1897).

16. Taha Toros, *Ali Münif Bey'in hâtıraları* (İstanbul: İsis, 1996), 48.

17. Boghos Markarian, *Ink'nakensagrut'iwn Pōghos Margareani: Ew ziwr ěntanik'i andamots' patmakann* (Pěrkěnfilt, Niw Chěrzi: [publisher not identified], 1951), 21.

18. The Yıldız Palace was the residence of the sultan and his court in the late nineteenth and early twentieth centuries.

19. BOA, DH.MKT 2434/140 (21 Teşrîn-i Sânî 1316/4 December 1900). See also BOA, DH.MKT 2445/108 (5 Kânûn-ı Evvel 1316/18 December 1900).

20. BOA, DH.MKT 2006/33 (13 Şubat 1316/26 February 1901).

21. BOA, BEO 1602/120138 (16 Kânûn-ı Evvel 1316/29 December 1900).

22. BOA, BEO 1618/121311 (30 Kânûn-ı Sânî 1316/12 February 1901).

23. He left the church and married in 1928. See Keleshian, *Sis-Matean*, 236.

24. Seropian refutes these claims. See Moushegh Yebisgobos (herafter Seropian), *Atanayi jardĕ ew pataskhanatunerĕ* (Gahire: Tparan Ararat-S. Darbinean, 1909), 11. For the French version of the book, see Seropian, *Les vêpres ciliciennes: Les responsabilités, faits et documents* (Alexandrie: Typo-Lithographie Centrale I. Della Rocca, 1909).

25. Moushegh Seropian, *Ink'nakensagrut'iwn*, vol. 2, (unpublished manuscript), 214. Seropian's memoirs consist of seven volumes located at the Nubarian Library in Paris. They were written sometime after World War 1. I would like to thank Vahé Tachjian for providing me with these memoirs.

26. On his first meeting with the vali, see Seropian, *Ink'nakensagrut'iwn* 2:345–47.

27. BOA, BEO 2401/1824 (12 Ağustos 1320/25 August 1904).

28. Levon Kirishdjian, a Hnchak activist born in Samatia in 1875, was a graduate of Robert College in İstanbul. He was the editor of the Reformed Hnchak organ *Dzayn Hayreniats*. Nazaret Daghavarian was born in Sivas in 1862. He was a physician, a member of the Ottoman Parliament (1908), and a public figure who played an important role in Armenian political life.

29. BOA, DH.TMIK.M 214/35 (10 Kânûn-ı Evvel 1321/23 December 1905).

30. BOA, Y.MTV 291/66 (25 Teşrîn-i Sânî 1322/8 December 1906).

31. On the work of Seropian, see Markarian, *Ink'nakensagrut'iwn Pōghos Margareani*, 21–23.

32. The market was built on the old Armenian cemetery. See Mixed Council meeting, 16/19 November, Archives of the Armenian Diocese of Adana, Madenataran Library (AADA).

33. *Zhamanak*, June 15, 1909, no. 191, 1–2.

34. Seropian, *Atanayi jardĕ ew pataskhanatunerĕ*, 15.

35. Ibid.

36. BOA, DH.MKT 908/17 (15 Mart 1322/28 March 1906).

37. See the telegram from the Ministry of the Interior to the province of Adana. BOA, DH.MKT 1902/103 (7 Kânûn-ı Evvel 1307/19 December 1891).

38. See BOA, DH.MKT 1973/18 (4 Temmuz 1308/16 July 1892); BOA, BEO 140/10474 (2 Teşrîn-i Evvel 1308/14 October 1892); and BOA, BEO 140/10474 (28 Eylül 1308/10 October 1892).

39. BOA, DH.MKT 225/10 (31 Mart 1310/12 April 1894).

40. BOA, BEO 1857/13219 (19 Mart 1318/1 April 1902). For Bahri's other letters on the matter, see BOA, DH.ŞFR 286/85 (20 Mayıs 1318/2 June 1902); and BOA, DH.ŞFR 293/22 (9 Eylül 1318/22 September 1902).

41. BOA, A.MKT.MHM 554/21 (25 Kânûn-ı Sânî 1315/6 February 1900).

42. BOA, A.MKT.MHM 554/21 (17 Temmuz 1318/30 July 1902).

43. BOA, A.MKT.MHM 616/43 (8 Kânûn-ı Sânî 1311/20 January 1896).

44. BOA, A.MKT.MHM 616/43 (15 Kânûn-ı Sânî 1311/27 January 1896).

45. BOA, A.MKT.MHM 616/43 (3 Şubat 1311/15 February 1896).

46. BOA, A.MKT.MHM 554/21 (13 Mart 1318/26 March 1902). See also BOA, A.MKT.MHM 554/21 (17 Temmuz 1318 /30 July 1902).

47. BOA, A.MKT.MHM 554/21 (1 Teşrîn-i Evvel 1319/14 October 1903).

48. BOA, DH.TMIK.M 131/42 (8 Ağustos 1318/21 August 1902).

49. BOA, DH.TMIK.M 131/42 (9 Teşrin-i Evvel 1318/22 October 1902). The information provided by the vali in these letters demonstrates that, even when Gökderelian was in prison, Bağdadizade was inciting other inmates to attack him. This personal animosity would take a new form in the postrevolutionary period.

50. BOA, Y.MTV 273/157 (11 Nisan 1321/24 April 1905).

51. BOA, DH.TMIK.M 227/16 (15 Nisan 1324/28 April 1908).

52. Seropian, Ink'nakensagrut'iwn 3:527.

53. For a detailed description of Telan Farm, see the letter that was sent from the Armenian Patriarchate to the grand vizier on May 13, 1903. BOA, A.MKT.MHM 529/22 (30 Nisan 1319/13 May 1903).

54. On Kefsizian, see Keleshian, Sis-Matean, 246–57.

55. BOA, BEO 2855/214099 (9 Haziran 1322/22 June 1906).

56. See "Document No. 71 from Sahag to the Catholicos of Echmiadzin, May 31, 1903," in Zakaria Bzdigian, Kilikean kskidzner, 1903–1915 (Beirut: Hraztan Press, 1927), 9–36. On the properties belonging to the Catholicos of Sis, see ibid., 24–27. Sahag II Khabayan was born in Harput on March 25, 1849. In 1869, his father took him to Jerusalem. He was elected Catholicos in 1902, with the consecration taking place on April 20, 1903. For more information about him, see Keleshian, Sis-Matean, 261–87.

57. Bzdigian, Kilikean kskidzner, 25.

58. Ibid., 26.

59. BOA, DH.TMIK.M 225/20 (9 Haziran 1322/22 June 1906). The letter was sent to Adana on July 25.

60. Moushegh Seropian to Maghakia Ormanian, February 23, 1905, Adana, "A Letter Sent from Moushegh," no. 4, in Bzdigian, Kilikean kskidzner, 1903–1915, 52–55.

61. Ibid., 54.

62. Sahag II Khabayan to Maghakia Ormanian, October 25, 1905, Sis, "A Letter from Catholicos Sahag II to Maghakia, Patriarch of İstanbul," no. 665/386, in Bzdigian, Kilikean kskidzner, 1903–1915, 58–59.

63. BOA, A.MKT.MHM 529/22 (13 Nisan 1322/26 April 1906).

64. BOA, İ.HUS 142/79 (6 Haziran 1322/19 June 1906).

65. BOA, A.MKT.MHM 529/13 (24 Haziran 1322/7 July 1906).

66. BOA, A.MKT.MHM. 529/13 (12 Ağustos 1322/25 August 1906).

67. Seropian, Ink'nakensagrut'iwn 2:359–68.

68. BOA, A.MKT.MHM 529/13 (23 Kânûn-ı Sânî 1322/5 February 1907).

69. Ibid.

Chapter 3: Bad Blood, Thwarted Hopes

1. *Arewelk'*, July 31, 1908, no. 6862, 1.

2. *İtidal*, September 5, 1908, no.1, 1.

3. Along with İbrahim Şinasi and Namık Kemal, Ziya Paşa was a member of the Young Ottomans and one of the most important authors during the Tanzimat period of the Ottoman Empire. In 1867 he published a newspaper called *Hürriyet* (Freedom). His last administrative position was as vali of Adana.

4. Toros, *Ali Münif Bey'in hâtıraları*, 6.

5. For a detailed description of the event, see Arshag (Adana) to ARF Lernabard Auxiliary Body (*Leṛnapart Ōzhandak Marmin*), September 8 (21), 1908, ARF Archives, C/961–94; and ARF Gomideh (Adana) to Constantinople Responsible Body, September 8 (21), 1908, ARF Archives, C/ 951–93.

6. Arıkoğlu, *Hâtıralarım*, 45.

7. *Arewelk'*, September 4, 1908, no. 6891, 1.

8. Ibid.

9. *İtidal*, September 12, 1908, no. 2, 2.

10. See İbrahim Şahin, "Tevfik Nevzat'ın hayatı," *Bilim Yolu: Kırıkkale Üniversitesi Sosyal Bilimler Enstitüsü Dergisi* 2, no. 119 (1999): 95–118.

11. Arshag (Adana) to ARF Lernabard Auxiliary Body (*Leṛnapart Ōzhandak Marmin*), September 8 (21), 1908, ARF Archives, C/961–94.

12. *İtidal*, September 12, 1908, no. 2, 2.

13. *İtidal*, October 21, 1909, no. 5, 1.

14. Ibid.

15. During Bahri Paşa's reign, İhsan Fikri, Abdülkadir Bağdadizade, and Ali Gergerlizade were all exiled. See also *Zhamanak*, June 15, 1909, no. 191, 1–2.

16. Hagop Terzian, *Atanayi Keank'ē* (K. Polis: Tpagrut'iwn Z. N. Pērpērean, 1909), 36.

17. Ibid., 33.

18. Ibid., 35.

19. Seropian, *Atanayi jardē ew pataskhanatunerē*, 19. On the establishment of the Agricultural Club, see *İtidal*, September 22, 1908, no. 3, 2.

20. *İtidal*, December 17, 1908, no. 7, 2. See also *İtidal*, February 27, 1909, no. 22, 1.

21. Arıkoğlu, *Hâtıralarım*, 44.

22. *İtidal*, December 26, 1909, no. 9, 3.

23. Ibid.

24. *İtidal*, November 21, 1909, no. 5, 1.

25. Terzian, *Atanayi Keank'ē*, 41.

26. *İtidal*, January 20, 1909, no. 13, 1. See also *İtidal*, February 5, 1909, no. 17, 1.

27. Terzian, *Atanayi Keank'ē*, 42.

28. Toros, *Ali Münif Bey'in hâtıraları*, 50.

29. *İtidal*, March 27, 1909, no. 28, 1.

30. Terzian, *Atanayi Keank'ĕ*, 42.

31. Seropian, *Atanayi jardĕ ew pataskhanatunerĕ*, 43.

32. Z. Duckett Ferriman, *The Young Turks and the Truth about the Holocaust at Adana in Asia Minor, during April, 1909* (London: [publisher not identified], 1913), 9.

33. *İtidal*, December 26, 1908, no. 9, 2.

34. Ibid.

35. Ibid.

36. Ibid.

37. Keleshian, *Sis-Matean*, 377.

38. *Arewelk'*, March 20, 1909, no. 7955, 3.

39. Zakaria Bzdigian (Adana) to Agnuni, August 8, 1908, ARF Archives, C/951–70.

40. Zakaria Bzdigian (Adana) to Agnuni, August 19, 1908, ARF Archives, C/951–70.

41. Ibid.

42. The Gomideh of Khor Virab (Adana) to the Western Bureau, August 3 (16), 1909, ARF Archives, C/951–87.

43. The Gomideh of Khor Virab (Adana) to the Western Bureau, September 3 (16), 1909, ARF Archives, C/951–87.

44. The Gomideh of Khor Virab (Adana) to the ARF Lernabard Auxiliary Body (*Lernapart Ōzhandak Marmin*) (Adana), September 16, 1908, ARF Archives, 951/87. The Gomideh of Adana to the Constantinople Responsible Body, September 3 (16), 1908, ARF Archives, C/951–90.

45. The Gomideh of Adana to the Constantinople Responsible Body, September 8, 1908, ARF Archives, C/951–93.

46. The Gomideh of Adana to the Constantinople Responsible Body, September 24 (October 7), 1908, ARF Archives, C/951–106.

47. Ibid.

48. Ibid.

49. See Der Matossian, "From the Streets to the Ballots," in *Shattered Dreams of Revolution*.

50. The Gomideh of Adana to the Constantinople Responsible Body, September 8, 1908, ARF Archives, C/951–93.

51. Zakaria Bzdigian (Adana) to Agnuni, August 19 (September 1), 1908, ARF Archives, C/951–74.

52. The Gomideh of Khor Virab (Adana) to the Western Bureau, September 3 (16), 1909, ARF Archives, C/951–87.

53. The Gomideh of Adana to the Constantinople Responsible Body, October 1 (14), 1908, ARF Archives, C/951–112.

54. The Gomideh of Adana to the Constantinople Responsible Body, November 12 (25) 1908, ARF Archives, C/951–144.

55. *Biwzandion*, August 18, 1908, no. 3607, 1.

56. *Arewelk'*, September 4, 1908, no. 6891, 1.

57. *İtidal*, September 12, 1908, no. 2, 3.

58. Letter from Fr. Arsen (Deputy of the Prelate of Adana) to Armenian Auditory Club, Mersin, August 5, 1908, AADA.

59. Dr. G. Keshishian (Mersin) to Comrades, August 16, 1908, ARF Archives, C/951–71; and Rupen Shahbazian (Adana) to the Editorship of Droshak, August 22, 1908, ARF Archives, C/951–77.

60. Arshag to the Western Bureau, September 26, 1908, ARF Archives, C/951–107.

61. G. Keshishian (Mersin) to Comrades, November 2, 1908, ARF Archives, C/951–134; and K. Keshishian (Mersin) to Comrades, December 14 (28), 1908, ARF Archives, C/951–166.

62. The Gomideh of Adana to the Constantinople Responsible Body, September 8, 1908, ARF Archives, C/951–93.

63. The Gomideh of Khor Virab (Adana) to the ARF Lernabard Auxiliary Body (*Lernapart Ōzhandak Marmin*) (Adana) September 8 (21), 1908, ARF Archives, C/951–92.

64. Ferriman, *The Young Turks*, 8.

65. *Biwzandion*, September 22, 1908, no. 3635, 1; and *Biwzandion*, October 2, 1908, no. 3643, 1. See also *Son vak'anüvis Abdurrahman Şeref Efendi tarihi*, ed. Abdurrahman Şeref, vol. 2, *Meşrutiyet olayları, 1908–1909*, ed. Bayram Kodaman and Mehmet Ali Ünal (Ankara: Türk Tarih Kurumu Basımevi, 1996), 71.

66. Boghosian, *Hachěni ěndhanur patmut'iwně*, 566–67.

67. *Biwzandion*, September 22, 1908, no. 3635, 1.

68. *Biwzandion*, August 18, 1908, no. 3607, 1.

69. *İtidal*, January 15, 1909, no. 12, 2. See also Seropian, *Ink'nakensagrut'iwn* 3:522.

70. After the massacres, the Armenian writer Mikayel Souren explicated the argument that these innocent theatrical presentations were merely puffed-up romanticism about the past and were not considered as any type of provocations. See *Kohak*, May 29, 1909, no. 16, 335. Arıkoğlu claimed that these presentations had clear political intentions, as only Armenians were allowed to attend them. See Arıkoğlu, *Hâtıralarım*, 46.

71. Henry Charles Woods, *The Danger Zone of Europe: Changes and Problems in the Near East* (Boston: Little, Brown, 1911), 171.

72. *İtidal*, May 12, 1909, no. 39, 2–3. This report also appeared in Arabic; see *Al-Ittiḥād al-'Uthmānī*, May 31, 1909, no. 29, 3. A. Adossidès, *Arméniens et Jeunes-Turcs: Les massacres de Cilicie* (Paris: P. V. Stock, 1910), 19–20.

73. For the complete play, see Bedros Tourian, *Erkeri zhoghovatsu* (Erevan: Haykakan SSH GA Hratarakch'ut'yun, 1971–72), 67–131.

74. In the original play there are no spirits. Characters are represented as hope, disunity, misery, and love.

75. *İtidal*, May 12, 1909, no. 39, 3.

76. Seropian, *Ink'nakensagrut'iwn* 3:523.

77. Helen Davenport (Brown) Gibbons, *The Red Rugs of Tarsus: A Women's Record of the Armenian Massacre of 1909* (New York: The Century Company, 1917), 98.

78. *Biwzandion*, October 27, 1908, no. 3664, 3.

79. Terzian, *Atanayi Keank'ě*, 10.

80. Ibid.

81. *İkdam* dismissed these reports from the provinces as total fabrication for political aims. See *İkdam*, October 21, 1908, no. 5176, 3; and *İkdam*, October 22, 1908, no. 5177, 1. Even the Ladino newspaper *El-Tiempo* published the appeals of the Catholicos; see *El-Tiempo*, October 28, 1908, no. 10, 92.

82. *Biwzandion*, October 29, 1908, no. 3666, 1.

83. Sir. G. Lowther to Sir Edward Grey (Received January 25, 1909), January 18, 1909, Pera, no. 36, in *Further Correspondence respecting the Affairs of Asiatic Turkey and Arabia January–March 1909*. Foreign Office (FO), Public Record Office (PRO), London. See also Seropian, *Atanayi jardě ew pataskhanatunerě*, 24.

84. See M. Barré de Lancy, vice-consul de France à Mersine et à Adana à Son Excellence M. Pichon, ministre des Affairs étrangères à Paris, Mersine, le 23 octobre 1908, 84, Turquie-Politique intérieure: Arménie—Anatolie—Cilicie XIII, ministère de l'Europe et des Affaires étrangères, Centre des Archives diplomatiques de La Courneuve (CADC), nouvelle série (NS) Turquie 83-P-16742. See also Şeref, *Son vak'anüvis Abdurrahman Şeref Efendi tarihi*, 72.

85. M. Barré de Lancy, vice-consul de France à Mersine et à Adana, à Son Excellence M. Pichon, ministre des Affairs étrangères à Paris, Mersine, le 23 octobre 1908, 84, Turquie- Politique intérieure: Arménie—Anatolie—Cilicie XIII, CADC, nouvelle série (NS) Turquie 83-P-16742.

86. *Biwzandion*, November 3, 1908, no. 3670, 2.

87. Vice-Consul Doughty-Wylie to Sir G. Lowther Konia, October 31, 1908, enclosure 2 in no. 46, in *Further Correspondence, October–December 1908*. See also Şeref, *Son vak'anüvis Abdurrahman Şeref Efendi tarihi*, 71.

88. Vice-Consul Doughty-Wylie to Sir G. Lowther Konia, October 25, 1908, enclosure 1 in no. 46, in *Further Correspondence, October–December 1908*.

89. From Moushegh to Minas Soghomonian, Kessab Efendi, January 26, 1909, no. 304, AADA.

90. From Moushegh to Fr. Vahan Der Sdepanian, Prelate of Bahçe, January 23, 1909, no. 300, AADA.

91. From Moushegh to the Armenian Patriarchate, January 31, 1909, no. 328, AADA.

92. *Zhamanak*, March 3, 1909, no. 105, 2.

93. *Biwzandion*, November 12, 1908, no. 3678, 1.

94. *Dzayn Hayreniats'*, October 23, 1908, no. 1, 8.

95. BOA, DH.MKT 274/78 (29 Kânûn-ı Evvel 1324/11 January 1909); and *Zhamanak*, January 22, 1909, no. 72, 2. See also *İtidal*, January 6, 1909, no. 11, 2.

96. Letter from Cathilocos Sahag II to the Armenian Patriarch of İstanbul, January 20, 1909, file II, no. 190, Izmirlian Archives, Madenataran Library (IA).

97. Ibid.

98. Letter from the Armenian Patriarch to Cathilocos Sahag II of İstanbul, January 20, 1909, file II, no. 191, IA.

99. Seropian, *Ink'nakensagrut'iwn* 3:502.

100. Seropian, *Atanayi jardĕ ew pataskhanatunerĕ*, 19. See also Seropian, *Les vêpres Ciliciennes*, 18–20.

101. Seropian, *Ink'nakensagrut'iwn* 3:505. See also Seropian, *Atanayi jardĕ ew pataskhanatunerĕ*, 26.

102. Seropian, *Atanayi jardĕ ew pataskhanatunerĕ*, 28.

103. Ibid., 30.

104. Ibid., 31.

105. Seropian, *Atanayi jardĕ ew pataskhanatunerĕ*, 32; and Seropian, *Ink'nakensagrut'iwn* 3:506–7. In a letter sent to Fr. Vagharshag Arshaguni, the deputy of the Catholicos, on January 2, 1909, Seropian raised the issue of ten Mauser revolvers that were bought by the women with a sum that was collected for the Armenians of Zeitun. Each weapon came with seven hundred bullets. See From Moushegh to Fr. Vagharshag Arshaguni Deputy of the Catholicos, January 2, 1909, AADA; and Mehmed Asaf, *1909 Adana Ermeni olayları ve anılarım*, ed. İsmet Parmaksızoğlu (Ankara: Türk Tarih Kurumu Basımevi, 2002), 22. See also Şeref, *Son vak'anüvis Abdurrahman Şeref Efendi tarihi*, 75.

106. Seropian, *Ink'nakensagrut'iwn* 3:509; 518–19.

107. Seropian, *Les vêpres Ciliciennes*, 22. On the report submitted to the government, see appendix A in the same book, 71–76.

108. Şeref, *Son vak'anüvis Abdurrahman Şeref Efendi tarihi*, 76.

109. Terzian, *Atanayi Keank'ĕ*, 43.

110. Asaf, *1909 Adana Ermeni olayları ve anılarım*, 32.

111. Ibid.

112. On the issue of Seropian going to Egypt, see the minutes of the meeting of the Armenian Diocese Assembly, February 27, 1909, no. 31, AADA; and Seropian, *Ink'nakensagrut'iwn* 3:531–33.

113. Seropian, *Atanayi jardĕ ew pataskhanatunerĕ*, 39.

114. See, for example, Asaf, *1909 Adana Ermeni olayları ve anılarım*, 33.

115. Zakaria Bzdigian (Adana) to the Western Bureau, September 2, 1908, ARF Archives, C/951–86. See also The Gomideh of Khor Virab (Adana) to the Western Bureau, September 3 (16), 1909, ARF Archives, C/951–87.

116. ARF Gomideh (Adana) to Constantinople Responsible Body, September 8 (21), 1908, ARF Archives, C/ 951–93.

117. ARF Gomideh (Adana) to Constantinople Responsible Body, October 9 (22), 1908, ARF Archives, C/ 951–113.

118. ARF Gomideh (Adana) to Constantinople Responsible Body, October 15 (28), 1908, ARF Archives, C/ 951–122.

119. ARF Gomideh (Adana) to Constantinople Responsible Body, October 29, 1908, ARF Archives, C/ 951–130.

120. Dr. G. Keshishian (Mersin) to Comrades, November 2, 1908, ARF Archives, C/951–135.

121. From H. Kalfayan to Mar, January 11 (24), 1909, ARF Archives, C/953–13.

122. From Bedros (Sis) to the Western Bureau, January 14, 1909, ARF Archives, C/953–16.

123. Under Ottoman Law, *mahlûl* lands referred to the uncultivated *miri* (state-owned) lands that would revert to the Ottoman state after three years.

124. *Zhamanak*, January 29, 1909, no. 78, 2.

125. From Moushegh to *Locum Tenens* Ghevond (İstanbul), February 7, 1909, AADA. See also Seropian, *Ink'nakensagrut'iwn* 3:526.

126. Seropian, *Ink'nakensagrut'iwn* 3:527.

127. Cited in *Zhamanak*, February 25, 1909, no. 100, 2.

128. Ibid, 2–3.

129. Ibid.

130. *Zhamanak*, April 17, 1909, no. 141, 1.

131. *İtidal*, February 27, 1909, no. 22, 1

132. Ibid.

133. Ibid., 2.

134. From the Resigned Catholicos, Sahag, to Priest Kiwd, April 19, 1906, Adana. A copy of the letter appears in Bzdigian, *Kilikean kskitsner*, 59–60.

135. Ibid.

136. Donald Horowitz and Ashutosh Varshney, "Lethal Ethnic Riots: Lessons from India and Beyond," *United States Institute of Peace Special Report* 101 (February 2003).

137. M. Barré de Lancy, vice-consul de France à Mersine et à Adana, à Son Excellence M. Pichon, ministre des Affairs étrangères à Paris, Mersine, le 23 octobre 1908, CADC, 84.

138. Arıkoğlu, *Hâtıralarım*, 45.

139. *Zhamanak*, March 17, 1909, no. 177, 2.

140. Ibid.

141. *İtidal*, March 9, 1909, no. 24, 4.

142. Ibid.

143. *İtidal*, March 4, 1909, no. 23, 4

144. Hagop Terzian, *Kilikioy aghetë: Akanatesi nkaragrut'iwnner, vawerat'ught'er, pashtonakan teghekagirner, t'ght'akts'ut'iwnner, vichakagrut'iwnner, amenēn karewor pat-kernerov* (İstanbul: Tpagr. H. Asaturean ew ordik', 1912), 12.

145. *İtidal*, March 4, 1909, no. 23, 4.

146. Ferriman, *The Young Turks*, 14.

147. Seropian, *Atanayi jardë ew pataskhanatunerë*, 36; Terzian, *Atanayi Keank'ē*, 44. See also the letter from the resigned Catholicos of Sis, Sahag II, to Bishop Moushegh, February 10, 1909, Adana, a copy of which appears in Bzdigian, *Kilikean kskitsner*, 73–74.

148. *İtidal*, March 24, 1909, no. 27, 4.

149. *İtidal*, April 28, 1909, no. 35, 4.

150. Seropian, *Atanayi jardë ew pataskhanatunerë*, 22.

151. See Asaf, *1909 Adana Ermeni olayları ve anılarım*, 21–28.

Chapter 4: An Imagined Uprising

1. Susanne Karstedt, "'Violence Is Difficult, Not Easy': The Emotion Dynamics of Mass Atrocities," in *Emotions and Crime: Towards a Criminology of Emotions*, ed. Michael Hviid Jacobsen and Sandra Walklate (London and New York: Routledge, 2019), 65.

2. Randall Collins, "The Invention and Diffusion of Social Techniques of Violence: How Micro-Sociology Can Explain Historical Trends," *Sociologica* 2 (Maggio–Agosto 2011): 5.

3. Dadrian, "The Circumstances Surrounding the 1909 Adana Holocaust," 11.

4. BOA, DH.MKT 2761/101, From Cevad Bey, the Vali of Adana, to the Ministry of the Interior (Dâhiliye Nezâreti) (24 Şubat 1324/9 March 1909).

5. BOA, DH.MKT 2761/101 (24 Şubat 1324/9 Mach 1909).

6. Hagop Terzian, *Kilikioy aghetë*, 13.

7. Ibid.

8. Ferriman, *The Young Turks*, 15. On the list of assaults prior to the massacres, see Terzian, *Kilikioy aghetë*, 9–23. See also Seropian, *Atanayi jardë ew pataskhanatunerë*, 44–47.

9. See the letter that was sent by the prelate of, Haçin Fr. Nerses Tanielian, to *Biwzandion* that appeared on March 31, 1909. It was translated by the Ministry of the Interior; see BOA, DH.MKT 2783/4 (19 Mart 1325/1 April 1909).

10. See the telegram from the Austro-Hungarian consul in Mersin to the ambassador in İstanbul, April 15, 1909, supplement to report no. 32 D ddo. cos-pel 16 IV 1909, From Austrian Ambassador in Constantinople to the Foreign Minister Alois Lexa von Aehrenthal, April 16, 1909, Constantinople, in Artem Ohandjanian, *Österreich—Armenien: 1872–1936 Faksimilesammlung Diplomatischer Aktenstücke*, vol. 4, 1897–1909 (Wien: Ohandjanian, 1995), 3367.

11. See *Biwzandion*, April 22, 1909, no. 3809, 2. Vahe Minas, the author of the article, claims that Ohannes was an ARF member. See also Terzian, *Kilikioy aghetĕ*, 18–19. A French source claims that the event occurred on April 9; see *Les massacres d'Adana: Avril 1909* (Burxelles: Joseph Polleunis Editeur, 1909), 5. See also Şeref, *Son vak'anüvis Abdurrahman Şeref Efendi tarihi*, 82.

12. From Gabriel Bie Ravndal, Beirut, Syria, to the Assistant Secretary of State, Washington, DC, April 25, 1909, Records of Foreign Service Posts, Consular Posts, Beirut, Lebanon, vol. 145, RG 84, USNA. In this letter Ravndal quotes Rev. T. D. Christie, President of the American St. Paul's Collegiate Institute in Tarsus, who explains the origin of the Adana tragedy.

13. From Daniel Miner Rogers to [recipient's name does not appear, but was most probably his wife Mary], April 14, 1909, in Thomas and Carmelite Christie and Family Correspondence, April–July, 1909, Minnesota Historical Society (MHS).

14. Ibid.

15. Mr. Ravndal to Mr. Leishman (April 17, 1909), Records of Foreign Service Posts, Consular Posts, Beirut, Lebanon, vol. 145, RG 84, USNA. See also Şeref, *Son vak'anüvis Abdurrahman Şeref Efendi tarihi*, 82.

16. On public demonstrations and the conversion of hostility to violence, see Donald L. Horowitz, *The Deadly Ethnic Riot* (Berkeley, CA: University of California Press, 2000), 285–90.

17. From T.D. Christie, May 6, 1909, to Gabriel Bie Ravndal, American Consul of Beirut, in Gabriel Bie Ravndal, American Consul of Beirut, Syria, to the Assistant Secretary of State, Washington, DC, May 11, 1909, Records of Foreign Service Posts, Consular Posts, Beirut, Lebanon, vol. 145, RG 84, USNA.

18. *Biwzandion*, April 22, 1909, no. 3809, 2.

19. From the Austro-Hungarian Consul of Mersin to the Consul of Aleppo, Mersin, April 15, 1909, no. 3368, in Ohandjanian, *Österreich—Armenien: 1872–1936*, 3368.

20. Terzian, *Kilikioy aghetĕ*, 20.

21. Ferriman, *The Young Turks*, 21.

22. From William Nesbitt Chambers to Barton, Adana, April 15, 1909, FO 195–2306.

23. Hampartsoum H. Ashjian, *Atanayi egheheṛnĕ ew Gonyayi husher* (New York: Kochnak Dbaran, 1950), 16.

24. Terzian, *Kilikioy aghetĕ*, 21.

25. Ferriman, *The Young Turks*, 22.

26. Asaf, *1909 Adana Ermeni olayları ve anılarım*, 10–11.

27. Karabet Çalyan, *Adana Vak'ası ve mesulleri* (Dersaâdet [İstanbul]: 1325/1909), 47. See also Manuk Chizmejian, *Patmut'iwn Amerikahay k'aġak'akan kusakts'ut'eants': 1890–1925* (Fresno: Tpagrut'iwn Nor Ōr-i, 1930), 174.

28. Sources indicate that the telegram sent from the Ministry of the Interior ordered the vali to protect the foreign subjects but not the Armenian inhabitants, thus raising the suspicions of Armenians that it constituted the orders for the massacres. See, for example, Suren Bartevian, *Kilikean arhawirkʻě* (G. Polis: Nishan-Babigian Press, 1909), v; and Seropian, *Les vêpres Ciliciennes*, 50.

29. Seropian, *Les vêpres Ciliciennes*, 52.

30. Kaiser, "Baghdad Railway Politics," 37.

31. *Biwzandion*, April 19, 1909, no. 3806, 2.

32. For a detailed description of the hardships of the migrant workers, see *İtidal*, December 17, 1909, no. 7, 3.

33. From the Consul of Austria-Hungary in Mersin to His Excellency Marquis von Pallavicini Ambassador Extraordinary and Minister Plenipotentiary of His Majesty, Mersin, April 30, 1909, in Ohandjanian, *Österreich—Armenien: 1872–1936*, 3397. White bandages have been used in other instances as a way of distinguishing members of the mob from others.

34. See "Allegato, rapporto Les evenemeuts d'Adana del 2 giugno 1909, scritto da un sacerdote armeno cattolico, G. H.," in *La Questione Armena*, vol. 3, *1908–1925, documenti dell'archivio della congregazione per le Chiese Orientali* (ACO), ed. Georges-Henri Ruyssen (Roma: Ed. Orientalia Christiana, 2014), 58. See also Woods, *The Danger Zone of Europe*, 129.

35. Seropian, *Atanayi jardě ew pataskhanatuneŕe*, 44–47 and Terzian, *Kilikioy aghetě*, 21.

36. Terzian, *Kilikioy aghetě*, 24. See also From William Nesbitt Chambers to Barton, Adana April 15, 1909, FO 195–2306; and Boghos Markarian, *Inkʻnakensagrutʻiwn Pōghos Margareani*, 30.

37. In an earlier article, Hagop Terzian, writing under the penname of "Hagter," did not mention Bağdadizade's name when discussing the murder of Urfalian. See *Zhamanak*, May 1, 1909, no. 154, 1. See also Markarian, *Inkʻnakensagrutʻiwn Pōghos Markariani*, 1.

38. For a detailed description of the conflagration in the Armenian Quarter, see Sabatier, "Precis des évènement d'Adana et de ses environs du 14 avril au 1er mai 1909," in *Missions de Syrie d'Egypte et d'Arménie*, 145a-223, tome 281, Archives jésuites, Vanves (AJV). See also Ferriman, *The Young Turks*, 24.

39. From Deputy Consul Dabbas to the American Embassy, April 15, 1908, Records of Foreign Service Posts, Consular Posts, Mersin, Turkey, vol. 012, RG 84, USNA.

40. Terzian, *Kilikioy aghetě*, 33.

41. On the looting, see Doughty-Wylie to the British Ambassador in Constantinople, 21 April 1909, FO 195/2306. See also Sabatier, "Precis des évènements d'Adana et de ses environs du 14 avril au 1er mai 1909."

42. *Biwzandion*, April 30, 1909, no. 3815, 3.

43. From Stephen Van R. Trowbridge to Mr. Peet (American Bible House, Constantinople), Adana, April 19, 1909, FO 195–2306.

44. On participatory violence, see Christian Gerlach, *Extremely Violent Societies: Mass Violence in the Twentieth-Century World* (Cambridge; New York: Cambridge University Press, 2010), 17–122.

45. Doughty-Wylie to the British Ambassador in Constantinople, 21 April 1909, FO 195/2306.

46. Rigal (P.), "Adana. Les massacres d'Adana," *Lettres d'Ore, relations d'Orient* [revue confidentielle des missions jésuites éditée par le siège de Lyon et publiée à Bruxelles], Novembre 1909, 9–16.

47. See *Arewelk'*, April 28, no. 7072, 1. See also A. Sabatier, "Some Facts of the Adana Massacres: Report of Three Fathers Returned from Adana," *The Woodstock Letters*, vol. 39. no. 1 (1910): 35–56; and Sabatier, "Precis des évènements d'Adana," AJV.

48. "Araxi (Bzdigian) Boyadjian's Memoir," (unpublished manuscript, Lanarca, 1948), 70. The memoir is written in colloquial Western Armenian.

49. Ibid., 91.

50. Ibid., 96.

51. On the attacks on the French mission, see *Les massacre d'Adana et nos missionaries: Recit de temoins* (Lyons: Imprimerie Vve Paquet, 1909), 9–23. See also "22 Aprile 1909—Rapporto di Mgr Giannini, Delegato apostolico in Siria, al Cardinale Gatti, Prefetto della Congregazione di Propaganda Fide, Armeni del Patriarcato 1891–1926, rubr. n° 105, 3, 11° 26397, Beirut, 22 aprile 1909 (n° 504)," in Ruyssen, *La Questione Armena* 3:29–30, ACO.

52. On the attacks on the French mission, see *Les massacre d'Adana et nos missionaries*, 9–23, AJV, 12 RA; and *Les massacres d'Adana: Avril 1909* (Burxelles: Joseph Polleunis Editeur, 1909), AJV, 12 RAr. See also "Lettres au R. P. Andre sur la massacres d'Adana by P. Benoit, Adana 19 Avril 1909," in *Missions de Syrie d'Egypte et d'Arménie*, 145a-223, tome 281, AJV; and "Lettres au R. P. Andre by P. Tabet, Adana 22 Avril 1909," in *Missions de Syrie d'Egypte et d'Arménie*, 145a-223, tome 281, AJV.

53. On the circumstances of their murder, see From Stephen Van R. Trowbridge to Mr. Peet (American Bible House, Constantinople), Adana, April 19, 1909, FO 195–2306. See also Doughty-Wylie to the British Ambassador, April 21, 1909, FO 195–2306; and Rose Lambert, *Hadjin and the Armenian Massacres* (New York; Chicago: Fleming H. Revell Company, 1911), 99–106.

54. Doughty-Wylie to the British Ambassador in Constantinople, April 21, 1909, FO 195/2306.

55. Fonds Ankara, Vice-Consulat d'Alexandrette et de Mersine, 6- Lutifk Khoubesserian-Adana, à Consul A. Jeannier 14 April 1909, Vice-Consulat d'Alex et de Mersin; Lutifk Khoubesserian-Adana, à Consul A. Jeannier 15 April 1909,

Vice-Consulat d'Alex et de Mersin; Lutifk Khoubesserian-Adana, à Consul A. Jeannier 16 April 1909, Vice-Consulat d'Alex et de Mersin; Lutifk Khoubesserian-Adana, à Consul A. Jeannier 17 April 1909, Vice-Consulat d'Alex et de Mersin, CADN.

56. Doughty-Wylie to the British Ambassador in Constantinople, April 21, 1909, FO 195/2306.

57. *Takvim-i Vekayi*, May 6, 1909, no. 202, 13.

58. Ibid.

59. On the massacres of Hamidiye, see Zabel Yesayan, *Aweraknerun mēj* (K. Polis: Hayots' Hratarakch'akan Ěnkerut'iwn, 1911), 268–74. See also Terzian, *Kilikioy aghetĕ*, 189–95.

60. BOA, BEO 3536/265127 (2 Nisan 1325/15 April 1909).

61. BOA, BEO 3536/265127 (2 Nisan 1325/15 April 1909).

62. BOA, BEO 3536/265144 (2 Nisan 1325/15 April 1909).

63. See Dr. H. Belart to the Deutsche Bank, April 16, 1909, in the Deutsche Bank [Vutz] to the Legationsrat Zimmermann in the Foreign Office, Politisches Archiv des Auswärtiges Amt (DE/PA-AA/R), R: Reich; General Files, 13184.

64. From the Consul of Austria-Hungary in Mersin to His Excellency Marquis von Pallavicini Ambassador Extraordinary and Minister Plenipotentiary of His Majesty, Mersina April 30, 1909, in Ohandjanian, *Österreich—Armenien: 1872–1936*, 397.

65. BOA, BEO 3535/265123 (4 Nisan 1325/17 April 1909).

66. BOA, BEO 3536/265166 (5 Nisan 1325/18 April 1909).

67. Dr. Kevork Keshishian (Mersin) to Constantinople Responsible Body, April 16, 1909, ARF Archives, C/953–13.

68. Woods, *The Danger Zone of Europe*, 133.

69. *Zhamanak*, May 1, 1909, no. 154, 1. Markarian, who played an important role in convincing Osman Bey to intervene on behalf of the Armenians, provides a very detailed account of these negotiations in his memoirs. See Markarian, *Ink'nakensagrut'iwn Pōghos Markariani*, 33–40.

70. Cypher Telegram from Captain Doughty-Wylie, Adana, April 17, 1909, FO 195/2306. See also Terzian, *Kilikioy aghetĕ*, 54; and Doughty-Wylie to the British Ambassador in Constantinople, April 21, 1909, FO 195/2306.

71. From William Nesbitt Chambers to Barton, Adana, April 15, 1909, FO 195–2306.

72. *Droshak*, May 1909, no. 5, 56. Doughty-Wylie was educated at Winchester and the Royal Military College, Sandhurst. He was a member of the Royal Welch Fusiliers and a decorated war hero who had served in South and East Africa, India, and China; see Tusan, *The British Empire*, 105–6.

73. S. Z., *Adanskie chernye dni* (Baku: Baku, Electric Printing House of the Newspaper Baku, 1909), 7.

74. From William Nesbitt Chambers to Barton, Adana, April 15, 1909, FO 195–2306.

75. Ferriman, *The Young Turks*, 26.

76. Ibid.

77. From Stephen Van R. Trowbridge to Mr. Peet (American Bible House Constantinople), Adana, April 21, 1909, FO 195–2306.

78. *Biwzandion*, April 19, 1909, no. 3806, 2.

79. Seropian, *Ink'nakensagrut'iwn* 3:546–50.

80. Krikor Chiftjian, "Atanayi Kotoradzin Aknarkuti'wnnerĕ Aṛachnort Moushegh Epis. Serobiani Dzots'atetrin Mēj (1909)," in *Hask: Hayakitakan Taregirk* 12 (2009–10): 122. In this article, Chiftjian reproduces Seropian's entire journal.

81. Ibid., 120–26.

82. From William Nesbitt Chambers to Barton, Adana, April 15, 1909, FO 195–2306.

83. From Stephen Van R. Trowbridge to Mr. Peet (American Bible House, Constantinople), Adana, April 19, 1909, FO 195–2306.

84. From the Consul of Austria-Hungary in Mersin to His Excellency Marquis von Pallavicini Ambassador Extraordinary and Minister Plenipotentiary of His Majesty, Mersina April 30, 1909, in Ohandjanian, *Österreich—Armenien: 1872–1936*, 3399.

85. Sir G. Lowther to Sir Edward Grey (Received May 3), Pera, April 28, 1909, in *Further Correspondence, April–June 1909*.

86. Command SMS *Loreley* G. J. no. 35, military police report on the events at Mersina, Mersina, April 23, 1909, in the Chief of the Navy's Admiral (Baudissin) to the State Secretary of the Foreign Office (Schoen), DE/PA-AA/R 13184. See also From the Consul of Austria-Hungary in Mersin to His Excellency Marquis von Pallavicini Ambassador Extraordinary and Minister Plenipotentiary of His Majesty, Mersina April 30, 1909, in Ohandjanian, *Österreich—Armenien: 1872–1936*, 3397.

87. Story of R. Constant, head of the Capucins in Tarsus, April 24, 1909, *Les missions Catholiques* 41, no. 2084 (May 14, 1909): 230.

88. Letter of R. P. Jerome, head of the Capucins of Syria, Tarsus, April 24, 1909, *Les missions Catholiques* 41, no. 2084 (May 14, 1909): 230.

89. Ibid., 116.

90. *Horizon*, April 30, 1909, no. 3815, 1.

91. Terzian, *Kilikioy aghetĕ*, 166. The American deputy consul of Adana provides a different figure; according to him, the whole Armenian Quarter of Tarsus, consisting of five hundred houses, was burned down. He estimates that fifty Armenians were killed in the city and many more in the villages. The number of refugees was approximately three thousand. See From Dabbas Deputy Consul to American Embassy, April 20, 1909, Records of Foreign Service Posts, Consular Posts, Mersin, Turkey, vol. 012, RG 84, USNA.

92. Woods, *The Danger Zone of Europe*, 147.

93. From T. D. Christie to Gabriel Bie Ravndal, American Consul of Beirut, May 6, 1909, in Gabriel Bie Ravndal American Consul of Beirut, Syria, to the Assistant Secretary of State, Washington, DC, May 11, 1909, Records of Foreign Service Posts, Consular Posts, Beirut, Lebanon, vol. 145, RG 84, USNA.

94. *Arewelk'*, April 27, 1909, no. 7972, 1. On the condition of the Armenian refugees in the Catholic and Protestant missions, see "Story of the R. Constant Head of the Capucins in Tarsus, Tarsus, April 24, 1909," in *Les missions Catholiques* 41, no. 2084 (May 14, 1909): 231.

95. From the American Embassy in İstanbul to Philander Knox, Secretary of State, April 28, 1909, 1906–1910 numerical file, National Archives Microfilm Publication M 862 roll 718, file 10044/215–217, RG 59, USNA.

96. Teotig, *Amis më i Kilikia*, 203. On Muslims rescuing Armenians, see Abdulhamit Kırmızı, "Feelings of Gratitude: Muslim Rescuers of Armenians in Adana 1909," in *History from Below: A Tribute in Memory of Donald Quataert*, ed. S. Karahasanoğlu and D. C. Demir (İstanbul: İstanbul Bilgi University Press, 2016), 643–60.

97. Vice-Consul Doughty-Wylie to Sir G. Lowther, Adana, April 24, 1909, enclosure 2 in no. 84 in Sir. G. Lowther to Sir Edward Grey (Received May 11, 1909), no. 324, Constantinople, May 4, 1909, in *Further Correspondence, April–June 1909*.

98. *Arewelk'*, April 27, 1909, no. 7072, 1.

99. Giligian (Mersin) to Taparig, April 18, 1909, ARF Archives, C/953–74.

100. Ibid.

101. Asaf Bey was the previous kaymakam of Jaffa and was appointed as the mutasarrıf of Cebel-i Bereket on October 6, 1906. See BOA, BEO 3395/254623 (21 Eylül 1322/4 October 1906).

102. Sir G. Lowther to Sir Edward Grey (Received May 3), no. 304, Pera, April 28, 1909, in *Further Correspondence, April–December 1909*. In his memoir, Asaf Bey says that there were three thousand prisoners in the Payas prison, all of whom escaped during the disturbances. See Asaf, *1909 Adana Ermeni olayları ve anılarım*, 14.

103. *İtidal* also claims that the Armenians were surrounding Cebel-i Bereket from four sides. See *İtidal*, May 1, 1909, no. 36, 3.

104. BOA, DH.MKT.PRK 2826/95 (3 Nisan 1325/16 April 1909).

105. From the Mutasarrıf of Cebel-i Bereket Asaf Bey to the Ministry of the Interior, Erzin, April 3, 1325. Copies of these telegrams appear in Terzian, *Kilikioy aghetë*, 292–95.

106. Ibid.

107. BOA, BEO 3535/265123 (4 Nisan 1325/ 17 April 1909).

108. BOA, BEO 3669/275159 (4 Nisan 1325/17 April 1909).

109. BOA, BEO 3669/275159 (4 Nisan 1325/17 April 1909).

110. BOA, BEO 3669/275159 (4 Nisan 1325/17 April 1909).

111. BOA, BEO 3669/275159 (4 Nisan 1325/17 April 1909).

112. BOA, BEO 36692/75159 (4 Nissan 1325/17 April 1909). See also "Petites relations d'Orient: Les massacres d'Adana et nos missionaries: Recit d'un temoin," in Mission d'Arménie, Arménie Avant, 1914-Adana, JAV/RAr 25/5.

113. From the Consul of Aleppo to the Imperial and Royal Ambassador in İstanbul, April 22, 1909, in Ohandjanian, *Österreich—Armenien: 1872–1936*, 3420.

114. In his memoir, Asaf Bey claims that the Armenians of Dörtyol were preparing an uprising to reestablish the Kingdom of Cilicia. See Asaf, *1909 Adana Ermeni olayları ve anılarım*, 7.

115. A letter sent by Vartevar Kuyumdjian to the Armenian Patriarchate of İstanbul a few weeks after the event puts the number of those that gathered and received weapons at 2,500. See Letter from the Member of the Church Committee of Osmaniye in the district of Maraş, Vartevar Kuyumdjian to the Armenian Patriarchate of İstanbul, BOA, DH.MKT 2837/31 (8 Mayıs 1325/21 May 1909). See also Letter from Christie to Gabriel Bie Ravndal Tarsus, May 6, 1909, and from Gabriel Bie Ravndal, Beirut, Syria, to the Assistant Secretary of State, Washington, DC, May 11, 1909, USNA; Terzian, *Kilkyo Aghede*, 150–51; and "Petites relations d'Orient: Les massacres d'Adana et nos missionaries: Recit d'un temoin," in Mission d'Arménie, Arménie Avant, 1914- Adana, AJV, RAr 25/5.

116. From the Member of the Church Committee of Osmaniye in the district of Maraş Vartevar Kuyumdjian to the Armenian Patriarchate of İstanbul, BOA, DH.MKT 2837/31 (8 Mayıs 1325/21 May 1909). See also Yesayan, *Aweraknerun mēj*, 224–25.

117. See Z., *Adanskie chernye dni*, 13–14. F. W. Maccalum lists the pastors and preachers killed in Osmaniye; see From F. W. Maccalum to James Barton, Adana, April 22, 1909, Central Turkey Mission, vol. 15, reel 660, the American Board of Commissioners for Foreign Missions (ABCFM) Archives. See Mrs. S. V. R. Trowbridge to Her Family, Adana, April 21, 1909, in Central Turkey Mission, vol. 15, reel 660, ABCFM Archives. See also Pamphlet Written by Rev. William U. Chambers of Adana, Enclosed in the Letter from the American Consul of Aleppo Jesse Jackson to the Secretary of State, May 12, 1909, 1906–1910 numerical file, National Archives Microfilm Publication M 862 roll 718, file 10044/262–263, RG 59, USNA.

118. Terzian, *Kilikioy aghetĕ*, 151.

119. From the Member of the Church Committee of Osmaniye in the district of Maraş, Vartevar Kuyumdjian to the Armenian Patriarchate of İstanbul, BOA, DH.MKT 2837/31 (8 Mayıs 1325/21 May 1909).

120. Terzian, *Kilikioy aghetĕ*, 152.

121. See also Letter from Christie, Tarsus to Gabriel Bie Ravndal, sent on May 6, 1909, enclosed in From Gabriel Bie Ravndal, Beirut, Syria, to the Assistant Secretary of State, Washington, DC, May 11, 1909, Records of Foreign Service Posts, Consular Posts, Mersin, Turkey, vol. 012, RG 84, USNA.

122. Terzian, *Kilikioy aghetĕ*, 153.

123. Ibid., 153.

124. "Petites relations d'Orient: Les massacres d'Adana et nos missionaries: Recit d'un temoin," in Mission d'Arménie, Arménie avant, 1914- Adana, AJV, RAr 25/5.

125. See Letter from a Couple of Signatories to the Armenian Patriarchate of İstanbul, İskenderun, 20 April (May 3, 1909), in Terzian, *Kilikioy aghetĕ*, 317.

126. *Biwzandion*, May 26, 1909, no. 3836, 1.

127. Report on the Armenian Massacres in Bahçe in April 1909, Copies of the Descriptions of Their Experiences, Submitted by Engineers of the Baghdad Railway Study at the Consulate, to Submit Obediently, Namely, the Chargé d'Affaires of the Embassy Constantinople (Miquel) to the Chancellor of the Reich (Bülow), June 19, 1909, DE/PA-AA/R 13187.

128. Vice-Consul Doughty-Wylie to Sir G. Lowther, Adana, May 6, 1909, enclosure 2 in no. 103, Sir G. Lowther to Sir Edward Grey (Received May 24, 1909), no. 346, Pera, May 17, 1909, in *Further Correspondence, April-June 1909*.

129. Ibid.

130. Krikor G. Koudoulian, *Hay leṛē: Karmir drwakner Kilikioy aghētēn* (İzmir: Tpagr. Mamurean, 1913), 40.

131. Vice-Consul Doughty Wylie to Sir G. Lowther Adana, May 6, 1909, enclosure 2 in no. 103, Sir G. Lowther to Sir Edward Grey (Received May 24, 1909), no. 346, Pera, May 17, 1909, in *Further Correspondence, April-June 1909*. See also Report on the Armenian Massacres in Bahçe in April 1909 by Engineers of the Baghdad Railway Study at the Consulate, June 19, 1909, DE/PA-AA/R 13187.

132. Koudoulian, *Hay leṛē*, 44–45.

133. Ibid., 44–47.

134. Report on the Armenian Massacres in Bahçe in April 1909, Copies of the Descriptions of their Experiences, Submitted by Engineers of the Baghdad Railway Study at the Consulate, to Submit Obediently, Namely, the Chargé d'Affaires of the Embassy Constantinople (Miquel) to the Chancellor of the Reich (Bülow), June 19, 1909, DE/PA-AA/R 13187.

135. Ibid.

136. Ibid.

137. "Petites relations d'Orient: Les massacres d'Adana et nos missionaries: Recit d'un temoin," in Mission d'Arménie, Arménie avant, 1914- Adana, AJV, RAr 25/5.

138. BOA, BEO 3535/265096 (4 Nisan 1325/17 April 1909). See also *Biwzandion*, April 19, 1909, no. 3806, 3. Sahag also sent a telegram to the Armenian Patriarchate; see From the Catholicos of Cilicia, Sahag, to the Armenian Patriarchate in İstanbul, Sis, April 4, 1909. A copy of the telegram appears in Terzian, *Kilikioy aghetě*, 305. See Also *İkdam*, April 21, no. 5354, 3.

139. *Biwzandion*, April 19, 1909, no. 3806, 2.

140. From Mrs. S. Van R. Trowbridge to Family, Mersine, Wednesday, May 5, 1909, Central Turkey Mission, vol. 15, reel 660, ABCFM Archives.

141. Terzian, *Kilikioy aghetě*, 226–32. See also Woods, *The Danger Zone of Europe*, 147.

142. See Consul Fontana to Sir G. Lowther Aleppo, May 27, 1909, enclosure in no. 13, in Sir. G. Lowther to Sir Edward Grey (Received June 25, 1909), no. 146, in *Further Correspondence, April-June 1909*.

143. Ibid.

144. See Houri Azezian, "Yerit. Tʻurkerĕ ew Halepi Vilayeti Haykakan Kotoradznerĕ (1909 t.)," in *Hask: Hayakitakan Taregirk* 12 (2009–10): 155–88.

145. BOA, DH.MKT.PRK 2828/82 (7 Nisan 1325/20 April 1909).

146. Ibid.

147. See Hagop Tcholakian, "Armenian Settlements in the Region of Antioch," in *Armenian Communities of the Northeastern Mediterranean: Musa Dagh—Dört-Yol—Kessab*, ed. Richard G. Hovannisian (Costa Mesa, CA: Mazda Publishers, 2016), 47–49.

148. *Horizon*, May 12, 1909, no. 20, 560.

149. "3 maggio 1909- Lettera di Mgr Sayegh, Arcivescovo armeno catlolico di Aleppo, al Cardinale Gotti, Prefetto della Congregazione di'Propaganda Fide, Armeni del Patriarcato 1891–1926, rubr. 11 ° 105, 3, 11° 26491," in Ruyssen, *La Questione Armena* 3:30–31, ACO.

150. Vice-Consul Douek to Acting Consul Catoni, Antioch, April 30, 1909, enclosure in no. 115, in Sir. G. Lowther to Sir Edward Grey (Received June 1, 1909), no. 382, in *Further Correspondence, April-June 1909.*

151. *Biwzandion*, May 14, 1909, no. 3827, 1.

152. Vice-Consul Douek to Acting Consul Catoni, Antioch, April 30, 1909, enclosure in no. 115, in *Further Correspondence, April-June 1909.*

153. DE/PA-AA/R, 13186, May 5, 1909. This report was sent to Tischendorf, the German consul in Aleppo, who forwarded it to the imperial chancellor (Bülow).

154. DE/PA-AA/R, 13186, May 5, 1909. Tischendorf forwarded this report to the imperial chancellor (Bülow).

155. Ibid.

156. Ibid.

157. Ibid.

158. Copy of a telegram from Belfante, Imperial Vice Consulate in İskenderun, dated April 24, 1909, enclosure 2, April 25, 1909, DE/PA-AA/R 13185.

159. The Consul in Aleppo (Tischendorf) to the Chancellor (Bülow), June 6, 1909, DE/PA-AA/R 13187. The total number provided by the consul is around 187. Other sources put the figure at 200. See also *Horizon*, May 12, 909, no. 20, 561. The British vice-consul Douek estimated the number to be between 200 to 350, and in the near neighborhood, 100; see Vice-Consul Douek to Acting Consul Catoni, Antioch, April 30, 1909, enclosure in no. 115, in *Further Correspondence, April-June 1909.*

160. "3 maggio 1909- Lett era di Mgr Sayegh, Arcivescovo armeno catlolico di Aleppo, al Cardinale Gotti, Prefetto della Congregazione di'Propaganda Fide, Armeni del Patriarcato 1891–1926, rubr. 11 ° 105, 3, 11° 26491," in Ruyssen, *La Questione Armena* 3:30–31, ACO.

161. Terzian, *Kilikioy aghetĕ*, 255–56.

162. *Biwzandion*, May 11, 1909, no. 3824, 1.

163. For more on Kessab, see Tcholakian, "Armenian Settlements in the Region of Antioch," 49–51.

164. Cipher telegram sent by Reşid Paşa, the Vali of Aleppo, to the Grand Vizier, May 10, 1909, BOA, DH.MKT 2812/57 (27 Nisan 1325/ 10 May, 1909).

165. Hagop Cholakian, *K'esap* (Ant'ilias: Metsi Tann Kilikioy Kat'oghikosut'iwn, 2015), 164.

166. FO 195/2306; see the pamphlet *The Sack of Kessab* by Stephen Van R. Trowbridge.

167. P. Sabatino del Gaizo, the head of the Kessab Mission, also attested to Hasan Ağa's role in the massacres along with the other notables of Ordu. See P. Sebastiano le supérieur de la mission Kessab à consul général de France à Beyrouth, Beirut, 7 May, 1909, ambassade de Constanitnople /E/129, CADN.

168. An urgent telegram from Reşid Paşa, Vali of Aleppo, to the Ministry of the Interior; see BOA, DH.ŞFR 412/66 (26 Nisan 1325/9 May 1909).

169. Alber Temirian, *K'ēsap: 1909–1946* (Pēyrut': Tparan K. Tōnikean, 1956), 51.

170. Cholakian, *K'esap*, 166.

171. Temirian, *K'ēsap: 1909–1946*, 52.

172. From Effie Chambers to Dr. Barton, Kessab, July 22, 1909, Central Turkey Mission, vol. 17, reel 662, ABCFM Archives.

173. "14 giugno 1909—Rapporto di Mgr Giannini, Delegato apostolico in Siria, al Cardinale Gotti, Pref etto della Congregazione di Propaganda Fide, Armeni del Patriarcato 1891–1926, rubr. n. 105, 3, n. 26719," in Ruyssen, *La Questione Armena* 3:39–45, ACO.

174. Temirian, *K'ēsap: 1909–1946*, 53.

175. Stephen Van R. Trowbridge, *The Sack of Kessab*, FO 195/2306.

176. Ibid. N. Vitale, vice-consul-general, puts the number of Armenians killed at eight hundred. See N. Vitale, Vice-Consul-General to Consul-General Cumberbatch, Lattaquie, May 3, 1909, enclosure 6 in no. 103 in Sir G. Lowther to Sir Edward Grey (Received May 24, 1909), no. 346, Pera, May 17, 1909 in *Further Correspondence, April–June 1909*.

177. From H. G. Gibbons to Stephen Van R. Trowbridge, May 1910, enclosed in Stephen Van R. Trowbridge to Dr. Barton, Latakia, May 19, 1909, Central Turkey Mission, vol. 20, reel 665, ABCFM Archives. *İkdam* reported that 1,500 houses were burned down; see *İkdam*, April 30, 1909, no. 5361, 3.

178. Mr. Ravndal to Mr. Leishman (April 24, 1909), in Telegrams regarding Murder and Pillage in Asia Minor and Syria from April 14th to April 25th, 1909, From Gabriel Bie Ravndal, Beirut, Syria, to the Assistant Secretary of State, Washington, DC, April 25, 1909, Records of Foreign Service Posts, Consular Posts, Beirut, Lebanon, vol. 145, USNA, RG 84.

179. Telegram from Mr. Ravndal to Mr. Leishman (May 11, 1909), in From J. M. Balph to G. Bie Ravandal (US General Consul), May 3, 1909, Latakia, Syria, 1906–1910 numerical file, National Archives Microfilm Publication M 862 roll 718, file 10044/236–39, RG 59, USNA.

180. Stephen Van R. Trowbridge, *The Sack of Kessab*, FO 195/2306.

181. Fouques Duparc Consul de France à Beyrouth à l'Ambassade de France à Constantinople, April 29, 1909, no. 59, ambassade de Constantinople /E/129, CADN.

182. Mattie R. Wylie and Zada Patton to Friend, from Latakia to Friends, in *Olive Tree: A Monthly Journal Devoted to Missionary Work in the Reformed Presbyterian Church, U. S. A* no. 7 (July 1909): 151.

183. Ibid.

184. Cholakian, *K'esap*, 176.

185. Stephen Van R. Trowbridge, *The Sack of Kessab*, FO 195/2306.

186. Mattie R. Wylie and Zada Patton to Friend, *Olive Tree* 7 (July 1909): 151.

187. Vice-Consul-General to Consul-General Cumberbatch, Lattaquie, May 3, 1909, enclosure 6 in no.103, in *Further Correspondence, April-June 1909*.

188. From Miss Effie Chambers, Missionary in Charge at Kessab to Jesse Jackson, American Consul in Aleppo, May 5, 1909, in 1906–1910 numerical file, National Archives Microfilm Publication M 862 roll 718, file 10044/313–314, RG 59, USNA.

189. "29 maggio 1909- Rapporto di Mgr Giannini, Delegato apostolico in Siria, al Cardinale Gotti, Prefetto della Congregazione di Propaganda Fide, Armeni del Patriarcato 1891–1926, rubr. n. 105, 3, n. 26610," in *La Questione Armena* 3:39–45, ACO. See also Cholakian, *K'esap*, 176; and N. Vitale, Vice-Consul-General to Consul-General Cumberbatch, Lattaquie, May 3, 1909, enclosure 6 in no.103, in *Further Correspondence, April-June 1909*.

190. On Dörtyol, see Kojayan, "The Chork-Marzban/Dort-Yol Armenians: Three Episodes of Self-Defense," in Hovannisian, *Armenian Communities of the Northeastern Mediterranean*, 327–56.

191. On the destitute condition of these refugees, see From Dörtyol to the Responsible Body in Constantinople, May 9, 1909, ARF Archives, C/953–88. See also Minas Khabrig, *Et'ē Ch'ork'-Marzpanē intsi het khōsēr*, 58–60.

192. For details about their self-defense, see Khaprig, *Et'ē Ch'ork'-Marzpanē intsi het khōsēr*, 60–82. See also Minas Kojayan, *Patmut'iwn Ch'ork'-Marzpani* (Los Anchelēs: Los Anchelēsi Ch'ork'-Marzpani Hayrenakts'akan Miut'iwn, 2005), 68–91.

193. BOA, DH.MKT.PRK 2829/124 (7 Nisan 1325/20 April 1909).

194. DE/PA-AA/R 13185, April 30, 1909. According to a German diplomatic source, twenty thousand rounds of ammunition had been delivered along with the weapons from the depot at İskenderun itself to the besiegers of Dörtyol. The local commander in İskenderun admitted to the dragoman of the German vice-consulate that

these weapons had been delivered to the *redifs*, who had joined the gangs ravaging the region. See Confidential Report Th. Belfante German Vice-Consul in İskenderun to the German Consul in Aleppo Tischendorf, April 26, 1909, enclosure 1 in The Consul General in Aleppo (Tischendorf) to the Chancellor (Bülow).

195. Memorandum by the Rev. S. H. Kennedy respecting the Siege and Relief of Dörtyol, enclosure 2 in no. 138, Sir. G. Lowther to Sir Edward Grey (Received June 21, 1909), no. 442, Therapia, June 15, 1909, in *Further Correspondence, April-June 1909*. Others put the figure at four thousand people in the mob. See DE/PA-AA/R 13185, April 25, 1909.

196. Memorandum by the Rev. S. H. Kennedy respecting the Siege and Relief of Dörtyol, enclosure 2 in no. 138 in *Further Correspondence, April-June 1909*. See also Kojayan, *Patmut'iwn Ch'ork'-Marzpani*, 81–83.

197. DE/PA-AA/R 13185, April 25, 1909. The dragoman of this ship, Vice-Consul Balit, was invited to be part of the group by the local authorities. See German Vice-Consul in İskenderun (Belfante) to the Consul General in Aleppo (Tischendorf), April 23, 1909, in enclosure 3, in Consul General in Aleppo to the Chancellor (Bülow), April 25, 1909. See also Kojayan, *Patmut'iwn Ch'ork'-Marzpani*, 88–89.

198. Memorandum by the Rev. S. H. Kennedy respecting the Siege and Relief of Dörtyol, enclosure 2 in no. 138 in *Further Correspondence, April-June 1909*.

199. BOA, DH.MKT 2798/95 (19 Nisan 1325/2 May 1909).

200. DE/PA-AA/R 13185, April 25, 1909.

201. Khabrig, *Et'ē Ch'ork'-Marzpanē intsi het khōsēr*, 85–90. See also no 138, Sir G. Lowther to Sir Edward Grey (Received June 21), no. 442, Therapia, June 15, 1909, in *Further Correspondence, April-December 1909*.

202. See the telegram sent by the Ministry of the Interior to the province of Adana on May 5, 1909, regarding the disarming of the Armenian population of Dörtyol. BOA, DH.MKT 2802/51 (22 Nisan 1325/5 May 1909).

203. See Consul Fontana to Sir G. Lowther, Aleppo, May 27, 1909, enclosure in no. 146, Sir. G. Lowther to Sir Edward Grey (Received June 25, 1909), no. 456, in *Further Correspondence, April-December 1909*.

204. From Raphael Fontana to Sir Edward Lowther, Aleppo, July 15, 1909, FO 195/2307. Fontana reported this based on an oral conversation with an English missionary in Aintab.

205. *İkdam* first reported on the matter on April 17, with news taken from *Biwzandion*. See *İkdam*, April 17, 1909, no. 5350, 3.

206. See *Arewelk'*, April 16, 1909, no. 7064, 3.

207. Ibid.

208. *Zhamanak*, April 18, 1909, no. 142, 3. The *şeyhülislam* was the head mufti and top religious authority.

209. *Biwzandion*, April 19, 1909, no. 3806, 2.

210. Italics were used in the original.

211. Ibid.

212. Ibid.

213. For the telegram, see *İtidal*, April 7, 1909, no. 33, 1.

214. *Biwzandion*, April 19, 1909, no. 3806, 2. A copy also appeared in *İkdam*, April 18, 1909, no. 5351, 3.

215. *Biwzandion*, April 19, 1909, no. 3806, 2.

216. Copies of the telegram appeared in *Osmanlı* and *İkdam*. The Austro-Hungarian consul also referred to this order in his report sent to the Austro-Hungarian embassy; see From the Consul of Austria-Hungary in Mersin to His Excellency Marquis von Pallavicini Ambassador Extraordinary and Minister Plenipotentiary of His Majesty, Mersina April 30, 1909, in Ohandjanian, *Österreich—Armenien: 1872–1936*, 3399.

217. *Biwzandion*, April 19, 1909, no. 3806, 2.

218. From Bishop Moushegh to the Ambassador of Austro-Hungary in Constantinople, Cairo, May 4, 1909, in Ohandjanian, *Österreich—Armenien: 1872–1936*, 3413.

219. *Takvim-i Vekayi*, April 23, 1909, no. 190, 1. The reaction of the Armenian daily *Arewelk'* toward Adil Bey's telegram to Adana was similar to that of *Biwzandion*. See *Arewelk'*, April 16, 1909, no. 7064, 3.

220. *Takvim-i Vekayi*, May 6, 1909, no. 202, 12.

221. Ibid., 13.

222. *Biwzandion*, April 20, 1909, no. 3807, 3.

223. See *Azkayin ëndhanur zhoghov*, Nist ZhT' [Session XIX], April 24, 1909, 300.

224. Ibid., 301.

225. Ibid.

226. Ibid., 299–303.

227. Ibid., 302–3.

228. *Arewelk'*, April 19, 1909, no. 7066, 3.

229. *Biwzandion*, April 20, 1909, no. 3807, 3.

230. *Biwzandion*, April 20, 1909, no. 3807, 3. See also *Arewelk'*, April 20, 1909, no. 7967, 3.

231. BOA, BEO 3538/265305 (7 Nisan 1325/20 April 1909).

232. *Biwzandion*, April 21, 1909, no. 3808, 3. See also *Arewelk'*, April 21, 1909, no. 7068, 3.

233. *Zhamanak*, April 21, 1909, no. 146, 3.

234. *Azkayin ëndhanur zhoghov*, 315.

235. From the Austro-Hungarian Consul of Mersin to the Consul of Aleppo, Mersin, April 15, 1909, no. 3368, in Ohandjanian, *Österreich—Armenien: 1872–1936*, 3368.

236. Doughty-Wylie to the British Ambassador in Constantinople, April 21, 1909, FO 195/2306. Another source estimates the number to be 2,500 Armenians and 200–300 Muslims. See *Les massacres d'Adana: Avril 1909*, 26.

237. From the Russian Embassy to the Austro-Hungarian Embassy, April 22, 1909, in Ohandjanian, *Österreich—Armenien: 1872–1936*, 3381–82.

238. Doughty-Wylie to the British Ambassador in Constantinople, April 21, 1909, FO 195/2306.

239. *Biwzandion*, April 23, 1909, no. 3810, 3. See also *Arewelk'*, April 27, 1909, no. 7072, 1.

240. Varuzhan Herkelean, ed., *Atanayi vkanerĕ ew Surb Step'anos vkayaranĕ, 1909, Larnaga* (Nicosia: [publisher not identified], 2010), 11.

241. For copies of dispatches exchanged with local authorities, see Austrian Embassy in Constantinople, April 19, 1909, Austro-Hungarian Consul of Mersin to the Consul of Aleppo, Mersin, April 15, 1909, no. 3368, in Ohandjanian, *Österreich—Armenien: 1872–1936*, 3374.

242. Ibid.

243. Ibid.

Chapter 5: False Protection

1. Doughty-Wylie to the British Ambassador in Constantinople, April 21, 1909, FO 195/2306.

2. Cyphered Telegram from Major Doughty-Wylie, April 19–20, 1909, FO 195/2306.

3. BOA, BEO 3539/265358 (5 Nisan 1325/18 April 1909).

4. Ibid.

5. BOA, BEO 3538/265303 (8 Nisan 1325/21 April 1909).

6. BOA, BEO 3537/265251 (8 Nisan 1325/21 April 1909).

7. From April 14 to April 24, the Armenian Patriarchate sent financial aid to Cilicia amounting to 1,600 GL. The aid was sent to Aleppo, Adana, Cyprus, Tarsus, Sis, Maraş, Latakia, and Adana. 930 GL from Cairo, Manchester, and İzmir was sent directly to Adana. See *Azkayin ĕndhanur zhoghov*.

8. From Stephen Van R. Trowbridge to Mr. Peet (American Bible House Constantinople), Adana, April 21, 1909, FO 195–2306.

9. Terzian, *Kilikioy aghetĕ*, 59.

10. Rigal (P.), "Adana. Les massacres d'Adana," 46. Dr. Habib Abu al-Rus, an Arab who found shelter in the Jesuit church, estimated the number of the refugees to be ten thousand. See *Lisān al-Ḥāl*, April 27, 1909, no. 6003, 3.

11. Surgeon Connell to Captain Thursby "Swiftsure," at Ayas Bay, May 19, 1909, enclosure 5 in no. 25, in Admiralty to Foreign Office (Received July 19), Admiralty, July 13, 1909, C.I. Thomas, in *Further Correspondence, July–September 1909*.

12. Ibid.

13. See *Les massacres D'Adana: Notes sur l'hopital* (Lyon: P. Grange & Refoubelet, 1910).

14. Sabatier precis des évènements d'Adana et de ses environs du 14 avril au 1er mai, 1909, in Missions de Syrie d'Egypte et d' Arménie, 145a-223, tome 281, AJV.

15. *Les massacre d'Adana et nos missionaries: Recit de temoins* (Lyons: Impremerie Vve Paquet, 1909), AJV, 12RAr. Marist Fathers is an international Roman Catholic religious congregation, founded in Lyon in 1816 by Father Jean-Claude Colin and a group of other seminarians.

16. Ibid., 24.

17. Ibid., 25.

18. From the Consul of Austria-Hungary in Mersin to Ambassador Marquis von Pallavicini, Mersin, April 30, 1909, in Ohandjanian, *Österreich—Armenien: 1872–1936*, 3394–3406.

19. *Zhamanak*, April 21, 1909, no. 3808, 3.

20. Ferriman, *The Young Turks*, 26.

21. *Zhamanak*, June 1, 1909, no. 179, 1–2; see also the lengthy article by Suren Bartevian about *İtidal*, in *Biwzandion*, May 19, 1909, no. 3831, 1.

22. Sémelin, "In Consideration of Massacres," 384.

23. Terzian, *Kilikioy aghetë*, 62.

24. *İtidal*, April 20, 1909, no. 33, 1.

25. Ibid.

26. Ibid., 3.

27. Ibid., 2.

28. Ibid., 4.

29. Ibid.

30. Ibid.

31. Even after the second wave of massacres, İhsan Fikri continued to claim that the main reason for the disturbances was the quest of the Armenians of Adana to reestablish their kingdom. See *İtidal*, May 4, 1909, no. 37, 1–2.

32. *İtidal*, April 20, 1909, no. 33, 1–2.

33. Ibid., 2.

34. Ibid.

35. Ibid.

36. *Al-Ittiḥād al-ʿUthmānī*, April 30, 1909, no.184, 1–2; *Al-Ittiḥād al-ʿUthmānī*, May 1, 1909, no. 185, 1; and *Al-Ittiḥād al-ʿUthmānī*, May 11, 1909, no.193, 2–3. *Al-Ittiḥād al-ʿUthmānī* was published by Ahmad Hasan Tabbara in Beirut after 1908.

37. See in particular his lengthy reports on the causes of the strife in Adana. *Al-Ittiḥ ād al-ʿUthmānī*, June 7, 1909, no. 30, 1–4, weekly edition; *Al-Ittiḥād al-ʿUthmānī*, June 14, 1909, no. 31, 3–5; *Al-Ittiḥād al-ʿUthmānī*, June 14, 1909, no. 31, 7–8; and *Al-Ittiḥād al-ʿUthmānī*, June 21, 1909, no. 32, 4–5.

38. For the full official report of the Inquiry Commission to Adana, see *Zhamanak*, August 2, 1909, no. 232, 3. See also Ferriman, *The Young Turks*, 137–50.

39. Terzian, *Kilikioy aghetë*, 94. See also Markarian, *Ink'nakensagrut'iwn Pōghos Markariani*, 43.

40. These battalions were the first of the 81st Regiment of the Second Army, the second of the 83rd Regiment, and third of the 10th Regiment. See *Ìtidal*, April 28, 1909, no. 35, 3.

41. *Droshak*, May 1909, no. 5, 56.

42. Terzian, *Kilikioy aghetĕ*, 101.

43. Ibid., 102.

44. Ibid., 105.

45. On April 26, 1909, Marist Antoine Ressicaud succeeded in saving two thousand Armenians refugees in Surp Step'anos Church from massacre. For this act he was awarded the Medal of Honor by the president of the Republic of France. See Ministère des Affaires étrangères à M. Bompard, ambassadeur de France à Constantinople, 17 June 1910, no. 41, ambassade de Const/ E/129, CADN.

46. Terzian, *Kilikioy aghetĕ*, 106.

47. Ibid., 109; and Markarian, *Ink'nakensagrut'iwn Pōghos Markariani*, 44.

48. Terzian, *Kilikioy aghetĕ*, 118–119. See also Markarian, *Ink'nakensagrut'iwn Pōghos Markariani*, 45.

49. Markarian, *Ink'nakensagrut'iwn Pōghos Markariani*, 45.

50. Woods, *The Danger Zone of Europe*, 135.

51. Ashjian, *Atanayi eghehernĕ ew Gonyayi husher*, 55.

52. Z., *Adanskie chernye dni*, 8.

53. Ferriman, *The Young Turks*, 33.

54. SMS *Hamburg*, telegraph from Mersin, April 29, 1909, no. 202, in Ambassador in Constantinople (Marshal von Bieberstein) to the Foreign Office, April 30, 1909, DE/PA-AA/R 13184.

55. From Major Doughty-Wylie to Sir Gerard Lowther (Ambassador in Constantinople), April 28, 1909, FO 195–2306.

56. Vice-Consul Doughty-Wylie to Sir G. Lowther Adana, May 2, 1909, enclosure 2 in no. 96, Sir. G. Lowther to Sir Edward Grey (Received May 10, 1909), no. 334, Pera, May 11, 1909, in *Further Correspondence, April-June 1909*.

57. Vice-Consul Doughty-Wylie to Sir G. Lowther, Adana, May 6, 1909, enclosure 3 in no. 103, Sir. G. Lowther to Sir Edward Grey (Received May 24, 1909), no. 346, Pera, May 17, 1909, in *Further Correspondence, April-June 1909*.

58. Ibid.

59. From Stephen Van R. Trowbridge to Friends, Adana, May 1, 1909, in From Gabriel Bie Ravndal, Beirut, Syria, to the Assistant Secretary of State, Washington, DC, May 7, 1909, Records of Foreign Service Posts, Consular Posts, Damascus, Turkey, vol. 020, RG 84, USNA.

60. Mr. Hammann (Candidate Junior Barrister/*Dragomanats-Aspirant Referendar*) to the Consul of Beirut, Schroeder Beirut, May 19, 1909, in The Consul in Beirut (Schroeder) to the Chancellor (Bülow), May 29, 1909, DE/PA-AA/R 13186.

61. From the Consul of Austria-Hungary in Mersin to Ambassador Marquis von Pallavicini, Mersin, April 30, 1909, in Ohandjanian, *Österreich—Armenien: 1872–1936*, 3394–3406.

62. From Zavarian to the Responsible Body in İstanbul, June 8, 1909, ARF Archives, C/953–100. On Muslim rescuers of Armenians during the massacres, see Kırmızı, "Feelings of Gratitude."

63. BOA, BEO 3539/265356 (13 Nisan 1325/26 April, 1909). The same telegraph was sent to the president of the parliament. See *Takvim-i Vekayi*, May 5, 1909, no. 202, 4–5.

64. BOA, BEO 3539/265356 (13 Nisan 1325/26 April, 1909).

65. From Stephen Van R. Trowbridge to Mr. Peet (American Bible House Constantinople), Adana, April 21, 1909, FO 195–2306.

66. BOA, BEO 3539/265355 (14 Nisan 1909/27 April 1909).

67. BOA, BEO 3539/265357 (14 Nisan 1909/27 April 1909).

68. Woods, *The Danger Zone of Europe*, 137.

69. The Chief of the Naval Staff of the Navy (Baudissin) to the State Secretary of the Foreign Office (Schoen), May 3, 1909, DE/PA-AA/R 13184. See also The Ambassador in Constantinople (Marshal von Bieberstein) to the Chancellor (Bülow), May 4, 1909, DE/PA-AA/R 13185; Deutsche Bank (Gwinner) to the Foreign Office, May 12, 1909, DE/PA-AA/R 13185; and The Consul in Beirut (Schroeder) to the Chancellor (Bülow), May 29, 1909, DE/PA-AA/R 13186.

70. DE/PA-AA/R 13186, May 21, 1909. See German-Levantine Cotton Society m.b.H., Seventh Special Report to the Members of the Supervisory Board, May 5, 1909, in Deutsche Bank (Vutz) to the Foreign Office.

71. Armenian sources later argued that the Adana massacres were orchestrated by the CUP. Boghos Markarian, who was an eyewitness to the events, claims in his memoirs that the CUP was behind the massacres. See Markarian, *Ink'nakensagrut'iwn Pōghos Markariani*, 31.

72. *İtidal*, April (27?), 1909, no. 34, 2. The date is not mentioned in the printed version of the newspaper.

73. Ibid.

74. Ibid.

75. *İtidal*, April 28, 1909, no. 35, 2.

76. Ibid., 3.

77. *Droshak*, May 1909, no. 5, 56.

78. Ibid.

79. Society for the Propagation of Faith, *The Adana Massacres and the Catholic Missionaries: Account of Eye-Witnesses* (New York: Society for the Propagation of Faith, 1910), 11.

Chapter 6: After the Fact

1. Zabel Yesayan, in her monumental book, provides detailed information about the condition in Adana and the work that was carried out by humanitarian organizations; see Yesayan, *Aweraknerun mēj*. On Yesayan's own humanitarian work in Adana, see Watenpaugh, *Bread from Stones*, 72–74.

2. Rodogno, *Against Massacres*, 209.

3. Watenpaugh, *Bread from Stones*, 70–71.

4. Ibid.

5. Ibid., 12.

6. Ferriman, *The Young Turks*, 95.

7. Ibid, 21.

8. Telegram from Vice-Consul Doughty-Wylie to the Captain of Hamburg, May 7, 1909, May 18, 1909, DE/PA-AA/R 13186.

9. Copy to B. 1808. I. Command SMS. *Hamburg*, UK, no. 294, enclosure in The Chief of the Navy's Admiral (Baudissin) to the State Secretary of the Foreign Office (Schoen), April 18, 1909, DE/PA-AA/R 13186.

10. V. Man, Beirut, May 12, 1909, enclosure 1, in The Chief of the Navy's Admiral (Baudissin) to the State Secretary of the Foreign Office (Schoen), May 27, 1909, DE/PA-AA/R 13186.

11. For a detailed report on the ARC's relief work in Adana, see G. Bie Ravndal, "Turko-Armenian Relief," *American Red Cross Bulletin* 4, no. 4 (October 1909): 8–29.

12. On the British relief efforts, see Tusan, *The British Empire*, 112–18.

13. Vice-Consul Doughty-Wylie to Sir G. Lowther, Adana, May 5, 1909, enclosure 1 in no. 103, in Sir G. Lowther to Sir Edward Grey (Received May 24), no. 346. Pera, May 17, 1909, in *Further Correspondence, April–June 1909*.

14. From Dabbas Deputy Consul to American Consul General Beirut, April 30, 1909, Records of Foreign Service Posts, Consular Posts, Mersin, Turkey, vol. 012, RG 84, USNA. Mrs. Trowbridge states that a German doctor, the only physician present at the time, diagnosed the case as "smallpox," thinking it was the English word for "measles." When the English doctor from the *Swiftsure* arrived, he discovered the mistake, but too late to keep the false report out of the papers. See From Mrs. S. Van R. Trowbridge to Family, Mersine, May 5, 1909, Central Turkey Mission, vol. 17, reel 662, ABCFM Archives.

15. HMS *Swiftsure* at Mersina to the American Consul, April 29, 1909, Records of Foreign Service Posts, Consular Posts, Mersin, Turkey, vol. 019, RG 84, USNA.

16. Ibid., 23.

17. From American Consular Edward Nathan to American Ambassador John G. A. Leishman, May 7, 1909, Records of Foreign Service Posts, Consular Posts, Mersin, Turkey, vol. 012, RG 84, USNA.

18. From Stephen Van R. Trowbridge to Friends, Adana, May 1, 1909, in From Gabriel Bie Ravndal, Beirut, Syria, to the Assistant Secretary of State, Washington, DC May 7, 1909, Records of Foreign Service Posts, Consular Posts, Beirut, Lebanon, vol. 145, RG 84, USNA. See also, From Mrs. S. Van R. Trowbridge to Family, May 3, Mersin, 1909, Central Turkey Mission, vol. 17, reel 662, ABCFM Archives.

19. Ravndal, "Turko-Armenian Relief," 8.

20. Yesayan, *Aweraknerun mēj*, 74

21. Ferriman, *The Young Turks*, 98.

22. From Stephen Van R. Trowbridge to Friends, Adana, May 1, 1909, in From Gabriel Bie Ravndal, Beirut, Syria, to the Assistant Secretary of State, Washington, DC May 7, 1909, Records of Foreign Service Posts, Consular Posts, Beirut, Lebanon, vol. 145, RG 84, USNA.

23. *Spectator*, May 8, 1909, vol. 102, no. 4219, 725.

24. Vice-Consul Doughty-Wylie to Sir G. Lowther, Adana, May 5, 1909, enclosure 1 in no.10 in *Further Correspondence, April-June 1909*.

25. The German emperor had sent his own ship, the *Hamburg*, posthaste from Corfu to Mersin soon after the first massacre, and the supplies needed for the German hospital were to a large extent furnished from the ship's stores.

26. A Military Police (*militärpolitischen*) Report, SMS *Lübeck* about the Situation in the Vilayet Adana in the Chief of the Navy's Admiral (Baudissin) to the State Secretary of the Foreign Office (Schoen), May 29, 1909, DE/PA-AA/R 13186.

27. Ibid.

28. Ibid.

29. Ibid.

30. *New York Times*, November 27, 1909, 3.

31. Society for the Propagation of Faith, *The Adana Massacres and the Catholic Missionaries*, 66.

32. Ibid.

33. From Stephen Van R. Trowbridge to Friends, Adana, May 1, 1909, in From Gabriel Bie Ravndal, Beirut, Syria, to the Assistant Secretary of State, Washington, DC, May 7, 1909, Records of Foreign Service Posts, Consular Posts, Beirut, Lebanon, vol. 145, RG 84, USNA.

34. Ravndal, "Turko-Armenian Relief," 17.

35. See BOA, DH.MKT 2821/20 (8 Mayıs 1325/21 May 1909).

36. Ferriman, *The Young Turks*, 96. The Trappists are named after La Trappe Abbey, the monastery from which the movement and religious order originated. Officially known as the Order of Cistercians of the Strict Observance (*Ordo Cisterciensis Strictioris Observantiae*, OCSO), the movement began with the reforms that Abbot Armand Jean le Bouthillier de Rancé introduced in 1664. This led to the creation of

Trappist congregations. In 1892, they promulgated a formal constitution as a separate religious order.

37. Society for the Propagation of Faith, *The Adana Massacres and the Catholic Missionaries*, 71–72.

38. Rigal, "Adana. Les massacres d'Adana," 13.

39. G. Bie Ravndal, "Turko-Armenian Relief," *American Red Cross Bulletin* 4, (October 1909): 8.

40. *Washington Post*, May 16, 1909, 14.

41. *New York Times*, November 27, 1909, 3.

42. Ibid., 11.

43. Ibid., 14.

44. *Washington Post*, May 16, 1909, 14.

45. *Spectator*, June 5, 1909, vol. 102, no. 4223, 878.

46. On the reports of the activities of the International Relief Committee in different towns and cities of Adana, see Central Turkey Mission, vol. 15, reel 660, ABCFM Archives.

47. This was also reported in "The Adana Relief Funds," *Times*, June 2, 1909, 12.

48. Ferriman, *The Young Turks*, 97.

49. Ibid., 96.

50. From Vali Ahmet Djemal to Rev. W. N. Chambers, President of the Commission of Industries, Adana, Turkey, December 24, 1909, Records of Foreign Service Posts, Consular Posts, Mersin, Turkey, vol. 025, RG 84, USNA.

51. Terzian, *Kilikioy aghetē*, 815.

52. Ibid., 816.

53. Ferriman, *The Young Turks*, 96.

54. Konstandnupolsoy Patriark'ut'iwn, *Npastits' handznazhoghov: Hashuets'uts'ak ew teghekagir, 1897–1908* (K. Polis: Tpagrut'iwn "Shant'," 1911), 15.

55. Ibid., 19.

56. Ferriman, *The Young Turks*, 94.

57. Raymond H. Kévorkian and Vahé Tachjian, eds., *The Armenian General Benevolent Union: One Hundred Years of History*, vol. I, *1906–1940*, trans. G. M. Goshgarian (Cairo: AGBU Central Board, 2006), 26.

58. Ferriman, *The Young Turks*, 98.

59. Konstandnupolsoy Patriark'ut'iwn, *Npastits' handznazhoghov*, 11.

60. See *Mshak*, May 28, 1909, no. 112, 1.

61. From Patriarch Haurtyun Vehabedian to the Armenian Catholicos of Cilicia Sahag II, April 27, 1909, Correspondences, 1909, no. 123–24, no. 39, 1909, Archives of the Armenian Patriarchate of Jerusalem (AAPJ).

62. BOA, BEO 3540/265467 (20 Nisan 1325/3 May 1909).

63. BOA, BEO 3542/265632 (23 Nisan 1325/ 6 May 1909).

64. A Military Police (*militärpolitischen*) Report, SMS *Lübeck* about the Situation in the Vilayet Adana in the Chief of the Navy's Admiral (Baudissin) to the State Secretary of the Foreign Office (Schoen), May 25, 1909, DE/PA-AA/R 13186.

65. BOA, DH.MKT 2801/99 (19 Nisan 1325/2 May 1909).

66. Ibid.

67. BOA, BEO 3541/265560 (21 Nisan 1325/4 May 1909).

68. BOA, DH.MKT 2808/57 (28 Nisan, 1325/11 May 1909).

69. BOA, BEO 3596/269676 (13 Temmuz 1325/ 26 July 1909).

70. Ibid.

71. Ibid.

72. Yesayan, *Aweraknerun mēj*, 30–80.

73. Ferriman, *The Young Turks*, 100–101.

74. P. Zhak Sayabalian, *Teghekagir ayriakhnam handznazhoghovi: 1910 Sept.11—1912 Sept. 11* (Ghalat'ia: Tparan "Shant'," 1912), 9.

75. Ferriman, *The Young Turks*, 99.

76. Terzian, *Kilikioy aghetě*, 831–33.

77. Kilikioy Orbakhnam Kedronakan Handznazhoghov, *Teghekagir 1909 Ōgostos 7–1910 Dektember 31* (K. Polis: Tparan ew Kazmatun Ō. Arzuman, 1911), 31. This was the report of the Armenian Patriarchate Orphanage Committee (APOC).

78. On the orphans and their condition in the post-massacre period, see Kilikioy Orbakhnam Kedronakan Handznazhoghov, *Teghekagir: 1909 Ōgostos 7–1910 Dektember 31*. On the Cilician orphanages, see Yesayan's articles in *Aragadz*, August 17, 1911, no. 13, 196–97; *Aragadz*, August 24, 1911, no. 14, 212–13; *Aragadz*, August 31, 1911, no. 15, 228–29; *Aragadz*, September 7, 1911, 244–45, no. 16, 196–97; and *Aragadz*, September 14, 1911, no. 17, 257–61.

79. Nazan Maksudyan, "New 'Rules of Conduct' for State, American Missionaries, and Armenians: 1909 Adana Massacres and the Ottoman Orphanage (Dârü'l-Eytâm-ı Osmânî)," in *L'ivresse de la liberté: La révolution de 1908 dans l'empire Ottoman*, ed. François Georgeon (Paris: CNRS, 2012), 43. Maksudyan provides an excellent analysis of the condition of the orphans, the efforts of the missionaries, and Cemal Paşa's orphanage.

80. Kilikioy Orbakhnam Kedronakan Handznazhoghov, *Teghekagir: 1909 Ōgostos 7–1910 Dektember 31*, 14. See also Divan of the Catholicos of All Armenians, Fond 57, Ts'uts'ag 5, Gordz 14, Resigned Patriarch of İstanbul, Yeghishe Tourian, to the Armenian Catholicos of Echmiadzin, December 31, 1909, no. 417, Armenian National Archives (ANA).

81. On the relief efforts of Armenian women in the post-massacre period, see Anna Aleksanyan, "Hay kanants' hasarakakan kordzuneyut'iwnĕ Kilikyayum 1909 t' kotoradznerits hedo (Z. Yesayan ew A. Teotiki Orinakov)," *Ts'eghaspanagitakan handes* 1, no. 1 (2013): 8–13.

82. State orphanages were established in Haçin and Dörtyol; English and French ones in Aintab; a German one in Maraş; an American one in Haçin; Catholic, Jesuit, and Protestant ones in Adana; German ones in Beirut, Urfa, Germany, İzmir, and Talas; a Catholic one in Aleppo; and a Jesuit one in Bethlehem. In addition, there were orphanages under the auspices of Baghdasarian in Bursa, Dbrots'aser Tiknats' (Ladies Who Love School) in İstanbul, Tiknats' Miyut'iwn (Ladies Union) in İstanbul, the Jerusalem Seminary, and one in Rodosto. See Kilikioy Orbakhnam Kedronakan Handznazhoghov, *Teghekagir: 1909 Ōgostos 7–1910 Dektember 31*, 39; Terzian, *Kilikioy aghetě*, 819–20; Adana Relief Committee Fourth Instalment Account, Adana, June 15, 1909, Records of Foreign Service Posts, Consular Posts, Mersin, Turkey, vol. 012, RG 84, USNA; and Ferriman, *The Young Turks*, 98.

83. Maksudyan, "New 'Rules of Conduct,'" 162.

84. Ibid., 163.

85. Report of the Adana Relief Committee, Adana, July 31, 1909, by Doughty-Wylie, Central Turkey Mission, vol. 15, reel 660, ABCFM Archives.

86. *Biwzandion*, May 8, 1909, no. 3822, 3.

87. *El Tiempo*, May 11, 1909, no. 91, 859–60.

88. *Journal de Salonique*, July 6, 1909, no. 1483, 1.

89. *Journal de Salonique*, August 12, 1909, no. 1500, 1.

90. BOA, BEO 3596/269676 (7 Haziran 1325/20 June 1909).

91. *Lisān al-Ḥāl*, May 21, 1909, no. 6024, 1–2; and *Lisān al-Ḥāl*, May 28, 1909, no. 6030, 1.

92. *Lisān al-Ḥāl*, May 28, 1909, no. 6030, 1.

93. *Lisān al-Ḥāl*, June 11, 1909, no. 6041, 1.

94. *Lisān al-Ḥāl*, June 11, 1909, no. 6043, 1.

95. *Lisān al-Ḥāl*, June 11, 1909, no. 6041, 1.

96. *Al-Muqtabas*, April 24, 1909, no. 111, 1.

97. *Al-Muqtabas*, August 8, 1909, no. 194, 2–3.

98. *Ṣada Bābel*, September 3, 1909, no. 4, 4.

99. Ibid.

100. See *Al-Ittiḥād al-'Uthmānī*, May 3, 1909, no. 26, 10–14; and *Al-Ittiḥād al-'Uthmānī*, May 31, 1909, no. 29, 3.

101. *Al-Ittiḥād al-'Uthmānī*, June 7, 1909, no. 30, 2.

102. Ibid., 3.

103. *Al-Ittiḥād al-'Uthmānī*, June 14, 1909, no. 31, 7–8.

104. Ibid., 8.

105. *Al-Ittiḥād al-'Uthmānī*, June 21, 1909, no. 32, 4–5.

106. *Ha-Po'el ha-Tza'ir*, May 2, 1909, no. 15, 14.

107. *Ha-Zvi*, November 26, 1909, no. 50, 2.

108. *Ha-'Olam*, July 13, 1909, no. 25, 12.

109. *Ha-Ḥerut*, May 18, 1909, no. 3, 2.

110. *Ha-Ḥerut*, July 29, 1909, no. 26, 3.

111. *Journal de Salonique*, May 21, 1909, no. 1448, 1.

112. Ibid.

113. *Journal de Salonique*, August 12, 1909, no. 1500, 2.

114. Ibid.

115. *Neue Freie Presse*, April 18, 1909, no. 16041, 1.

116. *Kurjer Lwowski*, April 16, 1909, no. 176, 5; *Kurjer Lwowski*, April 19, 1909, no. 180, 2; and *Kurjer Lwowski*, April 21, 1909, no. 183, 2.

117. *Wiener Zeitung*, May 1, 1909, no. 99, 12.

118. *Wiener Zeitung*, May 2, 1909, no. 100, 16.

119. *Proodos*, April 15, 1909, no. 1602, 3; *Proodos*, April 19, 1909, no. 1606, 2; *Proodos*, April 20, 1909, no. 1607, 3; *Proodos*, April 24, 1909, no. 1611, 1; *Proodos*, April 25, 1909, no. 1612, 3; *Proodos*, April 27, 1909, no. 1614, 3; *Proodos*, May 1, 1909, no. 1618, 2; *Proodos*, May 3, 1909, no. 1620, 2; and *Proodos*, May 4, 1909, no. 1621, 4.

120. *Proodos*, April 14, 1909, no. 1601, 3.

121. *Proodos*, April 16, 1909, no. 1603, 3.

122. *Proodos*, April 24, 1909, no. 1611, 1.

123. *Skrip*, April 7, 1909; *Skrip*, April 5, 1909, 4.

124. *Empros*, April 13, 1909 [April 26, 1909], 4; and *Empros*, April 23, 1909 [April 6, 1909], 4

125. *Empros*, April 12, 1909 [April 25, 1909], 2; and *Empros*, April 25, 1909 [May 8, 1909], 1.

126. *Empros*, April 13, 1909 [April 26, 1909], 4.

127. *Empros*, April 19, 1909 [May 2, 1909], 4.

128. *Empros*, May 27, 1909 [June 8, 1909], 2.

129. *Empros*, April 21, 1909 [May 4, 1909], 3.

130. Walter Siehe lived from 1897 in the Cilician region of southern Turkey. He regularly collected plants in the mountains of Adana and neighboring regions, sending his collections to European herbaria. He also exported bulbs for cultivation and submitted a series of papers on his botanical explorations to the *Sammler* and *Allgemeine Botanische Zeitung*, under the title "Botanische Forschungsreise nach Kleinasien."

131. *Berliner Tageblatt*, May 1, 1909, no. 218, 1.

132. *Berliner Tageblatt*, May 19, 1909, no. 251, 1. On Chambers, see *New York Times*, July 11, 1909, SM 1.

133. *Berliner Tageblatt*, June 4, 1909, no. 277, 1.

134. *Berliner Tageblatt*, June 10, 1909, no. 288, 1. See also Edward Mygind, "Roar from Adana," *Berliner Tageblatt*, July 7, 1909, no. 333, 1. On an analysis of Germany's attitude towards Armenians, see Stefan Ihrig, *Justifying Genocide: Germany and the Armenians from Bismarck to Hitler* (Cambridge, MA: Harvard University Press, 2016).

135. *Berliner Tageblatt*, June 15, 1909, no. 297, 1.

136. From 1893 to 1919, Cochin represented Paris in the French National Assembly. He was the principal spokesman of the Catholic party defending the religious educational liberties and congregations against the attacks of the administrations of Pierre Waldeck-Rousseau and Émile Combes.

137. *Le temps*, May 15, 1909, no. 17492, 6.

138. Ibid.

139. *Le temps*, May 19, 1909, no. 17493, 3.

140. *Le temps*, May 29, 1909, no. 17503, 4.

141. *Le temps*, October 15, 1909, no. 17641, 1.

142. Ibid.

143. Ibid.

144. Antonio Scarfoglio (1886–1969) was the son of Edoardo Scarfoglio and Matilde Serao, both well-known Neapolitan writers at the turn of the century and founders of *Il Mattino*, the Neapolitan daily newspaper. Antonio became a reporter for that paper. In June of 1909, he reported on the Adana massacres.

145. *Le matin*, May 31, 1909, no. 9225, 4.

146. *Le matin*, June 5, 1909, no. 9230, 3.

147. *Gazette de Lausanne*, May 5, 1909, no. 105, 1.

148. Ibid.

149. *Gazette de Lausanne*, July 24, 1909, no. 173, 2.

150. *Journal de Geneve*, May 8, 1909, no. 125, 1.

151. *Journal de Geneve*, June 17, 1909, no. 163, 1.

152. *Manchester Guardian*, May 8, 1909, 7. See also Utudjian's letter to the Armenian Catholicos Izmirlian on May 1, 1909, in Letter from Archbishop Kevork Utudjian the Primate of the Armenians in Europe (Manchester), April 18/May 1, 1909, IA.

153. *Manchester Guardian*, June 2, 1909, 3. This appeal also appeared in "The Adana Relief Funds," *Times*, June 2, 1909, 12.

154. For more examples, such as the reaction of the Boston press to the Adana massacres, see Lilian K. Etmekjian, "The Reaction of the Boston Press to the 1909 Massacre of Adana," *Armenian Review* 40 (1987): 61–74.

155. *Washington Post*, April 17, 1909, 1; *Washington Post*, April 24, 1909, 1; and *Washington Post*, May 1, 1909, 1.

156. *Washington Post*, April 19, 1909, 1.

157. Ibid.

158. *Washington Post*, April 22, 1909, 1.

159. *Washington Post*, May 1, 1909, 4; and *Washington Post*, May 5, 1909, 5.

160. *Washington Post*, May 11, 1909, 9.

161. *Washington Post*, April 21, 1909, 1.

162. *New York Times*, April 21, 1909, 2.

163. *New York Times* April 25, 1909, 1.

164. *New York Times*, April 30, 1909, 2.

165. *New York Times*, July 11, 1909, SM 1. Gibbons, from Philadelphia, was the son of Rev. Gibbons. A graduate of the Princeton Theological Seminary, he married a Bryn Mawr graduate and went to Tarsus, the birthplace of St. Paul, to teach while still pursuing his studies.

166. *New York Times*, August 1, 1909, SM 8.

167. *New York Times*, August 29, 1909, SM 4.

168. *New York Times*, August 22, 1909, SM 2.

169. Rodogno, *Against Massacre*, 204.

Chapter 7: Justice on Trial

1. The district of İçil was not included in the state of siege. The thirteen articles of the state of siege were based on those that were ratified on October 2, 1877. On state of siege in the Ottoman Empire, see Noémi Lévy-Aksu, "An Ottoman Variation on the State of Siege: The Invention of the *İdare-i Örfiyye* during the First Constitutional Period," *New Perspectives on Turkey* 55 (2016): 5–28.

2. Article 113 of the Ottoman Constitution states, "In the case of the perpetration of acts, or the appearance of indications of a nature to presage disturbance at any point on the territory of the empire, the Imperial Government has the right to proclaim a state of siege there. The state of siege consists in the temporary suspension of the civil laws. The mode of administration of localities under a state of siege will be regulated by a special law. His Majesty the Sultan has the exclusive right of expelling from the territory of the empire those who, in consequence of trustworthy information obtained by the police, are recognized as dangerous to the safety of the State." See https://www.anayasa.gov.tr/tr/mevzuat/onceki-anayasalar/1876-k%C3%A2n%C3%BBn-i-es%C3%A2s%C3%AE/.

3. Major Doughty-Wylie to Sir G. Lowther, Adana, June 14, 1909, enclosure in no. 149, in Sir. G. Lowther to Sir Edward Grey (Received June 29, 1909), Constantinople, June 22, 1909, in *Further Correspondence, April–June 1909*.

4. Ferriman, *The Young Turks*, 104.

5. Vice-Consul Doughty-Wylie to Sir G. Lowther, Adana, May 8, 1909, in enclosure 4 in no. 103, in Sir G. Lowther to Sir Edward Grey (Received May 24, 1909), no. 346, Pera, May 17, 1909, in *Further Correspondence, April–June 1909*.

6. Ferriman, *The Young Turks*, 104.

7. The British vice-consul at Mersin informed the British ambassador that the number of Armenians arrested was three hundred. See Sir. G. Lowther to Sir Edward Grey (Received May 10, 1909), Pera, May 11, 1909, no. 96, in *Further Correspondence, April–June 1909*. Zabel Yesayan, who frequently visited the Armenian prisoners, provides a detailed description of the horrific conditions in the prison. See Yesayan, *Aweraknerun mēj*, 134–54.

8. Terzian, *Kilikioy aghetě*, 340–64. Terzian also wrote for *Zhamanak* under the pen-name Hag Ter. His reflections on the prison experience appeared first in *Zhamanak*.

9. Terzian, *Kilikioy aghetě*, 358.

10. Ferid Jemil (Mersin) to A. Agnuni, May 16, 1909, ARF Archives C/953–94. See Bartevian, *Kilikean Arhawirk'ě*, 74–75.

11. Artin Arslanian, *Adana'da adalet nasıl mahkûm oldu* (Le Caire: [publisher not identified],1909 [1325]), 7.

12. Ibid., 8.

13. Ibid., 11.

14. BOA, DH.MKT 810/74 (29 Nisan 1325/12 May 1909).

15. BOA, DH.MKT 2838/100 (21 Mayıs 1325/3 June 1909).

16. See Sir. G. Lowther to Sir Edward Grey (Received May 24, 1909), no. 346, Pera, May 17, 1909, in *Further Correspondence, April–June 1909.*

17. Major Doughty-Wylie to Sir G. Lowther, Adana, June 14, 1909, enclosure in no. 149, in Sir. G. Lowther to Sir Edward Grey (Received June 29, 1909), no. 474, Constantinople, June 22, 1909, in *Further Correspondence, April–June 1909.*

18. *İkdam*, May 1, 1909, no. 5362, 4.

19. Terzian, *Kilikioy aghetě*, 368–69.

20. Woods, *The Danger Zone of Europe*, 181.

21. BOA, DH.MKT 2826/53 (17 Mayıs 1325/30 May 1909).

22. Asaf, *1909 Adana Ermeni olayları ve anılarım*, 15.

23. Ibid., 46.

24. Terzian, *Kilikioy aghetě*, 393–99. The letter was signed by the Armenian Catholic bishop, Boghos Terzian; the vice-prelate of the Armenian Orthodox Church, Fr. Arsen; the vice-patriarchate of the Chaldeans, Rev. Stephan Maksoubi; the Armenian Protestant minister Ashjian; the vice-patriarch of the Syrian and Greek Catholics, Fr. Philipos Shakkal; the vice-prelate of Greek Orthodox in Adana, Baba Avraham; and the Old Syrian vice-patriarch, Fr. Mansour.

25. Terzian, *Kilikioy aghetě*, 393–99.

26. From Austro-Hungarian Consul in Mersin to Ambassador Marquis von Pallaviccini, Mersin, May 30, 1909, Beilage zu Bericht, no. 46 a h D ddo. Cos-pel 9-6-1909 in Ohandjanian, *Österreich—Armenien: 1872–1936*, 3425–3429.

27. BOA, DH.MKT 2836/86 (24 Mayıs 1325/6 June 1909).

28. Minutes dated May 20, 1325 (June 2, 1909), Drawn Up by the Adana Court-Martial, Sent to Sir G. Lowther, enclosure in no. 131, Sir. G. Lowther to Sir Edward Grey (Received June 29, 1909), no. 434, Therapia, June 21, 1909, in *Further Correspondence, April–June 1909.*

29. Major Doughty-Wylie to Sir G. Lowther, Adana, July 19, 1909, enclosure 2 in no. 43, in Sir. G. Lowther to Sir Edward Grey (Received June 29, 1909), no. 622, Therapia, August 4, 1909, in *Further Correspondence, July–September 1909.*

30. Major Doughty-Wylie to Sir G. Lowther, Adana, June 14, 1909, enclosure in no. 149, in Sir. G. Lowther to Sir Edward Grey (Received June 28, 1909), no. 474, Constantinople, June 22, 1909, in *Further Correspondence, April-June 1909.*

31. BOA, BEO 3570/267681 (24 Mayıs 1324/6 Haziran 1909).

32. *Tasvir-i Efkâr,* June 8, 1909, no. 39, 1–2. Kemal claims that Babigian returned early due to health reasons. See also Yusuf Kemal Tengirşek, *Vatan hizmetinde* (İstanbul: Bahar Matbaası, 1967), 121.

33. M. Barre de Lancy, vice-consul de France à Mersine d'Adana à Monsieur Boppe chargé d'Affaires de France pres la Porte Ottomane, Mersine, 3 July 1909, Turquie, ambassade de Constantinople, série E, 129, confidential, no. 30, CADN.

34. Babigian to the Grand Vizierate, June 7, 1909, in Armenian Patriarchate, *La situation des Arméniens en Turquie exposée par des documents 1908–1912,* vol. 3 (Constantinople: [publisher not identified], [1913?]), 29–30.

35. Ibid.

36. *Takvim-i Vekayi,* May 23, 1909, no. 219, 1.

37. *Zhamanak,* June 5, 1909, no. 183, 2.

38. *Takvim-i Vekayi,* May 30, 1909, no. 226, 2–3.

39. Seven of these were only peasants, inhabitants of a village called Çakallı, forty miles from Adana. See The Armenian Prelate of Cyprus Rev. Hovhanness Chahinian to Mr. Minister of Foreign Affairs of Austro-Hungary, Vienna, Larnaca, July 9, 1909, in Ohandjanian, *Österreich—Armenien: 1872–1936,* 3442.

40. See *Tanin,* June 3, 1909, no. 270, 1; *Tanin,* June 9, 1909, no. 276, 1; and *Tasvir-i Efkar,* June 10, 1909, no. 940. The names of those who were hanged appeared in *Tanin.* See *Tanin,* June 11, 1909, no. 278, 2–3.

41. Terzian, *Kilikioy agheté,* 403–5.

42. BOA, BEO 3582/2686351 (4 Haziran 1325/17 June 1909).

43. BOA, DH.MKT 2861/16 (17 Haziran 1325/30 June 1909).

44. BOA, BEO 3621/271523 (24 Haziran 1325/7 July 1909). See also *Azatamart,* July 17, 1909, no. 22, 3. The report appeared in *Tanin* in seven installments: *Tanin,* July 30, 1909, no. 326, 1; *Tanin,* July 31, 1909, no. 327, 1; *Tanin,* August 1, 1909, no. 328, 1; *Tanin,* August 2, 1909, no. 329, 1; *Tanin,* August 3, 1909, no. 330, 1–2; *Tanin,* August 4, 1909, no. 331, 1; and *Tanin,* August 6, 1909, no. 333, 1.

45. BOA, BEO 3621/271523 (24 Haziran 1325/ 7 July 1909).

46. *Azatamart,* July 6, 1909, no. 12, 1; *Azatamart,* July 20, 1909, no. 24, 1; and *Azatamart,* July 21, 1909, no. 25, 1. See also *Tanin,* June 11, 1909, no. 278, 2.

47. Divan of the Catholicos of All Armenians, Fond 57, Ts'uts'ag 5, Gordz 14, Resigned Patriarch of İstanbul, Yeghishe Tourian to the Armenian Catholicos of Echmiadzin, December 31, 1909, no. 416, ANA.

48. The report appeared in *Tanin* in six installments: *Tanin,* July 30, 1909, no. 326, 1; *Tanin,* July 31, 1909, no. 327, 1; *Tanin,* August 1, 1909, no. 328, 1; *Tanin,* August

2, 1909, no. 329, 1; *Tanin*, August 3, 1909, no. 330, 1–2; and *Tanin*, August 4, 1909, no. 331, 1.

49. Ferriman, *The Young Turks*, 151.

50. See *Zhamanak*, July 10, 1909, no. 213, 1. The editorial suggested that Babigian should be the governor of Adana. See also Bartevian, *Kilikean arhawirk'ě*, 105. Babigian was born in Edirne on February 23, 1856, and graduated from the local French school. In 1877, he worked in Bosnia as an assistant to the Foreign Ministry management. Then, for two years, he worked in Edirne as the secretary of the commercial court, after which he worked as a member of the appeals court in Edirne. In 1891, he began working in Edirne as a lawyer. He was elected as a deputy in 1908. He left four daughters and two sons. See Hagop Babigian, *Atanayi egheṛně: Niwt'er Hay martirosagrut'ean patmut'eamn*, trans. Hagop Sarkissian (İstanbul: Artsakank Press, 1919). The introduction of the book was written by Francis de Pressensé.

51. *Zhamanak*, July 29, 1909, no. 229, 1.

52. *Yeni Tasvir-i Efkâr*, July 2, 1909, no. 39, 1–2.

53. Ibid. 2.

54. *Yeni Tasvir-i Efkâr*, July 12, 1909, no. 43, 2.

55. *Yeni Tasvir-i Efkâr*, July 21, 1909, no. 52, 4–5. See specifically the telegram included in the article.

56. BOA, BEO 3607/270490 (6 Temmuz 1325/19 July 1909). See also *Yeni Tasvir-i Efkar*, July 21, 1909, no. 52, 5.

57. BOA, BEO 625/271854 (6 Temmuz 1325/19 July 1909).

58. For Vali Mustafa Zihni's telegram to the grand vizier dated July 19, 1909, see BOA, BEO 625/271854 (6 Temmuz 1325/19 July, 1909).

59. *Yeni Tasvir-i Efkâr*, July 21, 1909, no. 52, 4.

60. *Yeni Tasvir-i Efkâr*, July 12, 1909, no. 43, 1–2.

61. The vali of Adana, Mustafa Zihni, also disagreed with the figures provided by Babigian; see his cipher telegram sent to the grand vizier: BOA, BEO 3621/271522, (27 Haziran 1325/10 July 1909). However, the figures that were provided by the government investigation commission were based on the population registrars (*nüfûs defterleri*), which did not include many people who were not registered and thousands of other laborers and visitors. See *Tanin*, May 24, 1909, no. 260, 1.

62. *Yeni Tasvir-i Efkâr*, July 12, 1909, no. 43, 1.

63. Ibid.

64. *Yeni Tasvir-i Efkâr*, July 31, 1909, no. 61, 4–5.

65. BOA, BEO 3580/268483 (9 Haziran 1325/ 22 June 1909).

66. In his introduction to the Babigian report published in 1919, Hagop Sarkissian says that, once Babigian was done with his report, "black hands arrive[d] in mysterious death [*khorhrdawor mahov*] to put an end to his life." See Babigian, *Atanayi egheṛně*, 6. Sarkissian notes that the original version of the report has remained secret, while the

report of Yusuf Kemal was burned in the fire of Çırağan Palace. According to him, the Adana massacres demonstrate the responsibility of the government led by the CUP. He says the only way to solve the situation of Armenia is to give Adana a status like that of Lebanon or Samos.

67. This document was found after Babigian's death among the papers that were handed over to the Armenian Patriarchate. An article in the *Times* titled "A Secret Report on the Adana Massacres" appeared on March 14, 1913, indicating the publication of the report. See *Times*, March 14, 1913, no. 40159, 7. The *Times* was probably referring to the French version of the report, which appeared in 1913. See Armenian Patriarchate, *La situation des Arméniens*, 5–31. It was also published in *Pour les peuples d'Orient*, May 10 and 25, July 25, and August 10, 1913. An Armenian translation of this version appeared in 1919. See Babigian, *Atanayi Egherně*.

68. Woods, *The Danger Zone of Europe*, 182.

69. Babigian, *Atanayi egherně*, 12.

70. Ibid., 12.

71. Ibid., 15.

72. Ibid., 16.

73. Ibid., 18.

74. Ibid., 36. Italics in the original.

75. Ibid., 36–37.

76. Ibid., 37.

77. Ibid., 35.

78. Ibid., 39.

79. This concluding section does not appear in Hagop Terzian's excerpts.

80. Babigian, *Atanayi egherně*, 42.

81. The prelate of Adana, Seropian, accused the government of being complicit in the massacres by noting, among other points, the light sentence that Vali Cevad received from the court-martial, the fact that Adil Bey retained his position in the Ministry of the Interior, the role of the battalions from the Second and Third Armies commanded by officers belonging to the CUP, the bias of the courts-martial in their proceedings, the role of the local CUP members in the reactionary movement, and the reluctance of the Young Turks to unveil the true origin of the massacres. See Seropian, *Les vêpres Ciliciennes*, 55–59.

82. The Armenian daily *Zhamanak* criticized this theory; see *Zhamanak*, August 5, 1909, no. 235, 1. See also Ashjian, *Atanayi egheherně ew Gonyayi husher*, 52; and Yeghiayan, *Atanayi Hayots' patmut'iwn*, 261.

83. Interview with Alice (Babikian) Maremetdjian, May 25–26, 1980. The unpublished interview was conducted mostly in French, and Sylvie L. Merian translated it into English. I would like to thank Sylvie for providing the original audio recording and the transcription of the interview.

84. *Zhamanak,* August 3, 1909, no. 233, 3. *Yeni Tasvir-i Efkar* claimed that he died from chest pain (*ihtinâk-ı sadr*); see *Yeni Tasvir-i Efkar,* August 4, 1909, no. 65, 3.

85. *Zhamanak,* August 4, 1909, no. 234, 1.

86. *Yeni Tasvir-i Efkar,* August 4, 1909, no. 65, 3.

87. *Zhamanak,* August 4, 1909, no. 234, 1.

88. Terzian, *Kilikioy aghetě,* 399–400.

89. The decision of the government to try these men led to some debate in the parliament. The deputy of Gümülcine, İsmail Bey, sent a question to Grand Vizier Hüseyin Hilmi Paşa regarding the arrest of Abdülkadir Bağdadizade and İhsan Fikri. On July 22, 1909, Hüseyin Hilmi responded that, based on the investigations of Haziran 24, 1325 (July 7, 1909), their influence on the events of Adana had been proven. On July 10, Bağdadizade, Fikri, and others were arrested and handed to the court-martial in accordance with the decision of the Council of Ministers. See *Takvim-i Vekayi,* August 3, 1909, no. 292, 6–7.

90. M. Barre de Lancy, vice-consul de France à Mersine d'Adana à Monsieur Boppe chargé d'Affaires de France pres la Porte Ottomane, Mersine, 13 July 1909, Turquie, ambassade de Constantinople, série E, 129, no. 14, CADN.

91. M. Barre de Lancy, vice-consul de France à Mersine d'Adana à Monsieur Boppe chargé d'Affaires de France pres la Porte Ottomane, Mersine, 16 July 1909, Turquie, ambassade de Constantinople, série E, 129, no. 16, CADN.

92. M. Barre de Lancy, vice-consul de France à Mersine d'Adana à Monsieur Boppe chargé d'Affaires de France pres la Porte Ottomane, Mersine, 20 July 1909, Turquie, ambassade de Constantinople, série E, 129, no. 17, CADN.

93. Terzian, *Kilikioy aghetě,* 405–14.

94. *Takvim-i Vekayi,* August 13, 1909, no. 300, 1.

95. Ibid. A similar statement was made by the Ministry of the Interior. See BOA, DH.MKT 2902/98 (2 Ağustos 1325/15 August 1909).

96. BOA, DH.MKT 2909/34 (7 Ağustos 1325/20 August 1909).

97. Ibid.

98. BOA, DH.MKT 2909/34 (10 Ağustos 1325/23 August 1909).

99. BOA, BEO 3661/274536 (14 Ağustos 1325/27 August 1909).

100. Ibid.

Chapter 8: The Form of Justice

1. See Gary Jonathan Bass, *Stay the Hand of Vengeance: The Politics of War Crimes Tribunals* (Princeton, NJ: Princeton University Press, 2002).

2. Djemal Pasha, *Memories of a Turkish Statesman, 1913–1919* (Hutchinson & Co.: London, 1922), 259–61.

3. Rudolph Peters, *Crime and Punishment in Islamic Law: Theory and Practice from the Sixteenth to the Twenty-First Century* (Cambridge: Cambridge University Press,

2007), 127–33. See also John Alexander Strachey Bucknill and Haig Apisoghom Sdepan Utidjian, *The Imperial Ottoman Penal Code: A Translation from the Turkish Text, with Latest Additions and Amendments, Together with Annotations and Explanatory Commentaries upon the Text and Containing an Appendix Dealing with the Special Amendments in Force in Cyprus and the Judicial Decisions of the Cyprus Courts* (Oxford: Oxford University Press, 1913), xii.

4. Ibid., xiii.

5. Kent F. Schull, *Prisons in the Late Ottoman Empire: Microcosms of Modernity* (Edinburgh: Edinburgh University Press 2018), 27.

6. Bucknill and Utidjian, *The Imperial Ottoman Penal Code*, xiv.

7. Schull, *Prisons in the Late Ottoman Empire*, 29–30.

8. This was essentially the version of IPOC that was used in 1909.

9. Bucknill and Utidjian, *The Imperial Ottoman Penal Code*, 1–36.

10. Ibid., 37–123.

11. Ibid., 124–98.

12. Ibid., 199–208.

13. BOA, DH.SYS 54–1/2–1 (10 Kânûn-ı Evvel 1326/23 December 1910).

14. A different list provides the total number convicted by the courts-martial of Adana, Maraş, Antioch, Cebel-i Bereket, Manastır, İstanbul, and Kosovo as 489. The list does not include the death sentences. The sentences ranged from one to six years in prison with hard labor to two years in exile. The fewest number convicted were in İstanbul (ten), Manastır (ten), and Kosovo (seven). See BOA, BEO 3785/283810. (10 Temmuz 1326/23 July 1910).

15. Osman Köksal, "Tarihsel süreci içinde bir özel yargı organı olarak divan-ı harbi örfiler (1877–1922)," (PhD diss., Ankara University, 1996), 133.

16. Quran, surah Al-Baqara: 179. See also *Tanin*, June 3, 1909, no. 270, 1.

17. On the massacres of Abdioğlu and Misis, see Terzian, *Kilikioy aghetě*, 176–88. See also Z., *Adanskie chernye dni*, 10–13; and Yesayan, *Aweraknerun měj*, 97–99.

18. From Zavarian to the Responsible Body in İstanbul, June 22, 1909, ARF Archives, C/953–107.

19. BOA, DH.SYS 54–1/2–1 (10 Kânûn-ı Evvel 1326/23 December 1910).

20. Le Contre-Admiral Pivet, Commandant l'escadre Ligue de la Méditerranée à Monsieur l'Ambassadeur de France à Constantinople, Mersine, 1 July 1909, Turquie, ambassade de Constantinople, série E, 129, confidential, no. 30, CADN.

21. See Arslanian, *Adana'da adalet nasıl mahkûm oldu*, 13. Zabel Yeseyan provides detailed information about the reaction of the Armenians of Adana to the hanging of the six Armenians and describes the condition of Missak's mother; see Yesayan, *Aweraknerun měj*, 155–62.

22. BOA, DH.MKT 2885/33 (14 Temmuz 1325/27 July 1909).

23. BOA, DH.SYS 54-1/2-1 (10 Kânûn-ı Evvel 1326/23 December 1910).

24. Bucknill and Utidjian, *The Imperial Ottoman Penal Code*, 48.

25. Ibid., 136–37. Kyurek (*kürek*) is "a Turkish word, the original meaning of which is an oar or shovel. It later obtained the meaning as given by Redhouse, 'the galleys, as a punishment' and hence generally roughly corresponds to 'imprisonment with hard labour.'" Bucknill and Utidjian, *The Imperial Ottoman Penal Code*, 6.

26. Ibid., 129.

27. BOA, DH.MKT 2893/4 (23 Temmuz 1325/5 August 1909).

28. Bucknill and Utidjian, *The Imperial Ottoman Penal Code*, 49.

29. BOA, DH.MUİ 22/58 (26 Eylül 1325/9 October 1909).

30. BOA, DH.SYS 54–1/2–1 (10 Kânûn-ı Evvel 1326/23 December 1910).

31. BOA, DH.MUİ 25/56 (7 Teşrîn-i Evvel 1325/20 October 1909).

32. Bucknill and Utidjian, *The Imperial Ottoman Penal Code*, 150.

33. Ibid., 152.

34. BOA, DH.MUİ 26–2/8 (10 Teşrîn-i Evvel 1325/23 October 1909).

35. BOA, DH.MUİ 29–1/35 (17 Teşrîn-i Evvel 1325/30 October 1909).

36. *Tanin*, October 4, 1909, no. 392, 3.

37. Asaf Bey complained to the Ministry of the Interior about his retrial on July 15, 1909. See BOA, BEO 3600/269949 (31 Temmuz 1325/13 August 1909).

38. BOA, BEO 3669/275159 (16 Teşrîn-i Sânî 1325/29 November 1909).

39. BOA, BEO 3693/276930 (13 Kânûn-ı Sânî 1325/26 January 1910).

40. BOA, BEO 3897/292264 (11 Mayıs 1327/24 May 1911).

41. Woods, *The Danger Zone of Europe*, 187.

42. *Zhamank*, June 12, 1909, no. 189, 2.

43. BOA, DH.MUİ 23–2/21 (5 Teşrîn-i Evvel 1325/18 October 1909).

44. BOA, DH.MUİ 23–2/21 (28 Kânûn-ı Sânî 1325/10 February 1910).

45. BOA, BEO 3650/273706 (27 Eylül 1325/10 October 1909).

46. BOA, DH.MKT 2885/15 (27 Haziran 1325/10 July 1909).

47. *Tanin*, July 14, 1909, no. 311, 1.

48. BOA, BEO 3661/274503 (21 Teşrîn-i Evvel 1325/3 November 1909).

49. BOA, DH.SYS 63/2–1, no. 56 (4 Teşrîn-i Sânî 1325/17 July 1909).

50. BOA, DH.SYS 63/2–1, no. 60 (4 Teşrîn-i Sânî 1325/17 November 1909).

51. Ibid.

52. BOA, BEO 3650/273706 (8 Eylül 1325/21 September 1909).

53. BOA, BEO 3647/273481 (22 Eylül 1325/5 October 1909).

54. Terzian, *Kilikioy agheté*, 416–20.

55. Ibid., 422–38.

56. Divan of the Catholicos of All Armenians, Fond 57, Ts'uts'ag 2, Gordz 14, 1–6, ANA.

57. BOA, BEO 3662/274622 (31 Teşrîn-i Evvel 1325/13 November 1909).

58. BOA, BEO 3535/265082 (29 Teşrîn-i Sânî 1325/12 December 1909).

59. Toros, *Ali Münif Bey'in hâtıraları*, 53–55.

60. Ibid., 56.

61. BOA, BEO 3683/276211 (26 Kânûn-ı Evvel 1325/ 8 January 1909).

62. See BOA, DH.SYS 63/2–1, nos. 62–99.

63. BOA, DH.SYS 63/2–1, no. 32 (15 Nisan 1326/28 April 1910).

64. BOA, BEO 3667/274990 (11 Teşrîn-i Sânî 1325/24 November 1909).

65. BOA, DH.SYS 63/2–1, no. 54 (12 Nisan 1326/25 April 1910).

66. BOA, DH.SYS 63/2–3, no. 41 (10 Mayıs 1327/23 May 1911).

67. BOA, DH.SYS 63/2–3, no. 19 (24 Nisan 1327/7 May 1911).

68. BOA, DH.MKT 2892/34 (22 Temmuz 1325/4 August 1909). Ahmed Cemal, born in Mitilin, the capital city of the Island of Lesbos, was the son of a military pharmacist. He attended a military high school academy (*Harbiye Mektebi*) and a staff officer school in İstanbul. He received his first career post in 1895. He was appointed to military posts in the European provinces of the empire. While serving in Salonica, he joined the CUP. He took an active role in the revolution as well as in the Action Army that subdued the counterrevolutionaries in the capital. After serving as the district governor of Üsküdar for three months, he was appointed as the governor of Adana in the post-massacre period.

69. M. Barre de Lancy, vice-consul de France à Mersine d'Adana à Monsieur Boppe chargé d'Affaires de France pres la Porte Ottomane, Mersine, Mersine, 20 August 1909, Turquie, ambassade de Constantinople, série E, 129, no. 27, CADN.

70. Ibid.

71. M. Barre de Lancy, vice-consul de France à Mersine d'Adana à Monsieur Boppe chargé d'Affaires de France pres la Porte Ottomane, Mersine, 7 September, 1909, Turquie, ambassade de Constantinople, série E, 129, no. 34, CADN.

72. BOA, DH.MKT 2914/1 (11 Ağustos 1325/24 August 1909).

73. M. Barre de Lancy, vice-consul de France à Mersine d'Adana à Monsieur Boppe chargé d'Affaires de France pres la Porte Ottomane, Mersine, 24 August 1909, Turquie, ambassade de Constantinople, série E, 129, no. 28, CADN.

74. BOA, DH.MKT 2914/9 (17 Ağustos 1325/30 August 1909).

75. Ibid.

76. BOA, BEO 3661/274536 (17 Teşrîn-i Evvel 1325/30 October 1909).

77. Djemal Pasha, *Memories of a Turkish Statesman*, 262.

78. Ibid.

79. BOA, BEO 3650/273706 (15 Eylül 1325/28 September 1909).

80. Maksudyan, "New 'Rules of Conduct,'" 154.

81. Ibid., 165.

82. See Nazan Maksudyan, "Cemal Bey' in Adana Valiliği ve Osmanlıcılık İdeali," *Toplumsal Tarih* 176 (2008): 22–28.

83. Ibid., 188.

Conclusion

1. Yesayan, *Aweraknerun mēj*, 16.

2. On the literary importance of Yesayan, see Marc Nichanian, *Writers of Disaster: The National Revolution* (Princeton, NJ: Gomidas Institute, 2002), 187–243. The only non-Armenian book that describes the condition of Adana Province in a literary style is Jean d'Annezay, *Au pays des massacres: Saignée arménienne de 1909* (Paris: Bloud, 1910). Jean d'Annezay (pseudonym of Jean de Beaucorps) was born on May 15, 1883, in Château de La Chesnaie (Loir-et-Cher, France), and died on November 2, 1914, in Saint-Eloi (Belgium). He was a traveler who visited Egypt, Sudan, Syria, and Palestine, among other places. After the massacres, d'Annezay visited İskenderun, Mersin, and Adana.

3. ARF Archives, Doc 1719 Kim-13, in Yervant Pamboukian, *Niwt'er Hay heghap'okhakan dashnakts'ut'ean patmut'ean hamar*, vol. 6 (Peyrout': Hamazgayini Vahē Sēt'ean Tparan, 2010), 266–27. On the ARF-CUP agreement, see Vahan Papazian, *Im husherě*, vol. 2 (Beirut: Hamazgayin, 1952), 123–30. See also Dikran Mesrob Kaligian, *Armenian Organization and Ideology under Ottoman Rule: 1908–1914* (New Brunswick, NJ: Transaction Publishers, 2008), 45–53.

4. Kaligian, *Armenian Organization and Ideology*, 46.

5. Ibid., 53.

6. Ibid., 63.

7. See Hans-Lukas Kieser, Mehmet Polatel, and Thomas Schmutz, "Reform or Cataclysm? The Agreement of 8 February 1914 Regarding the Ottoman Eastern Provinces," *Journal of Genocide Research* 17, no. 3 (2015): 285–304.

8. See Kévorkian, *The Armenian Genocide*; Uğur Ümit Üngör, *The Making of Modern Turkey: Nation and State in Eastern Anatolia, 1913–1950* (Oxford: Oxford University Press, 2012); Taner Akçam, *The Young Turks' Crime against Humanity: The Armenian Genocide and Ethnic Cleansing in the Ottoman Empire* (Princeton, NJ: Princeton University Press, 2012); and Donald Bloxham, *The Great Game of Genocide: Imperialism, Nationalism, and the Destruction of the Ottoman Armenians* (Cambridge: Cambridge University Press, 2005). For a review of the historiography of the Armenian Genocide, see Bedross Der Matossian, "Explaining the Unexplainable: Recent Trends in the Armenian Genocide Historiography," *Journal of Levantine Studies* 5, no. 2 (Winter 2015): 143–66.

9. One of the most important books on the Armenian Genocide that does not adhere to the continuum approach is Suny, *"They Can Live in the Desert."*

10. Kévorkian, *The Armenian Genocide*, 594.

11. Bardakçı, *Talât Paşa'nın evrak-ı metrûkesi*, 109. On Talat Paşa, see Hans-Lukas Kieser, *Talaat Pasha: Father of Modern Turkey, Architect of Genocide* (Princeton, NJ: Princeton University Press, 2018).

12. Kévorkian, *The Armenian Genocide*, 594.

13. Ibid., 595.

14. On the Armenian Legion, see Vahé Tachjian, *La France en Cilicie et en Haute-Mésopotamie: Aux confins de la Turquie, de la Syrie et de l'Irak (1919–1933)* (Paris: Karthala, 2004), 39–45. See also Dickran Boyadjian, *Haykakan lēgēonĕ: Patmakan hushagrut'iwn* (Niw York': Hratarakut'iwn Haykakan Baregortsakan Ĕndhanur Miut'ean Kedronakan Varch'akan Zhoghovi, 1965); and Susan Paul Pattie, *The Armenian Legionnaire: Sacrifice and Betrayal in World War I* (London: Bloomsbury Publishing, 2019).

15. Ibid., 748. On the French occupation of Cilicia, see Tachjian, *La France en Cilicie*.

16. Ibid., 174.

17. Garabed K. Moumjian, "Cilicia under French Administration: Armenian Aspirations, Turkish Resistance, and French Stratagems," in *Armenian Cilicia*, ed. Richard G. Hovannisian and Simon Payaslian (Costa Mesa, CA: Mazda Publishers, 2008), 457–94.

18. Talât Paşa, *Talât Paşa'nın hâtıraları* (İstanbul: Cumhuriyet, 1998), 16.

19. Ibid., 17.

20. Ibid.

21. Steven J. Zipperstein, *The Jews of Odessa: A Cultural History, 1794-1881* (Stanford, CA: Stanford University Press, 1985).

22. See Robert Weinberg, *The Revolution of 1905 in Odessa: Blood on the Steps* (Bloomington, IN: Indiana University Press, 1993); and *Antisemitism: A Historical Encyclopedia of Prejudice and Persecution*, vol. 2, L–Z, ed. Richard S. Levy (Santa Barbara, CA: ABC-CLIO, 2005), s.v. "Odessa Pogroms."

23. See Klier and Lambroza, *Pogroms: Anti-Jewish Violence in Modern Russian History*.

24. Robert Weinberg, "Workers, Pogroms, and the 1905 Revolution in Odessa," *Russian Review* 46, (1987): 58.

25. Robert Weinberg, "The Pogrom of 1905 in Odessa: A Case Study," in Klier and Lambroza, *Pogroms: Anti-Jewish Violence in Modern Russian History*, 251.

26. Robert Weinberg, "Anti-Jewish Violence and Revolution in Late Imperial Russia," in Brass, *Riots and Pogroms*, 58–59.

27. Weinberg, "The Pogrom of 1905 in Odessa," 255–56.

28. Ibid., 256.

29. Weinberg, "Anti-Jewish Violence," 62.

30. Ibid., 66.

31. Weinberg, "The Pogrom of 1905 in Odessa," 260–62.

32. Ibid.

33. Weinberg, "Anti-Jewish Violence," 76.

34. Po'alei Zion, *Odesskiĭ pogrom i samooborona* (Paris: Libr. A. Schulz, 1906).

35. Weinberg, "The Pogrom of 1905 in Odessa," 265.

36. Weinberg, "Anti-Jewish Violence," 74.

37. Weinberg, "The Pogrom of 1905 in Odessa," 267.

38. See Ornit Shani, *Communalism, Caste and Hindu Nationalism: The Violence in Gujarat* (Cambridge: Cambridge University Press, 2007); Parvis Ghassem-Fachandi, *Pogrom in Gujarat: Hindu Nationalism and anti-Muslim Violence in India* (Princeton: Princeton University Press, 2017); Raheel Dhattiwala and Michael Biggs, "The Political Logic of Ethnic Violence: The Anti-Muslim Pogrom in Gujarat, 2002," *Politics & Society* 40, no. 4 (2012): 483–516; and Raheel Dhattiwala, *Keeping the Peace: Spatial Differences in Hindu-Muslim Violence in Gujarat in 2002* (Cambridge: Cambridge University Press, 2019).

39. On the Anandpur Sahib Resolution, see Khushwant Singh, *A History of the Sikhs*, vol. 2 (Princeton, NJ: Princeton University Press; London: Oxford University Press, 1984), 337–51.

40. Giorgio Shani, *Sikh Nationalism and Identity in a Global Age* (New York: Routledge, 2008), 51–53.

41. On Jarnail Sing Bhindranwale, see Singh, *A History of the Sikhs* 2: 324–36.

42. Virginia Van Dyke, "The Anti-Sikh Riots of 1984 in Delhi: Politicians, Criminals, and the Discourse of Communalism," in Brass, *Riots and Pogroms*, 203.

43. Mark Tully and Satish Jacob, *Amritsar: Mrs Gandhi's Last Battle* (New Delhi: Rupa, 1985), 147.

44. Singh, *A History of the Sikhs* 2:352–72.

45. Ibid., 364. See also Poonam Taneja, "Why 1984 Golden Temple Raid Still Rankles for Sikhs," *BBC*, August 1, 2013, https://www.bbc.com/news/world-asia-23514583.

46. *The White Paper on the Punjab Agitation* (New Delhi: Printed by the General Manager, Government of India Press, 1984).

47. Singh, *A History of the Sikhs* 2:363.

48. Ibid., 367–68.

49. Shani, *Sikh Nationalism and Identity*, 61.

50. Singh, *A History of the Sikhs* 2:375.

51. Jaskaran Kaur, *Twenty Years of Impunity: The November 1984 Pogroms of Sikhs in India* (Portland, OR: Ensaaf, 2006), 45–61.

52. Kaur, *Twenty Years of Impunity*, 27.

53. Ibid., 37–39. See also Jaspreet Singh, "India's Pogrom, 1984," *International New York Times*, October 31, 2014, 7.

54. Singh, *A History of the Sikhs* 2:377.

55. Kaur, *Twenty Years of Impunity*, 31–32.

56. Singh, *A History of the Sikhs* 2:377.

57. Van Dyke, "The Anti-Sikh Riots of 1984 in Delhi," 208.

58. Ibid.

59. Ibid., 215.

INDEX

Note: page numbers in italics refer to figures. Those followed by n refer to notes, with note number.

Balkan Wars of 1912–13, and revival of
Armenian Question, 225
Balph, James, 122
Başıbozuks (irregular soldiers), participation in violence against Armenians,
102, 103, 110–11, 119, 145
Bayrakdar, Bekir, 77
Bayram Efendi, Mahmud, 78
Bayramian Ağa, Mkrtich, 41
Belart, H., 106
Belfante, Theodor, 120, 124
Berberian, Arakel, 85–86
Bereketzade, Rifat, 120
Berliner Tageblatt (newspaper), 173–75
Bhagat, Hari Krishan Lal, 238
Bhavnani, Ravi, 14, 93
Bhindranwale, Jarnail Singh, 236–37
Biwzandion (newspaper), 54, 78, 80, 83, 85, 127, 128
Bockelberg, Dr., 155, 157
Borel, Lucie, 177–78
Bouthiller, Dr., 157
Boyadjian, Araxi, 103–4
Boyadjian, Hampartsoum, 78
Boyadjian, Mihran, 103–4
Brass, Paul, 6
British: ambassador's reports of impending attacks on Armenians, 84; and Armenian Question, engagement with, 25; consulate, forced turnover of Armenians sheltered in, 186–87; and economic development in Cilicia, 40; efforts to stop violence, 124; and humanitarian concerns about Ottoman Armenians, 17–18; medical aid to Armenian wounded, after first wave of massacres, 136; and Ottoman railroad development, 38; participation in relief efforts, 157; press, coverage of Adana massacres in, 179; sheltering of Armenians, in second wave of massacres, 144; support for Armenian revolt, rumors

of, 53, 54. *See also* Doughty-Wylie, Charles (British vice-council)
Brudholm, Thomas, 14
Bulgarian independence, CUP response to, 70–71
burning of Armenian homes, businesses, and churches, 3, 231–32; in first wave, 103, 106, 110, 111, 114, 119, 122, 281n91; in Muslim version of events, 140; in second wave, 145, 146, 147, 148
burning of Christians' public buildings, 151
burning of hospitals and churches with Armenians inside, in second wave, 142–43, 144, 145, 146, 157
burning of mills and bakeries, food shortages resulting from, 151, 157
Butler, Nicholas Murray, 180
Byzantine Empire, Seljuk invasions of, and Armenian migrations, 28
Bzdigian, Krikor, 34, 103
Bzdigian, Samvel, 104
Bzdigian, Zakaria, 75–76, 186

Calhoun, Craig, 11, 252n32
Catholic churches: loss of all buildings in massacres, 151; sheltering of Armenians, 111, 136. *See also* Terzian, Paul
Catholic missionaries: aid in post-massacre relief efforts, 159–60; history of, 29; sheltering of Armenians, 111
Catholicosate of the Great House of Cilicia: and *derebeys*, conflict among, 30; and importance of Cilicia to Armenian national past, 23; lands seized from, given to Muslim refugees, 43, 48; move to Sis, 29; and Telan Farm controversy, 63–65
Catoni, Joseph, 124
Cebel-i Bereket: court-martial in, 186; massacres in, 111–12, 126

CPSIA information can be obtained
at www.ICGtesting.com
Printed in the USA
JSHW022153200323
39178JS00001B/3